The Well-Tended Perennial Garden

TRACY DISABATO-AUST

THE WELL-TENDED PERENNIAL GARDEN

THE ESSENTIAL GUIDE TO PLANTING AND PRUNING TECHNIQUES

A Bestselling Classic, Completely Revised and Expanded

Timber Press
Portland, Oregon

Frontispiece: Hiddenhaven, the author's collection of gardens, was used to evaluate the majority of pruning techniques in this book. Here, the front walk flourishes in spring; the annual cutting garden can be seen in the distance.

Photo credits appear on page 395.
Copyright © 2017 by Tracy DiSabato-Aust. All rights reserved.
Third Edition.
Published in 2017 by Timber Press, Inc.
The Haseltine Building
133 S.W. Second Avenue, Suite 450
Portland, Oregon 97204-3527
timberpress.com

Printed in China
Text design by Carrie Hamilton
Cover design by Carrie Hamilton and Anna Eshelman
Color illustrations by Kerry Cesen
Black and white illustrations by Beth Ann Daye

Library of Congress Cataloging-in-Publication Data

Names: DiSabato-Aust, Tracy, author.
Title: The well-tended perennial garden: the essential guide to planting and
    pruning techniques / Tracy DiSabato-Aust.
Description: Third edition. | Portland, Oregon: Timber Press, 2017. | "The
    bestselling classic, completely revised and expanded." | Includes
    bibliographical references and index.
Identifiers: LCCN 2016027264 (print) | LCCN 2016028654 (ebook) | ISBN
    9781604697070 (hardcover) | ISBN 9781604697872 (e-book)
Subjects: LCSH: Perennials. | Perennials—Pruning.
Classification: LCC SB434 .D37 2017 (print) | LCC SB434 (ebook) | DDC
    635.9/32—dc23 LC record available at https://lccn.loc.gov/2016027264

A catalog record for this book is also available from the British Library.

To my family, Team Austome: Jim, Zach, and Alyssa.
Love you forever, love you for always.

Summer vignette from the back gardens at Hiddenhaven. 'Gateway' Joe Pye weed (*Eutrochium maculatum* 'Gateway') and 'Herbstonne' coneflower (*Rudbeckia nitida* 'Herbstonne') were guinea pigs to test pre-emptive pruning (pruning prior to flowering) for height reduction and reduced need for staking.

CONTENTS

Lenten rose (*Helleborus ×hybridus*) is not just another pretty face in the perennial garden. It is long-lived, tolerant of heat and humidity, hardy in cold and drought, deer resistant, and free of pests and disease. It also requires minimal pruning and feeding and no staking.

Preface

We are thrilled to offer this information-packed, beautiful, and inspiring third edition of *The Well-Tended Perennial Garden*! In an effort to stay topical in the rapidly changing world of perennial gardening, we felt an update to the original edition from 1998 (that's right—can you believe it?) and the expanded edition from 2006 was in order.

Exciting changes to this edition include more than 50 new plant encyclopedia entries, dozens of new cultivars, scores of new photographs and illustrations, updates to some of my original garden design projects, and visual stories of new design projects. If you have the previous two editions of *Well-Tended Perennial Garden* you will also appreciate the updated *Perennials by Maintenance Needs*, which has been expanded in this third edition.

New perennials are being introduced daily and it's hard to keep up! Our goal isn't to provide every new perennial or cultivar (these are well covered in other publications), but to address these new plants from a maintenance perspective, which is a viewpoint unique to this book. What are the care, and more specifically, pruning, needs of these plants? Which cultivars are more reliable, hardier, or long-lived performers? Which ones have I used for years that still pass the test of a great plant?

Working in the horticulture industry for 4 decades now, I've seen many changes. I have always used native plants in my designs, but the emphasis on their use is even greater today. Perennials are being incorporated into rain gardens, rooftop gardens, container gardens, and mixed gardens. They are joining trees, shrubs, bulbs, annuals, and vegetables in the garden, rather than being strictly relegated to traditional perennial beds. There is the desire to grow dynamic yet low-maintenance plants that are deer resistant and drought tolerant, that don't require frequent pruning or care to look their best. Many new, safe organic fertilizers and pest controls are readily available. We address these issues here.

Thankfully, many of the sound horticultural practices that were discussed in the book's first edition still hold true today; you will find they remain in these pages, both in recommendations and in the examples of featured gardens.

Thank you for supporting this book and its mission all these years. Besides being one of the all-time bestselling and most-sustaining gardening publications available since it was first released, *The Well-Tended Perennial Garden* has been one of the most rewarding and cherished aspects of my career.

Today's world is hectic and filled with technology. People rarely look up from their cell phones or digital devices. We desperately need to fuel our souls, and an excellent way to do so is by connecting with plants and the earth through gardening. May this refreshed, more-relevant-than-ever guide help you navigate a joyful perennial gardening journey.

Spring at Hiddenhaven means fresh new growth on conifers and perennials. Colorful glass bobbles draw the eye, repeat the form of the ornamental onions (*Allium aflatunese* 'Purple Sensation'), and look great all season. Art in the garden requires minimal to no maintenance.

A well-tended garden need not be rigid. The arbor entrance to the back gardens at Hidden-haven is welcoming and free spirited, with just the right amount of openness to allow access.

BASIC PERENNIAL GARDEN PLANTING & MAINTENANCE

Design and Its Relationship to Maintenance

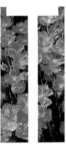

The amount of maintenance a garden requires depends precisely on how the garden was designed or planned. The chosen setting, style, size, and shape of the garden as well as the plant selection, arrangement, and spacing all intertwine to determine the type of care needed. Questions to be asked before the design stage include: How much time and money can be devoted to the upkeep? Who is going to do the maintenance—the owner, a professional crew, or a combination of the two? Whoever is doing it, do they know how to care for the plants chosen? Even the best-designed garden never lives up to what its creator visualized if it is poorly maintained.

There is no question that the planning stage of any perennial garden is thrilling; there are so many great plants from which to choose. The fact that many perennials require maintenance to one degree or another is usually overlooked at this stage, placed far away in the back of one's mind behind all the fantastic colors, cut bouquets, butterflies, fragrance, and other anticipated attractions. Such selective memory is not just the province of beginners; this thinking is true of my mindset as well when I'm planning gardens. Nonetheless, I don't feel that a garden should be planned solely around the premise of maintenance—this would be too limiting and inhibiting. I do believe in a balance, however, and this balance is going to be different for different people. For some, gardening 4 hours a week constitutes low maintenance; for others, anything over 30 minutes moves into the high-maintenance category. (Based on a 9-month period, I average 16 to 20 hours of gardening each month in my own garden, Hiddenhaven, which is about 4600 sq. ft.—of course certain months see more work than others.) Still, some gardeners are willing to invest time for maintenance in the spring, but prefer a golf club or a tennis racket to a pair of pruners in the summer. Such preferences need to be considered during the planning stages. For practical purposes we'll make the "mid-maintenance" garden the one to strive for in this book. Even better, let's not think of it as maintenance but as *gardening*! How much gardening are you or your clients willing to do?

In this chapter I will present general points that should be considered when planning a garden. The following chapters offer more specifics on the ins and outs

You will be rewarded manyfold for your time and effort to maintain a perennial garden, as shown here at Hiddenhaven in midsummer.

The main front border at Hiddenhaven gardens in the spring is lush and bursting with prospects, which will be showy for months to come.

of the various aspects of planting and maintenance. See the Encyclopedia of Perennials for information on specific plants as well as the extensive lists provided to find out which plants are best for certain conditions and requirements.

THE SITE

Let's look at some aspects of a garden and how they relate to maintenance, starting with the site. Considerations such as contour of the land, conditions of the existing soil, light exposure, and moisture conditions fall under this category. Before thinking about personal objectives, such as garden style or color and plant preferences, you must recognize that the site directly affects all these variables. Unfortunately, the site is not always given this preferential treatment, I suppose because it isn't really a fun thing to think about. You might visualize a vibrantly colored perennial garden full of fragrant dianthus and perhaps bright red beebalm, when in actuality the site is too shady to support either of these plants or these bright colors (most shade-loving plants bloom in soft pastel colors).

You need to take into account existing vegetation, buildings or structures, sun patterns, winds, soil conditions, and microclimates before you can start thinking about anything else. Are there trees that will compete with the perennials for moisture and sun? Is there an overhang on the house that will prevent rainfall or sun from reaching a 2- or 3-foot area of the garden? It's a waste of valuable resources to try to maintain moisture-loving plants in a dry location. Perennials such as *Symphytum grandiflorum* and species of epimedium and lamium will compete with trees for moisture without requiring large amounts of supplemental watering. And the solution for moisture-blocking overhangs is to start the

planting out from underneath the overhang, which can also provide a useful 2-ft. catwalk for maintenance along the back of the border. There are perennials suited for just about any location; you simply need to make the correct choices.

The back gardens at Hidden-haven in the autumn are rich and breathtaking, accented by the colors of the surrounding woodlands.

Soil conditions

What is the soil like where you want to plant the garden? Is it wet or dry? Clay or sand? Remember that you can find perennials for almost any soil condition. If you have a spot that is extremely wet or extremely dry, rather than trying to fight it by significantly changing the site to grow plants not suited to the natural conditions, why not grow plants that will take the conditions you have? Turn a wet clay area into a beautiful prairie or meadow full of plants native to those conditions. Neil Diboll of Prairie Nursery has an extensive list of natives that he refers to as "clay busters," which you'll find in the Perennials by Maintenance Needs section following the A–Z Encyclopedia. If you have an area that is constantly dry, select drought lovers. A wooded setting would be a good spot for woodland natives. Besides being of great benefit to the local ecosystem, native plants that are adapted to both your region and your particular site conditions can cut down on your maintenance requirements. Once established, they should be able to get by on only the amount of rainfall that nature provides, for example.

Do keep in mind, though, that when it comes to soil, most perennial plants—be they native or exotic—would prefer to have a soil high in organic matter for establishment and further growth. Except for plants that are adapted to dry-summer areas (such as lavender) and prefer a lean soil, just about all perennials appreciate compost-enriched soils. Most perennials also prefer a well-draining

BASIC PERENNIAL GARDEN PLANTING & MAINTENANCE

soil, and many garden sites need to be modified to meet this need. Can organic matter be incorporated in the soil to improve the conditions and meet the needs of the plants you are interested in growing? I discuss soil in detail in the next chapter, and I urge you to read this information before preparing your garden.

Light conditions

How much sun does the proposed garden area receive? People are too often "in the dark" when it comes to this question. They think an area receives full sun when in actuality the area receives sun only in the late afternoon, which happens to be the time they are home from work. Most often people just haven't taken the time to think about light conditions. Sometimes they are simply deceived by sun-blocking trees or buildings. Whenever existing trees, buildings, and other structures or the angle of the house raise questions about the amount of light exposure, I have my clients observe what I call sun patterns, or I do so for them. This involves tracking sunlight on an area throughout an entire day. It is the only way to truly evaluate light conditions. Sometimes such a survey can uncover some pretty complex patterns, particularly in large gardens with existing scattered mature trees. I have seen cases where areas of a garden that are in full sun for a good part of the day are directly next to areas that are in shade for most of the day. It is also important to remember that 3 hours of cool morning sun are quite different from 3 hours of hot afternoon sun. To me, knowing the amount of sun an area receives is crucial in planning the proper perennials for a site. If the wrong plant is selected for a shady area, it can lead to leggy plants that may not flower and will require pruning or staking for height control or support. In an

This garden at Hiddenhaven was designed for winter interest and is viewed from our conservatory, where we spend a good deal of time during the cold months in Ohio. It is the lowest-maintenance garden at Hiddenhaven, and a real treat! It features shrubs underplanted with 15 different species of ornamental grasses and sedges en masse.

(opposite) Autumn is a fantastic time in the perennial garden if the plants have been properly maintained throughout the season.

Take photographs on initial visits to new sites to help remember light patterns, existing conditions, and original plantings. This rather typical "ho-hum" foundation planting desperately needed an upgrade.

During bed preparation and planting.

overly sunny area, scorched plants might need pruning to remove damaged leaves or require more water in an effort to grow against the odds. All this means more maintenance than would have been necessary had the sun patterns been determined initially. It is best to evaluate the sun patterns during the growing season, as the angle of the sun in late autumn or winter is very different from the angle of the sun during the summer.

Other factors to keep in mind

Winds also can be an important factor in considering a site. If your gardens are exposed to high winds, as some of mine are, tall perennials that are noted for not requiring staking may in fact need support in your windy site. *Boltonia asteroides* 'Snowbank' and *Rudbeckia nitida* 'Herbstsonne' are perennials that require staking or pruning in my gardens to keep them from falling over, while they are happy to stand on their own with no supplemental treatment in some of my clients' gardens.

The newly transformed, vibrant foundation planting 3 months later! These types of images are rewarding to share with clients.

You may be dealing with several different soil conditions and sun patterns in a single garden as well as a variety of microclimates. Learn which areas are sheltered and warmed by the morning sun, for instance, and which areas are frost traps that remain colder than others. The sheltered sites are great for experimenting with tender perennials that perhaps are not normally hardy to your growing zone. The known cold areas should be devoted to reliably hardy species.

When evaluating the site take note of heat pumps, air conditioners, and any other eyesores that need to be hidden. Take photographs to work with later while designing; pictures help you to avoid ignoring such considerations. They also make great "before" shots for record keeping and self-satisfaction to see your accomplishment, or as additions to a professional portfolio of client "befores" and "afters" as you see in this book.

Beds and borders

Will you create a border or island bed? A border is a garden that is bordered by a wall, fence, or hedge. As I mentioned before, it is a good idea to leave a 2-ft. catwalk at the back of the border to assist with maintenance. Otherwise it can be difficult to reach the plants in the back, and these same plants often will lean

The site of Hayden Run Garden in Hilliard, Ohio, before weed control, grading, and soil preparation. This massive community garden is 300 yards long and about a football field wide.

The beginnings of a section of Hayden Run Garden—some soil preparation and stone wall construction in the autumn, to space out the work, prior to a very busy spring of further bed prep and planting. In large gardens, installing in phases can ensure proper execution.

over the shorter ones in front for light. Plants can also suffer from disease as a result of lack of air circulation in the back of the border. With the catwalk, an 8-ft.-wide border gives you 6 ft. of growing space that can easily be reached from either side of the bed, preventing excess compaction on any one side. The only problem is that 6 ft. isn't really much space when you start putting a garden together. So, as with many so-called design rules, this one is sometimes meant to be broken—but such rules do give the beginner a place from which to start. You will invariably step into your garden while working or cutting flowers anyway, so you might as well make the bed a bit wider. You can reduce the incidence of compaction by avoiding stepping on the bed while it's wet, or using small pieces of wood to step on and distribute your weight. I design small paths of stepping stones or mulch into large beds to assist with maintenance. You can also aerate

the bed by light forking or hoeing if it has received a good deal of traffic.

The island bed—surrounded by lawn or maybe pavement—was popularized by English perennial aficionado Alan Bloom. Many gardeners have observed that plants grown in island beds are sturdier and less susceptible to disease because of more even sunlight and air movement. According to the rules, an island is supposed to be 3 times as long as it is wide. So, for example, a 6-ft.-wide bed would be approximately 18 ft. long. For proportion, the tallest plant in the center ideally should be half the width of the bed, so a 6-ft.-wide bed would have about a 3-ft. plant for its tallest inhabitant. Again, this gives you somewhere to start, but have fun experimenting.

You may not have an area for either an island bed or a border, but the garden may be an area in a naturalized setting (an area of existing trees and native plants). Congratulations! Utilize that natural space for cultivated woodland perennials or introduce other natives or use a combination of the two. This is a garden style in itself.

It goes without saying that the larger the garden, the more time and effort is required for maintenance. Of course, a large garden can be very rewarding. It is easier to achieve a long season of interest in a large garden, and plenty of space allows you to follow many of the standard design principles, such as repetition and rhythm.

The same area the following July, just 2 months after a spring planting.

If you only have a small lot, you can overcome limitations by devoting the entire space to plants and do away with the lawn. Some of my favorite garden creations are no larger than 20 ft. × 20 ft. or 30 ft. × 16 ft. Small gardens require more prudent plant selection. Each plant needs to provide a long season of interest to earn a place in a small garden.

My favorite garden style is a mixed border combining perennials with shrubs, disease-resistant shrub roses, vines, grasses, pockets of unusual annuals, bulbs (especially the small or minor bulbs), and small trees where appropriate. Utilize the entire space by planting in layers and using any vertical space available: bulbs tucked under shrubs, vines growing on walls or in shrubs for support, and early season perennials that can be cut back to make room for late bloomers are all good uses of space. Most of the gardens I design are not simply for visual beauty but are also for cutting, for attracting butterflies and birds, and for providing fragrance. After all, these are the garden experiences that most of us want. By utilizing a variety of plant materials and having a decent amount of space with which to work, I'm easily able to accomplish these goals.

Massed plantings (large amounts of a limited number of different species) are often billed as low maintenance. But this depends entirely on the species selected. The massed style can be rather boring and limiting and is not appropriate in every situation. It is also frequently misused. This style can be appropriate in a commercial setting, in large gardens with large beds, or for a site located far from the house or prime viewing area, where larger masses are needed to carry the garden and provide proper scale.

SELECTING PLANTS

There are many things to consider when selecting plants for the garden, but foremost in many gardeners' minds are flowers. Flowers are a big part of what makes perennial gardens so enjoyable. During the planning stages of a garden, however, it's important to understand that flowers come with a certain amount of maintenance, depending on the plant's blooming habit. For example, many plants billed as long flowering may flower for a long period only if they are deadheaded or cut back. The gardener must be willing to perform this chore to extend the plants' season of interest. Another point to consider when selecting plants is that perennials that need to be cut back in order to rebloom will reflower at a shorter height than their original size. This trait can make possible interesting design combinations; shorter plants may be paired with rebloomers during their second flush.

All too often we focus on flowers to the exclusion of foliage, although foliage plays a big role in the perennial garden. It also comes with important design and maintenance implications. When selecting plants, we should ask questions like: Does the plant have attractive foliage? Does it die down gracefully, easily hidden by other plants after its decline? Does it need to be cut back to maintain decent foliage? It is important to think about what the plant looks like through the entire growing season. Foliage may change to scarlet or yellow in autumn on some perennials, and on others the foliage will hold its summer color into winter. Many plants simply need to be cut back once per season to maintain their attractive foliage. Others have foliage that is unattractive even with pruning. This needs to be considered at design time.

Maintenance factors

A number of variables determine what level of maintenance a perennial will require. Regional differences in climate and soil conditions dramatically affect a plant's performance. For example, 'Moonshine' yarrow (*Achillea* 'Moonshine') may do beautifully in a northern garden but is considered high maintenance in a southern garden, where it will melt out from the humidity. A perennial can be high maintenance in one area because it grows like a weed, while in another region it can be low maintenance because it grows at a modest pace. Then there are those plants that are high or low maintenance no matter where they are grown. So the "higher" and "lower" maintenance designations listed in the Perennials by Maintenance Needs section should be considered general guidelines only.

To my dismay, the first perennials that a beginning gardener usually wants in his or her border, often because of gorgeous pictures seen in English perennial books, are high-maintenance traditional perennials, such as the Pacific Giant

This small (14 ft. × 17 ft.) garden, located right next to a highly traveled sidewalk, requires close maintenance attention to keep plants reblooming and aesthetically pleasing all season for the many passersby.

Making more than 10,000 perennials and 3000 annuals fit properly into the huge Hayden Run Garden involved hours of layout—measuring and outlining each plant drift with lime or spray paint, then placing the pots at their proper spacing prior to planting.

(right) Four months after planting, the garden was thriving. Lower-maintenance, long-flowering, sun- and drought-loving plants were selected for this exposed, harsh, sloped site.

hybrid delphiniums. These delphiniums, for instance, generally are not cold, wet, or heat hardy; they are subject to a long list of disease and insect problems; they need to be staked, thinned, deadheaded, and cut back for best performance; and they require summer fertilizing to maintain vigor.

All perennials need some form of maintenance, and we would have a pretty short list of perennials from which to choose if we insisted that they possess all the characteristics of easy care. The typical lower-maintenance perennial will have most (approximately four-fifths) of the following traits:

- ❀ Life span of 5 or more years
- ❀ Cold hardiness
- ❀ Heat, humidity, and moisture tolerance
- ❀ Doesn't require frequent division
- ❀ Doesn't require daily deadheading
- ❀ Doesn't require staking
- ❀ Insect and disease resistance or tolerance
- ❀ Doesn't require numerous prunings to maintain acceptable foliage or habit
- ❀ Doesn't require heavy fertilizing
- ❀ Not invasive

A perennial that lives 5 or more years is considered a long-lived perennial. Some examples of long-lived perennials include peonies and species of *Baptisia* and *Dictamnus*. Some perennials are tolerant of extreme cold temperatures but are killed by wet soil conditions over the winter. Likewise, many perennials tolerate heat well but can be weakened or killed by summer humidity. Silver-foliaged plants are particularly susceptible to high humidity and can rot.

The U.S. Department of Agriculture's Plant Hardiness Zone Map is the most widely accepted resource for figuring out hardiness zones, and the updated map reflects the changes in climate regionally. Visit planthardiness.ars.usda.gov and find your exact zone by entering your zip code.

For a lower-maintenance perennial, look for one that can last at least 4 years before division is necessary. Some perennials don't ever need division and may even resent it.

Many *Coreopsis lanceolata* and *C. grandiflora* cultivars require daily deadheading to look their best. To call this high maintenance is an understatement. A better selection would be the *C. verticillata* cultivars, particularly 'Moonbeam', which can be sheared once for continual bloom for most of the summer.

Staking is an unpopular aspect of perennial gardening and consequently it is often put off until the last minute, when it is usually too late. Select a lower-growing cultivar if possible, or prune to reduce the need for staking. For example, *Gaura lindheimeri* 'Whirling Butterflies' would be a better choice than the straight species because it is more compact.

Perennials should be chosen that are resistant to disease and insects, or at least tolerant to the point that either they are not bothered to any great degree or they can be pruned to help recover from the problem rather than being sprayed. Spraying is an area where I will not compromise. I love gardening, but I hate spraying chemicals for pest control for many reasons. So I don't. I would rather do anything else as far as maintenance goes. This is another reason why proper plant selection is critical.

If a plant requires cutting back more than once or twice a season to look its best (above and beyond normal spring or winter cleanup), it moves into the higher-maintenance category. Some plants do best if cut back before flowering for height control. They may also require frequent deadheading. And then they may need cutting back once or twice to maintain a decent habit (the general form or shape of a plant) and to rebloom after flowering. This can involve a lot of work. You need to decide whether growing the plant is worth the extra work.

Perennials that need heavy feeding and a supply of supplemental nutrients through the season mean additional maintenance. A rich, high-organic soil and possibly a light spring fertilization is all that most perennials require.

An invasive plant can take over the world (or at least the garden) before you know it! Or at least it can seem that way when your monarda, a cute single-stemmed 4-in. plant, spreads by underground stems to fill a space 4 ft. × 4 ft. in your garden, devouring everything in its path. Certain species become invasive because of prolific reseeding. Timely deadheading can help prevent reseeding, but if this has been missed just once, populations can quickly get out of control. A great amount of time is often required to keep invasive species managed either by lifting seedlings or by digging out pieces of the expanding clump. Unless you enjoy that kind of thing, use invasive species with caution.

MAKING PLANTS "FIT"

Having considered the site and the types of plants you want to incorporate in the perennial garden, you now need to look at the arrangement and spacing of the plants. Proper spacing of perennials can be hard to determine even for the experienced designer. Even when you think you have it all just right, a plant grows larger than anticipated and another stays small, so at one time or another something is too close and something else a bit too far away. This is just the way of nature. Knowing the ultimate width of any perennials you want to use in your design is crucial to planning. One recommendation is to plant perennials in drifts (long-shaped planting of perennials) using odd numbers, preferably with at least three of a kind of a single species. (Planting in groups of odd numbers is based on the concept of "unity of three," as visually the eye will tend to draw a line between or divide even-numbered groupings of plants.) For genera like *Monarda*, however, using many plants together may mean you and your family moving out of your home to give your beebalm the space it will need. Even the lovely lady's mantle (*Alchemilla mollis*) can alarm the new gardener when its tiny 2 leaves turn into a 2-ft.-wide clump within a few years—normally a single plant repeated in several spots along a border is more pleasing than a single group of plants that would cover a 6 ft. × 6 ft. area.

I always keep the ultimate size of a plant in mind when designing, but I also space plants rather close to reduce weed competition and to produce the lush, full style I prefer within a short period of time. Closer spacing can require more maintenance in the long term in the form of pruning or transplant- ing (which I find more appealing than weeding), because plants may need to be trimmed to stay in their own space, or they may eventually need to be thinned or moved to maintain proper proportions—but results usually make it worth the effort.

It is hard to give specifics on spacing because of the many variables, such as initial plant size, regional differences, soil conditions, and so on. As a general guideline, small plants (under 1 ft. tall) or plants at the front of the border should be spaced 8 to 12 in. apart. Intermediate-sized plants (1 to 2½ ft. tall) are best spaced 15 to 24 in. apart. Spacing of 15 in. seems to work best for the majority of perennials, including plants in the genera *Coreopsis*, *Salvia*, and *Veronica*. I usually start the plants off in 1-quart containers (4¼-in. pots). When starting

with gallon sizes, I space similar species at 18 in. Larger-growing plants such as *Baptisia*, *Monarda*, ornamental grasses, and others I space 2 to 3 ft. apart. With *Baptisia* and *Monarda* I use single plants, giving them 2 or 3 ft. of space, then repeat them elsewhere in the border if appropriate.

When designing, you need to know the square footage of area your drift will cover. (I normally design on quarter-inch graph paper, with the scale ¼ in. = 1 ft., and then I can count the number of squares per drift to determine the square footage.) Once the square footage of area is determined, you can calculate the number of plants needed for that area by multiplying the area by the number of plants per square foot—that is, number of plants needed = square footage of area to be covered × number of plants per square foot. The following table shows the number of plants per square foot for a given spacing.

SPACING	NUMBER OF PLANTS PER SQ. FT.
12 in.	1.00
15 in.	0.64
18 in.	0.45
24 in.	0.25
36 in.	0.11

For example: to space plants 18 in. apart in an area of 7 sq. ft. would require 3 plants (7 sq. ft. of area × 0.45 plants per sq. ft. = 3 plants).

Now that you have taken the time to design an award-winning garden, take the time to properly prepare the soil, plant the perennials, and maintain the garden by reading the rest of the story presented in the following chapters. Good luck!

In this area of Hayden Run Garden, viewed mainly from distant balconies and roads, large drifts of plants—30 to more than 50 plants per drift—were required for proper visibility and scale. Interplanting different species within a drift (here *Liatris spicata* and *Lilium* 'Stargazer') creates exciting contrasts in color and form and prolongs interest, but also may space out maintenance requirements. As one species fades the other shines!

Bed Preparation: Insurance for Success

hile factors such as garden size, design, light exposure, and plant hardiness are undeniably important in preparing your garden for perennials, time spent properly preparing the planting bed is equally vital to the continuing health of your plants and is the key to reducing future maintenance. A perennial growing in healthy, nutritious soil will require less fertilizer and will be less stressed, thereby improving its ability to fend off attacks from disease and pests. Of course, some perennials can be temperamental and require coddling. Even if we do everything right and follow all the rules, we still lose them.

As much as 80 percent of all plant problems are related to poor soil. It is a waste of time, money, and valuable natural resources to try to "Band-Aid" an ailing plant by using a variety of chemical fertilizers or pesticides. Usually the problem could have been avoided initially by incorporating the proper amounts of organic matter and other soil amendments to provide additional nutrients and to alter the properties of the soil, which increases the availability of air and water to the plant. An amendment can be any material—such as compost, lime, or synthetic conditioners—that is worked into the soil to improve its conditioning properties. (Compost is defined here as an organic material rich in humus that is formed by decomposed plant material and other organic matter.)

Perennials can double or even triple in size in the first season if the beds in which they are growing are correctly prepared with sufficient organic matter. Unfortunately this critical step in the garden and landscape building process is often overlooked and given a lower priority than other tasks. Creating good soil is hard work, to be sure, and it will not win any popularity contests when compared to the joy of selecting which plants to use, or colors to combine, or all the other glamorous aspects of creating a garden. If you are an industry professional, you may need to take the time to educate your clients on the importance of investing in proper soil preparation. The most critical time to have good soil is while the plants are establishing themselves.

Healthy high-organic soils produce lush, healthy gardens. *Dianthus gratianopolitanus* 'Bath's Pink,' *Allium schubertii*, and *Digitalis purpurea* are on display.

Take the time to test the soil to determine what kind, and what amount, of organic matter is appropriate to the site. This is also a good time to eliminate perennial weeds, and to poke around for competing tree roots, rocks, and other often inevitable obstacles.

If possible, beds are best prepared in the autumn so that the new bed goes through the freeze-thaw cycles of winter to create a more structured, friable soil. I don't have this luxury in my business because we are so busy and people usually want as much done as possible when we are installing a garden in the autumn. One of my preferred approaches is to prepare the beds and plant the woody plants in autumn, come back the following spring to lightly retill the bed, if needed, and then plant the perennials.

In this chapter I am going to discuss soil (not dirt) requirements for perennial gardens in general. As always, we must remember the axiom "right plant for right place." Some perennials will tolerate poor clay soils, while others thrive in dry, sandy soils. The preparation process starts by determining the existing soil conditions. But, as I hope to make clear, we gardeners can improve on existing conditions to enable us to grow a much wider palette of plants, including many that may not be ideal for the original soil type.

Native plants are not to be overlooked in the selection process, as many outstanding species can tolerate a wide variety of less-than-ideal soil conditions. Yet, even for most of the natives, some bed preparation is beneficial if not vital to establishment.

KEY STEPS TO BED PREPARATION

A few basic steps should be followed to ensure successful bed preparation. Let's look at some key elements: (1) testing the soil; (2) eliminating perennial weeds; (3) making sure the soil drains well, yet is able to hold water and nutrients; (4) providing sufficient organic matter in the soil.

Testing the soil

Testing the soil is a step all too often ignored. Having worked with a variety of different sites for clients, I have become a firm believer in soil testing. It is the only way to effectively determine what soil conditions you are starting with. Experts say that in the United States alone there are approximately 15,000 different soil types. Soil should be tested to determine soil type (clay, sand, silt, loam, or a combination of these), pH (level of acidity or alkalinity), organic matter content, and available phosphate and potash. Phosphate is a form of

phosphorus that assists in strong root growth in plants; it is 1 of the 3 basic nutrients in fertilizers. Potash is a form of potassium that improves flowering and fruiting.

You can test the soil yourself using soil testing kits, or send it to soil testing labs or your county cooperative extension agency. These services can run various tests on your existing soil as well as on your chosen soil amendment, and they will make recommendations. Most soil tests are performed for field crops or vegetable garden plots; be sure to specify that you'll be growing herbaceous perennial plants or ornamentals, so that you'll receive the proper recommendations. It is also helpful to perform soil tests after the beds have been modified so that you can see the results.

With proper soil preparation, perennials thrive and flourish for many years beyond the first season. Here is the same garden 2 years later with no use of fertilizers or any additional topdressing.

The Perennial Plant Association (PPA) provides the following standards for perennial garden soils (these figures are the minimum for an amended soil): pH of 5.5–6.5, organic matter content of 5 percent (by weight), 50 pounds per acre (25 parts per million or 0.5 pounds per 100 sq. ft.) available phosphate, and 120 pounds per acre (60 parts per million or 1.2 pounds per 100 sq. ft.) available potash. I generally work with soils that are high in clay and low in organic matter (1–3 percent), which I find analogous to working with concrete. Most of us are working with problematic, disturbed urban soils, hence the importance of amending the soils properly.

Soil pH

I find that perennials tend to be rather flexible when it comes to soil pH. In central Ohio the pH is neutral to alkaline, about pH 7–7.8. (A pH of 7 is neutral; anything higher is alkaline and anything lower indicates acidity.) I never attempt to lower the pH to accommodate acid-loving perennials or to raise it for alkaline lovers. I have good success with both types as long as the other requirements are met—most critically, sufficient moisture in summer and good drainage in winter. Only if you are doing everything else right and are still having trouble growing acid- or alkaline-loving plants should you consider altering the soil pH to succeed with any particular plant. Lime can be used to increase soil pH and sulfur to decrease pH; the type and quantity needed to increase or decrease soil pH will be determined by your soil type. Refer to your soil test for pH recommendations.

A few perennials that prefer slightly acidic soil include *Iris ensata*, *Kirengeshoma palmata*, and *Asclepias tuberosa*; *Asclepias tuberosa* can have problems if the pH is above 6.5. Species of *Dianthus* and *Lavandula*, *Gypsophila paniculata*, and most silver-foliaged plants are examples of perennials that prefer alkaline soil.

Eliminating perennial weeds

Get rid of perennial weeds *before* you plant a garden full of desirable perennials—it will certainly make your life more enjoyable. Eradicating weeds is the one instance in which I will resort to the use of chemicals. When working with grassed areas that are to be turned into gardens or existing gardens full of weeds and undesirable plants, I apply glyphosate (Roundup; another option might be Finale) to new planting areas. Glyphosate is a nonselective, nonresidual herbicide that is systemic in its action (meaning it must come in contact with the shoots of the plant and then travels to its roots), so it is best applied when the plants are actively growing and when temperatures are above 50°F. I usually apply glyphosate in early April in Ohio for spring installations. For those with reservations about using Roundup, keep in mind that there are formulas available with less harmful surfactants, as well as products composed of strictly glyphosate, which many would consider safer to use than other products with added "inert" ingredients. I outline the shape of the new bed using a garden hose or a heavy-duty electric extension cord (which is lighter weight and more flexible than hose), and then spray within the outlined area to get the correct shape. After waiting about 14 days, to be certain all perennial weeds are killed, I go into the area and rototill directly through the dead vegetation, if it is not too heavy. (Seven days is the typical manufacturer's recommendation if the weeds are annuals or grasses.) Sometimes a good number of aggressive weeds are not destroyed by the first spraying and so it is necessary to come back for additional sprayings to ensure they have been killed. This step is not one you want to rush or else you will be fighting with those weeds for the rest of your life (or at least the life of the garden).

If you do not want to use chemicals, you can cover the bed area with several layers of moistened newspaper and mulch or other light-blocking material such as black plastic. (Some materials used as mulch include wood chips, bark, and pine needles.) Then wait, perhaps up to 6 months depending on the conditions, for the weeds to be destroyed.

Well-draining soil

More perennials are killed by wet overwintering conditions than by actual cold winter temperatures. This is why well-draining soil is essential for perennials. Part of the research for my master's degree focused on the cold hardiness of herbaceous perennials. ("Herbaceous" refers to a nonwoody plant that dies back to the ground every year.) Most of the species I studied were able to tolerate low temperatures when everything else was constant, but these same species did not survive in the field studies when exposed to excess moisture or fluctuating soil temperatures. Perennials can simply rot during the winter if the soil is not properly drained; this is often mistakenly attributed to cold temperatures, and they are labeled "not hardy." Yes, they are not hardy—to excessive moisture.

Perhaps you are one of the chosen few who have that perfect soil for perennials—a fertile loam that is well draining but also retains adequate moisture. If so, I am envious of you and wish you happy gardening! But most of us are not so blessed. My own soil and most of the soil I work with for clients is very poorly drained. Soil texture (the relative proportions of sand, silt, clay, and loam) can be an indication of what kind of soil drainage you have. Sandy soils are sometimes too well drained, requiring constant watering. On the other hand, if puddles tend to stick around for more than half a day following a rain, or if your soil is constantly soggy, you can be sure that you have a drainage problem (and probably lots of clay). Most of you probably know your soil type and are not happy with it. (If you're not sure of your soil type, you can run a percolation test, as described below.) In any event, let's discuss how to improve the drainage of your clay soil or to increase the moisture retention of your sandy soil.

To ensure well-draining soil, avoid low-lying areas. Add organic matter to the beds at the rate of approximately a third by volume, or 4 in. per 12 in. of soil—this will also improve moisture and nutrient retention in sandy soils. (I will discuss organic matter in greater depth later in the chapter, as it is so vital for all soils.) Creating a slightly raised bed will increase the gravitational pull of water down through the bed.

**A SIMPLE PERCOLATION TEST
TO CHECK FOR PROPER DRAINAGE:**

1. Dig a 12-in.-diameter hole the depth of the amended area.

2. Fill with water and let drain.

3. Fill with water again.

4. Wait 1 hour. If the water hasn't drained in less than 1 hour, drainage needs to be improved either with further soil preparation or with tiles.

Drainage tiles may be needed in some cases to improve drainage, but this should be considered only after you have considered all other factors. I have seen isolated instances where the compaction of the subsoil during construction of the home was so extensive that no matter what bed preparation was done, drainage tiles were still necessary to improve drainage. Tiles can be expensive and will often clog if not properly installed, so they are best used only as a last resort.

(top) Preparing the soil during renovation of sections of the back gardens at Hiddenhaven required time and hard work. The areas were tilled and soil amendments were added, based on calculations for the size of each area. There was no "shooting from the hip" or rushing the process.

(bottom) Plants were placed once the beds were prepared.

Organic matter

If you remember only one thing from this discussion of soil preparation for perennials, I hope it will be the importance of adding organic matter to the beds in sufficient amounts and to sufficient depths. Organic matter improves the physical, chemical, and biological properties of the soil. Research has shown that the application of organic matter can increase plant growth by anywhere from 20 to 100 percent while maintaining higher-than-average survival rates. The main focus in preparing soils for perennials should be improving soil structure, which is the capability of the soil to form aggregates (the natural grouping together of individual particles of sand, silt, and clay to form larger units). In clay soils, organic matter creates structure and increases air space. In sandy soils, it increases moisture and nutrient retention, reducing leaching. Organic matter also increases the availability of all necessary nutrients, and the microbial and

earthworm populations, which create a truly living, or biologically active, soil. Research throughout the United States has shown that most composts, if applied properly and at recommended rates, can reduce the incidence of many soil-borne diseases. This is due to the ability of composts to support beneficial microbes that suppress disease-carrying microbes. Finally, high levels of organic matter in the soil can reduce compaction and erosion and can buffer against toxic substances present in some soils.

The type of organic matter to use depends on soil type, local availability, economics, practicality of application, and personal preference. It is important to know the nutrient content of the organic matter. Any organic amendments should be tested before use. If you obtain compost from a soil company, the company should provide information on the nutrient content, pH, percentage of

Today, more than 15 years after planting, the back gardens at Hiddenhaven have flourished because of proper bed preparation and adequate organic matter being added to the gardens right from the beginning. Organic matter is continually added with each new planting and topdressing occurs every 5 years or more as needed.

organic matter, soluble salts (too high a concentration will hinder plant growth), and heavy metal content (if applicable). If they don't offer this information, I urge you to request a test to be run, because not all soil amendments are the same. Soil companies also will usually provide recommended application rates for their product; it is advisable to follow them. The higher the organic matter content of the material, the higher its soil-conditioning properties. For composts with a high nutrient content, overapplication of the product can injure or kill the plants. Work with your compost supplier to find the best product and to help determine the proper rate.

Organic amendments should be free of weeds, insects, diseases, and foreign material. I had the unfortunate experience of buying a compost that was full of weed seeds on one of my jobs. When the seeds began to sprout, well after planting, correcting the problem entailed having the weeds analyzed first to find out if they were annual or perennial (a key concern in this brand-new and large perennial planting), then trying to have the compost company stand behind its product, while satisfying the client at the same time. Definitely something to avoid if at all possible—know your source.

As I mentioned earlier, you can mix some of the soil amendment with your existing soil (in the proper proportions) and have the mixture tested by a soil testing lab for very specific and accurate recommendations.

Types of soil amendments

There are many different types of organic soil amendments from which to choose. Again, what you choose will depend greatly on what is locally available. I will share with you what is generally available in my area for landscapers and gardeners. I will also indicate the approximate nutrient analyses of these particular amendments. Remember, always test your own! I will not discuss the raw ingredients for various composts—leaves, grass clippings, sawdust, raw manure, hay, and others—as these materials should be composted first before being added to the perennial garden. Incorporating uncomposted woody (high-carbon) materials into your soil can rob nitrogen from the soil and starve your plants for a year or more as microorganisms work to break them down. Incorporating uncomposted high-nitrogen materials into your soil can burn sensitive plants.

LEAF HUMUS Supplies a wide range of essential plant nutrients. One leaf humus product that is available to me is about 38–43 percent organic and has pH 7.7, with a nutrient analysis of 1.0–0.4–0.5, referring to the percentage of nitrogen, phosphorus, and potassium (N–P–K) by weight. Keep in mind that oak leaves are acidic and maple leaves are more alkaline, so the incorporation of either in your humus will affect the pH of the material.

CANADIAN SPHAGNUM PEAT MOSS Provides very low nutrients (less than 1 percent N) and is acidic, with a pH of about 4. Canadian sphagnum peat moss is excellent for improving aeration of clay soils to increase drainage, and it improves the ability of sandy soils to hold water and nutrients. It is sterile and weed free. When used in combination with compost it helps reduce compaction that can sometimes occur when compost is used alone. Depending on the climate, peat can take several years to break down in the soil, as compared to composts (which can be partially broken down within months) and manures (which break down in several weeks). Canadian sphagnum peat moss, which grows at 50 times the rate at which it is harvested, has proved to be a sustainable resource. Its use is environmentally sound.

Sphagnum peat moss should not be confused with the dark black peat (muck soil) often sold and used like topsoil. Dark black peat is so far along in its decomposition that it does little to improve the structure of the soil. You want the bales of sphagnum peat, not the bags of muck peat.

COMPOSTED BIOSOLIDS This is the fancy "cocktail party" name for composted municipal sewage sludge. Composted biosolids can improve the physical structure of soil by increasing drainage, aeration, and moisture retention. They also recharge soil with microbial life. Sewage sludge is composted with different bulking agents, so again there will be differences in products from different sources. The one I use is composted with hardwood chips; others might be bulked with sawdust or other bulking materials. The pH is slightly above neutral, averaging pH 7.3–7.6, and the organic content is 56–72 percent. It contains a well-balanced macro- and micro-nutrient content (1.0–1.5 percent N, 0.4–2.0 percent P, 0.2–0.4 percent K) in organic forms, so the nutrients are released slowly over time and thus with no concern for burn, assuming the material has been applied at the recommended rates. Within the 1st year after application approximately 25 percent of the nitrogen is released, 10 percent in the 2nd and 3rd years, and 5 percent in the 4th and 5th years. During the 1st year approximately 30 percent of the phosphorous and 70 percent of the potassium are available. Because compost is high in phosphorus, supplemental phosphorus fertilizer might not be needed at bed preparation, depending on the quantity of composted biosolids used and the quantity of phosphorous present in the native soil. Composted biosolids are high in phosphorus and also supply good levels of calcium, magnesium, zinc, iron, and copper. Research has shown a 29 percent increase in dry weight of perennials when grown in soils amended with composted biosolids. Composted biosolids have also been shown to help suppress disease in turf. We as gardeners, landscape and horticulture professionals, and general stewards of the land have a commitment to our environment to utilize these alternatives for waste recycling.

Because of the varying composition of composts from different sources, I want to reemphasize the importance of requesting tests for nutrient content, pH level, and levels of soluble salts. Heavy metals, fecal pathogens, and parasites must be strictly controlled at all composting locations; detailed studies have shown that these factors do not pose a concern under existing regulations. Your supplier can provide you with information on these as well as on nutrient content, percentage of organic matter, and recommended application rates. Again, follow these recommended rates, because overapplication of compost can lead to many other problems.

MUSHROOM COMPOST A byproduct from mushroom production is another good amendment for improving soil properties. One available to me is a combination of steam-sterilized horse manure, sphagnum peat moss, brewer's grain, lime, and gypsum. It contains about 60 percent organic matter and has a pH of 7.8–8.2. High in nutrients, mushroom compost has a N–P–K content of 1.5–0.75–1.5, and it also supplies calcium. This is just one recipe, and not a common one at that. As always, request an analysis of the available product, including soluble salts, which can be high, and information about how it is processed. Not all products are the same.

BARK COMPOSTS Low in the nutrients they provide, bark composts are often used to improve the structure of soils. Bark compost material composed of large, coarse particles up to 2½ in. in size will help loosen heavy clay soils. Finer particles help bind sandy soils. Make sure it is composted, or you will need to add supplemental nitrogen. Studies have shown that hardwood bark compost can naturally suppress root rots, *Fusarium* wilts, and some nematode infections. The soil must be well draining in order for disease suppression to be effective.

COMPOSTED MANURE A valuable source of major nutrients, trace elements, and large populations of bacteria—bacteria that can help convert organic

material into humus. It's imperative that the manure has been composted to temperatures high enough to kill weed seeds, or major problems will arise. And all manure is not created equal, with chicken, horse, cow, swine, and sheep all offering varying levels of nutrients. Conditioning properties will depend on the animal source and on the bedding material used. Horse manure with straw bedding, which is high in fiber, helps hold clay particles apart. Users of cow manure swear by it, claiming that the nutrients are more readily available to the plants than in other manures.

COMPOST This catchall category includes homemade composts or commercial composts from mixed yard wastes. We are all aware of the environmental problem of solid waste. Today, we as a nation compost approximately 62 percent of all yard debris: a promising trend compared to just a few decades ago. Composting yard trimmings has evolved from a gardening novelty to a valuable practice for our plants and our planet. But there is still much room for improvement. Anytime we deadhead, prune, rake leaves, or collect and bag grass clippings and throw them away, we contribute to the problem of adding compostable waste to overflowing landfills. Approximately half of all states have enacted legislation banning yard debris from landfills. All gardeners and industry professionals must support this action by composting and by utilizing commercially available composts of yard wastes. Many soil companies and city landfills will take yard waste at no charge and transport it to composting

BASIC PERENNIAL GARDEN PLANTING & MAINTENANCE

facilities for processing. You can contact your local EPA office or cooperative extension office for guidelines.

Composts offer all the benefits mentioned for organic matter in general: wonderful soil conditioning, nutrient and microbial enrichment, and disease suppression. As with all soil amendments, knowing what a particular compost is made of and how it was composted is essential. What are its levels of nutrients? (The N–P–K nutrient analysis can range anywhere from less than 0.5–0.5–0.5 to 4–4–4.) Nutrient imbalances can exist in composts; for example, low levels of nitrogen are found in composts made from sources high in carbon, such as woody materials or leaves. But there can be significant differences in organic matter content with different types of compost, and one cannot truly know the benefits or shortcomings of a given compost without test results, finding out the same critical information as with the other amendments—organic matter content, nutrient content and availability, pH, and source. Remember that the organic matter content of compost affects its soil conditioning abilities. These variables also can affect the recommended rates of application of the material.

TOPSOIL Many people think bringing in some topsoil and dumping it on the garden-to-be is the solution to providing "good" soil for their plants. It is not. There are no government or trade standards that a topsoil provider must meet. Technically speaking, topsoil is the first 2 in. of the ground. This 2 in. may or may not be fertile soil, depending on the location. Topsoil can be low in organic matter and nutrients. If used by itself, topsoil may do little if anything to improve the soil. Sometimes it can take 10 yards of topsoil to equal the benefits in 1 yard of a composted material. Topsoil also can have the further disadvantage of containing weed seeds and herbicide or pesticide residues if it was scraped off farm fields. It is important to know your supplier and to ask for an analysis of the topsoil you buy.

Topsoil with a high organic matter content can be useful in blends with other organic materials where it serves as a stabilizer in otherwise light soil mixes. Other times it can be used independently as the base soil in raised planters to be topped off with a 6- to 8-in. layer of a good organic soil blend.

GYPSUM Gypsum, or calcium sulfate, is a commonly used soil conditioner for clay soils. It helps improve the structure of only certain types of clay soils found in the western United States. It does little or nothing to improve soils in the Midwest or East. It can aid in the removal of salt (sodium chloride) from soils.

SAND Another questionable soil amendment depending on your soil texture. Without delving into the soil triangle from old agronomy class days, I'll try to explain. If you have a soil that is already fairly high in sand, incorporating additional sand in the soil can improve it by moving your existing soil into another textural class—say, that of a sandy loam. But if you are working with a soil low in sand, such as a clay or clay-loam soil, adding a little bit of sand will make matters worse. In this texture of soil 6 to 8 in. (30 percent or more by volume) of a *very coarse* sand would be needed to improve your soil. Most people are not willing to add that much sand to their soils.

AGGREGATES Other coarse soil amendment products are occasionally used in perennial gardens to improve the aeration of heavy clay soils. Perlite, grower's grit (crushed limestone used in the agricultural industry as chicken feed), ceramics, fired-clay materials such as crushed brick, and fine gravels are a few such soil amendments that are available.

Variety seems to be the spice of an amended soil's life. Because of the wide scope of plants we use with very different needs, using a mixture of different organic amendments is most beneficial. You can see from the preceding discussion that each amendment has a little something special of its own to offer. Mixing different soil amendments gives us a bit of the best of each of them.

BED PREPARATION TECHNIQUES

Once you determine your soil type and what materials need to be added, it is time to prepare the bed for planting. As stated earlier, adding 4 in. of organic matter per 12 in. depth of soil is ideal. It is important to work the organic matter into the beds as deeply as is practically possible. The plants will root more deeply, thus improving their tolerance to drought, cold, and fluctuating temperatures. Organic matter also breaks down more slowly when incorporated into the soil, so the benefits are longer lasting than if it were just spread on top of the soil. Tilling will bring weed seeds to the surface, so you must be vigilant about weeding the bed during its establishment. Planting densely, mulching, and providing perennials with enough water and nutrients so that they will fill in quickly will ease the weeding burden.

Double digging is sometimes recommended for preparing a new perennial bed. If you haven't heard of this backbreaking technique, count your blessings. It involves removing 12 in. of soil, amending the subsoil with organic matter to an additional depth of 6 in., amending the removed topsoil, and then returning the amended topsoil to the bed. Double digging is said to be wonderful for the soil; I'm not so sure of the consequences to the digger. In fact, I've never noticed any differences in plants' performance when they are grown in double-dug beds as compared to those grown in rototilled beds.

I usually don't go the ideal 12 in. deep when preparing beds. I am able to work down 8–9 in. with a rototiller, which for practical purposes is what I do with my business. Only in the rare cases where we are renovating a perennial bed, and the beds had been worked and amended in previous years by the client, have we been able to till 12 in. deep. I have had great success with tilling to shallower depths and still adding 4 in. of organic amendments, which also serves to provide slightly raised beds. Going only 8 or 9 in. deep means organic matter is being added at approximately 50 percent by volume.

Adding the soil amendments is the most labor-intensive part of installation. First we till the existing soil, then we start adding our different amendments one at a time, re-tilling and blending these in with the existing soil. We make several runs over the beds, working to greater depths and blending each time until it is workable and ready for planting. The amendments are raked and leveled on the beds, with a final leveling with rakes when all the tilling is done. By the time the whole process is complete, it's like planting in chocolate pudding—truly a treat.

Wheelbarrows are usually sufficient for transporting the soil amendments to the beds. Construction equipment (such as a Bobcat tiller attachment) is required only with very large amounts of organic amendments or when there are long distances to travel. Heavy equipment can create compaction in the garden.

Care must be taken not to create a cleavage point where the good soil meets the poor existing subsoil, or a hardpan (a hardened or cemented soil layer) can develop. I generally do not experience this problem, but in cases where the tiller can't penetrate the existing soil, sometimes the subsoil must first be worked up by hand, using shovels and forks. Then you can get through it with the tillers. I have heard of cases where companies come in with a back hoe to loosen the existing compacted subsoil, then the soil is worked in by hand and with tillers to incorporate soil amendments and ensure organic matter to a greater depth in the soil. Sometimes the existing soil is removed completely from the site and new soil and organic matter is brought in. Very seldom do I have to do this, even in our poor clay soils. If this method is used, it is still important to make sure there is not a point at which the new soil meets with a hard layer of poor compacted subsoil.

The soil should be dry before you try to work it, but not too dry, as tilling soil when it is either too wet or too dry can damage the soil structure. Scheduling

The soil in this garden was poor draining and lacked nutrients. We removed 2 in. of it and added 6 in. of well-draining, nutrient-providing compost containing gravel. The compost and gravel was worked into the base soil, raising the beds about 4 in. Plants were then placed for planting.

installations around the weather is always a challenge in the spring and autumn seasons. I won't work in the beds if they are too wet from a previous day's rain. Not only does it further damage the structure of the soil, but it also increases labor time. If the bed is just slightly too wet, adding sphagnum peat moss first will help absorb some excess moisture and will make the beds workable. It is also important to stay off the beds as much as possible after preparation, especially if

Even after 10 years, the gardens look beautiful, with minimal additional organic matter added and only occasional fertilizer used on annuals.

the soil is moist, to avoid compaction. Walk around the outside of the beds or stay on the designated access paths, if possible.

The soil is said to have sufficient organic matter when you can work it with your hands. An abundance of earthworms is also a sign that the organic matter content is good. Our amended beds generally test out to approximately 16–18 percent organic matter, improved from the original 2–3 percent of the native soil. Remember, the PPA recommendation is a minimum of 5 percent organic matter. Most authorities say 6–8 percent is good for increased perennial plant growth. I have had great success with this higher amount of organic matter for both plant establishment and growth in later years. I find that it is about 4 to 5 years before I need to start adding more organic matter to the soil. But a word of caution: If you get above 20 percent organic matter, you are really working with what is considered more of a container mix, and your watering practices need to be monitored. You could be back to an overly moist soil because of the excess organic matter.

Some horticultural references suggest adding as much compost as you can get your hands on. This is unfounded advice—too much of a good thing is still too much. Too much organic matter can cause soil to become spongy. Also, excess quantities of certain composts can lead to increased disease and insect problems, and even death of the plants. From a business and economical view, the law of diminishing returns comes into play as well.

Calculating amounts of needed amendments

Adding the proper 4 in. of organic matter (30 percent by volume) requires a little of what I call "perennial gardener's math." It's no use to look at an area and guess how much organic matter to use—even after 40 years in the industry, I wouldn't trust myself to do it. Proper calculation helps ensure accuracy and takes little time. On landscape installations, where efficiency is profit, the proper amount of material must be ordered from your supplier. In most circumstances, you are not able to walk over to a compost pile and get more organic matter when you need it.

To accurately calculate the amount of organic matter required you will need to know the square footage of your bed. Square footage is determined by multiplying length by width. If you have an irregularly shaped bed, it is helpful to sketch it out on some type of grid paper (as discussed in the first chapter) so you can add up the grids to get your square footage. Following is an example of how I calculate the soil amendment needed for a 100-sq.-ft. (10 ft. × 10 ft.) bed. In this example I am incorporating 2 in. (or 0.166 ft.) of compost and 2 in. of sphagnum peat moss to get my 4 in. of needed amendments.

> 2 in. (0.166 ft.) of compost per 100 sq. ft. of bed =
> 0.166 ft. × 100 sq. ft. = 16 cu. ft.

Then, to calculate the amount of compost needed in cubic-yard units, divide by 27 cu. ft. (1 cu. yd.):

> 16 cu. ft. ÷ 27 cu. ft. = 0.6 cu. yd.

In this case I would go ahead and bump up my estimate and bring in 1 cu. yd. of compost.

> 2 in. (0.166 ft.) of sphagnum peat moss per 100 sq. ft. of bed =
> 0.166 ft. × 100 sq. ft. = 16 cu. ft.

Then divide by 4 cu. ft. to determine the number of 4-cu.-ft. bales of peat needed to cover the 16-cu.-ft. area:

> 16 cu. ft. ÷ 4 cu. ft. = four 4-cu.-ft. bales

The total cubic footage can also be divided by 6 cu. ft. because a 4-cu.-ft. bale of peat moss is compressed and can actually cover 6 to 8 cu. ft. Depending on how poor the soil is, I make my calculations based on 6-cu.-ft. coverage, so in this example I would use 2½ or 3 bales of peat.

You can see that an area as small as 100 sq. ft. requires quite a bit of soil amendment—1 cu. yd. of compost and a minimum of 2½ or 3 bales (each 4 cu. ft.) of Canadian sphagnum peat moss. An eyeball estimate for such an area probably would come up short of the actual organic matter needed, leaving the gardener wondering why the perennials didn't flourish despite the amendments to the new bed.

If you are amending several beds at one time and working with many yards of soil, keeping track of the number of wheelbarrow loads of soil that have been added is helpful for ensuring that the appropriate amount is incorporated in each bed. Approximately 4½ *heaping* 6-cu.-ft.-capacity wheelbarrows make 1 cu. yd.

Soil recipe for success

Different people swear by many different soil recipes. I will share the formula I have used in my own business, Horticultural Classics & Consultations. The perennials double or triple in size in their first year using these amendments and techniques.

Keep in mind that my technique might not be appropriate for all gardens in all areas. In arid gardens in the western United States, for example, less is more when it comes to organic matter. Plants adapted to lean soil like lavender, helianthemum, santolina, and some drought-tolerant western natives often perform poorly in organic-rich soils. However, this formula has given me great success in creating thriving perennial gardens.

HORTICULTURAL CLASSICS & CONSULTATIONS' SECRET RECIPE

2 in. of compost blend: ⅓ leaf humus, ⅓ composted biosolids, and ⅓ soil

(The soil portion contains a small percentage of composted yard waste and has a 5 percent organic matter content.)

2 in. of sphagnum peat moss

Although I am always looking at new methods and materials that may be better from a horticultural or economic perspective, I have been very pleased with the results of our soil preparation techniques. I have tried many different soil amendments and am happiest with this combination. I encourage you to experiment and find out what works best for you. After all, much of the fun of gardening is experimentation.

I hope this chapter has given you a better awareness of the importance of proper soil preparation. To summarize the steps of this fundamental element in perennial garden success:

1. Test the soil.

2. Outline the area with a garden hose and spray with glyphosate. Wait 14 days. Repeat the application if not all perennial weeds are killed.

3. Add 4 in. of organic matter (a variety of organic matter is best and it's best to have it tested to determine the nutrient analysis and organic matter content) and till it into the existing soil to a depth of 8 to 12 in. Creating slightly raised beds, perhaps outlined in stone, is often the best approach.

4. Plant, being careful to avoid compaction of the newly prepared bed.

5. Wait for outstanding results.

Planting and Renovation

PLANTING A NEW BED

Now that you have devoted time and money to preparing your site and creating fabulous soil for your perennials, you'll want to plant them properly. Many different variables need to be considered, such as plant size, time of year, and planting depths, in addition to the appropriate mulch, watering practices, and weed control.

Plant size

Once you have decided which types of plants you want to grow, you need to select the appropriate sizes for your garden area. You can choose from a variety of perennial sizes. The most common are 1-quart (sometimes called 4-in., or properly 4¼-in.) and 1- and 2-gallon sizes, and bare root (a plant that is sold without any soil around its roots). With a well-prepared soil and rapid growth of the perennials in the first season, starting with larger size plants usually is not necessary. I use predominantly 1-quart sizes. For ornamental grasses I like to use 2-gallon containers; it takes forever for a 1-quart miscanthus, for instance, to attain the scale and impact in the landscape that I am looking for, although it may be appropriate for other gardeners' needs. Out of desperation in those limited cases where the larger size of a grass wasn't available, I have used 3 or more smaller plants grouped together. Smaller-growing genera of grasses such as *Carex* and *Festuca* usually come in 1-quart or 1-gallon containers. Perennials like astilbes, hostas, and various ferns are most often available in the larger size pots, including 3-quart sizes. For autumn installations I use 1-gallon sizes, with the belief that the larger plant with a more extensive root system has a better chance of establishing and is less likely to heave (pop out of the ground) with fluctuating soil temperatures in winter. Irises, peonies, and poppies are often sold as bare root plants.

Keep in mind that a new perennial garden planted with quart-size plants is going to appear small immediately after installation. If you are in the horticulture or landscaping industry, it is good practice to show your clients photographs of previous jobs taken right after planting and then of what the same gardens looked like 3 months later, and so on. It will be more comforting for them than trying to visualize in their heads how a lush perennial garden will develop from such small plants.

This interesting and diverse mixed planting was a renovation of a stagnant garden filled with overgrown boxwood. It now features a weeping redbud, heirloom dahlias, zinnias, and asters.

This garden was planted with a variety of sizes of plants, including bare root, small quart size (4 ¼ in.), and 1-gallon plants.

Within 5 months, thanks to proper bed preparation, the plants doubled and tripled in size.

Timing

In central Ohio—which is plagued with wet, cold soil in the spring, hot and dry summers, often early frost in the autumn, and fluctuating winter temperatures without reliable snow cover—timing of planting can be a challenge. The best time for spring planting in this area is mid-April through May. With my business, we're usually still installing jobs into June and early July, and of course my own gardens don't see much planting until then, but the later we go into the summer, the harder it is for the plants to establish. The best time for autumn planting is from late August to early October. Ideally, planting should be finished by October 1, but we sometimes go until the 15th. I must admit that I prefer spring planting to autumn planting, although I do both. More plants seem to be available in the spring, and with the cool and moist conditions, the plants establish quickly and are sufficiently well rooted before winter. With our unpredictable Ohio autumns

and winters, fall plantings sometimes don't overwinter well here. Plants notorious for frost heaving, such as heuchera, and tender ones such as *Anemone ×hybrida* and kniphofia must be spring planted. In late October and early November I prepare beds and plant woody plants, and then come back in the spring to plant perennials. Pamela Harper and Fred McGourty, in their book *Perennials: How to Select, Grow and Enjoy*, indicate planting times favored by growers in different areas of the country: Northeast Coast (Boston to Philadelphia): April to May, September to mid-November; New England (inland): April to May, September; Mid-Atlantic Coast: October to November; Southeast: February to early April, October to November; Plains States: April to May, September to mid-October; Central (eastern slope of Rocky Mountains): April to May; Pacific Northwest (coastal): March, September to October; California: February to April, October to November; Southwest: February to April.

After 10 years, ongoing commitment and care in the same garden have paid off generously.

Laying out the plants

In a large, complex design like this walled heirloom garden, all the available plants are assembled together, pulled, and placed, starting at one end and moving down along the border. The largest woody plants were planted before the perennials and annuals and served as anchors. In addition, a single species was selected as an edging plant (similar to a low-hedge plant; usually mounded, providing softness to the margins of a bed or border) and was placed prior to the other herbaceous plants. This design took an assistant and me an entire day to lay out.

Before planting, it is important to lay out, or place, the plants, arranging them on the site according to your design. That way, any on-site adjustments can be made by simply shifting the pots around.

If you have a long border, start with a few key plants placed as anchors along the border, particularly the large-growing species such as great coneflower (*Rudbeckia maxima*), grasses, or maybe a shrub rose. Then start setting plants out at one end and work your way down. If you are working with a crew, they can be planting behind you. It is wise to run a 100-ft. tape measure along the edge of the bed to keep a check on where you are in the design. I measure the actual spacing between plants using a metal tape measure to follow the scale created during the planning stages. It is time-consuming, but is the only way I have found to do the job accurately on large, complex designs with a wide variety of species. I do the same in my own gardens when I'm putting in a new bed or adding several plants to an existing garden. Even after years of practice I still have the fear of getting to the end of the bed and running out of space or plants—and it has happened!

When working with several beds on a property, I try to stay ahead of the crew by placing a couple of the beds while the crew finishes preparing the soil in the others. That way, no one is standing around with nothing to do while I lay out the garden. It's also efficient to have another knowledgeable plant person on board who can help gather the plants and hand them to you as you are placing them in the bed.

As previously mentioned, try to stay off of the newly prepared beds as much as possible to minimize soil compaction. Walk around the outside of the beds or stay on the designated access paths when planting and mulching. I often lay small pieces of plywood down and stand on them when planting in large areas that are not accessible from outside the bed, or when the soil is moist.

Planting depth

Containerized perennials should be planted at the same depth at which they were growing in the pot. Plants placed too high can dry out; too low and they are more subject to collar rot. Dicentra plants, irises, and peonies have overwintering buds that sit on or near the soil surface; if planted too deeply, these perennials not only might not flower, they can also rot. Particular care must be taken with peonies not to plant with buds more than 2 in. below the soil in cooler climates (see discussion of *Paeonia* hybrids in the Encyclopedia of Perennials for more details). Bare root plants ideally should be soaked in a bucket of warm water for 30 to 60 minutes prior to planting. Also, any dry containerized perennials should be watered before planting.

Further notes on planting

The soil between newly planted perennials should be leveled before mulching. A small shrub rake is most effective for this. I leave only a single plant label per group of plants in the ground, which keeps the new planting from looking like a mouse cemetery with little white labels sticking up from the ground. In addition, the labels will not be pulled out by the rake and will not pop out with fluctuating temperatures. I also leave a label next to each very small plant, such as late-emerging platycodons, eutrochiums, or asclepias, so that these plants do not get covered with mulch.

If a containerized plant is root bound, make 3 cuts into the root ball to help promote branching of the roots into the newly prepared soil.

I prefer to use a trowel for most planting, although with the 1-gallon and larger perennials, transplant spades (sometimes called poacher spades) are a hot commodity. These are narrow, lightweight small spades (weighing only about 4 lb. and measuring 39½ in. long). They are great for larger-size plants, and some of my crew like to use them for quart-size plants as well. If any plants are root-bound, I make 3 cuts in the root ball with hand pruners before planting, to promote adventitious roots that branch into the newly prepared soil. (Adventitious roots originate from a stem or other part of the plant where roots do not normally occur.)

Plants can be firmed into the soil by pressing on them with your hands; larger grasses and perennials can be firmed in with your foot. Again, nothing dramatic is needed here, and be careful that a well-meaning crew member isn't stomping the perennials to death.

If a plant looks like it has become leggy in the container, cut it back by a third to half at planting to help create a fuller, healthier plant. *Artemisia absinthium* 'Lambrook Silver', for one, often needs this treatment.

When planting new perennials into an existing garden where the entire bed has not been prepared, be sure to dig a sufficient-sized hole, at least 2 times the size of the root ball. This helps prevent the plant's roots from growing into soil that has not been properly prepared while the new plant is establishing. Incorporate organic matter into the hole and the backfill during planting.

Amateur and professional gardeners alike have a tendency to accumulate used plastic pots and flats at an overwhelming rate. In many areas, pots can be recycled, and many nurseries accept used pots as well. I recycle my pots, and I urge you to do the same rather than throwing them out.

Transplanting

When transplanting perennials, it is best to water the plant the night before you plan to move it. Dig the hole as near to the size as you think you'll need, making any necessary adjustments immediately before planting. Take as much soil with the plant as possible. Add organic matter to the new hole and backfill. Firm the backfill in as you go, water when the root ball is covered, and then continue to fill the hole. Transplanting ideally should be done in early spring as new growth is emerging or in early to mid-September. It's best done after flowering, and plants should be cut back by half to two-thirds before transplanting if in a mature state. Transplanting can be done even when the plants are in flower, but they must be handled with extra care. Genera such as *Astilbe*, *Coreopsis*, *Geum*, and *Phlox* can handle transplanting while in flower. Larger plants as well as certain genera such as *Dictamnus* (which is difficult to move even under ideal conditions) and *Papaver* will have more trouble at such nonconventional times. Transplanting on a cloudy or overcast day with low wind is best. Plants may need to be shaded for a couple of days if transplanting is done during a period of high temperatures or if the plant is in a mature state. See the Encyclopedia of Perennials for transplanting requirements or limitations for particular plants.

MULCHING

We have become a society of overmulchers, feeling compelled to go out every spring and mulch, regardless of whether it's needed. Mulching makes the garden look neat and tidy, but we are suffocating our plants by piling the mulch up—especially on shallow-rooted woody plants like azaleas and rhododendrons—as well as potentially contributing to the rotting of our perennials.

A variety of different materials are available that can be used for mulching, but a light, fine-textured material is most suitable for perennials. I use a pine bark that is actually sold as a soil conditioner. It is similar to but slightly smaller than pine bark mini-chips and is dark, like the soil itself. Pine bark is easy to apply and to work with later for any additional planting. It can be worked directly into the soil. If I am applying a topdressing of compost, I do not use additional bark or other mulching products.

In the spring it is best to wait until the soil warms before mulching. No more than 2 in. of mulch should be applied, and it is most critical to keep the mulch away from the crowns of the perennials (where the stem meets the roots, usually found at soil level), as mulching over the crown will cause rot. I like to mulch the beds with 2 in. of material after planting, when the perennials are establishing. After that I use it with discretion, keeping the doses between 1 and 2 in., a sufficient amount to help control weeds, reduce moisture evaporation and temperature fluctuations, and protect against erosion and soil compaction. For perennials, I find that reducing winter temperature fluctuations in the soil is a primary benefit of mulching. Not only is frost heaving harmful to the plants, but research indicates that fluctuating temperatures also can cause certain physiological changes in herbaceous species that can weaken the plants and lead to death.

I rarely apply extra mulch for the winter. I only use perennials that can take our winters without this extra maintenance chore. Besides, I enjoy my perennial garden in the winter and don't like the idea of mounds of mulch or evergreens lying about. The exception would be for perennials transplanted or divided in autumn, which need 3 to 4 in. of mulch applied over their crowns after the ground has frozen. If you choose to grow marginally hardy perennials you will also need to follow this practice. In addition, certain subshrubs (plants that have a woody base but also have herbaceous shoots aboveground that die back annually) will burn if there is not persistent snow cover. They can be protected

with evergreen boughs, specifically old Christmas trees, cut into manageable pieces. Be sure they are light and open, such as pines. Rodents can also be a problem under the covers.

Mulch is generally sold in 2- and 3-cu.-ft.-size bags; it is also available in bulk in 1-cu.-yd. increments. To calculate the total number of 3-cu.-ft. bags of mulch needed to apply 2 in. of material to an area, divide the total square footage of the planting bed by 18 sq. ft. To calculate the number of 2-cu.-ft. bags needed, divide the square footage by 12 sq. ft. If using bulk material, 1 cu. yd. of material will cover 162 sq. ft.

WATERING

Proper watering of the newly planted perennial bed is vital to establishment of the plants. It is a good idea to check the new bed every other day for the first month after planting, not only to help guard against plants drying out, but also to allow you to get in touch with your new garden. Plants should be watered well, by hand, immediately after planting and mulching. With hand watering, water can be directed under the foliage right on the root ball where it is needed. I like to use a water wand because it makes it easy to reach into the plants and apply the right amount of water. A water wand is a long plastic extension with a nozzle on the end that can be attached to the end of a hose to deliver a fine spray of water.

The rule of 1 in. of water per week holds true while the plants are establishing. Use a rain gauge to determine how much water is being applied. Cans set up in various areas can determine coverage if a sprinkler is being used for watering. When perennials are just establishing, shallower and more frequent watering is needed because the plants are not yet rooted very deeply. As the plants become more established, after the first month, less frequent, deeper waterings are required to encourage the perennials to root more deeply and increase their drought resistance. Watering in the morning helps reduce incidence of disease and water lost through evaporation. Keep a close watch on watering in the first year to ensure that plants are not overwatered or underwatered. In subsequent years, plants can become acclimated to drier conditions with less frequent

These plants are thriving
in a soil amended with nutrient-
providing compost that drains
well.

watering. In my own gardens, although I will coddle newly planted perennials, watering well until established, I irrigate established plants only when I think they can't possibly stand another dry day. This is sometimes after weeks with minimal rainfall. Sure, some plants will succumb to drought, but most tolerate these conditions. There is no need to waste a valuable resource such as water, particularly when large quantities of water are not necessary for a beautiful perennial garden. Don't try to keep a moisture hog, such as ligularia, alive in an extremely dry site at the expense of excess watering. I have been able to grow ligularia in soil that remains moderately moist by lining the planting hole with a plastic bag to create a bathtub effect, which holds more moisture around the plant and reduces the need for large amounts of supplemental watering. The plants still usually wilt midday on hot days, but they recover nicely by evening.

A garden, particularly a new garden, should be watered into autumn as long as it is dry but not frozen. Just as perennials need well-draining soil for proper overwintering, they have a better chance of survival if they don't go into the winter in a dry condition.

If you are using an automatic irrigation system, make certain that the timer is set for more frequent, shallower waterings when the plants are establishing. As the plants establish, adjust for deeper, less frequent waterings. This is often a problem with automatic systems, as contractors set the timers as they do for turf, which is not appropriate for perennials. Drip irrigation systems have the great advantage that they are more efficient at moisture conservation, but the disadvantage is that problems in the irrigation system can go undetected because you can't see them. Watch plants with subirrigation closely for signs of line failure, be it a leak or clog. Make sure that the irrigation system has a rain gauge so that if sufficient rain has fallen, your irrigation will shut off. Troubles with irrigation can be a big problem with perennial plantings during establishment and in subsequent years if not closely monitored. Whatever irrigation system you choose, if you are not setting it up yourself it is a good idea to meet with the irrigation contractor to review the garden design, with its varied cross section, *before* the system is designed and installed. If using above-ground systems, make certain that taller plants are not blocking the spray from adjacent shorter plants.

FERTILIZING

Most perennials do not require large amounts of fertilizing; some, in fact, may resent such treatment, responding by producing excessive vegetative or leggy rank growth, minimal or no flowers, and possibly stunted root systems due to the highly soluble salts in the fertilizer. Silver-foliaged plants are particularly sensitive to overly rich conditions.

If soil is prepared properly from the start with nutrient-providing organic matter, supplemental fertilizing or topdressing might not be necessary for several years after planting. Studies have shown that a soil amended at bed preparation with 20 percent well-aged, quality compost, with an analysis of 1 percent nitrogen, will be sufficient to support most annual, perennial, tree, and shrub growth for at least the first year without any additional fertilizer. Nitrogen availability from such a compost usually is 25 percent for the 1st year, 10 percent for the 2nd and 3rd years, and declining to 5 percent in the 4th and 5th years. This means that if 1 in. of compost is used at bed preparation, 4 lb. of nitrogen per 1000 sq. ft. will be available in the 1st year. This is remarkable because the general recommendation for perennials is 1 lb. of nitrogen per 1000 sq. ft. However, organic nitrogen is dependent upon warm temperatures and microbial activity for release; in cool conditions, a small amount of quick-release fertilizer at planting will ensure adequate nutrients until the nitrogen is released in the compost with the coming of warm temperatures.

Findings suggest by extension that the majority of plants would benefit from a 1- to 2-in. topdressing of compost about once every 3 years, when the nitrogen availability from the compost begins to decline to about 10 percent. The recommendation often found in reference books to top-dress a garden annually with 3 to 4 in. of compost may be more than is necessary in many cases. Keep in mind, though, that slightly higher amounts of compost might be needed in the South than in the North because the humus in the soil tends to break down more quickly in the heat.

Topdressing with compost appears to be the best method for providing sufficient nutrients for perennials, and I rarely use fertilizer in my own gardens. Most of my perennial beds go 5 years with no additional nutrients and show no visible signs of the need for it. After 3 years, 1 bed fertilized with a general-purpose granular fertilizer showed no noticeable difference from the beds that were not fertilized. After 5 years, when some plants started to show decline (and this was partly because of the need for division), I tested the soil and found that the organic matter content had fallen to 6 percent (from approximately 16 percent after bed preparation). I top-dressed with 2 in. of compost (a blend of composted bio-solids and leaf compost), and this had a noticeable effect on the plants, providing more robust growth and better flowering.

Occasionally—for example, in situations where gardeners have large expanses of naturalized gardens or informal beds of mostly native plants—it's possible to get an annual addition of organic matter from the plants themselves. Roy Diblik advocates mowing perennial beds in early spring and leaving the plant remains in place to break down over time. This is often not practical in more conventional perennial gardens, but where feasible, it can be an option.

For a garden initially prepared with less than 20 percent compost, which also started with an organic matter content of less than 5 percent, fertilizers can be helpful in providing some immediate nutrients while the organics are building up in the soil and are slowly becoming available to the plants. In such a garden, in temperate soils, 3 consecutive yearly 1-in. applications of compost may be added to build up the organic matter in the soil. Take care to scratch or incorporate the compost lightly into the soil. The soil should be tested before the 4th-year application. Once the soil reaches an organic content of approximately 8 percent, compost application can be spaced to about once every 3 years.

My personal experience is that perennials growing in a rich organic soil have no great need for additional fertilizer. But just for insurance in my clients' gardens, I use a light application of a general-purpose, quick-release fertilizer in the spring following the first year. My belief here is that if any additional nutrients are needed it will be in the spring, when the plants are going into rapid growth and the organic nutrients in the soil may not be available due to cool weather conditions. Sprinkle the fertilizer around the base of the plants, avoiding the new growth to prevent burning. Watering in the fertilizer or applying it when the soil is moist also reduces the chance of burn. Moist soil is generally not a problem in central Ohio at the end of March or early April, which is usually when I am applying fertilizer. I top-dress with 2 in. of compost in the 4th or 5th year after the initial planting, along with any divisions and renovations that may be needed.

Fertilizer needs and rates of application ideally should be based on soil tests, but tests are not always practical on an annual basis. I base my calculations of fertilizer needs on the general recommendation for perennials, which is 1 lb. of nitrogen per 1000 sq. ft. The quantity of fertilizer should be based on this rate rather than on the recommendations on the fertilizer bag, because the latter rates can be too high for most perennials.

The granular fertilizer I use has an analysis of 12–12–12 or 5–10–5. So to calculate, for example, the amount of 5–10–5 fertilizer needed per 100 sq. ft. of area, based on 1 lb. of nitrogen per 1000 sq. ft., start with the fact that 1/10 of the total, or 0.1, will be needed for 100 sq. ft. (Remember, too, that because the numbers for the fertilizer refer to percentage of N, P, and K by weight, a 5–10–5 fertilizer has 5 percent N, or 0.05.)

$$0.1 \text{ lb. N per 100 sq. ft.} \div 0.05 \text{ N} = 2 \text{ lb. fert. per 100 sq. ft.}$$

Next, convert pounds to cups for easy measuring. For the general-size pelleted material that I use, 1 lb. of fertilizer equals 1½ cups. (You should test and weigh your own material because different fertilizers will have differences in granular size and bulk density.) So the 2 lb. of fertilizer needed for a 100-sq.-ft. area translates to 3 cups of fertilizer per 100 sq. ft.

If you're using the 12–12–12 fertilizer, 0.83 lb. of fertilizer is needed per 1000 sq. ft. (That is, ⁵⁄₁₂ of 2 lb. is 0.83 lb.) I round up to 1 lb. per 100 sq. ft. when using 12–12–12.

I also use organic fertilizers, including cottonseed meal (6 percent nitrogen, 2–3 percent phosphorus, 2 percent potassium), colloidal phosphate (0 percent nitrogen, 18–22 percent phosphorus, 0 percent potassium, 27 percent calcium, 1.7 percent iron, plus silicas and 14 other trace minerals), and greens and (0 percent nitrogen, 1 percent phosphorus, 5–7 percent potassium, 50 percent silica, 18–23 percent iron oxide, and 22 trace minerals) as well as Earth-Right (a composted soil conditioner containing animal, mineral, and sea products that can be applied as a topdressing) as substitutes for chemical fertilizers.

Perennials such as delphiniums, peonies, chrysanthemums, daisies, phlox, astilbes, and repeat-blooming daylilies are heavy feeders and may need a spring application of fertilizer as well as a summer application with a water-soluble fertilizer, even in soils high in organic matter. Delphiniums, for example, produce pale green new growth after being cut back, and this is a sign that fertilizing is needed. Repeat-blooming daylilies, such as *Hemerocallis* 'Happy Returns', especially benefit from foliar feeding (spraying liquid fertilizer directly on the surface of the leaves when first in bud). A water-soluble chemical (Peters' 20–20–20 or something similar) or organic fertilizer (such as fish emulsion or a seaweed-based product) can be chosen for foliar feeding. Foliar feeding results in a quicker uptake of nutrients. It should be performed early in the morning on an overcast day to prevent burning.

Again I must stress that proper initial preparation of your beds with organic matter can save on time and maintenance later. This point is clearly displayed when it comes to fertilizing perennials. If the soil is rich and the growing conditions are good, supplemental fertilizer is not necessary for most perennials. Topdressing with 1 to 2 in. of a high-quality aged compost every 3 years is the best approach to providing nutrients to most perennials, with regional adjustments possibly necessary. Heavy feeders like delphiniums may need some supplemental fertilizing.

WEED CONTROL

Ensuring that a bed is free of perennial weeds *before* planting is the first critical step toward weed control. If you are going to skip this detail, surrender now!

Close spacing of perennials is of benefit not only to the commercial grower selling many plants, but also to the home gardener because it helps eliminate weed competition. The biggest battle with weeds will be fought in the early spring, when weeds have sufficient light and room to grow since the perennials are still small. In the spring it can be difficult for even the savvy gardener to distinguish between a weed and a desirable perennial: "If in doubt, don't pull it out." A bit later in the plant's growth you will be able to make a clear call. Try to keep up with the weeds, or a relatively easy, methodical task can turn into a procrastinator's nightmare.

BASIC PERENNIAL GARDEN PLANTING & MAINTENANCE

Identifying the beast as annual, biennial, or perennial and its growth habit as stoloniferous, rhizomatous, or clump forming is necessary for developing the proper battle plan. Annuals generally last 1 season, then die; a biennial completes its life cycle in 2 seasons, then dies; a perennial normally survives for 3 or more seasons. A stolon is a horizontal stem above or just below the ground that forms roots at its tip to produce new plants; stoloniferous plants bear these. Rhizomes are horizontal underground stems that have nodes (points on a stem where leaves are attached), buds, or scalelike leaves and often are enlarged for food storage. Clump-forming plants divide and fill in open areas, developing an extensive root system.

Pre-emergent herbicides such as DCPA (Dacthal) or trifluraline (Preen) are sometimes used on perennial plantings for control of annual weed seeds. The problem with these herbicides is that they are species-specific as to which perennials on which they are safe to use. In diverse plantings, there is the risk of injury.

Careful application of glyphosate (Roundup) using a paintbrush can be effective on perennial weeds. I also know of gardeners who prefer a technique that involves wearing a cotton glove over a plastic glove, dipping the cotton glove in the herbicide, and then wiping the growing tips of weeds with the glove.

Most of the time I simply weed by hand. I like to use what's referred to as a Japanese weeding knife, which works really well on even the deepest rooted weeds (and no one else will mess with you when you're using it). I stay away from the use of chemicals.

Avoid seed set on the weeds as much as possible. One year I had a fantastic specimen, a 6-ft. bull thistle (*Cirsium vulgare*) flowering in my garden that made quite a show at an open garden tour. Visitors looked at it questioningly, afraid to ask whether it was another unusual plant of some sort, although it looked strikingly familiar. Could it be a type of *Acanthus*, or *Cynara*? I deadheaded the early flowers before seed set so that I could enjoy the flowers (and this little game) before removing the entire weed plant from the garden. Not something I would recommend on a regular basis, but look at the choices pruning provides!

I believe in planting a garden densely, in many layers, not only for season-long interest but also to help keep weeds down. It's actually best if you have to shoehorn in new plants.

RENOVATION OF THE ESTABLISHED PERENNIAL GARDEN

Frequently I am called upon to help with an existing perennial garden; the call can come for a variety of reasons. The owners may have decided that they are tired of the existing planting. They may have planted the garden themselves, with little background knowledge, and it never quite measured up to their expectations, or the planting might have been pleasing at one time but is now overrun by aggressive weeds. Often the plant performance was less than optimal, either because of poor plant choices for the growing conditions, or more often than not, poor initial soil preparation. Usually the owners are attached to some of the plants in the garden but could do without others, opting for newer introductions with longer bloom times, more fragrance, or perhaps finer habits. They have moved and removed things, added and subtracted, but it still doesn't gel. What to do?

In such cases we opt to renovate the garden. You start with some of the existing plants, design in some new plants, and most important, amend the bed properly. It's a fun and at times daunting process, but one that is always worth the effort in the end.

The first step is to evaluate the site. How much sun does it really get? Have trees or shrubs matured in such a way that the sun patterns or moisture levels of the garden have changed since it was first planted? Has new construction changed any views?

This small (25 ft. × 13 ft.), uninspired condominium "garden," with a few token perennials and the "same old, same old" woody plants, was in great need of a makeover.

By incorporating a 3-foot winding path, trellis for vines, and espaliered cherry trees to utilize the vertical space next to the house, we start to see a real garden developing. The woody plants were placed and planted prior to herbaceous plants.

(opposite) The garden 1 month after planting.

Next, have the objectives or commitments of the owner changed? Is there now more or less time for maintenance? Are there new pets or new children? Perhaps interior redecorating, or taste, has changed the color focus of the garden. This is a good opportunity to think things over clearly and thoroughly. The advantage in garden renovation projects is that you know what has and has not worked, and this can help greatly with decision making.

A primary concern in deciding which plants make the cut in the redesign is the prevalence of weeds. If stoloniferous weeds have really gotten into a plant, it may be best to get rid of the plant and just buy a new one, or something else, rather than risk reintroducing a fragment of weed that will take over the world even faster in your nice new organic soil. There is no sense in going to all the trouble of redoing a garden and then putting the weeds or aggressive perennials right back into it. And you are not doing your family or friends a favor by giving them such a plant either.

Aside from concerns of weediness, a plant may simply be a "dog" and not worth the effort to replant. Perhaps it was purchased in a weak moment, or was

given to you by a well-meaning individual renovating his or her own perennial garden. It just might not fit into the new objectives for the garden.

In my business, I will visit the garden in the summer or early autumn when things are in active growth so that I can really see what is going on. (This is often to the dismay of the owner who has had to wait patiently since making his or her winter or early spring decision to "do something with the garden.") During this visit a list is made of everything in the garden, including approximate numbers or sizes of clumps and the condition and approximate location of the plants. Actual measurements help a lot, because when you are back at the drawing table months later, notes that say "a large clump of Siberian iris" or "a small clump of bergenia" lose all context and perspective. This preliminary visit is also the time to evaluate what plants should be considered for returning to the garden based on the owner's wishes and the plants' condition or worth. These notes will help during the re-design process, when it may be decided that additional plants also need to go. Even a plant that has been cut from the draft needs to be recorded for figuring labor and time involved in removing it from the garden, especially if the plant is to be spared for a friend.

After the initial note-taking visit to the site, I usually redesign the garden over the winter for renovation the following spring. Renovation can also be done in early autumn; particularly in areas with milder winters and in areas with very hot and dry summers, autumn may in fact be the preferred season. I am not comfortable with redoing an entire garden in the autumn, especially someone else's entire garden, not being sure of what the winter will bring. While redesigning you must decide how much of a plant is to be saved and where it can be used as well as where new plants can be integrated. This can be a bit challenging because you are not working with a clean canvas but rather trying to save and use as many of the existing plants as possible, yet incorporating new ones as well.

Ideally the plants should be lifted from the garden in early spring, when new growth is just emerging yet high enough that you can see what is what. Lay a tarp down to protect the grass and place the plants on it. If the plants need to remain out of the ground for longer than a day before replanting—that is, if more work, such as weeding, needs to be done at a later time to prepare the bed for planting—I put them into flats and pots. Flats are good for small and shallow-rooted perennials, and pots are for sizable clumps of large-growing species. If any divisions are to be made, they should also be done at this time. The plants should be placed in the shade and kept watered. Sometimes they need to be held there for up to 2 weeks. If replanting that same day, all plants are removed, divisions are made, and the beds prepared, planted, and mulched. Try to pick a cool and overcast day for garden renovation work.

If weeds or invasive perennials are a problem in the beds—and usually they are—the best approach is to remove the desired plants, then spray the entire bed with Roundup (glyphosate) or another nonselective, nonresidual systemic herbicide. Any plants that aren't to be saved for reuse or recycling can be sprayed along with the weeds. Then wait 2 weeks and replant as above.

How long a garden renovation will take depends on several factors, such as number of plants to be saved, the age of the clumps to be moved, the condition of the existing soil, and the speed and efficiency of the people doing the work. I figure approximately 1 hour of labor for every 16 to 22 sq. ft. of bed.

Small sections of a large garden can be renovated individually so that the work is phased. It is risky to do the herbicide spraying in such a case, though, with desirables all around the renovated area. Renovating a perennial garden, like renovating a room or a home, can be an involved project, but one that you'll be glad you ventured into when you sit back and enjoy the delightful results.

The same garden, more than a decade later. It's so rewarding to watch a garden grow and evolve and still maintain the original design integrity and vision.

Pests and Diseases

sually few major pest and disease problems will be encountered in perennial gardens if time has been put into the proper selection of insect- and disease-resistant species, as well as into locating plants in the proper sites for optimal growth. There should be no reason to grow plants that require serious chemical controls given that so many outstanding perennials are free of pests or are unlikely to be seriously damaged. Battling pests with the use of controls that aren't truly necessary is a waste of time and contributes to the destruction of our environment. We need to be tolerant of a few holes or spots on leaves, or even in some years the destruction of the whole plant. Remember, herbaceous perennials will often send up new foliage later in the season even if totally defoliated early on or if pruned down as a result of serious damage. They will at least be back the following year to give it another try. Give a plant a couple of seasons—it may be affected with ailments some years, while in others it sails through cleanly, usually depending on weather conditions. If all our efforts at proper plant selection, sound cultural practices, patience, and the use of environmentally sound control methods have failed, then I think it's time to ask the afflicted plant to leave the garden!

Perennials that are sharp or spiny, such as this globe thistle (*Echinops ritro*), are naturally deer resistant.

PEST AND DISEASE PREVENTION

A stress-free plant is less susceptible to disease and insects than one growing in a stressful environment. Proper soil and water management are crucial to reducing stress on perennials. Keeping the garden free of debris is also helpful. Some gardeners believe that yellow foliage attracts insects and so believe that deadleafing is vital to avoid welcoming trouble (although I have not found this to be the case). Many insects and diseases overwinter on decaying foliage of certain perennials, so infected foliage should be removed from the garden in the autumn—do not compost these materials if your pile does not reach temperatures high enough to ensure that the pests are killed. Avoiding overhead irrigation can help reduce the chance of disease and its spread. The spacing of perennials in the garden can affect certain species' susceptibility to pests. Having a diverse number of species in the garden is important because many pests and diseases are species-specific, and so your whole garden or a big part of it won't be wiped out if you include species that are not prone to the pest in question.

If we want beauties like these visiting our gardens we need to pay the price of some damage by their larvae.

IDENTIFYING THE PROBLEM

The next step in pest control is identifying the pest and determining if it's truly a problem. Too often, insecticide or fungicide is grabbed and sprayed on the plant without a clue as to the real problem. I have had perennials such as 'Silver Brocade' beach wormwood (*Artemisia stelleriana* 'Silver Brocade') and copper fennel (*Foeniculum vulgare* 'Purpureum') completely eaten by what appeared to be just some caterpillar. It turned out to be butterfly larvae. *Artemisia stelleriana*, along with species of *Anaphalis* (pearly everlasting) and *Antennaria* (pussytoes), are host plants of the American lady butterfly; fennel feeds black swallowtails in the East and anise swallowtails in the West. Several other perennials are favored caterpillar food: hollyhocks of painted lady butterflies, rue (*Ruta graveolens*) of giant swallowtails and black swallowtails, and milkweeds (*Asclepias* spp.) of monarchs. This demonstrates the importance of proper identification of the so-called pest in question. The plants may look a little rough at times, but who cares when it means more butterflies in the garden? Perennials usually recover from damage with fresh basal growth anyway, either that same year or the following season.

Beneficial insects

Likewise, when you see orange beetles on your echinacea and heliopsis, don't spray them with the fear that the beetles are going to destroy your perennials—let these beneficial soldier beetles do their part in helping combat pests. Beneficial insects can help you control pests in your garden naturally. Encourage them by planting perennials that produce a lot of pollen or nectar. Native plants in the daisy family (Compositae), such as species of *Achillea* (yarrow), *Coreopsis* (tickseed), *Eutrochium* (Joe Pye weed), *Solidago* (goldenrod), and *Symphyotrichum* (asters), are especially attractive to them. Parsley family (Apiaceae) members like fennel and dill will also bring in hardworking beneficials, as will many mint family (Lamiaceae) representatives such as our native anise hyssop (*Agastache foeniculum*). Let beneficial ladybugs, lacewings, hoverflies, tachinid flies, and parasitic wasps help keep harmful pests to a minimum.

Larvae damage and "droppings" on *Artemisia stelleriana* 'Silver Brocade'.

TAKING ACTION

If you have a problem you can't ignore or tolerate, you need to decide what form of control measures to take. Manual or mechanical control with hands, feet, strong sprays of water, pruners, and traps should be the primary control. This manual approach is normally the only one that I take in combating pests in my gardens and in my clients' gardens. Insecticidal soaps would be the strongest control worth considering in the perennial garden, and even these are necessary only in limited cases. Many of the pests discussed here can be controlled with such soaps if the gardener feels that it is finally necessary. A mask should be worn when spraying insecticidal soaps because they can irritate the lining of the lungs. Certain perennials, such as bleeding heart (dicentra and lamprocapnos) and ferns such as the Japanese painted fern (*Anisocampium niponicum* 'Pictum'), are sensitive to soap-based products. Test a small area first before spraying an entire plant or group of plants. Other chemical sprays and dusts, including naturally derived chemicals such as rotenone or pyrethrin-based products, are not necessary. Keep in mind that just because a product is naturally derived doesn't mean that it is not toxic to one degree or another, either to humans, fish, birds, pets, or beneficial insects.

It's worth remembering that phlox and mildew, hosta and slugs, bearded iris and borers, and columbine and leafminer are frequent companions. If you can't eradicate a problem completely, ask what can be done to reduce the problem, or consider how you can alter your attitude to accept some of it.

DISEASE PROBLEMS

Stem and root rots can occur in certain perennial species where soil conditions are too moist. Damaged plants should be removed, and soil drainage improved. Perennials troubled with different leaf spots should have the affected parts pruned off if they are a problem.

Peonies in particular can have a host of problems. They look tatty and start to decline with the heat of August. This is because new eyes, or dormant growth buds, start to form at this time, taking the strength from the foliar portion of the plant. Klehm Nursery, famous American peony growers, recommends that gardeners not prune the plants until after the first of September in zones 3, 4, and upper zone 5; until the end of September in the rest of zone 5; and until after early October in zones 6, 7, or below. Resist pruning back even if the plants look ugly, so they can continue to photosynthesize, which will usually mean healthier plants the following year.

Botrytis and *Phytophthora*

The red peonies, as well as the more fragrant forms, are always more susceptible to disease. Klehm Nursery explains that this is because the red peonies produce more carbohydrates (evident by sticky sugars on the buds). *Botrytis*, an airborne disease, sticks to these buds more easily. *Paeonia tenuifolia* 'Flore Plena' (double fernleaf peony), which is red, is very susceptible to disease, so it is recommended that this form be deadheaded immediately after flowering to prevent the entry of disease from the mushy dead flower into the soft stem. Soil should also be kept well drained. If peonies are infected with disease, prune off infected parts and remove any debris from the base of the plants. All foliage and debris from around the plants must be removed each autumn and destroyed, not composted, to remove the possible sources of the *Botrytis*.

Phytophthora is one of the most common causes of root and stem base decay in a wide range of trees and shrubs, and is often characterized by yellow or sparse foliage, wilting, and branch dieback.

Powdery mildew

Powdery mildew can rob a plant of water and nutrients and cause leaf yellowing and even distortion of the plant, though usually only in extreme cases. Let's start by selecting resistant plants. I know of more than 20 mildew-resistant *Phlox* forms, in a variety of flower colors, heights, and bloom times, and I'm sure there are many more; a fair number of mildew-resistant beebalm (*Monarda didyma*) cultivars are also available. Some of these phlox and beebalms might not be totally free of disease, and again, much depends on the weather conditions, but I think we can live with a light dusting or a spot or two—the plants definitely can. Phlox and monarda both can be cut to the ground if mildew is a problem. They will usually put up fresh, clean growth later in the season if provided with sufficient moisture and will not miss a stride the following year. When cutting down infected plants, it's a good idea to disinfect your pruners by dipping them in a 10 percent bleach solution (1 part bleach to 9 parts water) or at least wash them with soap and water after cutting to reduce the chance of continued spread.

Powdery mildew is a unique fungus in that its life cycle is not encouraged by free water but rather by high humidity and lack of air circulation, as well as

The foliage of 'Nice Gal' peony (top) holds up pretty well through the season compared to many other peonies, such as 'Festiva Maxima' (bottom), which exhibits the unsightly decline of many peonies.

temperature fluctuations, such as warm dry days and cool nights. Close spacing of plants can contribute to decreased air movement, so providing a bit more room for the plants and keeping them away from walls or thick hedges can help decrease problems. Thinning of mildew-prone perennials is often recommended to improve air circulation within the plant's structure, although with phlox I have not noticed any reliable difference between thinned plants and unthinned plants—both seem to get mildew equally well if the conditions are right. It seems that selecting resistant forms is the surest approach.

Other mildew-ridden perennials include species of *Pulmonaria* and *Chrysogonum*, which are often subject to attack in dry locations. Plants can be cut to the ground—sometimes new clean growth will be already evident under mildew-ridden foliage, but not always—and fresh clean leaves will emerge.

Rust

Rust diseases are rarely a problem with perennials. Improving air circulation around the plants and growing plants in lean, well-draining soil can help reduce the incidence of rust. If it does occur, the affected plant parts can be pruned off.

PEST PROBLEMS

One hopes that perennial gardens are full of people and friendly creatures. It is our duty as gardeners to minimize damage from pests by selecting resistant plants, practicing sound cultural habits, accurately identifying any problems, and then handling them with some tolerance and manual controls before resorting to any form of chemical control that might have negative long-lasting effects.

Slugs

A limited number of perennial genera are troubled by slugs—*Acanthus*, *Delphinium*, *Ligularia*, and *Hosta* come to mind. But because hostas are such a popular perennial in many gardens, slugs seem to be a rather prevalent problem.

Hostas with a thicker substance to their foliage and those whose leaves do not come in contact with the ground are usually less prone to slug damage, although this varies depending on location. How favorable are the conditions to slugs to begin with and how many of them are there? If a slug is hungry enough, I'm sure even the most discerning slug (if there are any) would eat the most thick-skinned hosta. (See the discussion of *Hosta* in the Encyclopedia of Perennials for slug-resistant types.)

All the usual remedies can be used against slugs, including the beer bash (stale beer in shallow containers) and salt shaker approach, although these are not always practical from a contractor's point of view. I use diatomaceous earth (crushed sea diatoms) in clients' gardens for *Hosta* and *Ligularia* plants that suffer a good deal of damage. Apparently slugs don't like to crawl over the rough surface of the diatoms (such delicate creatures!), so a collar of sand or ashes around the plants may have similar effect. Diatomaceous earth is helpful in curbing the problem, but doesn't eliminate it completely, and it needs frequent replenishment. Van Wade, one of the premier hosta growers in the United States, has found that mulching with pine needles helps reduce slug numbers. Copper strips (sold as Snail-Barr) will give slugs a mild electric shock if they crawl over them. I do not use any metaldehyde-based baits because of their toxicity to cats, dogs, birds, and toads—all which live in the gardens. In recent years, iron phosphate–based products like Sluggo have become popular weapons in the battle against slugs and snails, and are safer to use around pets than metaldehyde-based pesticides.

Fortunately I do not have many problems with slugs in my own gardens. This may be due to several factors: my gardens are generally on the dry side, and a bit of slug damage doesn't bother me. It may also be because I have a fair number of toads in my gardens, and toads are predaceous of slugs. I have heard that delphinium and monkshood (*Aconitum*) have their own self-defense mechanism: after the first set of leaves are lost to slugs, plants send out a second set that are supposedly toxic to slugs. (Interestingly, both of these plants are poisonous to humans if ingested.)

Borers

When it comes to iris and borers, I feel the easiest solution is to avoid, or at least limit, the use of bearded iris. I never use them in clients' gardens, and the only ones I have in my own gardens were either given to me by my grandmother or by a friend, or are reblooming forms I wanted to test. I enjoy them enough when they are flowering, but I don't find *Iris ×germanica* to be worth the trouble of the horrid leaves that follow. Of the reblooming forms, I have been happiest with one called 'Perfume Counter', a purple-flowered cultivar whose foliage holds up much longer than that of other forms.

I feel the best alternative to bearded irises are Siberian irises (*Iris sibirica*). They add such great vertical form to the garden, and the flowers are gorgeous. The seedpods can be even more interesting than the flowers, contributing to the garden for the entire summer and winter. (Cut them in the spring for use in dried arrangements.) The foliage turns yellow in the autumn, providing ornamental benefits in that season. And best of all—no pests!

Many people simply must have bearded iris, however, in which case a few tactics can be employed to fight the borer. If you can see it, crush the borer in the iris leaves. When the leaves are badly affected I cut them down to a few inches above the rhizome—it looks tacky, but better than the previous brown-spotted option. Cutting at an angle reduces the "crew cut" look. I also just pull out the brown, curled-up leaves at the base of the plants. In the autumn, it is important to cut down the leaves again, and remove any brown leaves at the base of the plant, because the borer eggs overwinter on them. Do not compost infected iris leaves. Planting the rhizome high so that it is exposed to the sun helps reduce bacterial soft rot (*Pectobacterium carotovorum*), which often sets in after the borers and in fact causes most of the trouble.

Leafminer

Leafminer can be handled simply by pruning off infested leaves or by cutting the entire plant to the ground when symptoms get severe. Do not compost leaves and be certain to clean up debris in the autumn. Trying to prevent leafminers is a waste of effort because they don't cause long-term harm to the plants.

Japanese beetle

The main pests I have to contend with in my gardens are Japanese beetles, fourlined plant bugs, and grasshoppers. If you have small numbers of Japanese beetles, you can pick them off and put them in soapy water. But is it possible to have small numbers of Japanese beetles? I never have. I get masses of them in disgusting numbers. They are so taken by my rugosa roses (*Rosa rugosa*), which they practically destroy each year, that they usually leave my perennials alone, except for *Kirengeshoma palmata* and *Alcea rosea*. When my son was young, he would start watching for the beetles in early June, and we both derived great pleasure from catching them, smashing them, or even more rewarding, putting them in one of his bug boxes, with plain water, and using them for fish bait in our pond. Bluegills and bass love them. Even the catfish go for them if they are hungry enough. We would throw clumps of Japanese beetles into the water like chum to attract the fish. It's a bit scary how gratifying this bit of gardener's revenge can be, particularly baiting the hook! The only problem is keeping up with the quantity that eventually descends on the gardens. I have tried using traps placed about a hundred yards away from the gardens, and this has some-times helped in reducing the numbers, but there is always some fish bait available even in September. If you live in a residential area, you probably will only attract more beetles to your garden with traps. If you do try them, the traps should be placed as far away from your beds as possible.

Fourlined plant bug

Fourlined plant bugs leave small, round, sunken tan spots on the leaves and sometimes cause stunted growth of my veronica, boltonia, and foxglove. Fourlined plant bugs are also particularly fond of members of the mint family (Lamiaceae). The nymphs are bright red and appear in May or June. The adults are greenish yellow and, as the name implies, have four black lines down the wings. There is only a single generation of fourlined plant bugs per year. I control them by smashing nymphs and adults, when I can catch them. Sometimes plants seem to grow out of the damage. Other times, if the damage is too severe, I prune off the damaged sections. Some gardeners control nymphs with insecticidal soaps. The bugs lay their eggs in the stems of host perennials to overwinter, so it is important to cut these plants to the ground in the autumn and clean up the debris. Do not compost the autumn debris.

Grasshoppers

Walking down my back garden path on a summer's day is like being in an Alfred Hitchcock movie, with scads of grasshoppers flying up at you. It truly adds another dimension to perennial gardening. On top of form, texture, color, movement, sound, and time, we have bombardment, and I could certainly do without it. Grasshoppers seem to like to eat just about everything. They likely are prevalent only in country gardens.

I have had some success with a garlic-based product to fight the grasshoppers. It curbs them a bit, but I have a hard time keeping up with all the repeat applications this method requires. I start spraying the first week of July and then seem to need to do it weekly through August and into September. Most recommendations for controlling grasshoppers suggest also controlling or spraying adjacent weeds, which can be the original source of the problem, but when you have over 30 some acres of weeds around your gardens, that's not a very practical approach.

Black blister beetles

One year I found, much to my horror, black beetles covering my Japanese anemones (*Anemone* ×*hybrida*) and ground clematis (*Clematis recta*). It was mid-July and they were doing a good job of completely decimating both species. I looked up the pests, only to discover that they were black blister beetles, which,

Black blister beetle damage on *Clematis recta.*

lo and behold, favor Japanese anemones and clematis as well as asters and dianthus. I also discovered that the larvae are in fact beneficial: they eat grasshopper eggs in the soil—amazing! So the dilemma was whether to attempt a major control effort of the beetles, or to use them as a natural defense against the grasshoppers and let them eat my anemones and clematis, which were the only plants they had harmed? Obviously the black blister beetles were there for a reason, and it felt wrong to me to mess with the intended natural balance. I did knock off as many as I could, with a booted foot, and smashed them. Do not handle the adults with your bare hands; the blister beetles get their name from a nasty chemical they spray, called cantharidin, which causes severe skin inflammation and blisters. You can also use chemical-resistant gloves to knock the beetles off into a bucket containing a solution of soap and water.

Interestingly, *Clematis recta* plants that had been cut to the ground earlier in July (to control their sprawling habit), before the appearance of the beetles, missed the damage of the beetles' attack. From now on I will prune clematis to the ground before the beetles attack. Any beetles that remain when the new growth emerges are easily knocked off and smashed. In fact, the pruned plants went on to bloom again sporadically in September.

For the anemone, you should prune to the ground the bare, brown, leafless stems that remain after the beetles have eaten all the leaves. New growth will emerge nicely, though my plants failed to flower. In future years, if the blister beetle numbers increase and spread to other species of perennials, I may need to resort to different tactics. But for now I want to see if the black blister beetles have any noticeable effect on my grasshopper population.

Chicken-wire fencing around an island bed of perennials can be used to keep rabbits at bay.

Aphids, spider mites, and more

Aphids, spider mites, and spittlebugs are sucking insects that sometimes affect perennials, although these pests generally don't do much damage to the plants. *Heliopsis*, for one, is often loaded with aphids without any sign of harm, at least not until early September, when most flowering is finished and the plants are beginning to decline a bit anyway. If aphid damage becomes evident after flowering, the entire plant can be cut to the ground. Aphids, spider mites, and spittlebugs can be washed off with a strong spray of water.

Thrips can damage flower buds or distort petals and stunt growth on perennials such as daylilies (*Hemerocallis*). Affected plant parts should be pruned off and destroyed. This might mean shearing down the troubled daylily, but it will develop new growth in a number of weeks, depending on the moisture it receives.

Lily leaf beetles

Lily leaf beetles, first spotted in the United States in the 1990s, have become a growing problem and are now found in the New England states, New York, and Washington state. These bright red beetles feed voraciously both as adults and as larvae on lilies (*Lilium* spp.) and fritillaries (*Fritillaria* spp.), occasionally dining on Solomon's seal, lily-of-the-valley, and hostas. Regular handpicking of adults, larvae, and eggs (found on the undersides of leaves) is the recommended form of control. It isn't a job for the squeamish, as the young cover themselves in their own excrement as a deterrent to predators. As adults, their defense mechanism is to drop to the ground when disturbed, sometimes emitting a little squeak. Researchers are working on finding a safe and effective biological control for this troublesome pest.

Other pests

Rabbits, raccoons, squirrels, chipmunks, and deer all add to the already challenging world of perennial gardening. Most of us have problems with at least one if not several of these beasts.

My best defense against most such garden intruders are my cats, which live exclusively in the gardens and woods of our property. They are of great benefit against the small rodent-type pests. I have had little problem even with rabbits, thanks to the cats, which is incredible considering our home's country setting. I have suggested that clients acquire cats if the rabbit damage is serious. If a cat isn't the answer—and cats aren't always the best solution, as they may wreak havoc on bird populations—another option is fencing the border with chicken wire. The fencing isn't visible from a distance once the perennials fill in, and it beats trying to use repellents against the rabbits, which wash off with the rains and need to be applied frequently to the emerging new growth of perennials, particularly pruned perennials. Composted sewage sludge used in soil preparation is said to help deter rabbits as well as voles.

Chipmunks and squirrels do their damage by digging around the roots of perennials, particularly over the winter. The roots are then exposed to freezing temperatures, which can be the cause of the plant's demise.

I have trouble with raccoons. Whenever I plant new perennials in the gardens, that very night (I'm sure they're watching me with binoculars from the trees) the raccoons dig up the plants and leave them lying on top of the soil. I have found that sprinkling black pepper on the soil around newly planted perennials usually prevents the damage. I buy pepper in the industrial size and in rather large quantities (the grocery clerks aren't sure what kind of cook I am!). I know of other gardeners who rely on black pepper to control moles, rabbits, ground hogs, and squirrels. Pepper needs to be reapplied to newly planted areas after a rain.

Dogs can be helpful in pest control. I was once blessed with a golden retriever who was also an exceptional listener. When she was young she learned quickly the importance of the command "no gardens," and so even if her Frisbee landed in the gardens she would wait on the outside until the launcher of the bum throw came to fetch it out for her. Many breeds of dogs are not so cooperative, however. For many, digging is preferred over Frisbees. Or simply lying on a prized perennial will suffice. In such cases I have had clients use either chicken wire around the border, if it is small enough, or yellow tape tied from stake to stake around the garden, which keeps the dogs out but also makes the garden look like it is constantly under construction. The surest approach is the use of an invisible electronic fence around the gardens.

Deer deserve a book of their own, and several are available. If you have problems with deer, I'm sure any of the above so-called pests seem like a piece of cake comparatively. Combining a variety of control measures, from cultural to mechanical, is the best approach to keeping deer away. The scent of a dog can help to deter deer, even if the dog isn't keen on patrolling the garden. Several different deer repellents are available, and Liquid Fence, made from plant oils, seems to be the most effective one currently on the market. You should alternate repellents so that the deer don't get accustomed to them. And of course the repellents need to be applied frequently to rapidly growing perennials. Milorganite, Milwaukee's composted municipal sludge, is sold as an organic fertilizer and has been shown to help keep deer away. Its effect is lessened in the autumn when the odor is less pronounced.

Black plastic mesh deer fencing comes in 7½-ft.-high rolls and is fairly inexpensive. It is practically invisible and lasts 10 years. Obviously, the entire area must be completely enclosed in order for the fencing to be effective. Some gardeners use a 4-ft. chicken wire "mulch" around plantings, and others place Vexar (a dark bird netting) over plants in bud or use it as a mulch.

Growing plants on the lean side, trying to avoid lush succulent growth, and growing a variety of plants may help in deer prevention. Deer usually avoid pubescent (covered with short, soft hairs), aromatic, spiny, or toxic plants. Damage from deer depends on many factors, including the size of the deer population, the amount of space available to them, other available food sources, weather conditions, and time of year. Certain plants that may never be eaten in one garden are the favorite treat of deer in another.

Staking

Staking is not my idea of fun. No matter what kind of stakes or technique I use, it's still a chore I could do without. One way to skirt the staking issue is to select tall plants that are self-supporting—but this isn't always a solution, because what is free standing in one situation might not be in another. A need for staking can be due to richer or moister soil, heavier winds or rains, more shade, the fact that division is needed, or sometimes I'd swear it's simply contrariness on the plant's part! Another way to get around staking is to use shorter growing cultivars. Planting tightly, so that neighbors can help hold up a falling individual, is a choice method for airy perennials. Heavier tumbling plants will simply pull their companions down with them. Sometimes plants need to be lifted up off smaller neighbors so the lesser counterpart doesn't remain completely hidden or rot from lack of light and high moisture under the canopy. Pinching or cutting back is one of the most effective ways to avoid staking. Unfortunately, even with all these alternatives, staking isn't always avoidable.

So, if it needs to be done, do it early, after the first flush of growth but before full growth. The stems need to be sturdy, and flower buds should not be formed yet. Stakes placed early are easily hidden by maturing foliage. Avoid waiting until it is too late, when the plants have already toppled over and the stems have started to be affected by polarity.

Staking should be done as naturally as possible, without adulterating the normal habit of the plant. Follow the natural line of the stem. Use natural materials such as branches whenever feasible, and for ties use jute or string that blends well and is biodegradable (plastic-coated twist ties are not!). Examine the plant closely. Perhaps only the center of the plant is falling open. In that case only the sagging section, not the entire plant, needs to be staked. Don't tie the stem so tightly that it looks restricted. Let stems have a bit of slack to allow some movement.

Single stakes such as bamboo or steel bamboo-look-alikes are most effective for plants with spiked flowers (a group of flowers on a single upright stem) or with single heavy flowers. Tie the jute or string around the stem first and then around the stake, or make a twist in the tie, so that the plant is not in contact with the stake. Sometimes the stem will need to be tied in several locations along the stake. The stakes ideally should end approximately 6 in. lower than the

Staking should be done as naturally as possible. Single stakes are effectively used on this foxglove (*Digitalis purpurea*).

flowers or about three-quarters the mature height of the plant. The exception would be large-flowered plants with weak stems, where the flowers simply snap at a spot above the stake, infuriating the gardener. Weak-stemmed perennials, including the large-flowered Pacific Giant hybrid delphiniums, need to be staked all the way to the tip of the flower to prevent this—I'd rather grow *Delphinium ×belladonna* 'Bellamosum', a reliable smaller plant with smaller and airier flowers, that doesn't need support all the way up the stems.

Hoops or rings are useful for full, bushy plants such as peonies. The hoops should stand at half the mature height of the plant. The plant should be allowed to mature and spread out above the hoop naturally.

Pea staking, or the use of fine, twiggy branches, is effective with light, airy plants such as *Clematis recta* (ground clematis) and *Gypsophila paniculata* (baby's breath). It's a good idea to cut the branches when they are dormant to prevent them from rooting and sprouting in the garden while they are holding up your plants. Ideally the branches should be 6 in. shorter than the mature plant. I learned of this technique while working in England, and it's by far my favorite.

Single-stake method. Note the twist in the tie to keep the plant from coming in contact with the stake.

Linking stakes are available in many different sizes to fit a variety of plant sizes and shapes. They can be difficult to get into the ground at times, and then when you succeed, they may not be even, making it a challenge to link the stakes together. Yet I like them, especially for taller plants like 'Alaska' Shasta daisies (*Leucanthemum ×superbum* 'Alaska'). Linking stakes have the advantage that they can be inserted when the plant is a bit more mature.

Other staking devices that can be used with perennials include chicken wire held up with stakes, especially for thin-stemmed species of *Symphyotrichum* or *Boltonia* (although neither of these genera require staking if pruned properly). The chicken wire cylinder should be shorter than the mature height of the plant and slightly narrower than the mature width. Tomato cages can be employed in a similar manner. Bamboo stakes

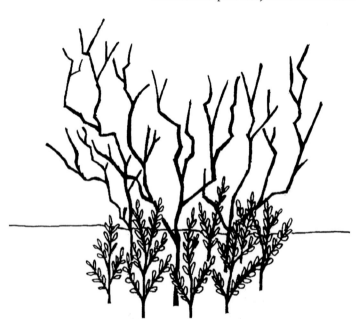

Pea staking.

connected by intricate crossing twine are useful for large perennials with numerous stems that require internal support. This technique can also be used effectively on perennials that were not staked and have fallen. If the stem tips have already started to bend, they may grow straight again if not too far gone, but

in most cases it's best to pinch or cut them off; the stems will branch and fill in. Criss-crossing bamboo stakes is an effective way to hold up sections of low-growing plants such as nepeta or geranium.

    If done properly, staking can help to greatly improve the appearance of many perennials. Don't let the plants fool you. One year my 'Alaska' Shasta daisies were looking stocky and upright, and I thought I was going to get away with not staking them. The gardens were to be photographed by a magazine, but that very night a major storm came through and knocked the plants silly. Needless to say, since then I have staked regardless of whether they looked like they were going to need it, because normally they do. Remember to remove the stakes after plants have been cut back. Empty stakes hovering over fresh new foliage is as obtrusive as any unstaked plant on its worst day.

Rudbeckia nitida 'Herbstsonne' cut back by half in early June produces a shorter, 4½- to 5-ft.-tall plant such as this, which won't require staking even in a garden exposed to winds.

Division

A perennial garden whose owner's primary objective for the garden is low maintenance simply should not contain plants that require division annually or even every couple of years. No worries though, as there are plenty of perennials that don't require division for 3 to 5 years. And many can go 6 to 10 years or even longer without division. In fact, several perennials would rather not be bothered at all. However, you should not let division requirements limit you too much in plant selection. It isn't as dramatic a procedure as it might first appear. In fact, it can be very satisfying, having a rejuvenating effect on perennial and gardener alike.

There is plenty to do in the perennial garden without going around needlessly dividing perennials. The growing conditions often will affect whether a plant is going to need division sooner or later. Some invasive plants can be more or less aggressive depending on the soil, amount of moisture available, and so forth. The plants will send signs when division is in order: the flowers may get smaller; the clump may take on the appearance of a traffic jam, with the stems and branches getting all tangled up; the plant may develop a hole in its center, taking on the form of a donut; the plant in general may have less vigor; it may flop more, requiring staking that it never needed in its prime; or it may need division to keep its spread in bounds. A perennial may also need division simply if the gardener decides he or she wants more plants, or if generous friends force that decision.

The perennial division gods once proclaimed that spring-flowering plants should be divided in the autumn, and autumn-flowering plants divided in the spring. This gospel stuck, and you see it stated in most of the literature. I'm not about to overturn tradition! But you gain an entire season of growth if early spring–flowering plants are divided right after flowering in April or May. If you don't mind sacrificing flowers for that year, the plants can even be divided in very early spring before flowering. Spring division also gives more time for establishment before winter. The tale holds true that autumn-flowering plants should be divided in spring, and this includes most ornamental grasses. For these reasons I tend toward spring division for almost everything, whenever possible.

Plants not suitable for spring division include fleshy rooted perennials such as peony (*Paeonia*), oriental poppy (*Papaver orientale*), and Siberian iris (*Iris sibirica*), which are best divided in autumn. Siberian iris will tolerate spring

When selecting perennials, consider how frequently they will need to be divided. Russian sage (*Perovskia atriplicifolia*) in the foreground and 'Milkshake' coneflower (*Echinacea purpurea* 'Milkshake'), midground, require infrequent division—sometimes not for 10 years. 'Lucifer' crocosmia (*Crocosmia* 'Lucifer'), in the background, may need more frequent division for best flowering; possibly every 3 years.

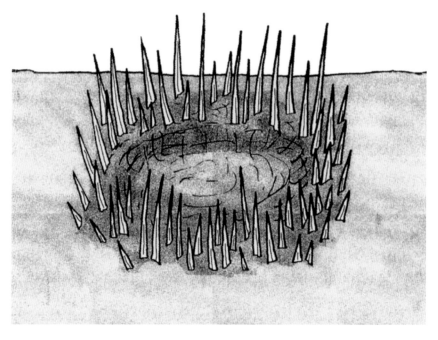

A sign that division is needed: when a hole or dead space develops in the center of the plant.

division only with sufficient moisture. In the Midwest, September is a good month for autumn divisions. Divisions should be done about 1 month before killing frost.

Most plants will not divide well in summer; an exception would be bearded iris, which is dormant in the summer and traditionally is divided in August. The tough nuts like hosta and daylily and a few other rugged perennials will take summer division. A hosta may respond by flopping, but by the next season it will regain its normal habit. When dividing in the summer and autumn it is best to cut the plants back by half to two-thirds to reduce transpiration (water loss by evaporation from leaves and stems). Cutting the plants back before division also makes it easier to see where to divide, although many gardeners cut back the plants after division. With summer divisions, extra care is needed to keep plants moist and shaded if hot and dry weather is expected.

Perennials with tough woody roots or taproots, such as species of *Actaea*, *Aruncus*, *Asclepias*, and *Echinops*, should be divided in early spring (before top growth emerges) or very early in the autumn. This also applies to plants in the genus *Filipendula*, except for *Filipendula vulgaris*, which divides easily. These so-called difficult-to-divide genera don't always live up to their reputations. I have had fairly good luck with dividing young plants of *Echinops ritro* 'Taplow Blue' in early spring when growth was approximately 3 in. high. I have not been so lucky with older plants, though I know of gardeners who have.

Ideally, spring divisions are made when the foliage is 2–3 in. high. In most cases the entire plant can be lifted from the ground using a spade or spading fork inserted into the ground about 1 ft. from the outside of the clump, depending on the species. Smaller-growing perennials don't have large root systems, so normally can be divided easily with a sharp nonserrated knife or sharp spade. If using a spade, work from the outside of the clump inward. Remember that the dead, woody center is tough and often hard to pierce, even with the strongest spade. Pulling apart clumps by hand is sufficient for genera with loose, spreading crowns and numerous shoots, such as *Monarda*, *Stachys*, and *Symphyotrichum*. If you are doing small divisions, you may need to wash the soil off the roots to see what you are doing. To divide large, thick clumps—especially of Shasta daisy (*Leucanthemum* ×*superbum*), hosta, daylily (*Hemerocallis*), and border phlox (*Phlox paniculata*)—the double-fork method is quick and easy. To use this method, first lift the entire clump from the ground with a spade. Then insert a spading fork into the center of the clump, and insert a second fork parallel to the first, setting the forks back-to-back with the tines of the forks intersecting. Pull the forks inward and then outward, and the clump will separate in two. You might have to repeat this process several times with a large clump. Once the large clump is broken up, a sharp nonserrated knife can be used for further divisions to obtain smaller pieces. Perennials such as peonies, which are fleshy rooted, do not divide well with the double-fork method and are best divided using a knife. *Astilbe* is also said to be a poor candidate for the double-fork method, but I successfully double-fork divided hundreds of them while working at a garden in Belgium (though it wasn't all that much fun!). Those astilbes must not have known better.

The number and size of divisions depends on your objectives. It is best to leave 3 to 5 healthy eyes (dormant growth buds) if you intend to rejuvenate the clump. Single eyes will give you the most divisions, but they will also give you small nonflowering plants that season. These small divisions are not recommended for the autumn.

If you simply want more plants from a perennial that doesn't need division, you can slice out sections of the plant early in the spring and it will fill in unnoticed. Groundcovers in particular or stoloniferous perennials that root freely at nodal joints can have these offshoots separated from the mother plant to decrease spread and give you more plants. This same technique can be used for plants that form new plantlets off the mother crown, such as foxgloves (*Digitalis*) or violets (*Viola*). Lift the new rosette and separate it from the older plant with a knife. You can also take cuttings of certain perennials to obtain more plants if division is not desired or is too difficult.

Plants should be kept moist and shaded during division. Discard the old, nonviable center portion of the crown and cut off any dead or damaged growth or roots. Spread roots out evenly in the hole. Water well after planting, and watch the new divisions for the next several weeks. Small divisions may need protection from wind and sun for the first several days. Within a few weeks after establishment, plants may benefit from a light fertilizing. Fertilizing at planting can burn the plant roots if the fertilizer comes in contact with the roots, unless a weak inorganic solution or starter organic solution is used. Dividing time is also a good opportunity to incorporate organic matter into the hole before replanting. Fall divisions should be mulched after the ground freezes.

Divided plants will reward you with an increase in vigor and flowering. Don't let this easy gardening technique intimidate you or limit your plant palette. Enjoy!

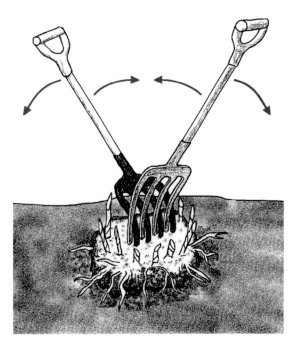

The double-fork method of division.

When making divisions, you should leave at least 3 to 5 healthy eyes, such as on this peony (*Paeonia*) division.

Silene dioica 'Firefly' is best cut back to its basal foliage after flowering.

PRUNING
PERENNIALS

Introduction to Pruning

Pruning is a term not normally associated with herbaceous plants, but when we deadhead spent flowers, pinch stems or buds, and cut back leggy plants, we are actually pruning. It also might be referred to as grooming, shaping, shearing, or snipping. Whatever you like to call it, the benefits to our perennial gardens are countless. Pruning is my favorite thing to do in my gardens, far surpassing in my heart planting, dividing, staking, or any other element of gardening (weeding is not even in the race). I get excited writing, lecturing, even just talking about pruning perennials because I believe that it is critical to maintaining the beauty in the gardens we create.

In your personal gardens, your objectives, mood, and family and work schedules will dictate if, when, and how often you're able to prune your plants. Sometimes I just don't have the time, or the desire, to get to all the pruning needed in my own gardens, and it shows. (That's when I tell visitors it's best to view the gardens from a distance.) I know my gardens can wait for the day when I can catch up with them. With the nature and siting of my house and gardens, I don't have to worry about keeping up with the neighbors, or even about their chatter when things get a bit wild. If your garden style is more formal, or is in a more formal setting (and you care what your neighbors think), or if you garden for a public garden with scrutinizing visitors, you will need to keep up with the pruning more diligently. If you get discouraged when you see pretty pictures of gardens in books or lectures and think yours doesn't stack up, remember that those gardens are photographed only on their "good hair" days.

Sometimes it bothers me to see my gardens unkempt, and if I have the time, I tear through them with shears and pruners flailing, trying to get everything looking just right—definitely a woman with a mission! At other times it doesn't bother me as much that things need to be pruned. Go with your mood, but always keep in mind that the time and hard work you put into your gardens will help them reach their full potential. A well-tended perennial garden shows. Too much neglect (for more than a year) will spell disaster.

In the landscape industry, a company can't afford to be relaxed about pruning their clients' gardens. The company's reputation depends on the appearance of those gardens. Proper pruning will make the difference between a fair garden and a distinctive one.

Enjoy the beautiful autumn season in the garden, as most perennials are best left up for the winter and pruned in the spring. The exceptions are perennials affected by pests or disease; cut these plants back in the autumn and remove the debris from the garden.

Lush foliage on perennials develops with pruning after flowering.

MORE THAN MEETS THE EYE

When I was first asked to write about pruning herbaceous plants for the Brooklyn Botanic Garden Record Book (*Pruning Techniques*), I thought it would be a straightforward topic. As I continued to work on the subject, writing a magazine article then beginning to lecture and to work on this book, I came to realize how very complex a topic it is because of the many variables involved.

Ironically, a great deal of pruning is based on common sense and comes naturally with experience working with the plants. Skill and art develops with practice. To me, part of the lure of pruning is working with your hands, as a sculptor might, shaping, forming, trimming. It can be a nurturing and gratifying (almost spiritual) experience. In my travels I have talked with gardeners from around the country, and it is always wonderful to watch how the best of them can look at a plant and naturally know how and when to prune it. This is part of the complexity of this topic, as the common-sense approach can be difficult to put into words with specifics. "Because you just do it" is not the best answer! This is not meant to intimidate the beginning gardener—just the opposite. Don't worry about hurting your plants by experimenting; you really can't do all that much harm. In most cases perennials are very forgiving.

I will share with you my personal experience as well as the experience of some of the best perennial gardeners in the United States. You will find that an individual perennial often can be pruned many different ways for similar results. There are also different ways it can be pruned for slightly different results. Certain tools or techniques may be preferred by some and not others. Use the information provided here as a guideline, then experiment, have fun, and learn as you go.

WHY WE PRUNE

What, how, and when to prune perennials varies from region to region, from year to year, and with the age of the plant. The condition of the plant, whether it is healthy or stressed, and the fertility of the soil will affect pruning requirements, as will weather conditions in a given year. Watch your plants closely: they usually will tell you by their appearance what kind of pruning is in order. If in doubt (and if I haven't given you the answer in the Encyclopedia of Perennials), just watch the plant and experiment—leggy, tatty old growth and new fresh growth at the base of a plant are red flags summoning the pruners. Pruning also depends on the individual gardener's objectives. I have listed below some important objectives in pruning; they are discussed in detail in the chapters that follow.

Extend bloom period or promote repeat bloom

Extending the bloom period or promoting repeat bloom is one of the most important reasons to prune perennials. Even though we all appreciate the many attributes of perennials, the beauty of their flowers is probably the primary reason that most people grow them. Most perennials only flower for 3 weeks, some for an even a shorter period of time, so if something can be done to extend the flowering season, it will be a worthwhile endeavor. Deadheading, the removal of faded or spent—basically dead—flowers, is a rather morbid name for a technique that can give life to your garden through prolonged bloom or repeat bloom of certain species. In many (but not all) cases, if the bloom is not allowed to go to seed, the plant will continue to put out new blooms in an attempt to complete the life cycle. When we deadhead, we force the plant to put its energy into new flower and shoot production, rather than into seed production.

Encourage lush new growth

Cutting plants back when old growth has become tatty can promote lush new growth from the base of the plant. This new growth contributes to the overall appearance of the garden, refreshing it and holding that spot in the overall design. Remember, foliage form, texture, and color contribute to the garden effect for a much longer period of time than do flowers.

Regenerate or extend the life of plants

Pruning is not simply cosmetic. Pruning can also increase the vigor and life expectancy of the plants, as well as improve their resistance to disease and harsh weather conditions. This is particularly true with woody perennials—perennials that have hard and thickened stems or trunks and do not die back to the ground.

For a wide range of short-lived, usually biennial species, life span can be extended by several years if the plants are cut down immediately after flowering. As discussed above, a plant's main biological goal is to produce seed, which will become the next generation. Unlimited seed production pulls strength from the plant and leads to death of these biennials. If the deadheads are removed before seeds start to set, the plants get confused, thus stimulating new shoot production and a further year of flowering. This can be an advantage or a disadvantage, depending on your objectives. I often prefer seeding some species for a more natural, unplanned look. Pruning allows us these choices.

(left) Regrowth and flowering on *Malva sylvestris* 'Zebrina' after being cut down to 8 in. following the initial bloom period.

(right) Balloon flower (*Platycodon grandiflorus*) responds well to cutting back before flowering to reduce height and eliminate the need for staking. These pruned plants matured to 18 in., compared to the normal height of 2 to 3 ft.

Some perennials can flower themselves to exhaustion and are then unable to form buds for the following year. To prevent this from occurring, the whole plant should be cut back to stimulate vegetative growth. This principle applies to a wide range of perennials. New growth produced from cutting back a plant early in the season is more vigorous and less stressed than the old dying foliage and is thus less likely to succumb to disease and weather damage.

Stagger plant heights or bloom times

For perennials growing in large groups, you can encourage the plants to mature to differing heights or to bloom at slightly different times by pinching or cutting back. This creates interesting gradations and extends the bloom time of a planting. You can delay flowering on a few stems of an individual plant to provide a longer bloom period at the expense of abundance.

Reduce plant height

Reducing plant height, thus eliminating the need for staking, is an important pruning principle. The little bit of time it takes you to cut back or pinch perennials before they flower, creating more compact plants, will save you the headache and time of having to stake plants later.

Keep plants in their own space

I like full, lush (some might call it crammed) gardens with as little ground or mulch showing and as diverse a palette of plants as possible. Such an approach requires some management of the planting to keep everyone in their own space. Sometimes this will mean the removal of a branch or several at the base of the plant or a few panicles off the top. (Panicles are branched groups of flowers on a single stem.) Other times it means cutting the whole plant down to the ground, after its show is finished, to let its neighbor have room to shine. Intricate gardens

This transplanted patch of beebalm (*Monarda didyma*) was cut back in stages to create a layered effect and a sequence of bloom. The flowering part of this clump, in the back, was left unpruned, the middle part of the clump was pruned on the first of May, and the front part of the clump was pruned on the first of May and again in mid-May.

with a high variety of plants often require this kind of policing. Mass plantings of only a couple of different species are far less likely to need the intervention.

Increase flower size or numbers

Pinching a plant will often cause it to produce more, but smaller, flowers than it might normally produce without pinching. Removing, or disbudding, the side buds of a plant will produce a single large flower on a long stem. If the terminal

The front of this beebalm plant, which received the most pruning, flowered about 3 weeks later than the other sections, and the decline of the foliage in the front is also delayed as compared to the back section.

(top) The appearance of *Pulmonaria* plants can be greatly improved by removing old flowering stems. The old stems have fallen to the outside of this clump of *Pulmonaria longifolia* 'E. B. Anderson'.

(right) The stems can be grabbed by the handful and pruned to the ground.

(growing at the tip of a branch or stem) bud is removed, side shoots will produce many small flowers. Disbudding is most often practiced by growers of show chrysanthemums, peonies, carnations and pinks. For certain plants the thinning of stems can produce larger flowers.

Prevention or control of pests

Thinning stems on mildew-prone perennials can increase the air circulation around the plant and decrease the incidence of disease. The arrival of pests may also be discouraged by better air flow. If a perennial has been infected with a disease or insects, pruning off the damaged foliage and removing it from the garden can often be an effective method of control and prevention of further pest invasion.

Such deadheading leaves a fresh-looking clump of foliage that contributes to the garden for the rest of the season.

Enhance the overall appearance (habit) of the plant

Cutting a plant back before it flowers not only creates a more compact plant but can help shape the plant's habit. By cutting outer stems lower than inner stems you can create a more mounded plant and reduce unsightly legginess. Pinching or cutting back a perennial when it is first planted normally improves its habit. Physiologically, pinching or cutting back perennials simply breaks the apical dominance (a condition wherein the terminal or apical bud inhibits the development of lateral buds that branch from the side of a shoot). The apical bud (a bud located at the tip of a stem or branch; terminal bud) usually grows more vigorously than lateral or axillary buds due to the higher concentration of auxin. If the dominant growing tip is removed, the auxin:cytokinin (growth hormones that control shoot growth and root formation) ratio is altered in the lateral buds, promoting their subsequent breaking and growth. Normally 2 branches will grow from each pinched stem, but sometimes more are produced. If a structured look is preferred in the garden, you can also shape plants after they bloom into neat rounded forms. Simply cutting off any deteriorating leaves, stems, or flowers can improve the overall appearance of a plant.

Remove unsightly or insignificant flowers

Some perennials are worth keeping more for their foliage than for their flowers. The poor flowers may even detract from the beauty of the foliage, either in their appearance alone or by causing a decline in the health of the foliage. Such unwanted flowers should be removed from the plant before the buds open.

Clean up the garden

Cutting plants to the ground in the autumn and spring is a significant part of cleaning up the garden, and most perennials are going to need it either before or after the winter. With certain species, cutting back before winter not only creates an orderly appearance in the garden, but is also vital for removing debris that might otherwise harbor insects or disease over the winter. Species that pose no threat of harboring pests will provide winter interest for humans, and food and shelter for the birds, and these species can wait to be pruned in the spring.

There is also just the general cleanup needed throughout the season. This might involve the removal of a few dead leaves from a plant or of browning stems from a clump of fresh green ones. It could be the cleaning out of an area around the base of a plant to make room for its seeds to drop. There is tidying up to be done in the garden at almost any time of year, including in winter when a little time spent in the garden is a welcome change.

Bond with your plants

Pruning is a form of meditation for me. I find it very relaxing to go out into my gardens, sometimes just for some light snipping, other times getting into major shearing, depending on how I'm feeling. It connects me with my plants. I can see who's sending up new growth or flower buds or forming intriguing seedheads. In my country garden pruning connects me with nature, as the bees, hummingbirds, butterflies, chickadees, wrens, bluebirds, frogs, toads, and hawks carry on with their world around me. In my clients' gardens I feel like I know more about what is going on after close inspection and caring for the gardens. This renewed sense of good health, that all is well in this sometimes crazy world, can't help but make you feel alive.

I'm sure that if I could prove this effect of pruning and gardening in general, I could go on the road with a bestseller and a prescription for good health: along with eating sensibly and aerobic workouts, prune your perennials at least 3 times a week—for mental and physical well-being!

Benefits to the landscape industry

A well-pruned perennial garden obviously is going to look and perform better than one that is not well tended, even if pruning may not be identified as the improving factor to the untrained eye. If you are a landscape or garden contractor, I would suggest that you not install perennial gardens unless you or someone you trust plans on maintaining them. Your reputation rests on how the gardens look. A neglected perennial garden is not a picture for the portfolio. If the client chooses to do his or her own maintenance, you should provide specifications on the proper maintenance of the garden, especially the pruning requirements, species by species (perhaps a copy of this book would be helpful!). Follow up with several visits to answer any questions on-site with your clients, and be certain they understand the maintenance requirements. If your work looks good and your clients are happy, then you will be happy and rewarded with numerous referrals.

TYPES OF PRUNING

Pruning takes a variety of forms in varying regularity and at various times of year. Cutting back during the summer can be done before or after flowering, or both. Deadheading is a constant throughout the season. Pinching and thinning and disbudding are performed less frequently, but still must be part of the program. Deadleafing is frequently done in late

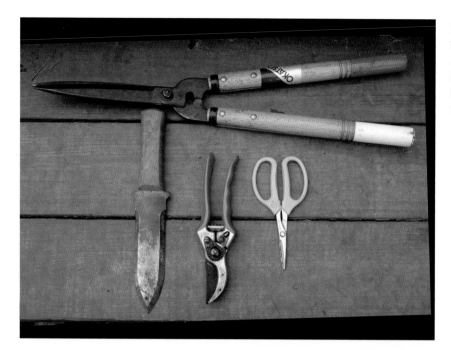

summer and into autumn, when plants are showing wear from the hot and dry weather. Pruning to prepare for winter and, more so, in the early spring are especially busy times. I will examine each of these pruning times and purposes in the following chapters.

Because of the complexity of the topic, it is difficult to make generalizations relating to all forms of pruning. For clarity I have tried to group the plants into categories, but remember that pruning perennials is very species-specific. You will want to refer to the Encyclopedia of Perennials for pruning and maintenance information for individual plants.

TOOLS OF THE PERENNIAL PLANT PRUNER

Bypass pruners, pruning scissors, and handheld hedge shears are the primary tools needed for pruning perennials. The bypass pruner is probably the most commonly used tool for deadheading and cutting back. Avoid anvil-type pruners, which can crush stems. Hedge shears have become a favorite tool of mine for cutting back or shearing perennials either before or after flowering. Hedge shears can be used for shaping plants, and they are also effective for spring or autumn cleanup in the garden. Very sharp pruning scissors, which are some-times sold as never-dull, bonsai, or grape scissors, are helpful and often essential when delicate deadheading of small flower heads is needed.

Pruning scissors are small and comfortable in smaller hands (and as an added bonus they come in attractive pastel colors). They are very sharp and can cut a variety of things in the garden, from heavy branches to fingers—so be careful. When I first bought a pair of these, they were so popular that there would be a rush for them among my crew to see who could get them first. In some cases, particularly for large jobs or mass plantings, string trimmers can be used. And don't rule out the usefulness of a sharp thumbnail for snapping off dead flowers. Electric hedge shears work wonders on ornamental grasses in the early spring. I have never had to resort to a chain saw, although the temptation has been there on occasion when the gardens have gotten totally out of hand! Throughout the following chapters and in the encyclopedia I will refer to the specific tool that I find works best for a given pruning job.

Deadheading

on't Be a Deadhead" is the title of one of my more popular lectures about pruning perennials and preparing planting beds. When I was preparing this talk for a mixed audience of both professionals and homeowners I asked my husband to listen to it and give me his opinion, representing the very novice gardener. In his usual, patient way he waited until I was completely finished with the 1-hour discussion, then said, "You better tell them what a deadhead is."

Fortunately no one left the room during my first talk when they found out that I was discussing the removal of old or spent dead flowers and not old or spent rock 'n' rollers (although the latter does sound somewhat more intriguing). I have been called the "deadhead queen" by various colleagues because of my work with pruning—I'm not sure if there is any deeper meaning to this. . . .

Deadheading is beneficial to most herbaceous ornamental plants. Usually there is deadheading to be done from spring to killing frost. You'll enjoy the process more and are less likely to feel overwhelmed if you keep up with it. There are many reasons for deadheading. Primarily, deadheading can prolong the bloom period for plants on which the flowers open over a period of several weeks, or it can initiate a second flush of smaller, sometimes shorter and less numerous blooms on plants that have a single heavy bloom. It can improve the overall appearance of the plant, giving a fresh new look to an otherwise finished or even distracting item. It can persuade biennials to behave like perennials. It can prevent self-seeding. I also like to remove deadheads or seedheads that weigh down the plant's foliage. Seed production can drain a plant's energy, and consequently, with certain perennials it can cause the foliage to deteriorate. Deadheading can promote vegetative and root growth rather than seed production and help retain the plant's healthy appearance.

The age of a plant greatly influences its deadheading needs. New plants give the gardener a grace period by requiring less frequent deadheading in their first year in the garden. The honeymoon, so to speak, is over after that first year, however, as deadheading hits full force the second season. Weather also greatly affects deadheading from season to season, with cool, moist weather extending the bloom life and sweltering heat and pelting rain decreasing it.

'Alpha' phlox being deadheaded to a lateral bud to extend the bloom period.

BASIC DEADHEADING METHODS

How to deadhead depends on the particular growth habit of the plant. The most common question I hear from people is how far down they should prune. Sometimes you need to remove individual dead flowers one at a time, or remove whole clusters of dead flowers, or cut off the entire flowering stalk. Because deadheading, like other forms of pruning, is so species-specific, it is difficult to categorize or group plants into neat compartments. A key thing to look for when deadheading is the presence of new buds or new flowers. If they are present, deadhead to the new buds or flowers. In the Perennials by Maintenance Needs chapter, lists 17 and 18, I indicate those perennials that should be deadheaded to a lateral flower, bud, or leaf and those that should be deadheaded to the ground

Basic botany for the perennial plant pruner, here showing the basic structures of Shasta daisy (*Leucanthemum* ×*superbum*).

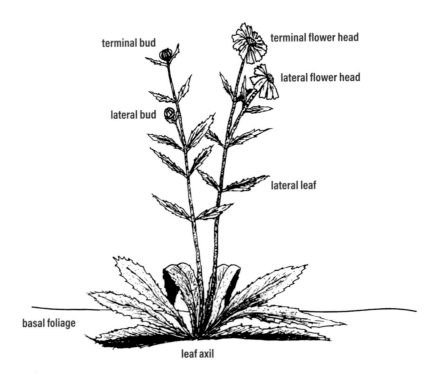

terminal bud

terminal flower head

lateral flower head

lateral bud

lateral leaf

basal foliage

leaf axil

or to basal foliage. These lists are intended as general guidelines only, and a few of the plants could be in either list; consult the Encyclopedia of Perennials for individual plant requirements. A review of some basic botany in the accompanying drawing may be helpful at this point.

Questions often arise about when to deadhead a plant that has a flower spike on which the flowers at the bottom of the spike open first, in which case the flowers at the bottom start to develop into seed while the flowers near the tip of the spike are still opening. (This flowering pattern is technically termed indeterminate.) If let go too long, such a plant will often produce rather long and gangly looking flower spikes, full of seed capsules and with 2 or so little flowers overwhelmed at the tip. This may be a personal preference, but it is best not to let things go this long. A rule of thumb would be to deadhead when the seedpods outnumber the flowers or when the spike is about 70 percent finished with flowering.

Deadhead to a lateral flower, bud, or leaf

The majority of perennials require deadheading to a lateral flower, bud, or leaf. Plants of this type include popular perennials like Shasta daisies, yarrow, salvia, and veronica (see Perennials by Maintenance Needs, list 17). After all flowering is finished, many of these perennials also require further cutting down to basal foliage (see Perennials by Maintenance Needs, list 27). To deadhead, prune off the dead flower stem to a new lateral flower or, if visible, to a lateral bud; if neither are apparent, cut the old flower off at the first lateral leaf. Many perennials can also be deadheaded by shearing, thus eliminating the tedious task of deadheading each individual old flower above a lateral leaf.

(left) Deadheading for perennials with foliage on the flower stem, here showing *Heliopsis helianthoides*.

(right) Deadheading for perennials with new buds adjacent to the old flowers, here showing *Campanula persicifolia*.

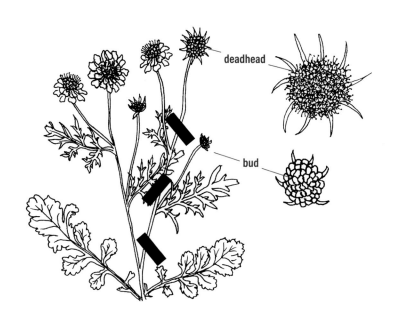

Deadheading for perennials with multibranched flowering stems, here showing *Scabiosa columbaria* 'Butterfly Blue'.

The ugly deadheads or "mush-mummies" of daylilies are not attractive additions to any garden and are best pruned off.

Snap the entire deadhead off daylilies with your fingers.

Plants like balloon flower (*Platycodon grandiflorus*) and peachleaf bellflower (*Campanula persicifolia*) require careful deadheading of each individual flower along the stem. New buds are produced adjacent to the old flowers along the stem, and if the stem is cut back to the foliage before this flowering is completed, the bloom period will be greatly shortened.

Perennials such as *Gypsophila paniculata*, *Scabiosa columbaria* 'Butterfly Blue', and species of *Aquilegia* and *Hemerocallis*, which have branching flowering stems, also require careful attention to detail when being deadheaded. Deadheading for these plants involves cutting the old flower and its stem down to a lateral flowering stem or bud; then, when this next lateral stem or bud is done flowering, it is cut down to another lateral flowering stem, if present, or, if not, to the basal foliage. With daylilies (species of *Hemerocallis*), the individual deadheads—which become wet, slimy, mummy-shaped dead flowers or, as I like to call them, "mush-mummies"—first should be pruned or snapped off using your fingers, taking care not to damage any of the new buds. When no more new buds are visible in the bud cluster, the entire flowering stem should be cut off at the base (see the Encyclopedia of Plants for more details).

Deadhead to the ground

Perennials with a single bare flower stem (sometimes with a few small insignificant leaves on the stem) should have their stem cut off close to the ground at the base of the plant when all flowering is finished. Heuchera, hosta, and kniphofia are examples of plants with this type of flowering.

The renowned author, lecturer, and perennial gardener Elsa Bakalar taught me that some plants, like lady's mantle (*Alchemilla mollis*) and certain geraniums, which would normally be deadheaded to the ground or to basal foliage, can also be deadheaded by pulling the old flowering stems out of the plant, right to the root. This way, these otherwise wide-growing plants can be kept in bounds and even thinned in the process. Pulled stems often have roots on them that will take if replanted.

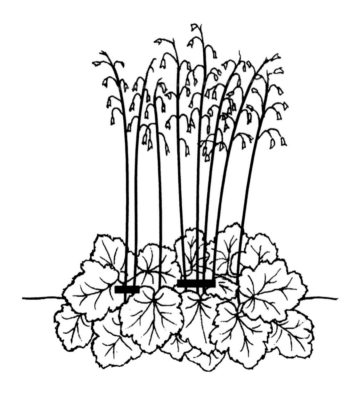

Deadheading for perennials with a single bare flower stem, perhaps with a few small leaves on the stem, here showing *Heuchera sanguinea*.

An alternative method of deadheading for wide-spreading mounded plants, here showing *Alchemilla mollis*. Twist and pull out the old flowering stem right down to the root.

Seedling variability
in *Phlox paniculata.*

(opposite) The
spontaneous purple and blue
provided by seeding of alpine
columbine *(Aquilegia alpina)*
and Hungarian speedwell
(Veronica austriaca subsp.
teucrium) add greatly to this
cottage garden.

TO SEED OR NOT TO SEED

The question of whether you should deadhead to prevent self-seeding depends
primarily on your objectives for the garden and how you want to spend your
time: deadheading or removing seedlings. The weather can influence deadheading needs because it affects the amount of reseeding that occurs; wet springs, for
example, can greatly enhance germination. Another consideration is whether
the seeds will develop into the desirable plant. Species forms will grow true to
type from seed, but cultivars may not and so allowing them to go to seed can be a
pitfall. Sometimes this provides the gardener with pleasant surprises, but
usually they are not so pleasant—these unpleasant progeny can take over the
desirable cultivar, leaving you wondering what you started with. This is often the
case with *Phlox paniculata.*

Personally, I like some seeding in my gardens to promote that "unplanned"
look. This approach can be promoted a bit too much, and I pay the price by
spending a great deal of time removing unwanted plants. On the other hand,
perennials such as columbine and rose campion *(Silene coronaria)* are rather
short-lived and readily perpetuate themselves if allowed to self-sow. Biennials
such as sweet William *(Dianthus barbatus)*, as well as some of my favorite annuals
like nigella or love-in-a-mist *(Nigella damascena)*, I treat as perennials because
they self-sow reliably. The nigella plants stay close by the feet of their original
parents. A point that also comes into play when deciding whether to allow plants
to seed is whether the seeds fall close to the parent (which won't mean too much
work) or scatter everywhere (which can result in a great deal of work). You can be
selective with your deadheading, particularly with prolific seeders, and remove
all but a few deadheads to allow smaller numbers of seedlings in. This is a good
approach but takes some forethought. If seeding is desired but the deadhead is
unattractive, as in the case of a spiked flower like digitalis, the spike can be
shortened, thus still allowing for some seeding but without being so obtrusive.

PRUNING PERENNIALS

Some years you may not need any new seedlings, in which case the plants should be completely deadheaded. A predominately self-sown garden can be an economical approach for the budget-conscious gardener, although it does require intervention to keep it managed.

So, in certain instances, reseeding can actually be a reason for not deadheading, such as when it makes for a more diverse or more economical planting. Attractive seedheads is another good reason. Many plants, such as *Anemone pulsatilla*, *Asclepias tuberosa*, *Dictamnus albus*, *Sedum* 'Autumn Joy', and most of the ornamental grasses extend their season of interest through the summer to the fall, perhaps even into winter, with their ornamental deadheads. Care must be taken, however, not to allow too much seed formation; even if you choose to allow seedheads to form because they are attractive, physiological concerns for the plant remain. The seeds are a sink for the plant's energy and the rest of the plant may suffer. I found this to be true with Siberian iris. I got greedy one year and left all the deadheads on the plants until the following spring, at which time I cut them and used them for dried arrangements. The plants were drastically weakened, opened up in the center, and had a significant reduction in the number of flowers produced—all the signs that division is needed. The plants were only 2 years old, and Siberian iris usually doesn't require frequent division, so I figured that this condition was related to the number of seedheads allowed to mature. Now I remove about two-thirds of the seedheads and allow a third to mature on the plants. This doesn't seem to drain them.

Coreopsis lanceolata requires frequent deadheading to keep up its appearance.

(opposite) This chance seedling of *Rudbeckia fulgida* var. *speciosa* in the front path of my garden is a charming and welcome surprise.

Some plants are just so willing to please that they offer us rebloom as well as pretty seedheads. In certain cases you can have both at the same time if you deadhead a few flowering stems and leave others to ripen. In most cases, though, you will need to deadhead the entire plant, let it rebloom, and allow this secondary display to ripen for your ornamental seedheads.

Some perennials have unattractive deadheads that require frequent (daily is best) deadheading to look decent. Most modern daylilies as well as *Coreopsis lanceolata*, *Hibiscus moscheutos*, and *Leucanthemum ×superbum*, to name a few, fall into this category. Plants of this nature are not good choices for the low-maintenance gardener. Older daylilies with smaller flowers, such as *Hemerocallis* 'Mme. Bellum', are exceptions, as they drop their old flowers cleanly.

Perennials such as gaura, linum, and tradescantia (whose flowers actually melt away) shed their petals discreetly, but they usually do this by the afternoon, thus leaving the evening devoid of their beauty—a letdown for the gardener who is away all day and can enjoy the garden only in the evenings after returning home. Other self-sufficient "petal droppers," including *Coreopsis verticillata*, *Iris domestica*, and *Silene coronaria*, hold their flowers for longer than 1 day. It should be noted that although these plants neatly dispose of their dead flowers, they still are producing seedheads that produce seed, and so they may require deadheading either to prevent seeding or to help produce or prolong bloom. But at least they don't require daily attention like some of the others.

Astilbe, baptisia, *Papaver orientale*, and others do not flower longer or repeat their bloom if deadheaded, so this extra work is not needed. It can also be beneficial to not deadhead perennials that flower late in the season, such as boltonia or *Heterotheca villosa*, as their entire structure, including seedheads, can be left for winter interest.

Certain silver-leaved perennials, such as the artemisias, *Santolina chamaecyparissus*, and *Stachys byzantina*, have foliage that will deteriorate if the plants are allowed to go to seed. Deadheading allows the plant's energies to stay directed toward foliage production. These plants often are not blessed with particularly outstanding flowers anyway, and usually I remove the flower buds before they

Siberian iris *(Iris sibirica)* seedheads are an attractive addition to the garden, although leaving too many can rob the plant of energy.

even open, keeping the plant in a strictly vegetative state.

Birds are another element to consider when deciding whether you are going to deadhead your perennials. Plants of genera such as *Echinacea*, *Heliopsis*, and *Rudbeckia* are attractive to goldfinches, and I have had flocks of goldfinches in my gardens happily munching away. Echinacea is a particularly favorite delicacy for the finches as well as for the juncos over the winter. The only problem is that echinacea will seed in outrageous proportions all over the garden. I tried hanging bundles of cut stems from a tree, but the finches didn't seem to be as attracted to those as to the ones in the gardens, so I always leave a few drifts up for them in various spots. Hosta seeds are savored by chickadees. Watching the birds in the gardens in the summer and winter adds a special dimension to perennial gardening.

Cutting Back

utting back refers to pruning a plant to renew its appearance or encourage a new flush of growth and flowering, or to control its height or flowering time. In contrast to deadheading, which is the removal of a dead flower and its stem and perhaps a few leaves, cutting back generally means removing foliage, even a significant amount, as well as possibly removing flower buds or deadheads. This technique can regenerate or extend the life of certain perennials. It can be used to remove unwanted flower buds on plants grown exclusively for their foliar effect. Cutting back or shearing can also be helpful for keeping plants within their assigned space in the garden.

To encourage varied plant heights and staggered bloom times, cut back perennials in stages and layers.

Under certain circumstances, it is necessary to cut perennials all the way down to the ground or to the foliage developing at the base of the plant. Plants that are to be cut to the ground need some coddling through such a traumatic experience. At the very least, keep them well watered. Aerating the soil with light forking or hoeing also seems to help. And sometimes a light topdressing with compost or liquid fertilizer gives a needed boost. Growth often will be slow on plants that are cut back and left in poor dry conditions, and new growth might not occur until cooler conditions return later in the season. Plants that are highly stressed may be greatly weakened and in severe cases may not return. In southern regions or in areas with very hot summers, cutting plants back before the heat of August is advisable. If pruning later than the end of July, do not prune off as much or as far back on the stems as you might with earlier pruning.

Cutting plants to the ground can be an unnerving and traumatic experience for some gardeners as well. To ease the process, plants can be cut back in stages, if desired. For example, cut half the plant down to the ground and pull the other half over the wounds; wait for new growth and then cut the remaining part of the plant. In addition to assisting the gardener through this troubling procedure, pruning in this fashion means there will not be as large a hole in garden because the entire plant is not being pruned at one time.

The typical pruning tools can be used for cutting back. Pruners work fine with small plantings, but on most jobs (including my own gardens) I resort to hedge shears. Grass shears or string trimmers for very large areas can also be used to help speed up this labor-intensive chore. Hedge shears and string trimmers don't cut as cleanly as pruners, but the plants help out by filling in rapidly after

Regrowth on *Symphyotrichum novae-angliae* 'Andenken an Alma Pötschke' 2 weeks after pruning.

pruning—usually within a week there will be new growth, and in 2 weeks you'll have a full, lush plant again. A word of caution is in order when it comes to using hedge shears or string trimmers: be sure that the individual wielding the tool is trained in the way the pruning should be performed, both from the plant's point of view as well as from the operator's, otherwise unintended cuts may be encountered. Unless you have a lot of time to spare—and most people don't these days—if using hand pruners, simply grab a handful of stems and snip, rather than doing an individual stem at a time.

I will discuss cutting back for maintenance and aesthetics, for height control, as a means of delaying or preventing flowering, and as a regenerative technique. Given the complexity of this topic, I have placed plants into categories based on their flowering time: spring, summer, or autumn. As with most living things, plants don't always fit into neat categories, but it does help in simplifying this otherwise confusing information. The Encyclopedia of Perennials provides detailed information on the best techniques for specific plants.

CUTTING BACK FOR MAINTENANCE OR AESTHETICS—PRUNE AFTER FLOWERING

Perennials that are being cut back for purposes of maintenance or aesthetics should be pruned after flowering. Generally when plants are cut back after flowering, the regrowth remains lower than the normal mature height of the plant, and if rebloom occurs, the flowers often will be smaller in number and sometimes in size. In many cases, when pruning after flowering it is best to cut down to the start of new growth developing at the base of the plant, or the basal foliage. Personally, I am more comfortable pruning a perennial down to basal foliage, rather than pruning to the ground when no signs of life are evident. Regrowth usually is much faster and generally is ensured if pruning is done when basal foliage is present. When cutting plants to the ground, do not cut flush to the soil; leave about 2 in. of stem, just in case new buds are present slightly above ground. They won't be damaged by shearing too close if a few inches of stem remain.

Spring-flowering perennials

Many spring-blooming, low-growing rock garden or edging plants should be cut back or sheared by half after flowering. This severe pruning promotes attractive new growth and sometimes sporadic rebloom, and it prevents the plants from becoming straggly or woody or opening up in the center (melting out). Plants that benefit from this type of pruning include maiden pink (*Dianthus deltoides*), evergreen candytuft (*Iberis sempervirens*), and moss phlox (*Phlox subulata*).

Although not a mat-forming perennial, Hungarian speedwell (*Veronica austriaca* subsp. *teucrium*) also benefits from a cut in half after flowering. Catmint (genus *Nepeta*) may flower sporadically throughout the summer if cut back by a third to half after the first spring bloom period. Plus, the plant's overall appearance is greatly enhanced by the pruning even if you don't get more blooms. If you miss the chance to cut back catmint in the spring and it starts to rebloom for you later in the summer, it will benefit from removal of the ratty foliage and dead flowers that will have fallen to the edges.

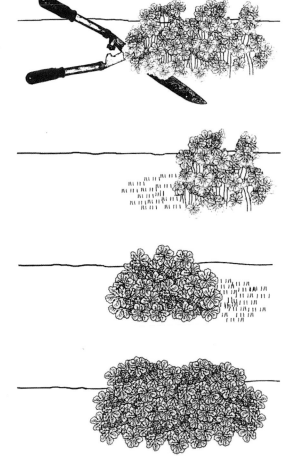

An alternate form of cutting back perennials, in stages to prevent a large hole in the garden or to assist a timid gardener through the operation, here showing *Geranium platypetalum*.

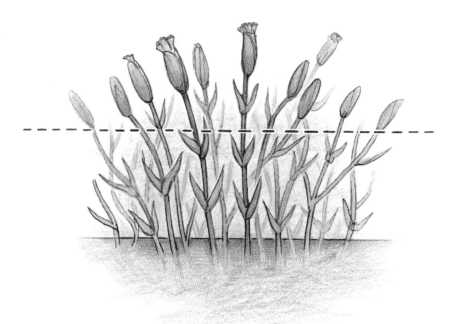

Pruning for spring-flowering perennials, here showing *Dianthus deltoides*.

Some gardeners have good luck with cutting oriental poppy (*Papaver orientale*) to the ground immediately after flowering. New basal growth appears and remains to fill in the space through the summer, rather than leaving a void for much of the summer, which happens if plants are allowed to mature and die back, and then are cut down. I have pruned back poppies right after flowering for several years now but have not had good luck. In my garden the new growth doesn't appear until autumn—which is the same time it appears when I don't cut the plants down right after flowering, but allow them to die down naturally and then prune them. Besides, not cutting them down after flowering allows me to enjoy the ornamental seedheads that develop.

(clockwise from top left)
Evergreen candytuft with deadheads; evergreen candytuft can be cut back by grabbing a handful of stems at a time; evergreen candytuft after being cut back.

Summer-flowering perennials

Summer-flowering perennials differ from the spring-flowering types in the amount of cutting back that is required after flowering. Some plants look best if cut to the ground, or to new basal foliage, whereas others require a cut by half or a third, and still others need 6 in. left on top. Here individual needs come into play. As with other pruning techniques, the cutting-back requirements of perennials is greatly affected by the age of the plant, weather conditions, and soil conditions. First-year plants may be vigorous and may flower most of the summer without any cutting back, though in subsequent years they usually demand it. If the weather has been extremely hot and dry, as in southern regions, the plants are going to show more wear and will benefit from a trim to bring some fresh new growth to the garden.

The degree of cutting back is also specific to each species. Looking at a few plants from the genus *Geranium* gives us a good picture of just how individual the plants can be in their needs. *Geranium endressii* 'Wargrave Pink' looks unsightly in our hot summers if all the old stems are not cut back to the ground where new basal foliage is forming; the closely related *Geranium* ×*oxonianum* 'Claridge Druce' and 'A. T. Johnson' need to be treated in a similar fashion. But *Geranium macrorrhizum* and *Geranium* ×*cantabrigiense* 'Biokovo' require nothing more than deadheading and maybe a touch of deadleafing.

Artemisia schmidtiana 'Nana' and *Thalictrum aquilegiifolium* are just a couple of other summer-flowering perennials that may benefit from being cut down to basal foliage after flowering. Some grasses may develop brown leaf tips by late summer; the cure for this is shearing or mowing them to the ground to promote healthy new foliage. Lamium, which gets tatty in midsummer, can be cut down to new basal foliage, and the attractive new growth will last into early winter.

Plants such as *Amsonia tabernaemontana*, *Baptisia australis*, and *Euphorbia epithymoides* get not only a cut but also a style when being pruned. These perennials may be formed into rounded shapes to add structure to a garden. Hedge shears are the better tool to use for shaping perennials. Shaping plants in this way is commonly done in public gardens where a bit more formality is in order. The pruning done in public gardens can serve several purposes, as cuttings are frequently taken for propagation in addition to pruning for aesthetics or regeneration. This is something to keep in mind in the home garden as well.

Cutting back to basal foliage after deadheading

Many summer-flowering perennials benefit from a couple of types of pruning to look their best. First they are deadheaded down to a lateral bud, flower, or leaf, which often means cutting them back by about a third to half; then, as new basal foliage starts to develop and all lateral flowering (if any) is finished, the plants should be cut back to the newly emerged basal foliage. Sometimes you will get an additional bloom on plants pruned in this way, though the flowers tend to be smaller and fewer than in the initial 2 flowerings. Popular perennials such as Shasta daisy, delphinium, and 'Moonshine' yarrow, as well as a slew of others, fit into this category. Remember that after cutting plants down to basal foliage they'll appreciate being kept moist, aerated, and perhaps topdressed with organic matter, which is nice but not absolutely essential. In the case of heavy feeders like delphinium, incorporating a topdressing or a light water-soluble fertilizer after cutting back is especially helpful for healthy growth and rebloom. In one mild year I still had a bloom (albeit only one) on my delphinium in December, which I proudly showed to some horticultural colleagues who were visiting for an early Christmas celebration (nothing like a little showing off!).

As always, the age of the plant and weather conditions will greatly influence

(left) Maiden pinks can be sheared with grass shears or hedge shears.

(right) Prune sprawling stems of *Geranium endressii* 'Wargrave Pink' that develop after the initial flowering.

Amsonia plants benefit from shearing back by a third and shaping after flowering, here showing _Amsonia elliptica_. The plant on the left was sheared by a third and shaped after flowering; the plant on the right was not pruned and has a tendency to open up.

whether this type of pruning is needed. I have some old _Salvia ×sylvestris_ 'East Friesland' plants that in most years do not produce many new flowers from lateral buds. Instead, after the initial bloom they open up in the center, begging to be cut back to new basal foliage, which in turn gives me some rebloom. Younger plants of the same cultivar produce nice lateral flowers, with deadheading, before needing to be cut down. Observing the plants and using a little common sense are usually your best guides to what type of cut is in order.

CUTTING BACK FOR HEIGHT CONTROL AND TO STAGGER OR DELAY BLOOM—PRUNE BEFORE FLOWERING

For many summer- and autumn-flowering perennials, cutting back before flowering can help limit the plant's height. Especially in areas of high winds, controlling mature height may be needed to prevent plants from flopping or to eliminate the need for staking. This approach to pruning can also be used to layer a planting by creating interesting gradations in heights. Furthermore, overly fertile soil and too much shade for a sun-loving plant will produce leggy growth, and cutting back before flowering will often produce plants with a nicer, fuller habit as a result of increased branching. Many times, depending on the species, cutting back before flowering will produce smaller but more numerous flowers. When perennials are first planted they often benefit from cutting back for fuller first-year plants.

Bloom time in the garden can be staggered by selective pruning, and this can be used to the gardener's advantage in several ways. Simply pruning separate plants of the same species a week or so apart, or pruning only part of a group and leaving the rest unpruned, will stagger flowering by delaying bloom in the pruned individuals. Individual plants can also be pruned so that their flowering will coordinate better with a later blooming species. Staggering or delaying bloom extends the season of interest in a garden, particularly in a mass planting, and the technique is often used by public gardens for this purpose. Of particular note is Stonecrop Gardens in Cold Spring, New York, where different "moments" are created in the garden by pruning certain plants for special flower or color effects at specific times. I too have employed this technique when I have put

together color combinations that I end up not liking. Though I may not want to move the plant because I like it where it's planted, I don't want it flowering at the same time as one of its neighbors, so I prune it back to flower later.

Individual plants will flower longer but not as profusely if a few stems are cut back to delay bloom. Many summer- and autumn-flowering plants can be delayed by cutting stems back by about 4 to 6 in. when the flower buds start to form. This can delay flowering by several weeks or more. If a 'Clara Curtis' mum (*Chrysanthemum rubellum* 'Clara Curtis') is sheared while in bud, for example, flowering can be delayed by 1 to 2 months. With some perennials, cutting the plants back when the flowers are forming will result in no bud development and consequently no bloom.

A delay in flowering can also be useful for the flower arranger who would like to have, perhaps, beebalm into August for arrangements. The smaller flowers that result from pruning before flowering are also often a better size for cut arrangements.

I have several clients who travel for several weeks or even a month during the summer. Often they will cut the majority of their garden down by about a third or half, depending on the time and the plants, before they leave. They return to lush new growth and flowering on plants that otherwise would have flowered with no audience and would have looked finished and shabby upon the owners' return.

Although in many cases either

Many perennials can be sheared and shaped after flowering, such as *Baptisia australis*.

Pruning summer-flowering perennials by cutting back (deadheading) by a third or half to a lateral bud, followed by cutting down to basal foliage, here showing *Achillea* 'Moonshine'.

pinching or cutting back can be used to achieve similar effects, I generally opt for cutting back rather than pinching. From a time standpoint, I prefer to cut something back once, rather than pinching and then having to come back and pinch again, and perhaps again, to create the desired effect. Certain perennials do seem to respond better to pinching than to cutting back, although from a physiological point they should be the same.

Most of my work concentrates on the effects of cutting plants back once before flowering. Perennials can be cut back at different times, or several times, for different effects, but in most cases pruning only once makes sense from a maintenance standpoint. Pruning of plants before flowering (by half or two-thirds) is generally done in early to mid-June, because this is also the time when many spring-flowering species can be pruned after flowering. It gives the landscape contractor, for example, a time frame in which a large number of perennials can be pruned during one maintenance visit to a garden. Keep in mind that, again, this is an attempt to simplify a rather complex area of pruning. Pruning in early June will delay the flowering of many summer bloomers, but pruning earlier in the season may be preferable if no delay is desired. In warmer climates you may need to prune earlier because of faster growth earlier in the season, and you also may need to prune plants more heavily in such climates to effectively reduce their height. The longer growing season in the South means late-flowering plants can be pruned later into the season to further delay flowering, while such pruning in cooler climates may result in plants that don't have a chance to flower before snowfall.

Timing of cutting back is an interesting issue and one that is open to lots of fun and experimentation. The cutoff date to stop pruning perennials so that they will flower before cold weather, or so they will or won't be delayed or by how much, is not known in most cases. General pruning dates are often given without sound experience, such as "don't prune after the 4th of July if you want flowers before frost." I have experimented with a variety of different pruning dates for different species, and the results are provided in the Encyclopedia of Perennials. With some plants, cutting back before flowering will decrease the floral display or the vigor of the plant or both. Some perennials, if cut back too often, or by too much, or too late in the season, may not flower nicely, or at all, or they may be stunted. Others may start flowering as soon as pruning stops no matter how late

in the season, within reason. Why perennials respond differently is not completely understood. As is emphasized throughout the book, regional differences, age and vigor of the plant, and weather conditions for the season, among other factors, can affect the results. Photoperiod (day length) and the obligatory cold period (vernalization) that many perennials require to induce flowering could also be responsible for differing results of different pruning techniques and different perennials.

An important thing to keep in mind is that often the more of a plant that is cut off or the closer it is pruned to its normal flowering date, the greater the delay in flowering. Also, the amount of delay is not directly related to the timing of the pruning. In other words, a plant cut back on the 30th day of the month will not necessarily have its flowering delayed 15 days longer than one cut back on the 15th day of the month. Also keep in mind the natural habit of the plant. Waiting until later to cut something back may result in a rather odd-looking shape to the plant. Plants that are cut back late may develop a tall single stem topped with a multibranched head, creating an awkward look to certain perennials, reminiscent of the standard look often used for woody plants such as lilac or fuchsia.

Summer-flowering perennials

It is well known that certain autumn-flowering perennials benefit from cutting back early in the season to reduce the need for staking, but it is not as well known that this can be done with several different species of summer-flowering perennials as well. Summer-flowering phlox respond well to cutting back before flowering and can be treated in a variety of different ways to reduce height and delay flowering. *Phlox maculata* 'Alpha', for example, cut back by half when in bud in early June may flower at 18 in. rather than at 2½ ft., and about 2 weeks later than usual. Heliopsis can also be pruned by half at the same time to flower at 2½ to 3½ ft., rather than at 5 ft., with about a 1½-week delay. Balloon flower (*Platycodon grandiflorus*) tends to flop, but pruning it back by half in early June can produce plants 1 to 2 ft. shorter than normal and with a 2- to 3-week delay in flowering.

Preventing flowering altogether, rather than just delaying it, by shearing or cutting off the flower buds may be desirable with certain perennials. I think of this pruning as a form of disbudding, although technically the term doesn't apply (disbudding traditionally refers to removing surplus buds to promote production of high-quality flowers or fruit)—but after all, it is removing the buds! This pruning technique is utilized when plants are grown mainly for foliar display or when the flowers are unsightly, distracting, or simply unwanted. *Heuchera micrantha* 'Palace Purple' and *Penstemon digitalis* 'Husker's Red' are a couple of examples; I don't want the flowers of these plants to compete with the attractive foliage, so most of the time I cut off the buds as they set. When plants like teucrium and others are grown for hedging purposes, the flowers are not desired. Removing the flower buds is also effective in stopping the decline in vigor of many silver-foliaged plants, particularly silvermound artemisia (*Artemisia schmidtiana* 'Nana') or lavender cotton (*Santolina chamaecyparissus*), which decline after flowering. The flowers on these 2 plants are not especially attractive anyway, so why bother to keep them? Preventing flowering can mean several shearings if new buds develop after the initial pruning.

Autumn-flowering perennials

Many late-flowering plants benefit from being cut back before they bloom. As with the summer-flowering plants that benefit from cutting back for height control, the late bloomers treated in this way will have a fuller and more

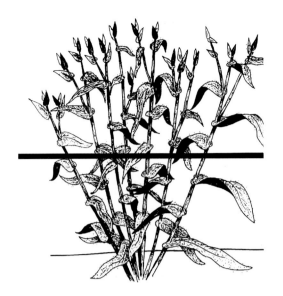 

Cutting back autumn-flowering perennials such as symphyo-trichum: **(left)** cut back by half to two-thirds in early summer for height control; **(right)** plants can also be shaped, if desired.

compact habit, less need for staking (if any is required), and staggered bloom time if desired.

Cutting back autumn-flowering plants for height control is normally done in mid- to late June in the Midwest, generally when the plants are 12–16 in. tall. Cutting back can be done later, depending on the usual variety of factors. Most of the time the plants should be cut back by half, but you can prune back two-thirds or more depending on the plant and your objective. Pruning later may involve simply removing 4–6 in. from the tips of the plants.

Asters are among the first autumn-flowering plants that come to mind for cutting back. They are one of several perennials for which pinching is often recommended, but that respond just as well or better to cutting back. I find that cutting back these late-season beauties by half or two-thirds when the plants are 12–16 in. tall is more effective than pinching. The outer stems can be cut lower than the inner ones to create a more rounded habit and reduce the ugly legs usually associated with asters. Cutting back can eliminate the need for staking on most *Symphyotrichum* cultivars, but some of the extremely tall ones may require it even with pruning, depending on the soil and weather conditions. Once cut back, they usually flower at a sturdy 3 ft. or so. You can also select asters that won't require cutting back. One I prefer is the late-season (mid-October for us) *Aster tataricus* 'Jindai'. It usually reaches only 4 ft. in height and doesn't need cutting back or staking. Lower growing forms can also be used, such as *Symphyo-trichum novae-angliae* 'Purple Dome', which reaches only 18 to 24 in. in height.

Sedum 'Autumn Joy' is often pinched for height control, but it can also be cut back by half in the spring, when plants are 8 in. tall (in the Midwest this is usually the first week of June). Plants will have more but smaller flowers. Pruning also helps prevent flopping on plants growing in part shade or very rich soils.

One usually associates chrysanthemums with pinching, but they can also be cut back effectively. I don't use many mums because of their lack of hardiness, but I have a few that I love that are tough as nails and quite attractive, and some do fine without any pinching or cutting back. I discuss these forms in more detail in the next chapter and in the encyclopedia.

When grown in the South, *Eutrochium purpureum* can be cut back to 12 in. in early June and will flower at about 3 ft. in early August, compared to its typical 15 ft. or more mature height. In the Midwest, I pinch *Eutrochium maculatum* 'Gateway' for outstanding full plants with smaller flowers. A variety of

This *Eutrochium maculatum* at Saul Nursery in Georgia was cut to 12 in. in early June. It flowered at about 3 ft., rather than the typical 15 ft.

techniques can be used on other natives to control their heights, and this is true of many perennials.

Gardeners sometimes have different techniques for the same plants, depending on their objectives or their situations. For instance, boneset (*Eutrochium perfoliatum*), great blue lobelia (*Lobelia siphilitica*), and ironweed (*Vernonia altissima*) can be cut back by half when 4 in. tall and then by half again when 16 in. tall. Or, great blue lobelia can be pinched around the first of July, and ironweed can be cut to the ground when 2 ft. tall or cut back by 1 or 2 ft. when 4 ft. tall to stagger and delay flowering. A good way of demonstrating that pruning methods, as with many gardening techniques, are not set in stone.

CUTTING BACK TO REGENERATE OR EXTEND THE LIFE OF PLANTS

A regenerative pruning cut can lead to a more vigorous plant and even a longer life in certain species. Richard Hansen and Friedrich Stahl, in their book *Perennials and Their Garden Habitats*, write that certain short-lived perennials—*Centranthus ruber*, *Coreopsis grandiflora* 'Badengold', *Coreopsis lanceolata*, *Gaillardia* ×*grandiflora*, and *Leucanthemum maximum* among them—flower themselves to exhaustion and are consequently unable to form buds for the following year's shoots. To avoid this situation, Hansen and Stahl recommend that the whole plant be cut back to stimulate vegetative growth. In the Midwest, cutting back in late August or early September should allow enough time for growth to emerge before cold weather. This same principle could apply to a wide range of perennials. New growth produced from cutting a plant back is more vigorous and less stressed than the old dying foliage, and it is likely to be less prone to disease and weather damage.

PRUNING PERENNIALS

Woody-stemmed perennials (or subshrubs) should be cut back to about 4 to 6 in. in the spring or early summer to midsummer if they have started to die back or grow leggy. Plants in this category include sunroses, St. John's wort (*Hypericum calycinum*), lavender cotton (*Santolina chamaecyparissus*), germander (*Teucrium chamaedrys*), and thymes. This also applies to lavender (*Lavandula*), which may need a hard cutting back in the spring every 2–3 years to hold a decent habit if the plant has become open and leggy. Many of these species tolerate cutting back so well that they can be used for low hedging.

The life of a whole range of short-lived, otherwise biennial species can be prolonged by several years if cut down immediately after flowering, before seeds set; hollyhock (*Alcea rosea*), foxglove (*Digitalis purpurea*), and dame's rocket (*Hesperis matronalis*) fit into this category. As mentioned in the chapter on deadheading, a plant's primary biological goal is to produce seed to become the next generation. If this goal isn't accomplished, the plants put their energy into vegetative growth, thus extending the life of the existing plant.

Wait until new growth has broken from the old stems of lavender before pruning out damaged sections.

PRUNING TECHNIQUES FOR LONG PERFORMANCE DURING PEAK SEASON

I like to look at spiderwort (*Tradescantia* ×*andersoniana*) as an example of a plant that benefits from several different pruning techniques to perform its best. When the plants are 12 in. tall (early May in the Midwest), cut them back by half to reduce legginess; after the first flowering, deadhead the plants, again cutting

them back by about half. Be certain to prune above new lateral buds, if they are present. Be patient when deadheading spiderwort; the flowers melt away by afternoon, but many new buds still remain in the flower cluster, so make sure the plant is finished flowering. After the second bloom from lateral buds, spiderwort plants may require cutting back by two-thirds or more for healthy new growth and possibly for another smaller show of flowers. Plants often need to be cut back by two-thirds or to the ground after the first flowering, skipping the deadheading step, depending on the growing conditions and the age of the plant. This is particularly true of older plants subjected to dry conditions, which look pretty tacky by midsummer. *Tradescantia* species produces new growth and often will rebloom with sufficient moisture.

Pruning techniques for long peak-season performance, here showing *Tradescantia* ×*andersoniana*: **(left)** reduce height by half in early May; **(middle)** reduce height by half after first bloom by deadheading to lateral buds; **(right)** reduce height by two-thirds or more if necessary after all flowering is completed.

Pinching, Disbudding, Thinning, and Deadleafing

PINCHING

Pinching is one of the best-known forms of pruning perennials, associated in particular with garden mums (*Chrysanthemum ×morifolium*). Anyone who considers themselves so much as a weekend gardener knows the supposed attributes and glories of pinching mums. But very few gardeners take full advantage of this valuable technique, which can enhance the habit and flowering effect of innumerable other perennials. Pinching is also a good alternative for the timid gardener who may be hesitant to do dramatic cutting back for height control. Pinching allows for experimentation; you can pinch just a few stems on a plant, observe, and then decide what approach to take in subsequent years. If in doubt, you may not want to pinch an entire plant, although a bit of adventure is healthy. Always remember that perennials will come back next year in their original state—it's not like an apple tree, which may be marred for life with a single improper pruning.

As with cutting back, pinching can be used to help keep plants in bounds, to prevent plants from growing tall and straggly, and to stagger the bloom period of an individual plant or a group of plants. Pinched perennials often produce more, but smaller, individual flowers than a plant that hasn't been pinched. You can also shape a plant by pinching the outer stems shorter than the central stems. Flowers will be distributed more evenly over the entire plant with shaping, and plants will have leaves to the ground rather than bare lower stems, which often require a hiding facer plant. This problem is sometimes overlooked during the design process, so pinching can compensate for that oversight.

Although pinching and cutting back are often talked about interchangeably, the practices differ in the amount of plant material that is removed and the tools that are used to remove it. Pinching usually involves removing only the growing tips and first set of leaves, or approximately ½–1 in. (at the most 2 in.), of each shoot. Fingers work best for this task and are the most portable garden tools available. A sharp thumbnail is particularly handy, and I know some perennial

Gorgeous in bud, flower, and fruit, solitary clematis (*Clematis integrifolia*) benefits from deadleafing after flowering to look its best later in the season.

producers who grow their thumbnails longer just for this purpose. Cutting back, on the other hand, involves removing more than 2 in. of growth, sometimes 4 in., 6 in., or even 1 ft. or more, and pruners are generally the best tool for this. Pinching involves less time initially, as it is fast work to go through a plant and pinch it. A plant may require a second or third pinching as well, so in the long run more time may be required when pruning a plant by pinching as compared to simply cutting a plant back by half once. As with other forms of pruning, pinching is best done by cutting the stem just above a node. Ideally the top bud should point outward; this prevents new stems from growing inward and creating an entangled, unproductive mess.

It is difficult to generalize as to the best time to do pinching. As with any form of pruning, when to pinch varies according to several factors, among them climatic conditions, seasonal weather, soil fertility, plant individuality, and the gardener's objectives. Pinching usually is performed in May or early to mid-June in the Midwest; earlier if you are in a warm climate such as California or the South. If you wish to retain normal bloom time, pinching must be done early in the season; early spring pinching will be necessary for plants that bloom in late spring. Any subsequent pinching should be done after 2 or 3 nodes' growth. If a delay in flowering is the objective, pinching close to bloom time will give the desired results. Pinching can be used to stagger bloom time: for example, pinch a third of the plants in the bed well before normal blooming time; 1 week later pinch another third; and pinch the rest a week after that. Even pinching plants a few days apart will create an extended bloom season, though at the expense of a single abundant display. Pinching perennials when they are first planted often produces a more compact habit and better branching on first-year plants. With some perennials, long internodes are a sign that pinching will help improve growth habit. *Perovskia atriplicifolia*, for one, should be pinched when it is 12 in. tall to help control flopping. *Physostegia virginiana* should be pinched in early spring to control lankiness, whereas *Helianthus salicifolius* can be pinched in early July to create smaller plants for smaller spaces. More exact guidelines are given for individual plants in the Encyclopedia of Perennials, including approximate height, time, and frequency of pinching.

Pinching is most commonly used on branching perennials. If we look closely at our plants, common sense tells us that it would be of no use to try to pinch an iris, for example, or a daylily, or crocosmia, or any other single-stemmed perennial. Pinching is of no benefit to plants growing from rhizomes, bulbs, or corms or to plants that form basal rosettes. Heuchera does not need its foliage pinched, and we all can figure out the consequence of pinching the flower stems. Pinching is not for the rhizomatous polygonatum, either. Some gardeners feel that plants with a spike or single large head of flowers are ruined if they are pinched, because the big show will have been pinched off. The pinched plants may produce smaller lateral flower spikes, but not always. Some gardeners might find the smaller flower spikes to be an advantage. I like to pinch or cut back certain spiked plants, such as *Alcea rosea* and *Lobelia cardinalis*. Yes, the flower spikes are smaller, but they are more in scale with the smaller plant that is produced from pinching. In some cases, such as with digitalis or verbascum, pinching may simply result in no bloom.

Pinching, here showing chrysanthemum.

As has been emphasized throughout this book, often several different pruning techniques can be used for the same plant. Many perennials can be either cut back or pinched depending on the desired results, timing, season, gardener's mood, and so forth. *Sedum* 'Autumn Joy', for example, can be cut in

half when 8 in. tall or it can be pinched. I know several gardeners who prefer pinching 'Autumn Joy' sedum because they claim that cut-back plants look too rough, or the stalks are tough and callused and thus break off easily. I have favored the results I have gotten from pinching, rather than cutting back, with perennials like Shasta daisy (*Leucanthemum ×superbum*) and 'Gateway' Joe Pye weed (*Eutrochium maculatum* 'Gateway'). Species of *Symphyotrichum* and *Artemisia*, as well as *Boltonia asteroides* 'Snowbank', are just a few other plants that can be either pinched or cut back, again depending on the intended result (and, again, refer to the encyclopedia for specifics).

I feel obliged when writing about pinching to cover mums in greater detail. Despite the fact that advice on pinching has been covered in every article ever written on mums, in every introductory horticulture or master gardener class,

(clockwise from top left) *Sedum* 'Autumn Joy' pinched; 'Autumn Joy' sedum pinched and used as a low hedge is outstanding even without flowers at Boerner Botanical Gardens in Wisconsin; even more dramatic is the show that pinched 'Autumn Joy' sedum plants provide in flower at Boerner Botanical Gardens.

Eutrochium maculatum 'Gateway' pinched stem on the left, unpinched stem on the right.

and passed along from every mum-growing mum to mum-growing daughter, hopefully a speck of something new will be provided in this rendition. With that I'll add that I don't pinch my mums anymore, but rather cut them back by half in early June. I also use what I consider special mums, not your typical garden-center varieties. These special types are extremely hardy and some don't even need to be cut back. They look more natural to me than most, either because of their single flowers or their overall habit and appearance. *Chrysanthemum* 'Venus' is a nice, single pink that becomes leggy unless cut back by half, which can create a full, rounded plant to 2–3 ft. Two other hardy mums that I love are 'Viette's Apricot Glow' and 'Mei Kyo'. 'Viette's Apricot Glow' remains a compact 18–24 in. without pruning, and 'Mei Kyo' grows to about 2½ ft. but remains full and rounded with nice burgundy double blooms, without cutting back or pinching.

Nevertheless, if pinching is the pruning method of choice, then spring-planted garden mums should be pinched for the first time a few weeks after planting. If the plants have buds on them when you buy them in the spring, pinch these off. If you have overwintered your mums, pinch when shoots are 4–6 in. long and then again 2–3 weeks later. The last pinch date depends on the climate and the type of mum being grown and the individual objectives. Generally pinching should be stopped in about mid-July in midwestern and northern gardens, whereas pinching may continue until late July or early August in warmer regions. Most mums benefit from 3 to 4 pinches for height control,

except for the lower-growing cushion types, which require only 2 pinchings. The number of times and how late in the year you pinch your mums is something you will want to play around with. You may find that by pinching a bit later you can delay flowering to a more suitable time for your needs. Keep in mind, however, that if you get pinch happy you may pinch away any chances of flowering before cold weather arrives. Mums need several weeks to set bud after the final pinch.

Pinching can be an important aid in maintaining perennial gardens, but it should be used with discretion. Avoid trying to create a garden full of rounded forms, all the same height, covered from head to toe in flowers, at the cost of plants with natural graceful habits and just the right amount of bloom.

Thinning: before and after, here showing *Monarda didyma*.

THINNING

Thinning stems of perennials can help prevent disease, improve the overall appearance of the plant, produce sturdier stems, and in some cases, increase the size of flowers produced. Thinning allows more light and air into the plant and encourages better branching of the remaining stems. In addition to the removal of entire stems, thinning can mean removing flowers, leaves, or only certain branches, depending on the gardener's intentions.

Cut or pinch stems at ground level in the spring, when the plants are a quarter to a third their mature height. How many stems to thin depends on the type of plant and its size. In general, thinning 1 in 3 stems is sufficient. This can leave anywhere from 1 to 4 in. between the stems, depending on the species. Keep the stems fairly evenly spaced. Be sure to remove any weak or particularly thin stems as well. If in doubt as to how many stems to remove, remove more shoots, or else the thinning won't be effective and the time spent will be wasted.

Thinning is a useful tool to help the perennial gardener create desired shapes or appearances in the garden. I use thinning throughout the season if a plant has become too full or dense for the effect I hope to accomplish, and again this may mean thinning of flowers, leaves, or select branches and stems. When thinning in the summer, flowers, leaves, and select branches usually should not be cut to the ground—as entire stems should—but should stop at a lateral bud. An imbalance of weight in a garden may not be obvious on casual observation, but too much weight in the wrong spot will mar the overall appearance of the design. Scented oxeye (*Telekia speciosa*), for example, has very large, coarse leaves, and if it isn't balanced properly with sufficient quantities of plants with finer-textured leaves, I will thin some leaves and maybe some stems to lighten it up a bit. If I have used a taller or slightly denser plant near the front of the perennial border to create a more diverse cross section to the garden, I sometimes will need to thin its flowers or foliage to allow a view through it to the other plants. A plant's flowers may seem to outweigh the poor stems that are trying to support them, and in such a case, the plant itself is out of balance. Thin some of these flowers. Use them in the home in floral arrangements and you will be happier all around. Purple-foliaged plants add depth to garden designs, but too much depth can create a somber feeling. Remedy this with thinning. Remember to step back and look at the plant as you are thinning so that you see what you are creating.

Thinning can serve a variety of functions for a variety of plants. *Delphinium*, *Monarda*, *Phlox*, and *Symphyotrichum* are a few genera that may be less prone to mildew if their stems are thinned, although my experience has not shown much of a difference in the mildew on thinned phlox as compared to unthinned. Delphinium and phlox may also produce larger flowers if thinned by a third. Other perennials such as bugleweed (*Ajuga reptans*), lady's mantle (*Alchemilla mollis*), Bethlehem sage (*Pulmonaria saccharata*), lamb's ear (*Stachys byzantina*), and some hardy geraniums often benefit from a summer thinning to improve air circulation around the plant and prevent rot or mildew. I cut out some of the dense foliage on *Stachys byzantina* 'Helene von Stein' to open it up a bit when the humid weather comes, and this applies to other silver-foliaged plants as well. With *Alchemilla mollis*, *Geranium* ×*magnificum*, and *Pulmonaria* plants, you can pull out some stems while you are deadheading to thin the plants and reduce the incidence of disease when water accumulates in the dense foliage. This can keep plants from getting too large as well.

DISBUDDING

Disbudding, the removal of flower buds, is a pruning technique that is usually associated with growing plants such as mums, carnations and pinks, dahlias, and peonies for floral shows or arranging. When disbudding for shows, side buds are removed so that the plant's terminal bud will produce a larger flower on a longer stem. Disbudding at least 2 pairs of the side buds is best; for even larger blooms, remove 3 pairs. Removing the terminal bud will cause the side buds to produce smaller but more numerous flowers. Disbudding the terminal bud can also eliminate the need for staking in the garden. Removing side buds along the spikes of perennials such as lobelia or delphinium is not effective, but you can remove smaller side spikes from these plants and other spike-blooming plants such as aconitum for a larger terminal spike. Whatever the method or intention of disbudding, buds should be removed before they get too large, otherwise unsightly scars will appear.

Flower buds may be removed from perennials for different reasons, including distraction from the ornamental foliage of the plant. I often think of this as disbudding, because one is removing flower buds, but, as was previously discussed, it doesn't fit the technical horticultural description for disbudding.

DEADLEAFING

Charles Cresson, renowned horticulturist and author, popularized the term deadleafing. Appropriately enough, it refers to the removal of individual dead leaves. It is not cutting back stems. Deadleafing is the fine-tuning of the garden. The dead foliage has done its job. It's time to get rid of it and make room for any new foliage that may be ready to grow and contribute to the health of the plant. Deadleafing can mean removing yellowing and browning leaves for purely cosmetic purposes as well, as they are often distracting in the garden. A plant whose foliage is 30 percent dead leaves looks like it's had it—but removing those leaves can give the plant a fresh look and improve the appearance of the garden. In this sense, deadleafing is rejuvenating. Dead and dying leaves can also harbor insects and diseases.

Dead leaves sometimes are just the nature of the plant, no matter what the growing conditions. Most often, they are the result of some cultural condition. Dry or wet weather can cause leaves to yellow, scorch, or brown. Too much sun, heat, or humidity are other culprits. Placing the plant in the right conditions will minimize the problem. Of course, we have no control over droughts or monsoons, but if we stretch the growing conditions for the plant and increase its stress, we may have the added maintenance of deadleafing. Dying leaves on plants can also be a symptom of a larger problem that you may not be aware of, such as poor drainage, competition from a neighboring tree, or a break in an irrigation line. So think about the potential causes of dead foliage and what, if anything, can be done to correct the problem.

Pruning by deadleafing is done with many perennials. My gardens don't have ideal growing conditions for primula. The plants do well through the moist spring but start to fade with summer heat and drought. When summer comes, I simply cut the yellow leaves from around the base of the rosette to create a fresh new look. I have *Fragaria* 'Pink Panda' plants that invariably develop brown leaves by midsummer. I grab handfuls of leaves out of the planting, not concerning myself if I pull out a few fresh leaves or even plantlets, as new ones will be fast to follow. My lady's mantles (*Alchemilla mollis*) always need old leaves cut off in late summer because they are sited in full sun. I have 25 of them repeating along the edges of 2 of my front gardens. I love my lady's mantles and wouldn't think of giving them up, so my choice is deadleafing. For years I pruned each leaf individually with hand pruners. I was about at the point of learning to like the plants with the dead leaves on them. Brown is a color too, I told myself. Then I fortunately discovered that hedge shears would do the job, and now I use them to make quick work of this deadleafing task. New foliage waits below the old leaves to quickly fill in the space. I have seen this pruning of lady's mantle also referred to as shearing. Call it what you like, but you'll need to do it if they get too dry or receive too much sun.

A good deal of deadleafing is needed in the spring on evergreen plants such as *Asarum europaeum* and species of *Bergenia* and *Helleborus*. Their outer leaves deteriorate over the winter and removing them is all that is needed to start a new season. 'Elijah Blue' fescue (*Festuca glauca* 'Elijah Blue') is another plant that after most winters needs its dead leaves pulled out from within the clump in early spring.

Pruning to Prepare for Winter and Pruning to Prepare for Spring

WINTER PREPARATION

It used to be accepted practice to cut down most perennials in autumn. Strictly herbaceous gardens were left totally bare, a very depressing sight, while mixed borders may have had the odd conifer, woody shrub, or rose bush left on its own to provide winter interest. Fortunately, as our appreciation for the winter forms and colors of perennials is heightened, as well as our awareness and sensitivity to the habits of birds and butterflies, we no longer mindlessly go out and cut everything back, leaving the garden naked of any sign of dormant plants.

Winter interest—contrary to what is preached by many well-meaning individuals, those who usually have limited knowledge of perennials—is not provided solely by junipers, yews, pachysandra, English ivy, or the odd mugo pine (with the requisite accompanying rock!). Certain conifers, particularly some of the dwarf forms, and broad-leaved evergreens do add a special dimension to mixed herbaceous borders, but many perennials contribute greatly to the winter garden as well. Such contributions are not only in the way of attractive seed-heads. Form, structure, and foliage color are also notable perennial contributions during the winter season. Perennials and grasses, with their often intricate seedheads and outstanding habits, hold snow, frost, and ice in a way that is distinct from other plants.

In addition to their ornamental qualities, perennials in the winter landscape are important resources for birds and butterflies. Butterflies such as the viceroy pupate (in a sheltered spot for the winter), and other species of butterflies and moths lay eggs in the leaves of perennials for overwintering. If we cut down and compost these plants, we may be composting next year's generation of butterflies. A variety of birds frequent our feeding stations in the winter, and most of

At Hiddenhaven, there is a great deal of winter interest in the mixed gardens, from the conifers, boxwood, and the many perennials which remain. They are aesthetically pleasing, and also offer food and shelter for countless birds.

them also frequent the gardens. These visitors include finches (gold and house), red-breasted woodpeckers, juncos, chickadees, tufted titmice, cardinals, nuthatches, and sparrows (song and American tree). They visit to collect and eat seed from perennials (including fallen perennials) such as echinacea, heliopsis, and rudbeckia, or to use the perennials as cover and resting grounds. Some people bring cut branches into their garden areas for the birds. Don't think just because a perennial is going to fall that it should be removed from the winter scene. If the perennials weren't there, the birds would have fewer places to take refuge.

If you want some green in the winter, why not go for painted arum (*Arum italicum* 'Pictum')? In a protected site, painted arum will give you an almost tropical look with its lance-shaped, silver-marked leaves. I love the gray provided by lavender (*Lavandula*), common sage (*Salvia officinalis*), and lamb's ear (*Stachys byzantina*) during the winter, contrasted against the deep green of *Dianthus deltoides* or evergreen candytuft (*Iberis sempervirens*). Pair *Helleborus foetidus* (with its glossy purple-tinted foliage and yellow-green flower buds that form in the autumn and hold through the winter) with the scarlet-streaked, gray-green foliage of *Geranium macrorrhizum*, and you have a combination worth venturing out to see on an otherwise stay-huddled-in-the-house day. If the snow is too deep to allow you to enjoy these low-growing beauties, cross-country ski around a garden bearing grass genera such as *Calamagrostis*, *Miscanthus*, and *Panicum* highlighted by seedheads of *Iris sibirica* and *Rudbeckia nitida* 'Herbstsonne'.

There are many low-growing evergreen perennials as well as tall perennials with evergreen or semi-evergreen basal foliage. Some plants will be evergreen in milder climates or in winters with early and persistent snowfall. They may look a bit forlorn in more severe situations after snow, wind, and subzero and fluctuating temperatures take their toll. Yet they have provided interest in late autumn and early winter, so they have earned their keep as far as I'm concerned. Perennials that have not evolved to be evergreen yet behave like evergreens due to milder conditions may be shorter lived.

One year at the end of January, after a snow melt, I counted approximately 50 different species of perennials that had green basal foliage or evergreen to semi-evergreen leaves, or leaves that simply remained green under a month-long snow cover. It looked like spring green, with spiderwort (*Tradescantia ×andersoniana*) shoots 1 in. or so high and beebalm (*Monarda didyma*) with 4 healthy leaves per shoot. The list of green plants also included species of *Geum* and *Stokesia*, *Veronica austriaca* subsp. *teucrium* 'Trehane' (which was an outstanding bright yellow), *Veronica alpina* 'Alba', and basal foliage on *Rudbeckia triloba*. The foliage of oriental poppy (*Papaver orientale*), which is usually left over the winter as a living

My mixed borders in winter.

mulch, was exceptionally green, looking as though it would send forth a flower bud at any moment. Following a month of sporadic snow cover and temperature extremes from –10 to 50°F, by late February many of these 50 species had become bedraggled, turning to mush. Some still looked good, however, including the poppies, *Penstemon digitalis*, and *Phlox stolonifera*, with just a touch of bronzing on some of them.

With some plants, like pulmonaria, you can't be sure what they're going to do. I have several different species and cultivars of *Pulmonaria*, and sometimes they hold up nicely into the winter and other years they are black by late autumn. On some plants just the outer leaves blacken and the inner foliage is nice. I still leave them unpruned or just prune the outer foliage and either cut them down over the winter or in the spring.

Some perennials should not be cut down in the autumn because they can contribute aesthetically to the garden in winter. In other situations, certain tender perennials can be left up for the winter to ensure overwintering. Marginally hardy perennials, such as 'Mönch' aster (*Aster ×frikartii* 'Mönch'), tender ferns, and mums, benefit from leaving the old foliage on the plants to provide insulation for the crowns during cold weather. I leave the old fronds on all ferns until spring, whether they are tender or not, and some ferns, like the Christmas fern (*Polystichum acrostichoides*), are evergreen and hold up well through the winter regardless. An eye-opening research study out of Germany, conducted for Yoder Brothers, showed that mums that were not cut back in autumn resprouted substantially better and earlier in the spring than the plants that were pruned. Many of the cultivars tested had no overwintering losses if they were not sheared back in the fall, compared to 75–100 percent overwintering loss for those that were sheared. Wait until warm weather is ensured in the spring to prune mums.

Another reason to not cut down certain perennials in autumn is demonstrated by *Ceratostigma plumbaginoides*. This species emerges late in the spring, sometimes as late as June in our area. I like to leave the old stems over the winter and into the spring until the plant emerges. This way, the old stems serve as an indicator that something is growing there, ensuring that the soil isn't disturbed or something else isn't planted in its space while it's taking its time awakening from the winter.

On the flip side of all these reasons to *not* prune in the autumn, there are many reasons why pruning is necessary before the coming of winter. One important reason to cut certain perennials back is to avoid overwintering diseases or insects. Some notable examples include fourlined plant bug and mildew on monarda and other members of the mint family, botrytis on peonies, and borers on bearded iris. Removing foliage and stems of these plants from the garden in the winter can help reduce maintenance problems for the following year. In addition, removing excessive debris such as fallen leaves and fallen deadheads decreases other potential sites for pests. I recommend raking large leaves of maples or sycamores out of the garden in autumn, as these can mat down and hold water, contributing to the potential for crown rot on the perennials. Also, if large quantities of leaves litter the garden, most of them should be removed. It's not practical to get every leaf out—and what a bore it would be to try—but too many can be a problem.

Besides pruning in autumn to minimize the incidence of pests and disease, there are aesthetic reasons to prune before the coming of winter. Some perennials simply do not contribute much to the winter garden; in fact, they may detract from it. In such cases I opt to cut the plants down. This might include veronicas or geraniums that have blackened and turned to mush, or a great coneflower (*Rudbeckia maxima*) that has fallen onto a frequented path. Certain ornamental grasses are better cut down before the winter because they either break down in the winter or lose their good color. If a grass is not reliably hardy, it should be left unpruned for the winter.

The pruning done during the growing season can dictate whether a plant needs pruning in the autumn for winter. Many perennials cut back during the growing season remain as attractive, low green mounds into the winter. For example, if *Centaurea montana* is pruned back in the summer and all that remains is fresh low basal foliage in the autumn, it doesn't need to be pruned again for the winter. On the other hand, if the plant was not cut back heavily during the season, the tall stems and leaves will blacken and require pruning in late autumn. Also, if a perennial is deadheaded during the season, so reseeding is not a concern, the rest of the plant may be able to remain for the winter. If the plant wasn't deadheaded, it may be best to cut the entire plant down before winter to avoid reseeding, rather than deadheading at this point.

Pruning to prepare for winter is a matter of personal choice. What some find attractive, others may find distracting. With certain clients or certain styles of gardens, things need to be neat and tidy for the winter, and this involves more pruning in the fall. With others, a more natural look is acceptable and a "fallen soldier" here or there over the winter can easily be removed in the spring with no harm done. In my personal gardens I leave more perennials up in the back gardens, which are more natural and less visited by guests in the winter months, than I do in my front entrance gardens—although these too are rather wild looking over the winter. I also like the option of leaving some things unpruned; then if a plant declines by mid- or late winter I can go out and cut it down at that point. It gives me some gardening to look forward to during the winter when weather permits. Pruning selectively in the autumn or over the winter also helps ease the burden of spring cleanup. Your spring schedule may be an important factor in deciding what you leave during the winter.

In the encyclopedia, I have indicated whether pruning is needed for the winter for specific perennials. In the Perennials by Maintenance Needs chapter, list 33 includes some of the plants I don't prune for the winter. In this list it is assumed that the appropriate recommended pruning has been done during the season. You need to remember all the factors that come into play in determining whether a perennial should be pruned for the winter.

The intricate deadheads of *Eutrochium maculatum* 'Gateway' are dazzling when covered with frost.

Perennials that are to be cut down for the winter should be cut down when they are dormant; usually this is after several killing frosts. For me this is generally early November, when we are scheduling our autumn cleanup for clients, although in some years it has been late November. If perennials are cut down too early, when they are still actively growing, one concern is that they might put on new growth, use the carbohydrate reserves that were meant for the following season, be hit by a freeze, and not return the following year. Sometimes I will go ahead and cut down plants that are still very green or even flowering if I know that within a few days a freeze will come along and turn the plants to mush. If in doubt, you're better off leaving the plant up.

Plants should be cut back to within about 2–3 in. of the ground. Cutting back too close to the crown can cause certain plants to become damaged over the winter. On some perennials, the overwintering buds are not beneath the soil, but rather are either level with, above, or only slightly below the soil, so if you cut back too close you may be cutting into these buds. I once did this with some of my famous lady's mantles. I used a string trimmer and cut a few of them back too far. They were weak to emerge the following spring and parts of the crowns never regrew. I also know some gardeners in colder climates who leave about 6 in. of stems to help trap the snow, and then cut back again in the spring.

Hedge shears are useful for most of the autumn cleanup. It's quick work to shear the plants off at their bases, then follow up with a garden fork to pick up large piles of debris. Hand pruners may be needed on some very tough stems, and I sometimes use a weed whacker with a rigid plastic blade for mass plantings. Workers must wear protective clothing and safety goggles when using this kind of equipment.

Sedum 'Autumn Joy' being cut down in the spring. Note the light green nubs of new growth at the base of the plant.

EARLY SPRING PRUNING

Generally speaking, plants that are not pruned in the autumn need to be cut back, or possibly deadleafed, in the spring. Perennials like species of *Asarum*, *Bergenia*, *Helleborus*, and *Heuchera* need to have their dead leaves removed, particularly if they have been exposed to windburn or sunscald. Epimedium and helleborus need to be cut back early in spring so that the new flowers and leaves are not masked by the previous season's tattered remains. Rotary mowers can be used on large plantings of epimedium. The groundcover *Liriope spicata* also can be mown down in the spring. Moss phlox (*Phlox subulata*) may incur dead branches over the winter, or portions of the plant may die out, and these should be removed at this time. Evergreens may not need any additional pruning in the spring in some years, as their foliage can stay fresh over the winter. *Phlox stolonifera* and *Dianthus gratianopolitanus* are a couple that usually fair well. Most often, evergreen basal foliage doesn't need any additional pruning in the spring.

Certain subshrubs have their overwintering buds aboveground, which classifies them botanically as woody plants, but horticulturally they are classified with herbaceous perennials. They benefit from snow cover for protection and may experience tip dieback on the part of the plant above the snow line. Spring is the time to prune off those dead tips. This group includes evergreen candytuft (*Iberis sempervirens*), lavender, germander, and thyme. They may also need a hard cutting back in the spring if they start to grow leggy. Lavender normally only needs its dead tips cut off in late spring or early summer, once all the woody growth has had a chance to break. Often the beginning gardener will prune back lavender hard before winter, only to be disappointed that it doesn't return at all the following spring. Lavender may need a hard cutting back (down to 4–6 in.) in spring every 2–3 years to hold a decent habit if it has become open and leggy, or if it's being used as a hedge. It can be cut back hard annually for hedging. Perovskia can be cut to the ground to encourage sturdier plants; I prefer to cut mine down to live buds, which can be 6 in. or more aboveground.

Electric hedge shears work best for ornamental grasses on large jobs. First tie the grasses together, which keeps excessive debris to a minimum, and then cut it down. It helps to have two people working together on this. Handheld hedge

Electric hedge shears do an efficient job of cutting down ornamental grasses in the spring.

shears do the trick on small quantities. A weed whacker with a rigid plastic blade can also be used. I've even heard of people using chain saws, but I've never needed such heavy machinery, even for very large grasses. Do wear gloves, as the grass blades can cut like razors. *Festuca glauca* 'Elijah Blue' normally only needs dead blades pulled from within the clump by hand. After severe winters I have had to cut 'Elijah Blue' fescue back because of excessive tip burn on the blades.

I do most spring pruning early on, before new growth begins, usually sometime in late March or early April. Gardeners in milder climates may need to get an earlier start. You don't want a lot of new growth in the way while you are trying to clean up the old stems and leaves. If some new growth is hit during spring cleanup, no harm done—perennials are very forgiving and will be quick to fill in, but if you cut too late you may be altering the plant's ultimate height, and even flowering time on early-blooming species.

Many native plants such as Joe Pye weed (*Eutrochium maculatum*), heliopsis (*Heliopsis helianthoides*), and purple coneflower (*Echinacea purpurea*) respond to pruning prior to flowering, either to reduce the need for staking or to delay flowering.

ENCYCLOPEDIA OF PERENNIALS

Guide to Using the Encyclopedia

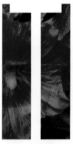he pruning and maintenance information in this encyclopedia is based primarily on my personal experiences. I have actually performed the different pruning techniques for the various plants as well as done the follow-up "research," if you will, by tracking bloom dates, measuring plant heights and flowering size, and so forth. Many of the techniques I have tried were suggested to me by gardeners from across the country, or were gathered from my own extensive research. My goal was to test the various techniques as well as to try variations of my own—a very involved and complex process. My successes and failures are included with the plant entries. I have provided dates, plant heights, and other vital statistics whenever possible so that the information can be used as reference points. The perennials included in this encyclopedia, as well as other perennials, can be pruned in a variety of ways for similar or different results.

For the most part, the pruning that was performed on plants before blooming (in an effort to create more compact plants that don't require staking, or to experiment with bloom times) was done in early to mid-June. I picked this time partly because it is also the time when a good deal of spring-flowering species are pruned after flowering, thus giving the maintenance contractor or the busy gardener one key time of the season to keep in mind for pruning a wide range of species. It is also an appropriate time based on the growth habits of many summer- and autumn-flowering perennials.

In the first edition of this book, I called my efforts a pioneer project. I am still a pioneer today! Many questions about pruning perennials remain to be answered. Remember that what, how, and when to prune varies with weather conditions, regional variations, age of the plant, soil fertility, moisture availability, and the gardener's own objectives. The results of the pruning, such as amount of flower delay or time for regrowth, will also differ according to these variables. Gardeners in the South or the far North may need to adjust the timing a bit on certain pruning. You may need to prune slightly heavier in the South due to the longer season and the effects of the heat on producing taller and leggier growth.

In the North, a lighter touch may be more effective for accomplishing the pruning goals in a shorter season. Although the information should be used only as a guide, with necessary adjustments according to individual needs and conditions, it is my hope that the information included with each plant offers gardeners precise guidelines for pruning, rather than vague recommendations that don't provide specific how-tos or results. Take these, experiment, learn, and grow.

The descriptions for each plant in the encyclopedia are fairly brief. My objective in writing this reference book was not to write another descriptive manual—such manuals have already been successfully created. The objective of this book is to provide new, and easily referenced, material specific to maintenance and pruning of perennials.

Plant entries are listed alphabetically by scientific names. Immediately following the entry head is a list of key information: the plant's common name, the family to which it belongs, descriptive features, size, preferred exposure, blooming time if applicable, and hardiness zone(s). Height measurements given in parentheses indicate the height of the foliage and are provided only if the height is significantly different from the height of the plant in flower. Many perennials are cut down or deadheaded down to this foliage, so it is significant information to keep in mind while designing. Pruning and other maintenance information follows. Cultivars and related plants are mentioned if they offer something unique from a maintenance standpoint, as compared to the featured plant. In cases where a cultivar or variety is the perennial being featured, rather than the species form, more often than not it is because that is the form of the plant most commonly used in the industry. If you have difficulty locating information for a particular plant or cultivar, please consult the index, which may be able to direct you to the proper entry.

The chapters in the first two sections of this book will greatly aid you in a more thorough understanding of the pruning and maintenance information provided in the encyclopedia. They provide insight not always included in the specific plant entries; I strongly recommend that you read and familiarize yourself with the information provided in these chapters. The numerous lists at the end of the Encyclopedia of Perennials can also serve as a quick reference on many of these maintenance requirements. For example, which plants need cutting back after flowering? Which ones should be divided every year, or every 10 years, and so forth?

Pruning is often tailored to species. 'Carillon' yellow foxglove (*Digitalis grandiflora* 'Carillon') can be deadheaded to basal foliage for decent rebloom. Mountain bluet (*Centaurea montana*) is first deadheaded to lateral flower buds for prolonged bloom, then cut down to basal foliage for repeat flowering. Shown with *Allium* 'Firmament' and California poppies.

A–Z Encyclopedia of Perennials

Acanthus spinosus

Spiny bear's breeches
ACANTHACEAE

Spikes of mauve flowers;
shiny thistlelike leaves
3–4 ft. (2–2½ ft.) high; 3 ft. wide
Part shade
Blooms June–July
Zones 5–10

PRUNING Deadheads remain attractive for several weeks after flowering is finished. When they decline, cut to the ground. If plants become tattered after flowering in midsummer, they can be deadleafed or, if severe, cut to the ground for complete renewal of foliage. No additional flowering will occur. Foliage often remains healthy until late summer (early September), particularly if plants have received sufficient summer moisture, at which time the old declining foliage falls to the outside of the plant, revealing fresh, newly emerging basal growth. Hedge shears can be used to quickly remove the old leaves. The new growth may remain evergreen or at least semi-evergreen, depending on the severity of the winter. Do not cut back for the winter but cut off any damaged leaves in the spring if needed. If plants are grown for foliage alone, the flower

Acanthus spinosus

spikes can be easily pruned out when in bud—plants will not flower if the buds are removed.

OTHER MAINTENANCE Although generally listed as hardy in zones 7–10, *Acanthus spinosus* has proved to be reliably hardy in zone 5, though not remaining as evergreen in bad winters. Flowering is often reduced after cold winters. Can be invasive in light soils, and the spreading roots are difficult to remove completely. Stays well contained in clay soils and usually in dry soils. Benefits from morning sun and will take more sun and drier soils in cooler climates. Slug and snail damage is often a problem. Well-draining soil is critical. Benefits from a winter mulch in northern areas. Can be slow to establish. Spring division every 4–5 years.

RELATED PLANTS *Acanthus spinosus* 'Spinossisimus' is a much spinier form that isn't fun to prune or weed around.

Achillea 'Coronation Gold'

'Coronation Gold' yarrow
COMPOSITAE

Mustard-yellow flower heads; fernlike, scented gray-green foliage
2–3 ft. (1 ft.) high; 3 ft. wide
Full sun
Blooms June–August
Zones 3–8

PRUNING Deadhead to lateral buds, then after lateral buds finish blooming, cut stems down to basal foliage. Young plants usually repeat bloom for a long period with deadheading. Older clumps may not produce many lateral flowering stems; if this is the case, plants should be pruned down to basal foliage, skipping deadheading. Sporadic flowering may be produced from the basal foliage in some cases. Flowers are smaller in the second bloom phase. Yarrows bloom longer where summers are cool, only about half as long in hot regions. If foliage is infected with rust or other foliar diseases, deadleaf or prune off affected parts. Leave basal foliage over the winter as it holds up better than that on most forms. Cut out dead foliage in the spring if needed.

OTHER MAINTENANCE Well-draining soil is the main element for survival. Usually trouble free if given full sun and well-draining soil; will tolerate dry soil. Normally does not need staking unless grown in excessively rich soil or too much shade. Divides easily in the spring or autumn, every 4–5 years. Relatively low-maintenance plant. One of the best yarrows for hot and humid conditions.

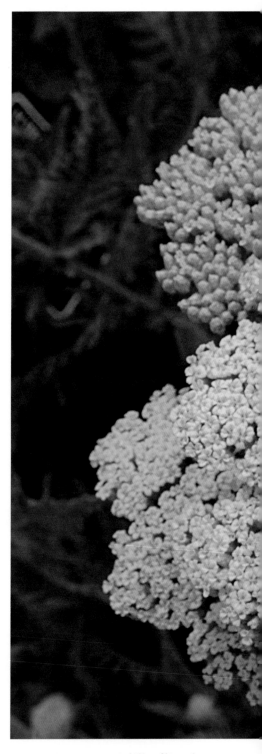

RELATED PLANTS *Achillea filipendulina*, fern-leaf yarrow, is one of the parents of *Achillea* 'Coronation Gold' (the other is *A. clypeolata*). It usually requires staking unless given full sun and dry soil. *Achillea filipendulina* 'Altgold', 3-ft.-tall free standing, is a reblooming cultivar with deadheading.

Achillea filipendulina 'Credo' has large yellow flowers and strong stems that don't require staking. Achillea filipendulina 'Gold Plate', 4½–5 ft. tall, usually requires staking. Achillea filipendulina 'Parker's Variety', 3½ ft. tall, is very tough, drought tolerant, and free standing even with winds in the Midwest, but may need staking in areas with hot, humid summers. Produces abundant flowers for a long period with deadheading.

Achillea 'Coronation Gold'

Achillea millefolium

Achillea millefolium
common yarrow
COMPOSITAE

Flat heads of red, white, or pink flowers; ferny, dark green leaves
2–3 ft. high; 2 ft. wide
Full sun
Blooms June–August
Zones 4–8

PRUNING Young plants can be deadheaded to lateral buds for summer-long bloom. With age or when grown in conditions that promote leggy growth, such as very wet conditions or hot weather early in the season, plants may need to be cut back (hedge shears work well) by a third to half after first bloom to prevent flopping, then sheared again down to basal foliage as the second bloom phase is completed. Plants often send up sporadic small blooms from basal foliage. Deadheading prevents seeding. Cutting plants back by half or two-thirds before flowering in early June, or when about 18 in. tall, can produce shorter, stockier plants that are self-supporting early in the season, though they may still flop slightly by late season, depending on other growing conditions. Flowers are smaller but more numerous on cut-back plants and flowering may be slightly delayed. Cutting back after flower buds form may mean no bloom for the season. These aggressive yarrows often need pruning to keep them in their own space. Cut foliage and roots back, if necessary, to give neighboring perennials room. Leave basal foliage over the winter. Cut back any damaged sections in the spring if needed.

OTHER MAINTENANCE Invasive habit, plants can spread 2–3 ft. in a season, and a good deal of maintenance is required to keep plants in bounds. Plants require staking if not cut back for height control. Division in spring or fall every couple of years keeps plants vigorous.

RELATED PLANTS The Galaxy Hybrids (*Achillea millefolium* × *Achillea* 'Taygetea') offer a variety of outstanding colors, but the plants are short-lived in my experience and flop and spread like the species. *Achillea millefolium* 'Fire King' is a long-blooming cultivar with dead-heading that can go strong for 6 weeks and then sporadically for a total of 15 weeks. May need staking, but more self-supporting than others. The stout stems of *Achillea millefolium* 'Apple Blossom' usually don't require staking.

Achillea ×kellereri requires the old blossoms and a third to half of the foliage to be cut after flowering.

Achillea ptarmica, sneezewort, is invasive and lanky and contracts mildew in hot, humid conditions.

Achillea 'Taygetea', 1½ ft. tall, flowers from May to hard frost with deadheading. Remove the flowers when they start to turn dingy.

Achillea 'Moonshine'
'Moonshine' yarrow
COMPOSITAE

Sulfur-yellow flower heads; fernlike silver foliage

24 in. (12 in.) high; 18 in. wide

Full sun

Blooms June–August

Zones 3–8

PRUNING As the flowers fade, dead-head to lateral buds; when lateral flower stems finish blooming, cut down to basal foliage. Foliage remains attractive into winter. In early spring cut off any dead or old foliage, leave new growth at base. In areas with high heat and humidity, thinning plants can reduce moisture around crown and help prevent disease. Prune out diseased sections as needed; do not compost infected material.

OTHER MAINTENANCE Requires well-draining soil to ensure perennial nature and to prevent melting out. Pythium and botrytis can be a problem in the South. Planting and mulching with coarse grit may aid survival in heavy soils. Avoid high-fertility soils and shade or plants will require staking. Not invasive like some other yarrows. Seems to weaken after a couple years of strong flowering; at that point divide in the spring or autumn. Plants sustaining winter injury (from wet soils or fluctuating temperatures) may not flower the following season.

RELATED PLANTS *Achillea* 'Anthea', 18–20 in. tall, has light yellow flowers and silver-green foliage. It performs for long periods without division and the growth habit is more upright than 'Moonshine', not requiring staking. It produces numerous secondary flower heads that start to bloom just as the primary ones begin to fade. (Dead-heading of the primary flowers keeps plants tidy, although the flowers are fairly attractive even after they have faded.) Also, 'Anthea' is not prone to melting out in hot, humid climates as is 'Moonshine'.

Achillea 'Moonshine'

Achillea ×lewisii 'King Edward' should be deadheaded to lateral buds to prolong bloom, then cut to new basal foliage when secondary flowering is completed. Well-draining soil is essential.

Aconitum napellus

monkshood
RANUNCULACEAE

Blue-violet spikes of hooded flowers;
deep green palmately divided foliage (lobed
or divided as in the shape of a fan)

3–4 ft. high; 1 ft. wide

Part shade

Blooms July–August

Zones 4–8

Aconitum napellus

PRUNING Most parts of the plant are toxic if ingested. When pruning or handling do not get juice from the plant into your mouth or open wounds, and be certain to wash your hands immediately after cutting back plants. Deadhead to lateral buds for a smaller second flowering. When secondary flowering is finished, cut down to new basal foliage if the old foliage declines, and fertilize if plants are pale. Sporadic small flowering may occur from the basal growth. Leave basal growth over the winter, and prune off in the spring. Plants can be cut back or pinched to control height, although this usually means removal of the large terminal spike. This will produce smaller but more numerous, and possibly later, flowers on sturdier plants. New plants can be cut back by half at planting for a better branching, slightly shorter first-year plant. Established plants can be cut back by half when 18 in. tall to increase fullness. Some gardeners cut plants back by 6 in. when plants are 2½ ft. tall and again by 6 in. when 3½ ft. tall. Staking may be necessary even with any of these pruning techniques used for height control, depending on conditions. If plants are not pruned for height control, side flower spikes can be pinched out to increase the size of the terminal spike if desired.

OTHER MAINTENANCE Prefers a rich, high-organic, moist soil. Avoid hot locations and burning sun; water during dry periods. Won't tolerate tree root competition. Division can be done in early spring or fall, but plants are slow to establish, so best left undisturbed for many years. Requires staking.

RELATED PLANTS *Aconitum* ×*cammarum* 'Bressingham Spire' is a 2½- to 3-ft.-tall selection by Alan Bloom that doesn't require staking. A good choice since pruning is not necessary.

Aconitum carmichaelii 'Arendsii' is a late-flowering monkshood that doesn't require staking, thanks to its strong stems, even though it reaches 3–4 ft. tall.

Aconitum henryi 'Spark's Variety' grows 4–5 ft. tall. Plants cut back by half when 15 in. tall, at planting, flowered at 3 ft., as compared to unpruned plants that flowered at 4 ft. The flowers on pruned plants were slightly smaller and bloomed 14 days later. Pruned plants still require light support from surrounding perennials.

Aconitum septentrionale 'Ivorine' is a lovely cultivar with creamy flowers and upright growth to 2 ft., not requiring staking. Flowering usually starts in late

May or early June. Tough to establish, but once it takes hold 'Ivorine' even seeds itself a bit if not deadheaded.

Aconogonum 'Johanniswolke'

(syn. *Persicaria polymorpha, Polygonum polymorphum*)

white fleeceflower
POLYGONACEAE

Large fluffy panicles of tiny white flowers that age to dusty pink; lance-shaped green leaves
4–6 ft. high; 4–5 ft. wide
Full sun–light shade
Blooms June–September
Zones 4–8

PRUNING White fleeceflower blooms most of the summer without deadheading, the inflorescences remaining attractive into fall, when they turn a tawny pink color. Where winters aren't too punishing, plants may continue to supply some structural interest into December and January. Reseeding isn't an issue, so there's no hurry to remove the spent flowers. Cut plants to the ground any time before growth resumes in early spring. Height may be reduced and bloom time delayed by cutting plants back by half in early summer when they reach 2–3 ft., though this shrublike perennial becomes truly spectacular when allowed to reach its full 6-ft. potential.

RELATED PLANTS 'Johanniswolke' is an adaptable plant but needs protection from wind. It requires only full sun and average soil for a stellar performance, and possesses some drought tolerance, but is better in moist soils. Staking shouldn't be necessary. Unlike some of its *Persicaria* kin, this selection is noninvasive, though it does fill in quickly and makes a substantial clump by its 2nd year.

Aconogonum
'Johanniswolke'

Actaea racemosa

Actaea racemosa

black cohosh
RANUNCULACEAE

White, bottlebrush-shaped, ill-scented
flowers; ferny leaves
4–6 ft. (3 ft.) high; 2–4 ft. wide
Part shade
Blooms June–July
Zones 3–8

PRUNING Allow seedheads to remain
on black cohosh for winter interest.
Cut back in early spring. If plants
receive too much sun or are allowed to
dry out, scorching of the leaves may
occur and deadleafing will be necessary to improve appearance.

OTHER MAINTENANCE This
woodland-edge native does best in
fertile, moist, high-organic, acidic
soil—with the emphasis on moist.
Avoid hot afternoon sun. Individual
flower spikes may need support.
Division is difficult due to the thonglike roots, but it is rarely needed,
as clumps can remain undisturbed
forever. If desired, divide clumps
carefully in the fall. Plants are
slow growing.

RELATED PLANTS *Actaea pachypoda*,
white baneberry, and *A. rubra*, red
baneberry, are North American
woodland wildflowers for the shady,
rich, moist, well-drained border. They
both stay under 3 ft. tall and have
white flowers in spring and colorful
but poisonous berries in late summer
and fall.

Actaea pachypoda 'Misty Blue' has glaucous blue-green leaves.

Actaea simplex, Kamchatka bugbane, resembles *A. racemosa* but is autumn flowering and is sensitive to early frosts. It is more tolerant of basic soils. *Actaea simplex* is especially coveted by gardeners in its many dark-foliaged forms, which go by names like 'Black Negligee', 'Brunette', 'Chocoholic', and 'Hillside Black Beauty'. Prune and maintain as for *A. racemosa*. *Actaea simplex* 'White Pearl' (3 ft.) doesn't require staking.

Agastache 'Blue Fortune'
'Blue Fortune' anise hyssop
LAMIACEAE

Tall spikes of lavender flowers; licorice-scented foliage

2–3 ft. high; 1½–2 ft. wide

Full sun–light shade

Blooms June–August

Zones 4–8

PRUNING 'Blue Fortune' anise hyssop is a short hybrid with extra-long lavender-blue flower spikes. Preemptive pruning is not needed. If you get the genuine article, it shouldn't reseed. Plants may need deadheading when blooms begin to look tired in August, to lighten the load and encourage rebloom in late September. Shears make short work of this task. Plants may also be pinched in late May for a bushier habit.

Wait until spring to cut back agastaches to improve chances of overwintering. When new buds appear, cut old top growth down to within 6 in. of the ground. Plants will self-sow prolifically, so remove spent flower spikes in early fall if reseeding is a concern, although finches will visit the seedheads if they're left standing over the winter.

OTHER MAINTENANCE A native Midwestern prairie plant, anise hyssop prefers moist, well-drained soil, but can handle drought when established. It's likely to lean or flop in shade. Division is possible in spring, but because plants self-sow so abundantly, it's easier to replace declining or dead plants with volunteers. They grow quickly and often bloom their 1st year. Unwanted seedlings are easily pulled up.

RELATED PLANTS *Agastache foeniculum* 'Golden Jubilee' is shorter (to 3 ft.) and has bright yellow spring foliage that fades to yellow-green. Seedlings come true to type. Agastaches with pink, orange, or yellow flowers, like cultivars 'Tutti

Agastache 'Blue Fortune'

Frutti' (pink) and 'Tango' (orange), are usually selections or hybrids involving Western species. With these Western types, sharp drainage is especially crucial to winter survival. Plants may be short-lived even under ideal circumstances.

Ajuga reptans
bugleweed
LAMIACEAE

Blue, white, or pink flowers; green, variegated, or purple leaves
6–9 in. (2 in.) high; 24 in. wide
Full sun or part shade
Blooms May–June
Zones 4–9

PRUNING Deadheading prevents excessive seeding and improves the overall appearance of the plant. Hedge shears or a weed whacker can be used for large plantings. Plants usually can even tolerate occasional, but not repeated, mowing. Cut back runners drastically whenever necessary to keep plant from spreading too far. Thinning of plants can reduce the incidence of crown rot; if plants are infected, prune out diseased sections. Plants are evergreen; do not prune for winter. Deadleafing may be required to clean

Ajuga reptans 'Catlin's Giant'

up plants a bit in the spring or occasionally through the growing season.
OTHER MAINTENANCE Invasive groundcover, but fairly easily pulled to keep under control in gardens; avoid spread into turf areas. Unwanted seedlings are best removed when young. Crown rot is a significant problem, particularly in southern gardens. Plant in areas with good air circulation and divide every 2–3 years

to help reduce the problem. Tolerates poor soil.

RELATED PLANTS Purple-leaved forms hold up best against both cold and heat, except for *Ajuga reptans* 'Catlin's Giant', which gets battered by 0°F temperatures. 'Burgundy Glow', a silver variegated form, is often killed by cold. 'Cristata' holds up very well, even in harsh winters.

Ajuga pyramidalis, upright bugleweed, is more upright than *A. reptans* and is slower spreading. Will seed strongly; deadhead to reduce the problem.

Alcea rosea
hollyhock
MALVACEAE

Spiked single or double flowers in a wide range of colors; large, palmate, coarse leaves
3–8 ft. high; 3–4 ft. wide
Full sun–part shade
Blooms June–August
Zones 3–8

PRUNING Biennial hollyhocks act perennial in nature if they are deadheaded and then cut down to new basal foliage as soon as all flowering is completed. Flowers from the bottom of the spike open first. Deadhead plants to lateral buds when the seed capsules (on the bottom half) outnumber the new flowers (on the tip). Plants frequently seed if not deadheaded; leave the seedheads if that is the desired way to perpetuate the plant in the garden. Deadleafing is needed to remove yellowing leaves, starting in June, and leaves damaged by Japanese beetles or rust. Destroy rust-infested leaves. Cut out all old flowering stems and old basal leaves to expose clean basal foliage in late summer when flowering is completed. The plants look so horrendous by this time that such pruning can be a welcome relief. The new foliage holds up well into the winter and may remain semi-evergreen under consistent snow cover or in mild winters. Remove any winter-damaged leaves in the spring. Tall-growing forms can be cut down

once or twice before flowering to create later blooming, shorter plants that don't require staking. Flower spikes will be smaller but more in scale with the shorter plants, and more useful for smaller flower arrangements.

OTHER MAINTENANCE Hollyhock is definitely in the high-maintenance weight class. A choice plant of a variety of insects and diseases, and it's particularly demolished by Japanese beetles and rust. Staking is usually required unless plants are pruned or lower-growing forms are selected. Rich moist soil and good drainage are essential.

RELATED PLANTS *Alcea rosea* Chater's Series is a double perennial form. *Alcea rosea* 'Old Farmyard' is a single, 6- to 8-ft.-tall perennial form. Plants may be cut back by half in about mid-May, or when 15–18 in. high, and then again when in tight bud around mid-June, or when 3 ft. tall—the last

pruning is usually necessary because the plants may still be spindly. Pruning in this way will mean that plants flower at approximately 3½ ft. tall, rather than the typical 6–7 ft., and about 3 or 4 weeks later, starting around July 20 and continuing, although only lightly, into early October. Also, plants generally aren't as badly affected by Japanese beetles at this later date. Such pruning makes the plant usable in my front border, which adds to the cottage garden look, and it doesn't need to be relegated to a cutting garden once it is "reformed." A few branches can be left uncut at the second pruning in June to allow some flowers to bloom then and to provide color in the gardens and for cutting.

Alcea rugosa has pale yellow flowers and is resistant to rust. Doesn't fall over. Deadheading prolongs bloom into autumn. Grows 4 ft. tall.

Alcea rosea

Alchemilla mollis

lady's mantle
ROSACEAE

Frothy chartreuse flower heads; round, scalloped, soft, smoky yellow-green leaves
15–18 in. (12 in.) high; 24 in. wide
Part shade or sun
Blooms June–August
Zones 4–7

PRUNING Lady's mantle can be deadheaded in a couple of different ways. The most common method is to cut the old flowering stem down to the basal growth. The other approach is to pull the old flowering stem out at the base, which serves the additional purpose of thinning the plant a bit, and if some root is pulled out along with the stem it can be propagated. Self-seeding can be a problem in some gardens; if this is the case, seedheads should be removed before they mature. I don't have heavy seeding in my gardens, even with 20 or more plants, and the few seedlings that I get are welcome, so I prefer to leave the heads on until they are brown, as I enjoy them at this stage as well. Plants may bloom sporadically later in the season if deadheaded. Leaves will scorch if grown in too much sun or in dry conditions. Deadleafing usually is necessary. Leaves can be removed individually with pruners, or if scorch damage is severe, foliage can be sheared, with hedge shears, to a

couple of inches from the base early in the season, soon after flowering. Do not shear too close to the crown, or plants may be killed. Plants can also be deadleafed lightly as needed early on, and then sheared to the lush new basal foliage, which develops under the old tatty leaves, in late summer. I opt for this latter approach because I don't like the hole that is created by shearing the plant low early in the season. I have found regrowth to be slow on plants sheared low too early on, often delayed by a month or more, particularly when the pruning is followed by hot and dry weather. The plants seem to overwinter better if they are not cut back in the autumn. Hedge shears make quick work of dead leaf cleanup in the spring, but again it is important to avoid cutting close to the crown. Thinning the plants as described or by removing some of the leaves can reduce moisture trapped in the foliage, which can lead to disease problems, particularly in southern gardens. Plants are wide spreading and some outer leaves may need to be removed to keep plants off of their neighbors.

OTHER MAINTENANCE Plants prefer rich, moist soil in areas not exposed to hot afternoon sun. They will grow in sun or shade, but require pruning as described above to keep them looking decent. Divide in spring or fall every 6–10 years. Lady's mantle is very effective when repeated along a border.

Amsonia tabernaemontana
Eastern bluestar
APOCYNACEAE

Light blue star-shaped flowers; glossy leaves that may turn yellow in fall
2–4 ft. high; 2–4 ft. wide
Full sun–part shade
Blooms May–June
Zones 3–9

PRUNING When grown in too much shade or in overly rich soil, or where a more structured look is desired in the garden, bluestar will benefit from shearing back by a third to half and shaping after flowering. Hedge shears do the trick. Cut outer branches slightly lower than inner branches to shape plants. Plants fill in nicely in 2–3 weeks at about 1 ft. shorter than original size if cut back by a third. Pruned plants add a neat, rounded, shrublike structure to the garden as compared to their flopping and open unpruned counterparts. Look at the plant: sometimes just a little cut off the top, such as 4–6 in. off the tips, is enough to remove the weight and allow the plant to stand upright again, particularly if the plant is in a fair amount of sun. In some years, particularly those with moist springs, plants can seed by the hundreds; fortunately seeds will usually drop directly at the base of the plant. Cutting plants back after flowering and removing seedpods at the same time will eliminate this concern. Plants can be cut down to 6–10 in. above the ground to improve growth habit, which may be needed in warmer climates or in areas of deep shade. Plants grown in full sun may not require cutting back, although deadheading may be necessary if seeding is a problem. Seedpods can be snapped off easily with a sharp thumbnail. Shorter growing forms like 'Short Stack' or 'Blue Ice' should be selected if you want to avoid pruning.

Amsonia tabernaemontana

Eastern bluestar carries its shrub form into the winter, but it may break down in heavy snows. Cut plants down in the spring. Some people are highly sensitive to the milky sap produced by amsonia, which can cause itching or burning upon contact; protective clothing should be worn while pruning the plants.

OTHER MAINTENANCE This is an easy-to-grow, hardy, low-maintenance plant. It tolerates both dry and wet soils for short periods, but generally prefers evenly moist conditions. Division is easy, in late spring or fall, but isn't necessary for 6–10 years or longer. It will require staking if grown in shade and not pruned.

RELATED PLANTS *Amsonia ciliata*, downy amsonia, is a fine-leaved, feathery form that opens up a bit after flowering. I shear 4–6 in. off the tops of plants grown in full sun, shaping them into a better habit.

grown in shade, prune it as you would *A. tabernaemontana*.

Amsonia hubrichtii, Arkansas bluestar (zones 5–9), is primarily grown for its feathery foliage that turns a rich gold in fall. In fact, *A. hubrichtii* has begun to eclipse other *Amsonia* species in popularity thanks to its outstanding foliage and autumn color. It is drought tolerant once established and grows to 3 ft. in dry soils and to 4 ft. in moister sites. It can become chlorotic in high pH soils.

Anaphalis triplinervis
three-veined everlasting
COMPOSITAE

Papery white flower heads; woolly (long and entangled soft hairs), 3-veined leaves; zigzag stems

12–18 in. high; 12–15 in. wide

Full sun–part shade

Blooms August–October

Zones 3–8

PRUNING Three-veined everlasting has long-lasting flowers and a long bloom period. Deadhead to lateral

Amsonia hubrichtii

Anaphalis triplinervis 'Sommerschnee'

Amsonia elliptica has wider, glossier leaves than *A. tabernaemontana*. Its rounded, shrubby form holds up fairly well in full sun with no pruning. It tends to be a heavy seeder in moist years and should be deadheaded before pods mature. When

buds when flowers fade to keep plants looking fresh. Foliage declines if grown in too dry a soil, thus requiring deadleafing. If damage is severe, cut plants down to basal foliage. Plants may also need pruning back due to damage from painted lady butterfly larvae.

OTHER MAINTENANCE One of the few gray-foliaged plants that doesn't rot in moist soils or humid conditions; in fact, this species requires evenly moist soils, or the foliage will decline. Clumps increase at a moderate rate, but plants do not send out invasive stolons like other *Anaphalis* species. Divide every 4–5 years in early spring. Do not prune for winter; cut back in early spring.

RELATED PLANTS *Anaphalis triplinervis* 'Sommerschnee' has whiter flowers than the species and is more compact (8–10 in.).

Anaphalis margaritacea is an invasive, higher-maintenance plant, but it will take drier conditions than *A. triplinervis*. Native species appropriate for native setting.

Anchusa azurea
Italian bugloss
BORAGINACEAE

Tiny bright blue flowers; large coarse leaves
4–6 ft. high; 2 ft. wide
Full sun–part shade
Blooms May–June
Zones 3–8

PRUNING Deadhead plants to lateral buds to prevent excessive seeding and to prolong bloom. Foliage declines after bloom period. The plant's life expectancy can be prolonged by several years if cut back hard to the ground immediately after flowering; or, even better, cut back into the crown, going ½–¾ in. under the soil surface right to the roots. Do not prune again for the winter. Clean up if needed in the spring.

OTHER MAINTENANCE Plants require staking, particularly in high-fertility soil. Can be invasive in rich soil. Tolerates short periods of drought; rots in wet soils. Italian bugloss is a high-maintenance,

(**left**) *Anchusa azurea* 'Loddon Royalist'

(**right**) *Anchusa azurea* 'Dropmore'

short-lived perennial that deteriorates after the 2nd year and must be divided. Plants do not respond well to autumn planting. Heavy seeders.

RELATED PLANTS *Anchusa azurea* 'Dropmore' is floppy and requires staking, but has gorgeous sky-blue flowers. 'Little John' grows 12–18 in., usually not needing staking. 'Loddon Royalist', 3 ft. in height, may need staking, particularly in wind and storms.

Anemone ×hybrida
Japanese anemone
RANUNCULACEAE

White, pink, or rose flowers; trifoliate leaves
2–4 ft. (1¼–1½ ft.) high; 2 ft. wide
Full sun–part shade
Blooms September–October
Zones 4–8

Anemone ×hybrida 'Bressingham Glow'

PRUNING Japanese anemone doesn't require deadheading to prolong bloom, but the old flowers tend to detract from the beauty of new buds and flowers. I usually deadhead once early in the bloom period, and then let the rest of the deadheads remain on the plants. The seedheads do not turn cottonlike, as do the flowers of many other members of the genus. Plants blacken and become quite unattractive with a hard frost, and are probably best cut down for the winter. Can be completely defoliated by black blister beetles in July. The remaining bare stems of infected plants should be cut to the ground. New basal foliage quickly returns, but the plants most likely will not flower that season. Take care when pruning down stems after beetle damage to wear gloves and protective clothing, as a few beetles may still be on plants and can cause blisters on the skin upon contact. Japanese beetles also can do major damage to Japanese anemone leaves. I consider the damage from the Japanese beetles to be pruning for height control as my *Anemone ×hybrida* 'Queen Charlotte' flowered at 2½ ft., rather than its typical 3½ ft., with little delay in the flowering time as a result of Japanese beetle feeding in June. The overall vigor of the plant was reduced, however. I assume gardeners may be able to prune similarly by cutting back by half in early June when plants are 12 in. tall; my attempts at finding out the results of this have been hindered by black blister beetle damage on pruned plants.

OTHER MAINTENANCE Plants prefer rich, well-draining organic soil. Often killed by wet overwintering conditions. Avoid periods of drought. Can be short-lived and requires mulching for the winter in northern gardens. Often slow to establish, but once Japanese anemone takes hold it can be invasive, requiring digging out to keep plants in their intended space and to control spread. I have grown them successfully in sun or shade, although morning sun is preferred to hot

afternoon sun in hot locations. Divide every 10 years in the spring if needed to renew clump. Fall transplanting is fatal; spring planting is advised. Tall-growing cultivars (4–5 ft.) may need staking.

RELATED PLANTS I have tried approximately 10 different cultivars of *Anemone ×hybrida* and I find the old standbys 'September Charm' (single pink) and 'Honorine Jobert' (single white) to be the longest lived and most tolerant to sun and drought once established. Both can be invasive. 'Bressingham Glow' is a semi-double with rose-pink petals.

Anemone tomentosa 'Robustissima' can be invasive but is well behaved in dry shade. Also afflicted by black blister beetles. More tolerant of temperature extremes than *Anemone ×hybrida*. Hardy to zone 3.

Anemone pulsatilla

pasque flower
RANUNCULACEAE

Cupped purplish-red flowers; silky hairs on foliage
12 in. high; 12 in. wide
Part shade
Blooms April–May
Zones 5–8

PRUNING Leave deadheads on the plant because they mature into fantastic fluffy, multispined creatures resembling clematis seedheads. The leaves usually disappear in the summer after the seedheads emerge.

OTHER MAINTENANCE Plants are short-lived unless provided with well-draining soil, particularly over the winter. Tolerates drought in cooler regions. Plants do not require division for many years; once plants are well established, divide carefully after flowering, if desired.

Anemone pulsatilla

Angelica gigas

purple angelica, Korean angelica
APIACEAE

Bold dissected foliage; 4- to 8-in.-wide
burgundy flower heads
3–6 ft. high; 2–3 ft. wide
Part shade
Blooms July–August
Zones 4–8

Angelica gigas

PRUNING *Angelica gigas* is monocarpic, meaning it dies after setting seed, so the flower heads should be cut off as soon as the flowers fade to prevent seed maturation. This extends the life of this normally biennial, or short-lived perennial, species.

Deadhead to a lateral bud. If allowed to go to seed, it may produce offspring with great ambition if the conditions are favorable, but in my gardens only minimal offspring are produced (I wish there were more!).

Flowers are attractive to beneficial insects. Deadleaf older yellowing leaves in late summer. All leaves drop off the stem after a frost, and unless the seedheads have been allowed to remain, the plant should be cut down at that time.

OTHER MAINTENANCE Will grow in full sun but best performance is in locations with afternoon shade. Moist fertile soil enhances growth. May be affected by mites or leaf miner, but not of significant concern. It is a self-supporting giant that does not need staking.

RELATED PLANTS *Angelica archangelica*, archangel, has the same pruning and maintenance requirements as *A. gigas*.

Aquilegia hybrids

columbine
RANUNCULACEAE

Wide range of colors and bicolored flowers; gray-green compound foliage
1–3 ft. (1 ft.) high; 1 ft. wide
Full sun–part shade
Blooms May–June
Zones 3–9

PRUNING First deadhead to lateral flower buds, then cut old flowering stems to the ground when all flowering is finished to prevent seeding, which often results in undesirable strains. Deadheading can prolong bloom, particularly on young plants. Deadleafing keeps plants in good condition, but if severely affected by leaf miner or other pests, plants can be cut to the ground. A fresh mound of foliage will develop from the pruning. Do not be concerned if it takes several weeks or longer for new foliage to emerge, particularly under dry conditions. The clean fresh mound of foliage can remain for the winter. If plants have leaf miner or other pests in the autumn, they should be cut down for the winter; clean up all debris from around the plant. Destroy any and all pest-infested leaves.

OTHER MAINTENANCE Plants do best with evenly moist, rich soil. Overly dry soil will take its toll, as will overly wet soil, which leads to crown rot. Avoid locations with hot afternoon sun. Taller forms will need staking. If columbine gets infested with borers, dig out and destroy the entire plant. Plants can be divided, with care, in the summer, although it usually is not required. Columbine is short-lived, normally persisting only 3–4 years. Natural hybridization will occur between species. Planting in different areas of the garden can reduce the cross-hybridization. Also, planting among other perennials that will fill in after the columbine is finished flowering will help to hide ugly or cut-back foliage.

RELATED PLANTS *Aquilegia* McKana Group (hybrids) are commonly available 30-in.-tall plants, usually requiring staking.

Aquilegia Biedermeier Group are compact 12-in. cultivars. No staking needed.

Aquilegia alpina, alpine columbine, is my favorite species. Will seed, but not to nuisance level. Grows 18–24 in., needs no staking, and is longer lived.

Aquilegia canadensis, Canadian columbine, reseeds heavily to colonize an area. Native, easy to grow, less troubled by leaf miner.

Aquilegia flabellata, fan columbine, is 8–12 in. high, requires no staking, and is longer lived.

Aquilegia vulgaris, granny's bonnet, is a classic form often found in old gardens.

Aquilegia hybrids

Arisaema triphyllum

jack-in-the-pulpit
ARACEAE

Single green "flower" with purple-striped hood; large trifoliate leaves
12–24 in. high; 12–18 in. wide
Part shade–shade
Blooms April–May
Zones 3–9

Arisaema triphyllum

PRUNING Jack-in-the-pulpit makes only 1 set of leaves each year, and cutting down foliage early robs the plant of energy needed for growth and winter survival. Allow foliage to die down naturally in summer and fruit to form. Orange-red fruit ripens on female plants in August, but plants may not bear every year, as this species has the ability to change sex from year to year.

OTHER MAINTENANCE Plant this native wildflower in moist, organic-laden soil in dappled to full shade. Companions such as ferns or hostas are useful in hiding the gaps left by dormant jacks. To increase stocks, established clumps may be divided just after they enter their dormancy period in midsummer, or plants may be simply left in place and ants will disperse the seeds.

RELATED PLANTS *Arisaema candidissimum*, white jack-in-the-pulpit (zones 5–7), is one of many dramatic Asian species available and sports a pink-and-white-striped spathe and huge leaves. It doesn't emerge until May or even June; be patient. Like most of the Asian species, it needs excellent drainage. This plant can multiply quickly in a favorable site, but is never a nuisance.

Arisaema ringens, cobra jack (zones 5–9), is one of the easiest arisaemas to grow. It emerges early, and the large, glossy leaves may need protection from late frosts. It doesn't go dormant until fall.

Arisaema sikokianum, gaudy jack (zones 4–9), is a showstopper with a purple-black "pulpit" (spathe) and a snow-white "jack" (spadix). This one also emerges early; give it protection from late frosts in spring. This species doesn't produce offsets, so new plants must be raised from seed. It will go dormant in late summer.

Armeria maritima

sea pink
PLUMBAGINACEAE

Round, bright pink flowers on long stems; grasslike mounded foliage
12 in. (3 in.) high; 12 in. wide
Full sun
Blooms May–June
Zones 4–8

PRUNING Requires little pruning other than clipping off unsightly faded flowers and stalks down to basal foliage. Deadheading keeps young plants flowering through the summer and causes sporadic rebloom on older clumps. If no new buds are evident with the dead flowers, grab a handful of deadheads and prune off all at once, or use hedge shears to ease the labor in large plantings. Plants are evergreen. Do not prune for winter, but sections may need to be pruned off in the spring if there is winter damage.

OTHER MAINTENANCE Performs best in poor and dry soils. Mats rot in the center in heavy clay, poorly drained, or overly rich soils, and plants are usually short-lived (3–5 years) under such conditions. Division is needed when cushions open up and

decline, but division is often hard to do successfully, so it's best to replace plants at this time.

Artemisia abrotanum
southernwood
COMPOSITAE

Gray-green, finely divided foliage; nonornamental yellow flower heads
3–4 ft. high; 1½–2 ft. wide
Full sun
Blooms July–August
Zones 5–9

PRUNING Cut back tips by 6–8 in. in spring or early summer to prevent plants from getting rangy. If prone to very weedy growth, perhaps in rich soil, plants can be cut back even harder, taking them to within a foot of the ground. Avoid cutting into the old woody part of stems, which may result in the death of the plant. Hedge shears are useful for shaping and cutting back plants. Removing the flowering stalks before the flowers open helps keep plants in good form. If allowed to flower, deadheading and shaping with shears can be done after flowering. Do not cut back hard after August as plants may not have time to regrow and harden before winter. Do not prune for winter.

OTHER MAINTENANCE Best in well-draining or dry sites; wet soil or extreme humidity will cause the plant to open in the middle.

Armeria maritima

Artemisia abrotanum

Artemisia absinthium
'Lambrook Silver'

Artemisia absinthium **'Lambrook Silver'**

'Lambrook Silver' artemisia
COMPOSITAE

Gray, deeply divided foliage; yellow flower heads

2 ft. high; 2 ft. wide

Full sun

Blooms August–September

Zones 4–9

PRUNING When half their mature height (normally in early June), plants can be pinched, or cut back by half, and shaped with hedge shears to reduce height and to prevent flopping later in the summer. I usually cut off the flower heads as soon as I see them forming to better enjoy the silver foliage. A second trim may be necessary to keep plants looking good. Plants that are allowed to flower should be deadheaded to prevent seed set, otherwise foliage will deteriorate at the sake of seed production; deadheads also add a tarnished look to

plants. Neglected plants may be killed if cut back too hard to old wood if no new buds are breaking. It's best to not prune hard after August as plants may not have time to harden for the winter. 'Lambrook Silver' artemisia is semi-evergreen, so do not prune for winter. When planting it is useful to cut back or pinch new plants for fuller, more compact first-year growth.

OTHER MAINTENANCE Prefers poor, well-draining, even dry soil with an alkaline pH. It is an easy artemisia to grow, and it doesn't spread invasively by underground runners like *Artemisia ludoviciana* 'Silver King' and others. Best artemisia for northern gardens if good winter drainage is assured.

RELATED PLANTS *Artemisia stelleriana* 'Silver Brocade', also known as 'Silver Brocade' beach wormwood, requires excellent drainage for survival. Pinch plants to keep full and to prevent flowering. If allowed to bloom, deadhead before seed set. Cut back to control spread. Deadleafing of

foliage at the base may be necessary. Do not prune for winter. I have had plants totally defoliated by larval feeding in summer.

Artemisia lactiflora

white mugwort
COMPOSITAE

Ornamental creamy white flower heads; green divided leaves

4–6 ft. high; 3 ft. wide

Full sun or light shade

Blooms August–September

Zones 4–8

PRUNING Plants provided with sun and moist soils become surprisingly large (6 ft. tall) and require staking. Height and legginess can be controlled if thinned and pinched or cut back by 4 in., or even by half, depending on how unmanageable it tends to become, in late May or early June. Under dry conditions or poor soil, plants usually attain a manageable 3½- to 4-ft. height and require no pruning, thinning, or staking. In autumn, cut plants down to basal rosette, which remains fairly evergreen.

OTHER MAINTENANCE Staking is required in conditions of moist, rich soil. Divide every 4–5 years. Long-lived.

Artemisia ludoviciana 'Silver King'

'Silver King' artemisia
COMPOSITAE

Woolly, gray, lance-shaped leaves; insignificant yellow flower heads

2–3 ft. high; wide-spreading clump

Full sun

Blooms August–September

Zones 3–8

PRUNING If grown for foliar effect alone, plants should not be allowed to flower, which can lead to decline. Plants can be sheared back by half or two-thirds at the end of May or in early June to control flopping; they may benefit from another cut in half in mid-July. Plants can be selectively pruned to keep in shape. Plants that fall over in summer can be sheared back by a third to half at that time and will return to good form. Although the height of 'Silver King' artemisia can be controlled, it is difficult to control the spread of this plant just with pruning, and it usually involves digging out the invasive roots. If grown for wreath making (which I feel is this plant's main attribute), pinching early in the season will keep plants fuller and will ensure flowering. Cut stems while in bud before flowers mature, in early to

Artemisia lactiflora Guizhou Group

Artemisia ludoviciana 'Silver King'

Artemisia 'Powis Castle'

mid-September in the Midwest, for best effect in wreaths.

OTHER MAINTENANCE Plants are very invasive. As tempting as it is to grow this plant in the perennial border for the wonderful silver foliage, it isn't advisable. Best given a bed by itself where it can run and be used for cutting and yet will not take over the rest of the world. Some gardeners are experimenting with new commercially available barriers. Also, with its tendency to flop, it can do so in peace if given its own out-of-the-way space. Plants may rot in excessively moist soils or in regions with high humidity. If grown in the border, plants will require frequent (annual) lifting and dividing in the spring or autumn to control spread.

RELATED PLANTS *Artemisia ludoviciana* 'Silver Queen' has foliage that is slightly less dissected. It is a fast spreader as well. 'Valerie Finnis', when sheared (with hedge shears) by half in early June, grew to 15 in. tall at maturity. Plants sheared by half in June and again in mid-July formed a nice 8- to 12-in.-high groundcover,

compared to the flopping 3-ft.-high unpruned plants. Plants did not bloom under either pruning regimens. Some claim it is not invasive, although it is for me even in clay soil.

Artemisia 'Powis Castle'

'Powis Castle' artemisia
COMPOSITAE

Finely cut silver foliage; insignificant flower heads
2–3 ft. high; 3–4 ft. wide
Full sun
Blooms August–September
Zones 5–8

PRUNING Little quart-size plants can become specimens that are 3 ft. high and wide in the first season, which creates much excitement. Pinch before planting if leggy. Do not prune in the autumn, but in early spring, plants can be cut back to control height and width. Make certain to not cut back too hard into the old wood, as this may kill the plant. Allow buds to start to break before pruning to provide a helpful reference point as to how far back to cut. Do not cut into wood that does not have live buds. Plants fill out quickly in a week or two after pruning. Hedge shears can be used during the summer to shape plants as needed and to keep them in their own space, as well as to remove flower buds before blooming, to help maintain the attractive appearance. If plants fall open in the summer, shearing back by a third or half will return them to good form, and soon after they won't even look as though they were pruned. Deadleafing may be necessary if plants have received too much moisture.

OTHER MAINTENANCE My biggest problem in the central Ohio area is lack of hardiness. I have tried it in several different locations in clients' gardens and my own, only to have it live for a year or two and then be killed over the winter. Planting in a protected site has allowed the longest life (3 years) in my experience. Division of this woody subshrub is difficult.

RELATED PLANTS *Artemisia* 'Silverado'—I'm not sure on the nomenclature of this plant, but I love it and use it anyway. Plants can be cut back by half at planting to promote fullness. Shearing back by half when just in bud, around early to mid-July, and then shearing off buds when they appear around the middle of August and again in the middle of September creates full, compact (8–10 in. rather than 18–20 in.), nonflowering plants that hold up well until the end of the season. The flowering stems are attractive, but if allowed to develop early in the season, plants will not be as full as pruned specimens. The flowering also causes decline of the plant. Cut off deadheads to the base of the plant. In hot summers, plants that have been allowed to flower may need to be cut back all the way to fresh basal growth that develops in August. You could always try for the best of both worlds: prune in July and August for full plants, and allow some flowering in September. I use chicken grit in the hole and as a mulch when planting *Artemisia* 'Silverado', to reduce losses from wet soil.

Artemisia schmidtiana 'Nana'

silvermound artemisia
COMPOSITAE

Finely cut silvery foliage; insignificant flower heads
12–18 in. high; 15–18 in. wide
Full sun
Blooms July–August
Zones 3–7

PRUNING Clumps usually open up in the center by midsummer, which is a good time to cut the plant back to the new basal growth. If you are weak at heart about cutting back so drastically, you can do it in phases. Cutting back in phases is particularly helpful since silvermound artemisia usually is located right in the front of the border, where dramatic pruning is obvious. You can delay the plants from opening up by preventing flowering, either by shearing (plants can be shaped at this time as well) or pinching when flower buds are first evident. As with most silver-foliaged artemisia, silvermound artemisia's habit is best maintained if flowering is prevented entirely.

OTHER MAINTENANCE Requires well-draining, low-fertility soil and good air circulation to prevent rotting; tends to rot in high humidity. High maintenance. I'm not sure how this plant ever gained so much popularity—I suspect it is simply the good fortune of being silver.

Artemisia schmidtiana 'Nana'

Arum italicum 'Pictum'
painted arum
ARACEAE

Spear-shaped, variegated deep green
leaves; orange-red berries;
jack-in-the-pulpit-type flowers
12–20 in. high; 18 in. wide
Part shade–full shade
Blooms May
Zones 5–9

PRUNING Painted arum may require
deadleafing when foliage dies down in
summer to tidy up the area and allow
the attractive fruit to be best displayed.
Often this entails simply pulling leaves
out gently by hand as they shrivel away.
Do not deadhead, or you will lose one
of the prime features of the plant: the
ornamental fruit. When the fruit
decline the stems usually become limp
and are hidden by returning autumn
foliage, so pruning of stems generally
is not needed. Plants are evergreen or
semi-evergreen, depending on the
climate—do not cut back in the
autumn. May need a bit of deadleafing
in the spring so as to not detract from
healthy foliage.

Arum italicum 'Pictum'

OTHER MAINTENANCE Best in moist
shady sites with soil high in organic
matter. Tolerates drier soils when the
leaves are dormant during the summer.
Summer is also the best time to divide
the plants, but this usually is not
necessary for many years (6–10 years).

Beautiful low-maintenance plant. Slow
to take hold, but long-lived once
established. Considered to be on the
hardiness borderline in zone 5, often
listed as zone 6–9, but has tolerated our
Midwest winters, though it often dies
down and comes back in the spring.

Aruncus dioicus
goat's beard
ROSACEAE

Plumelike creamy flowers; pinnately
compound astilbelike foliage
4–6 ft. high; 6 ft. wide
Part shade
Blooms June–July
Zones 3–7

PRUNING The plants are dioecious
(male and female flowers borne on
separate plants), and although the
male flowers are more attractive in
bloom, the female seedpods are more
attractive for the winter—what a
dilemma! Nurseries do not distinguish
between the sexes anyway, so you
usually don't get a choice. The
deadheads may weigh down the
foliage, which is an obvious sign that
deadheading would improve the
overall appearance of the plant.
Deadleafing may be required if
scorching or dry conditions are a
problem. Self-seeding may occur
where male and female plants are
grown together, but it is seldom
troublesome.

OTHER MAINTENANCE Staking is
not needed, but heavy rain when the
plant is in flower will weigh the great
plumes to the ground. Best in
moisture-retentive soil. Will take full
sun in cool summer climates. Tolerates tree root competition if soils are
high in moisture or in areas with
heavy rainfall, although the competition will curb the plant's size.
Although rarely required (every 10
years or more) and difficult to accomplish, division is recommended in the
spring. Tough roots. Not for use in
areas warmer than zone 6, where
performance is poor as a result of the
heat. It is slow growing in the first
season or two, but once it takes hold,

stand back, as it forms a large shrub. Allow plenty of space when planting (at least 4 ft. diameter), since the plant won't like being moved.

RELATED PLANTS *Aruncus aethusifolius* is a small 6- to 8-in. mound that should not be deadheaded because the seedheads are ornamental over the summer and winter.

conditions in my experience. Spreads slowly by rhizomes and can be divided in the spring or early fall, but division is rarely needed (6–10 years). Avoid planting too deep. Dies out in zone 8.

RELATED PLANTS *Asarum canadense*, Canadian wild ginger, is a native deciduous species that is more tolerant of alkaline conditions and heat and is more vigorous.

Aruncus dioicus

Asarum europaeum
European wild ginger
ARISTOLOCHIACEAE

Brown flowers hidden under shiny, kidney-shaped leaves

6–8 in. high; 12–15 in. wide

Part shade–full shade

Blooms April–May

Zones 4–7

PRUNING Minimal pruning is needed. Plants are evergreen or semi-evergreen, depending on the climate. Do not prune for winter, but deadleaf as needed in the spring.

OTHER MAINTENANCE Low-maintenance plant. Prefers rich organic, moist but well-draining, slightly acidic soil, although it has performed well in more alkaline

Asarum europaeum

Asclepias tuberosa

Asclepias tuberosa
butterfly weed
APOCYNACEAE

Orange flowers; narrow foliage
2–3 ft. high; 2 ft. wide
Full sun
Blooms June–August
Zones 4–9

PRUNING Deadheading results in rebloom about a month after initial flowering. Allowing some of the second bloom phase to mature into the ornamental fruit prolongs the season of interest. It is a heavy seeder. The fruit should be removed before it splits and spills the seeds, if seeding is not desired. Do not prune for the winter, cut back in the spring.

OTHER MAINTENANCE Butterfly weed is a native prairie plant that tolerates poor, dry soil and is drought tolerant. Well-draining soil is essential, particularly in the winter. Prefers acid soil. Can be slow to establish but is long-lived once it takes hold. Late to emerge in the spring. Divide in the spring only when new growth starts. Division is difficult due to the taproot, but fortunately it's seldom needed. Mulching helps prevent frost heaving. Low-maintenance plant. Do not collect from the wild.

Aster

(see also *Symphyotrichum*)

Aster ×*frikartii* 'Mönch'

'Mönch' Frikart's aster
COMPOSITAE

Lavender-blue flower heads; finely pubescent leaves and stems

Blooms July–October

2–3 ft. high; 2–3 ft. wide

Full sun

Zones 5–8

PRUNING This plant has a long bloom period even without deadheading. The new flower buds are borne close to the old flowers, so if you do choose to deadhead, you must take care to remove each spent bloom without damaging the new bud. Plants are often lanky; cutting back by half or more in late May or early June can improve the habit. It may also delay flowering. 'Mönch' aster is a tender perennial; several authorities recommend that it not be cut back for the winter in order to increase its survivability. Cut plants down in the spring after all danger of cold weather has passed.

OTHER MAINTENANCE 'Mönch' needs winter protection in zone 5, and it will not survive wet winters. Select a light mulch such as pine needles for protection to avoid crown rot. Provide light support such as pea stakes if pruning is not performed.

RELATED PLANTS *Aster* ×*frikartii* 'Wonder of Staffa' is even taller than 'Mönch' and requires pruning for height control.

Aster tongolensis, a compact summer-flowering aster known as East Indies aster, does not need pruning for height control. If deadheaded it may rebloom later in the season. The cultivar *A. tongolensis* 'Wartburgstern' (Wartburg star) grows to 18–24 in. with lavender-blue flowers.

Aster ×*frikartii* 'Mönch'

169

Aster tataricus 'Jindai'

'Jindai' Tatarian daisy
COMPOSITAE

Lavender-blue flower heads; large basal
leaves up to 18 in. long
Blooms September–November
3–4 ft. (2 ft.) high; 3 ft. wide
Full sun
Zones 4–8

PRUNING *Aster tataricus* 'Jindai' is a
self-supporting cultivar that normally
doesn't require pruning for height
control. It is a desirable plant, because
the only pruning it requires is cutting
back for cleanup in the spring.
Sections can be pruned before
flowering to layer the planting, if
desired. Cutting plants back by half in
mid-July produces 3-ft. rather than
4-ft. plants, but without any delay in
bloom. Deadheading in the autumn is
senseless, as the old flowering stems
remain upright and strong throughout
the winter. I have never had any
seeding of this cultivar.

OTHER MAINTENANCE 'Jindai' is an
easy-to-grow aster and one of the
coolest, latest-flowering perennials in
Midwest gardens. The clean foliage is
free of pests and disease. Spreading
underground stolons can be invasive;
divide in the spring every 3rd or 4th
year to control spread.

Aster tataricus 'Jindai'

RELATED PLANTS The straight
species form of *Aster tataricus* may
flower at 6 ft. in height. Cutting it back
as described for the cultivar will also
produce shorter plants. Lifting the
stolons and pruning them off can
control spread.

Asteromoea mongolica

(syn. *Kalimeris mongolica*)

double Japanese aster
ASTERACEAE

Numerous small white flowers; small
divided leaves
3–3½ ft. high; 2 ft. wide
Full sun–part shade
Blooms July–September
Zones 5–8

PRUNING This perennial has a long
bloom period even without deadheading. Old flowers simply dry up
unobtrusively. Plants can be left up for
winter interest and then cut down in
early spring. They respond well to
cutting back before flowering to
reduce height, which can effectively
layer the planting. Cutting back can
also be used to slightly delay flowering
on a few plants or on a few stems of an
individual plant. Plants cut back by
half in mid-June, when about 3 ft. tall,
flowered at 2½ ft. rather than 3 ft.;
they were also fuller than unpruned
plants and flowering was delayed by
about 1 week.

OTHER MAINTENANCE Fairly
low-maintenance plant except for its
spreading root system, which can be
easily controlled. This usually is
necessary in the spring in about the
plant's 4th year. Tolerant of a fair
amount of shade. Adaptable, pest free,
and normally no staking required.

RELATED PLANTS *Asteromoea incisa*
(*Kalimeris incisa*) grows 2 ft. tall and
has single flowers with a shorter
bloom period than the above species.
Shear off old flowering stems to a low
mound of deep green foliage after
flowering is completed in midsummer
to clean up the plant and for a possible
light rebloom in the autumn.

Astilbe ×arendsii

astilbe
SAXIFRAGACEAE

White, pink, red, even peach flowers; ferny, green or bronzy foliage
2–4 ft. high; 2 ft. wide
Shade
Blooms June–July
Zones 3–8

PRUNING Deadheading will not induce more bloom, and the dried seedheads extend the interest of astilbe through the season and even into winter. With certain cultivars or species of *Astilbe*, seeding can be a problem in some years, particularly if there is a moist spring. Once it is determined that seeding presents a problem, such plants can be dead-headed in the future. Deadleafing may be necessary to keep plants neat, particularly if subjected to dry conditions. If plants have totally "crisped" from prolonged drought, they can be cut to the ground for regrowth of fresh foliage later in the season with the return of cooler, moister conditions. Depending on the severity of the conditions, new growth may not return until the spring of the following season, if at all. *Astilbe* foliage can be subject to late-spring frost damage, particularly on *Astilbe* ×*arendsii* and *A. japonica* types; any such damage should be pruned off and plants will rebound nicely. Some gardeners remove the flowers of their astilbe when in full bud to delay bloom. I haven't had luck with this myself; when I remove the buds, the plants simply don't flower at all. Factors such as soil fertility and moisture level, as well as overall age or vigor of the plant and the particular species, most likely contribute to these different results. Do not cut back for winter, but prune in early spring. The old foliage may help protect the plant from winter damage in colder areas.

Asteromoea mongolica

Astilbe ×*arendsii* 'Hyazinth'

Astrantia major

OTHER MAINTENANCE Four key things to remember for best results with *Astilbe* plants are: (1) they are heavy feeders; (2) summer drought is their worst enemy—keep watered in July and August; (3) winter wetness is their next worst enemy; (4) and they should be divided every 3 years to maintain vigor. *Astilbe* needs high-nitrogen fertilization in the spring or autumn, either from composted manures or fertilizers or both. Dave Beattie, renowned astilbe grower, recommends using a general-purpose lawn fertilizer, such as a 20–10–10, in early October for best results. The overwintering structure of the plant increases in size in November, just before the last hard frost, so an October application of fertilizer will help its development. Also, early flowering astilbe form buds in the autumn for next year's flowers. All late-flowering *A. chinensis* types, such as *A. chinensis* 'Pumila', are more

tolerant of dry conditions; others should be kept moist during the summer. *Astilbe* plants will tolerate full sun if given plenty of moisture. In zones 3, 4, or 5, spring planting, or planting no later than September 1, is advisable or plants may heave, especially smaller-growing forms such as *A. simplicifolia* 'William Buchanan'. If crowns rise above the soil, gently press in, and top-dress with organic matter. Divide in the early spring or midsummer before September.

RELATED PLANTS *Astilbe* ×*arendsii* 'Hyazinth' is a sturdy-stemmed, abundantly flowered cultivar, with lavender-pink blooms that fade to white.

Astilbe biternata (false goatsbeard) is the only astilbe native to North America, and has long been underutilized. It is a bold plant, 3–6 ft. tall with feathery white panicles set above a 3-lobed terminal leaflet. Deadleafing is required midsummer for best appearance.

Astrantia major

masterwort
APIACEAE

Creamy white flowers with green, pink, or red bracts; palmately lobed leaves

2–3 ft. (1½ ft.) high; 2 ft. wide

Part shade

Blooms June–July

Zones 4–7

PRUNING Bracts are attractive for a long period. Deadheading can prolong bloom sporadically into September and prevent seeding, which under certain conditions can be prolific. Deadhead to lateral flower buds; when secondary bloom finishes and before seeds mature, cut down flowering stems to basal foliage. Yellowing of the foliage may occur in summer, particularly in dry conditions; deadleaf, or if severe, cut back to new growth at base of plant. Leave this basal growth for the winter. Prune in the spring.

OTHER MAINTENANCE Masterwort prefers moist, shady, high-organic-matter conditions. It can grow in sun if kept constantly moist and spreads rapidly by runners under good conditions. Divide plants in spring or fall every 4–5 years.

RELATED PLANTS Choose *Astrantia major* 'Hadspen Blood' or 'Moulin Rouge' for especially showy deep red flower bracts. 'Sunningdale Variegated' has pale pink flowers and foliage edged in creamy yellow, while 'Vanilla Gorilla' has soft pink blooms and leaves bordered with white.

Baptisia australis

false indigo
LEGUMINOSAE

Indigo-blue flowers on spikes; pealike blue-green leaves

Blooms May–June

3–4 ft. high; 3–4 ft. wide

Full sun–part shade

Zones 3–9

PRUNING Plants that are cut back by a third and shaped after flowering form fresh, rounded, shrublike plants that hold up well for the rest of the season. This eliminates the flopping and opening up of plants that normally necessitates staking, particularly when they are grown in some shade. Cutting back also keeps plants in their intended space. Hedge shears work well for this task. Plants fill in after 3 weeks or so. As expected, plants cut back by half grow even smaller and narrower than those cut back by a third, but in my opinion they are not as attractive and take longer to fill in.

Baptisia australis

Shearing plants normally eliminates seedpods at the same time, although reseeding usually doesn't occur with *Baptisia*, and the seedpods, which turn black with maturity, are attractive and useful in dried arrangements. Removal of deadheads may not be desirable for this reason, although plants may flower more profusely the following season if they are deadheaded. Foliage blackens with heavy frost, and plants fall over by mid-January or earlier depending on weather conditions. Still, I leave plants up for the winter. In a more formal setting it may be beneficial to cut *Baptisia* down after several killing frosts, or in January when falling occurs.

OTHER MAINTENANCE Although slow to establish, *Baptisia* is tough, drought tolerant, and low maintenance once it takes hold. It takes low-fertility soils very well. It prefers acidic soil but will tolerate higher pH conditions. Plants are slow growing and normally don't require division for 10 years or more, unless the expanding root system needs to be curbed. Normally difficult to transplant, *Baptisia* can be moved successfully if given plenty of soil and the roots are undisturbed, especially when plants are still relatively small. Personally, I like to transplant in early spring, but it can also be done in late fall. Good plant for zone 8. If pruning is not desired but plants require staking, peony hoops placed over the plants in early spring offer an easy solution.

RELATED PLANTS The genus *Baptisia* is undergoing a revolution. Using genetic material from purple- and blue-flowered species like *B. australis*, white species such as *B. alba*, and yellow ones like *B. sphaerocarpa*, breeders are hybridizing new forms in a myriad of flower colors. 'Purple Smoke' (lavender) and 'Carolina Moonlight' (light yellow) led the way, followed by selections like 'Twilite' Prairieblues (purple and yellow), 'Dutch Chocolate' (chocolate-purple), and 'Cherries Jubilee' (dusky rose-red and yellow). Care is the same as for straight *B. australis*. Most of the hybrids, such as *Baptisia* × *variicolor* 'Twilite' Prairieblues, will mature in the 3–4 ft. size range, although dwarf forms like *B. australis* var. *minor* 'Melissa Blue' (2 ft. × 2 ft.) are occasionally offered.

Begonia grandis

hardy begonia
BEGONIACEAE

Small pink flowers in drooping clusters; light green succulent leaves with red veins

24–30 in. high; 18 in. wide

Part or full shade

Blooms July–October

Zones 6–9

PRUNING Pinching encourages branching and keeps plants compact. Deadheading to lateral buds prolongs bloom, although hardy begonia has attractive pink seedpods that extend the interest of the plant. It is susceptible to stem rot, so when deadheading leave about 1 in. of flower stem on the plant. This will harden and fall off, thus avoiding fresh wounds on the main stem that can lead to infection. Dead leaves can also cause rot and should be removed. Do not prune off bulbils (small bulbs) that form in a leaf axil (the upper angle between a petiole and stem of the plant); allow these bulbils to develop to encourage some seeding of this tender perennial, especially in northern areas, which will ensure constancy in the garden. Plants blacken with heavy frost. Cut down for the winter, and clean up debris from the base of the plant.

OTHER MAINTENANCE Hardy begonia prefers moist, high-organic-matter soil. Will take some sun in cooler regions. At its hardiness limit in zone 6, where cool winters are common, it needs a winter mulch. Plants are late to emerge (as late as mid-June in central Ohio); do not disturb growing area in early spring. Seldom needs division, generally every 6–10 years.

Begonia grandis

Belamcanda chinensis

(see *Iris domestica*)

Bergenia crassifolia
heartleaf bergenia
SAXIFRAGACEAE

Pink flowers; shiny, round evergreen leaves
12–18 in. high; 12 in. wide
Part shade; full sun with moisture
Blooms April–May
Zones 3–8

PRUNING Deadhead to the ground to help maintain appearance. Plants remain semi-evergreen though are often damaged or bronzed over the winter. Do not cut back in the autumn; wait until early spring when faded leaves can be cut or pulled off the plant. Some deadleafing during dry summers, or if grown in too much sun, is usually needed to keep plants looking their best.

OTHER MAINTENANCE Adaptable to a variety of soils, including some tolerance to drought conditions, but does not tolerate overly wet conditions. Prefers moist soils high in organic matter. Tolerates alkaline soil. Divide in the spring when clump opens up in the center, about every 4 years or longer. Rhizome may require a topdressing of compost if it is pushing up out of the soil. Flower buds are damaged in harsh winters. Relatively low-maintenance plant.

RELATED PLANTS *Bergenia cordifolia* 'Winterglut' Winter Glow sports magenta-red flowers on 16-in. panicles. Its reddish autumn and winter foliage is beautiful in cut flower arrangements.

Boltonia asteroides 'Snowbank'
'Snowbank' boltonia
COMPOSITAE

Daisylike white flower heads; narrow leaves
3–5 ft. high; 3–4 ft. wide
Full sun–part shade
Blooms September–October
Zones 4–9

PRUNING Plants normally don't require staking if grown in full sun and sheltered from winds, but if grown in more exposed areas, or in part shade or overly rich soil, they have a tendency to fall over. Plants respond well to pruning before flowering, and it can be done in several different ways, depending on the final objective. Pruning of 'Snowbank' boltonia can be used to control height, stagger bloom, or to layer individual plants or a large planting. Plants can be cut back by half to two-thirds in early June and the outer stems layered for fuller, self-supporting plants that grow shorter than unpruned plants with minimal or no delay in bloom. Alternatively, plants can be cut back by about a third in mid-July, in which case they bloom at 2½ ft. tall, rather than 4 ft., and 1 week later than unpruned plants. It also creates an interesting layering effect. If less dramatic height control is desired, plants can simply be pinched or have a few inches removed in early July. I never deadhead *Boltonia* because it flowers late in the season until the frost takes it. Plants that are sturdy and self-supporting do not need

Bergenia crassifolia

to be cut back for the winter, but should be pruned down in early spring. If plants are floppy, cutting back before the winter may be desirable since more stems will fall with poor weather. **OTHER MAINTENANCE** Prefers well-draining, moist, organic soil, but will tolerate dry soil. Plants will be shorter if grown in prolonged dry conditions. Tolerates heat and humidity. Can spread rapidly in moist, sandy soil and will even fill a large area (4 ft. × 4 ft.) in clay soil within about 5 years, but not invasively so in either condition. May require staking. Divide in the spring or fall every 4–5 years or as needed to control spread. Low-maintenance, problem-free plant. **RELATED PLANTS** *Boltonia asteroides* 'Pink Beauty' usually grows only about 3½ ft. tall, but it can be leggy and flop. Plants grown in part shade and cut back by two-thirds in early June when 2½ ft. tall flowered at 2½ ft. but were still a bit floppy.

Brunnera macrophylla
Siberian bugloss
BORAGINACEAE

Small, true-blue flowers; coarse, heart-shaped leaves
12–18 in. high; 20 in. wide
Part shade–full shade
Blooms April–May
Zones 3–8

PRUNING Deadheading prevents reseeding, which can be abundant in moist locations but slim to none in dry sites. Most seeding occurs at the base of plant, and seedlings are easily removed or transplanted. Deadhead plants down to large basal foliage. Plants should also be deadleafed to remove foliage damaged by late-spring frosts, hot sun, or drought. Siberian bugloss can be cut back to the ground to stimulate lush new foliage if the old leaves start to decline severely in midsummer (mid-July in Ohio). Plants fill in nicely in about 3 weeks but will not return to full size that season. Keep plants moist after pruning. Brunnera foliage blackens with frost. Cutting back for the winter may be preferred. **OTHER MAINTENANCE** Plants prefer moist organic soil, and this is essential in southern areas. In northern gardens, however, plants will tolerate some

Boltonia asteroides 'Snowbank'

Brunnera macrophylla 'Jack Frost'

dryness as long as they are shaded; they often respond by producing smaller leaves, and if the drought is prolonged they may go dormant. Leaves usually burn in hot sun, but will tolerate more sun in cool, moist climates. Division generally is not needed for 6–10 years or longer, but if necessary it should be done in the spring.

RELATED PLANTS Several variegated forms of *Brunnera macrophylla* are available. My favorite is award-winning 'Jack Frost', with leaves like crackled porcelain. The foliage of 'Looking Glass' is almost completely white. All benefit from deadleafing or cutting back if the foliage deteriorates. Best growth is in shady, moist sites to prevent leaf scorching.

Campanula carpatica
Carpathian harebell
CAMPANULACEAE

Cup-shaped blue flowers; triangular leaves
6–12 in. (4–6 in.) high; 12 in. wide
Full sun or part shade
Blooms June–September
Zones 3–8

Campanula carpatica

PRUNING Young plants are little charmers that provide a long bloom period with minimal pruning other than deadheading, which will reduce seeding. Deadheading, and often cutting back, is needed in later years to keep plants attractive. Deadheading is a tedious task due to the delicate nature of the plants. Small sharp pruning scissors work well. Depending on the conditions, plants may require cutting back by about a third or more in midsummer for fresh growth and possible rebloom. Plants can be cut back in stages. For example, cut back a third of the plant by a third, allowing the other sections to continue blooming. As the pruned section starts to fill in, cut back another section of the plant. This prevents a void in the garden and keeps a part of the plant flowering most of the season. If foliage is severely tattered, or if plants open up in the center, plants will benefit from cutting to basal growth. Basal growth should remain for the winter. Cut back any dead foliage in the spring if needed.

OTHER MAINTENANCE Plants aren't particularly long-lived, succumbing to heat, high humidity, and dry or wet soils. Prefers a cool soil, and summer mulch is useful, particularly in southern gardens. Division is required every 2 years and is best done in the early spring or the late summer.

RELATED PLANTS *Campanula carpatica* 'Blaue Clips' ('Blue Clips') and 'Weisse Clips' ('White Clips') are more desirable than the species due to greater vigor.

Campanula poscharskyana, Serbian bellflower, is wonderful as a groundcover in dry conditions and part shade. If grown this way, plants can be deadheaded once with shears down to basal foliage when all flowering is finished. Foliage will remain semi-evergreen to evergreen over the winter. Can spread fairly quickly.

Campanula glomerata
clustered bellflower
CAMPANULACEAE

Purple or white flowers in clusters;
heart-shaped to oval green leaves
18–24 in. high; 18 in. wide and spreading
Full sun
Blooms June–July
Zones 3–8

PRUNING Deadhead plants to lateral
buds to prolong bloom. As foliage
starts to decline and when all flowering is completed, plants can be cut
down to fresh basal foliage. Do not
prune for the winter. Clean up as
needed in the spring.

OTHER MAINTENANCE Plants prefer
evenly moist, alkaline soil. Can be
somewhat invasive in rich soils,
though spread is minimal in poor soils.
Performs better in part shade in hot
climates. Often requires support to
keep upright. Divide in the spring or
autumn every 4–5 years or as needed
to control spread.
RELATED PLANTS *Campanula
glomerata* 'Superba' has greater heat
tolerance than the species.

Campanula persicifolia
peachleaf bellflower
CAMPANULACEAE

Spikes of bell-shaped blue flowers; narrow
leaves
2–3 ft. (⅔ ft.) high; 2 ft. wide
Full sun or part shade
Blooms June–July
Zones 3–7

PRUNING Most campanulas will
flower longer with regular deadheading. When pruning the peachleaf
bellflower it is important to not cut off
the new buds that form along the same
flowering stem as the previous flowers.
This pruning can be tedious since each
individual dead flower must be
removed without damaging the
yet-to-open new buds. I like to use
small sharp pruning scissors for this
task. Deadheading reduces seeding,
although some seeding should be
permitted to ensure persistence of this
rather short-lived perennial in the
garden. When all flowering is finished
the old flower stems should be cut
down to basal foliage. Basal foliage
persists for the winter and rarely needs
cleanup in the spring. Pinching plants
when the shoots are about 6 in. tall
may eliminate the need for staking.
OTHER MAINTENANCE Can natural-
ize by root spread and seeding, but not
a nuisance. Not particularly long-lived,
except in porous, sandy soils. Requires
moist, well-draining soil for best
growth, and afternoon shade in hot
climates. Plants usually need staking,
particularly in shadier spots. Divide
every 3–4 years in the spring.
RELATED PLANTS *Campanula
lactiflora*, milky bellflower, can be
deadheaded by cutting back by a third
after all flowering is completed, which
often induces sparser rebloom in the

Campanula glomerata

Campanula persicifolia

autumn and also prevents self-seeding. Old flowering stems and foliage often decline after blooming; if this occurs, cut down to the new basal foliage that has developed. Most cultivars flop. Cutting off 4–5 in. before flowering in early May creates fuller plants. Cutting plants back in late June or early July in an attempt to delay flowering and control sprawling habit proved ineffective—it did produce compact, 1-ft.-tall upright plants, compared to the flopping 2½-ft.-tall unpruned plants, but they never flowered. *Campanula lactiflora* 'Pouffe' is a dwarf, 10- to 18-in.-tall, self-supporting form. *Campanula latifolia*, great bellflower, requires deadheading before seeds mature to prevent numerous seedlings. If you don't want to do the tedious task of deadheading each individual flower, wait until the deadheads outnumber the new flowers and cut the entire stem down to the basal foliage. For height control cut back as for *C. lactiflora*. Great bellflower can spread aggressively.

Campanula rotundifolia 'Olympica'

Olympic Scotch bluebell
CAMPANULACEAE

Tiny, blue, bell-shaped flowers; round leaves often disappear by the time flowering occurs
6–12 in. high; 12 in. wide
Full sun–part shade
Blooms June–September
Zones 2–7

PRUNING Olympic Scotch bluebell is long blooming even without

deadheading, but deadheading prolongs bloom from spring to late summer on neater plants, and unless you're really quick to get them, seeding is usually ensured anyway, which in my area is essential to keeping plants in the garden. It can seed to nuisance levels under ideal growing conditions, but I never have enough of this perennial to make me happy. Seedlings are easily removed if it becomes a problem. Deadheading can be an extremely tedious job due to the delicate nature of the flowering stems and the large number of them. It is easiest to use small sharp pruning scissors. In late summer plants should be cut down to the tiny basal foliage to remove tatty old growth and seedheads. Hedge shears can be used at this stage. Basal foliage remains evergreen over the winter.

OTHER MAINTENANCE Very short-lived, usually only a couple of years. Good drainage is absolutely essential to survival. Alpine conditions are ideal. If you can keep plants for 3 or 4 years, division may be necessary to keep them under control.

Campanula 'Sarastro'

'Sarastro' bellflower
CAMPANULACEAE

Deep blue-violet bell-shaped flowers; heart-shaped green leaves
18–20 in. high; 18–24 in. wide
Full sun to part shade
Blooms June–August
Zones 3–8

PRUNING This handsome hybrid is the result of a cross between *Campanula punctata* and *C. trachelium* and is

Campanula rotundifolia 'Olympica'

sterile; thus deadheading is not required to prolong bloom, although you may want to remove spent flower stalks for the sake of appearance. Clean up as needed in the spring.

OTHER MAINTENANCE A well-behaved clump former, 'Sarastro' requires minimal attention. Often produces a second flush of flowers in well-nourished soil. Unlike many other bellflowers, it tolerates muggy, hot summers.

RELATED PLANTS *Campanula* 'Pink Octopus', a cross between *C. punctata* and *C. takesimana*, is similarly heat tolerant and reaches 15 in. in bloom, with a spread of 18 in. It produces masses of unusual, pendulous, narrow-petaled pink flowers, hence the cultivar name. Hardy in zones 5–9.

Centaurea montana
mountain bluet
COMPOSITAE

Fringed blue flowers; green leaves
1–2 ft. high; 1 ft. wide
Full sun or part shade
Blooms May–July
Zones 3–8

PRUNING Depending on the conditions (or I think even the disposition of the plant), repeat bloom can be

achieved simply by deadheading to lateral buds. Once all flowering is finished cut the old flowering stalks to the ground, leaving the fresh basal foliage. Plants are likely to rebloom in late summer. Older (or moody) plants, or plants growing in rich soil or overly shady conditions, usually become floppy and weedy after the first flowering. Cut entire plant back by two-thirds immediately after flowering for potential rebloom and a more compact habit. Deadheading or cutting back should be performed before seeds mature to prevent excessive seeding. If plants are cut back during the season, the low basal

(left) *Campanula* 'Pink Octopus'

(right) *Campanula* 'Sarastro'

Centaurea montana

foliage can remain for the winter. Plants that were not cut back usually blacken and turn mushy with frost and are best cut down at this point.

OTHER MAINTENANCE Best performance in poor, well-draining, alkaline soils. Tolerates some drought. Roots can spread rapidly to invasive proportions, particularly in cool northern gardens; not as hearty in the South. Requires division every 2–3 years in the spring or fall.

Centranthus ruber
Jupiter's beard
CAPRIFOLIACEAE

Fragrant pink or reddish flowers in clusters; gray-green leaves
18–36 in. high; 24 in. wide
Full sun
Blooms June–August
Zones 5–8

PRUNING Deadhead to lateral buds as flowers are spent, to encourage bloom from late spring to early summer and sporadically into August. Flowers longer in cool conditions. Plants are prolific seeders under favorable conditions; deadhead if seeding is not desired. Where plants bloom early and then stop in the heat of summer, or if plants fall after flowering, shearing by a third to half after the first bloom often results in a second crop in August. This perennial is often short-lived, and it may be that plants deplete their energy reserves with so much flower production and then are unable to form buds for the next season's shoots. To prevent this from occurring, the whole plant can be cut back to 6–8 in. in late August or early September to stimulate vegetative growth, which may increase the plant's overwintering survival. Do not cut again for the winter; clean up in the spring.

OTHER MAINTENANCE Prefers infertile, well-draining, neutral to alkaline soil. Divide in the spring or fall every 1–3 years.

Centrathus ruber

Cephalaria gigantea
Tatarian cephalaria
CAPRIFOLIACEAE

Yellow pincushion flowers on tall wiry stems; compound leaves

5–7 ft. (3 ft.) high; 3–6 ft. wide

Full sun

Blooms June–August

Zones 3–8

Cerastium tomentosum
snow-in-summer
CARYOPHYLLACEAE

Small white flowers; mat-forming silver leaves

4–8 in. high; 18 in. wide

Full sun

Blooms June

Zones 3–7

PRUNING Plants should be sheared back by a third to half and shaped after flowering to keep in good form and prevent open centers void of leaves. Hedge shears are the best tool for the task. The plant's typical "softness" will quickly return after shearing. Prune back whenever the plant gets out of bounds. Don't do any heavy shearing during hot, dry conditions. Do not prune for the winter. Prune out any damaged sections in the spring as needed.

OTHER MAINTENANCE Well-draining soil is essential for survival. Prefers infertile conditions. Often melts out in hot, humid weather. Spreads rapidly by underground roots. May require frequent division in spring or fall to keep in bounds; keep plenty of soil around the roots to ensure success. Often short-lived due to its tendency toward rotting.

RELATED PLANTS *Cerastium tomentosum* 'Yo Yo' and 'Silver Carpet' are more compact than the species.

Cerastium tomentosum var. *columnae* is also more compact.

Cephalaria gigantea

PRUNING Flowering stems are branched, so deadhead to lateral new flowers. After all flowering is finished, cut flowering stems down to the ground. Deadleafing may also be necessary as plants are usually tatty by late summer or early autumn, particularly with dry conditions. If damage is major, cut plants down to about 1 ft. above the ground. They are not especially attractive at this stage, so it would be a good idea to include late-blooming plants as companions to help hide pruned plants. Plants don't appear to respond to cutting back or pinching before flowering to reduce height or delay bloom. Plants should be cut down for the winter. Leaves of cephalaria have tiny bristly hairs that can irritate the skin when pruning.

OTHER MAINTENANCE Moisture is necessary to maintain health of the leaves. Sometimes requires staking. Divide every 2–3 years in the spring. Give plenty of space in the garden.

Cerastium tomentosum 'Yo-Yo'

Ceratostigma plumbaginoides

Ceratostigma plumbaginoides
plumbago
PLUMBAGINACEAE

Small blue flowers; small green leaves
8–12 in. high; 12–18 in. wide
Full sun–part shade
Blooms August–September
Zones 5–9

PRUNING The only pruning that this plant requires is cutting dead stems to the ground once new growth is visible in the spring. Plants are late to emerge, sometimes not until early June in central Ohio, so leaving the bare stems and seedheads over the winter and into spring marks their spot in the garden and avoids chance of disturbance.

OTHER MAINTENANCE Plants perform best with morning sun and afternoon shade. Well-draining soil is essential; it is tolerant of short periods of drought. Rhizomes can be invasive, making the plant suitable as a groundcover. In a mixed planting it will overtake low-growing perennials in its path, including *Coreopsis verticillata* 'Moonbeam'. Doesn't compete with tree roots. Usually considered a zone 6 plant, but it survives well in zone 5 with a light mulch or in a semi-protected area. Divide in spring as needed to keep in bounds.

Chelone lyonii
pink turtlehead
PLANTAGINACEAE

Pink turtle-shaped flowers; thick green leaves
3 ft. high; 2 ft. wide
Full sun or part shade
Blooms August–September
Zones 3–8

PRUNING Plants can be deadheaded if desired, but the seedheads are attractive and extend the interest of the plant so are best left on. Plants may flop, particularly if given too much shade. Plant height can be reduced by pinching in the early spring when plants are about 6 in. tall. For me, pinching in mid-June resulted in plants that never flowered. Do not cut back for the winter. Prune in early spring.

OTHER MAINTENANCE Plants are moisture loving and will form nice stands if sufficient moisture is available. Plants grown under drier conditions will be shorter and less vigorous. Prefers high-organic soil and tolerates light shade. Divide every 4 years, if needed, in the spring or after flowering in autumn.

Chrysanthemum ×*morifolium*

mum
COMPOSITAE

Daisylike flower heads; lobed leaves
1–3 ft. high; 1–3 ft. wide
Full sun
Blooms August–October
Zones 5–9

PRUNING Mums and pruning go hand in hand. Cutting back or pinching before flowering will create more compact plants, often with more numerous though possibly smaller flowers. Pinching or cutting back may also delay flowering if done late in the summer. Naturally low-growing forms don't need pruning for height control, but it may be desirable to delay bloom, such as with early blooming cultivars. Pinching is often associated with mums, and vice versa. The frequency and timing of pinching, whether employed for height control or to delay bloom, can be determined by experimenting according to your individual needs and expectations. Three or 4 pinchings is sufficient for controlling height on most mums, though lower-growing types generally need only 2 pinchings. For mums that have overwintered, pinching can be initiated when the plants are about 6 in. tall (May) and then again every 2–3 weeks. New garden mums planted in the spring should be first pinched a few weeks after planting. The cutoff date for pinching depends on the climate and the type of mum, be it early or late season. Mums need several weeks to set buds after the final pinching. For early season mums (most garden-center varieties are early) and in gardens north of the Mason-Dixon line (colder than about zone 6), the usual recommendation is for pinching until about mid-July. For northern gardens, stopping in mid-July will assure bloom before heavy frost. In the Midwest, though, for even later bloom or for late-flowering cultivars, pinching into

Chelone lyonii

late July may mean flowers in October rather than September. In the South pinching can go as late as mid-August, particularly for late-blooming cultivars. Pinching or cutting back plants too late may reduce the floral display. (Results of cutting back mums in August in the Midwest are noted below.) Although pinching directly above lateral leaves makes for a neat initial appearance, removing 1 in. of stem with hedge shears simulates a pinch and accomplishes it much more efficiently. The plants fill in quickly, hiding any cuts.

One alternative to pinching, which I prefer, is to simply shear the plants once by half or two-thirds in early to mid-June. In the South a second shearing may be necessary for best results. Cutting plants back in this way may delay flowering. If staggered bloom on a large planting of mums is desired, an additional 4–6 in. can be removed from some plants later in the season (mid- to late July or to mid-August depending on your climate, as discussed above) to further delay part of the planting.

Mums usually are disbudded if grown for shows to produce a larger terminal flower. Disbud mums by removing all buds along the stem, except for the top largest bud. Remove buds when plants are in tight bud with no color showing.

How to prune mums for winter may be as important as when to pinch or cut back for height control. Research in Germany, and confirmed in trials at Iowa State University, has shown that leaving the plants up for the winter greatly improves their overwintering survival rate. Do not cut down the plants until spring when all threat of cold weather has passed. Hedge shears, either hand held or electric, make for greater speed.

OTHER MAINTENANCE Unless cold-hardy forms such as those listed below are selected, most mums are best treated as annuals. Ed Higgins, from the mum-producing firm of Yoder Brothers, provided some further tips for successful overwintering: avoid planting mums in areas subject to cold, drying winds; mums are heavy feeders but fertilizing should be stopped, especially in the North, by the end of July to discourage new growth late in the season; to promote roots that are well established by winter, keep the soil moist but not soggy through the autumn; avoid wet overwintering conditions; in northern areas, provide loose winter mulch after the ground freezes. Divide in the spring every year or two to maintain vigor.

RELATED PLANTS The following *Chrysanthemum* cultivars have been reliably hardy in central Ohio, showing great vigor and requiring no additional feeding beyond good organic soil. These forms need no division for 4 or more years.

Chrysanthemum 'Mei Kyo', 2 ft. tall, offers deep rose or burgundy small double flowers in late October. Pinching is not required as plants are

Chrysanthemum ×morifolium 'Viette's Apricot Glow' (foreground), 'Mei Kyo' (middle ground), and 'Venus' (background)

naturally full and dense to the base. In fact, pinching or cutting back 'Mei Kyo' may delay the flowers too much in the North, since this is a late-blooming cultivar anyway. For trial purposes, I sheared plants by half in mid-June, and they started flowering in early November, rather than late October. They grew 15–18 in. tall, rather than 2 ft., and the floral display was a bit weaker than that on unpruned plants. Plants sheared by 4–6 in. on August 15 (these were not previously pruned) also flowered in early November, but the floral display was greatly reduced. These late-pruned plants experienced damage to the foliage tips from an early October frost, but the flowers were not harmed. A single plant can spread quickly, covering a 5 ft. × 5 ft. area in about 4 years. Division is seldom needed, but plants can be thinned by pulling out bunches of spent flowering stems, root and all, in the early spring.

Chrysanthemum 'Venus' has single soft pink flowers. Plants can be cut back by half to two-thirds in early to mid-June for 3-ft. compact growth and mid-October flowering. As a test to see if August pruning would be too late for flower formation in the Midwest, I sheared plants again by about 4–6 in. on August 5 and August 15. The plants flowered about 1 week later and at about 2 ft. high. Their habit was more desirable, their flowers delayed, and the floral display was only slightly reduced.

Chrysanthemum 'Viette's Apricot Glow' has single apricot flowers in mid-October. It is a compact 18- to 24-in. form that doesn't need any pruning to look spectacular.

Chrysanthemum rubellum 'Clara Curtis' has pink flowers in mid- to late summer and is more readily available. May require pinching or cutting back to control height, particularly if the soil is rich. Pruning for height control is usually not required in clay soils. If later flowering is desired, plants can be sheared by 4–6 in. after the buds form to delay flowering by 1 or 2 months, depending on the weather conditions for the year. Sporadic bloom may occur in the autumn if plants are allowed to flower in the summer and are deadheaded or cut back to basal growth. Very floriferous; may actually bloom itself to death. Divide every 2–3 years to maintain vigor and control spread. Very cold hardy.

Chrysogonum virginianum
golden-star
COMPOSITAE

Daisylike golden-yellow flower heads on prostrate stems
6–8 in. high; 12 in. wide
Part shade–full shade
Blooms May–June
Zones 5–9

PRUNING Periodic cutting back of old flowering stems down to basal foliage will tidy up the plant and prolong the bloom, but it doesn't seem to be critical

Chrysogonum virginianum

since sporadic flowering usually occurs into summer, before any major heat sets in, even without pruning. Flowering lasts longer in regions with cooler summers. Sporadic rebloom may occur again as the cool weather of autumn returns. Deadheading prevents seeding, but seedlings are easily removed and, especially in a woodland setting, may be welcome. Deadleafing is needed in the summer if plants dry out. Plants that get infected with mildew should be cut back to the base to prevent further infection. Remove and destroy pruned parts. Plants unaffected with mildew do not need pruning for the winter; clean up in the spring if needed.

OTHER MAINTENANCE Low-maintenance woodland or shade garden plant. Prefers moist, well-draining soil, but I have had good luck with golden-star in fairly dry shade locations, although rebloom is reduced. Plants may survive overwintering in zone 4 if given a winter mulch or consistent snow cover. Easily divided in late spring.

RELATED PLANTS Cultivars of golden-star flower longer than the species. *Chrysogonum virginianum* 'Alan Bush' and 'Mark Viette' are long-blooming cultivars of choice.

Chrysopsis villosa
(see *Heterotheca villosa*)

Clematis heracleifolia
blue tube clematis
RANUNCULACEAE

Blue flowers; coarse green leaves
3 ft. high; 4 ft. wide
Full sun–part shade
Blooms August–September
Zones 3–9

PRUNING *Clematis heracleifolia*, tube clematis, is somewhat woody in nature. Prune back hard in early spring to only a couple of nodes for more compact growth. The variety *davidiana* is more herbaceous. Cut to the ground in early spring. Pinching

plants when they are 12–15 in. tall can help control flopping. Deadleafing is needed to remove scorched leaves if plants dry out in the summer. Prune back as needed to keep blue tube clematis in its own space. Deadheads turn into cottony seedheads that are best allowed to remain.

OTHER MAINTENANCE Requires support, and pea staking is the recommended method. Flourishes in moist soils that are alkaline to slightly acidic, with high organic matter. Mulch to provide cool soil.

RELATED PLANTS Cultivars of *Clematis heracleifolia* such as 'Cassandra' and 'China Purple' share the woody nature of the straight species and should be treated similarly.

Clematis integrifolia is a solitary clematis—beautiful in bud, flower, and fruit. It benefits from light cross-staking May through June and in the autumn. A crowd favorite!

Clematis recta
ground clematis
RANUNCULACEAE

Fringed, fragrant white flowers; compound blue-green leaves
3–4 ft. high; 3 ft. wide
Full sun–part shade
Blooms May–June
Zones 3–7

PRUNING Plants can be cut down after flowering for lush new growth and rebloom and as a means of minimizing black blister beetle damage. Shearing plants to the ground in early to mid-July or when the first beetles are sighted will avoid most of the feeding of the beetles. A few beetles may still be around as the new growth starts, and these can be knocked off with a booted foot or gloved hand and then stepped on; any damage by beetles at this point won't be significant. Be certain to wear gloves when pruning or staking, as a stray beetle may be hiding under the foliage and can cause blistering on your hands. Lush new growth will return in about a month after shearing, and plants will grow to nearly full again and produce sporadic rebloom. Pea staking is required at this point, or plants can be left to crawl along the ground. Plants cut back by a third in early July received a good deal of beetle damage, but they put on new terminal growth after the beetles were gone. Still, plants didn't rebloom, had bare stems at their bases, and were never as attractive as plants sheared to the ground. Plants get mushy after a hard frost, and it may be desirable to cut them back at this time.

OTHER MAINTENANCE Plants can be left to crawl, although pea staking lifts flowers up to a more visible height and restricts the space occupied by ground clematis in the garden. Stake in late April or early May before flowering starts. Fairly tolerant of dry conditions, but prefers moist, high-organic soil.

RELATED PLANTS *Clematis recta* 'Purpurea' has purple stems and leaves that fade as they age, so cutting plants

Clematis recta

back after flowering, as described, can send forth a new flush of purple foliage in August.

Clinopodium grandiflorum
large-flowered calamint
LAMIACEAE

Tubular lobed pink flowers; aromatic toothed green leaves
Blooms June–September
18–24 in. high; 12–15 in. wide
Full sun–part shade
Zones 5–9

PRUNING Large-flowered calamint is valued for its long bloom time. Spent flowers are self-cleaning, shriveling and falling neatly from the plant. When blooms do begin to dwindle in late summer, shear plants to induce a flush of fresh foliage and possible rebloom. This species may reseed; promptly shear spent flowers if this is an issue. Cut plants to the ground in late winter.

OTHER MAINTENANCE This European native performs best in moist but well-drained soil in sun or dappled shade. Powdery mildew can be a problem; grow plants in an open

Clinopodium grandiflorum

area with good air circulation, especially in humid climates.

RELATED PLANTS *Clinopodium grandiflorum* 'Variegata', with white-flecked foliage, is more popular than the species. It's shorter and less vigorous than the type. Prune out all-green reversions as soon as they appear, or they may take over. If allowed to self-sow, this selection will likely produce variegated seedlings.

Clinopodium nepeta
lesser calamint
LAMIACEAE

Clouds of dainty white or pale blue flowers; Small fragrant gray-green leaves
Blooms July–October
12–18 in. high; 12–18 in. wide
Full sun
Zones 5–7

PRUNING Lesser calamint flowers for a long period even without deadheading. If plants do look spent or unshapely in late summer, tidy them up with hedge shears; flowering will resume about 6 weeks later if weather permits. Plants bloom until hard frost—often until November in mild climates. Lesser calamint sometimes reseeds; shear in early September before seed set if this is a problem. This species is frequently short-lived, however, and volunteer replacements are usually welcomed. Leave plants standing over the winter and cut back any remaining dead top growth in early spring.

OTHER MAINTENANCE This unassuming perennial isn't overwhelming in flower, but it makes a useful filler, edging, or container plant and boasts an exceedingly long bloom time. Lesser calamint flourishes in well-drained soil on the dry side and is drought tolerant once established.

RELATED PLANTS 'White Cloud' and 'Blue Cloud' are popular selections. 'Montrose White' is a sterile form.

Coreopsis grandiflora
tickseed
COMPOSITAE

Golden-yellow flower heads; narrow green leaves on bushy plants
2–3 ft. (⅔–1 ft.) high; 1 ft. wide
Full sun
Blooms June–August
Zones 4–9

PRUNING Tickseed needs daily deadheading. Cut the entire flowering

Clinopodium nepeta

stalk to new lateral flower buds, if present, or to the basal foliage if no side flowering is evident. Deadheading keeps plants flowering and looking decent, prevents seeding, and reduces potential disease sites. Plants may need to be cut back in midsummer if they sprawl. *Coreopsis grandiflora* and its cultivars can flower themselves to exhaustion and thus will have trouble forming buds for the following year's growth. Cutting all the flowering stems down to the basal foliage at the end of August or in early September will stimulate new vegetative growth and may increase the plant's overwintering survival rate. Do not prune for the winter. Cut back as needed in the early spring before new growth begins.

OTHER MAINTENANCE Requires well-draining soil for overwintering survival. Drought tolerant. Not long-lived; tends to be good for 2 or 3 seasons, and then needs division in the spring. Plants may flop; select lower growing cultivars.

RELATED PLANTS *Coreopsis grandiflora* 'Early Sunrise' is the longest flowering cultivar and is more compact (to 18 in.). Prune as described above for the species. 'Goldfink' is more compact (9 in. high) and may need annual division to perform its best.

Coreopsis lanceolata, lanceleaf coreopsis, is similar to *C. grandiflora* and actually may be synonymous in the trade. Prune as above.

Coreopsis tripteris
tall tickseed
COMPOSITAE

Yellow daisies with brown centers; pinnate leaves in pairs along tall, stiff stems
Blooms July–September
4–8 ft. high; 2–5 ft. wide
Full sun
Zones 3–8

PRUNING Deadhead to discourage reseeding, which can be excessive in favorable sites, or plant this North American native in spacious naturalistic gardens where it has room to roam. In areas where self-sowing isn't a problem, leave plants standing over the winter, and finches will feed on the seeds. Otherwise, cut tall tickseed down during the late fall cleanup.

OTHER MAINTENANCE An adaptable plant, *Coreopsis tripteris* will grow in a variety of soil conditions as long as it receives full sun and sufficient moisture during establishment. Although it is strikingly tall (typically 7 ft.), it is largely self-supporting; only on very windy, wet sites is it likely to need staking. Division every few years

Coreopsis grandiflora

Coreopsis tripteris

Coreopsis verticillata

threadleaf coreopsis
COMPOSITAE

Yellow flower heads; feathery green leaves
2–3 ft. high; 2 ft. wide
Full sun
Blooms June–October
Zones 3–9

PRUNING First-year plants may flower all summer long even without deadheading, but older plants require deadheading for best performance. They flower in early and midsummer and then sporadically, or they may rest totally in August and then rebloom in September and October. For a stronger and more attractive rebloom in autumn, plants can be sheared in August to remove deadheads, along with the few flowers that may be blooming at the time, using hedge shears or even a string trimmer for large plantings. Clean up pruned branches by hand or with a small shrub rake. Deadheading also prevents reseeding. Plants with deadheads left on from the second bloom phase contribute to winter interest. Unless you want to avoid seeding, do not prune again until early spring. If seeding is a concern, cut down in autumn—string trimmers can be used at this time as well.

OTHER MAINTENANCE Can spread invasively by underground stems, particularly in moist, sandy soils. Divide as needed every 2–3 years in spring or autumn. Long-lived. Requires well-draining soil, and is drought tolerant. Overly fertile soil leads to sprawling habit. Cultivars perform better than the species in areas warmer than zone 6 or 7.

RELATED PLANTS Cultivars of *Coreopsis verticillata* should be pruned as described above for the species, although I have not witnessed reseeding of cultivars so I leave them for winter interest. It should be noted that first-year plantings usually don't need any deadheading to be attractive throughout the entire season. 'Golden Showers' most likely needs staking.

will keep plants vigorous, though an easier solution is to let self-sown seedlings take the place of tired plants.

RELATED PLANTS *Coreopsis tripteris* 'Lightning Flash' sports glowing yellow foliage in spring which fades to green in summer. It may flop during flowering. 'Flower Tower' reaches 8 ft. and has thick, sturdy stems to support its tall bouquet of late summer blossoms.

Cota tinctoria

(syn. *Anthemis tinctoria*)

golden marguerite
COMPOSITAE

Golden-yellow flower heads; fernlike foliage with woolly undersides; aromatic when touched

2–3 ft. high; 2 ft. wide

Full sun

Blooms June–August

Zones 3–7

PRUNING Plants can be cut back or pinched before flowering to help control flopping habit and to create fuller plants. One effective way to cut plants back is to prune off 6 in. in early to mid-May and then cut off another 6 in. in early June; this may delay flowering. After flowering but before seeds mature, deadhead to lateral buds for continued bloom. After secondary flowers fade, cut plants down to new basal foliage. A few sporadic blooms usually will be produced from basal growth. Unlimited seed production robs the plant of energy and can lead to death. Cutting plants back in late summer, usually late August or early September, allows more vigorous vegetative basal shoots to develop for overwintering, which may help prolong the life of the plant. The basal growth remains fairly evergreen; do

Coreopsis verticillata 'Moonbeam'

'Moonbeam' is an outstanding cultivar, but it lacks a bit in winter hardiness. Winter losses occur with unmulched plants in zone 5. Seems to prefer a bit more moisture than the species. Benefits from afternoon shade in warmer climates. Divide every 2–3 years to keep vigorous. I have never had self-seeding with this cultivar. Leave for winter interest. 'Rosea' spreads very quickly to take over large areas, so it is not recommended for use in a mixed perennial border but rather on its own as a groundcover. 'Zagreb' grows to 12 in. and requires no staking. Appears more cold hardy than 'Moonbeam'. Very drought tolerant. 'Creme Brulee' is very popular and has soft yellow flowers. It is a bit more vigorous than 'Moonbeam', but I still see overwintering issues after a couple years, even in well-maintained gardens.

Cota tinctoria 'Golden Rays'

not cut back further for the winter. Prune off any damaged growth in the spring. If allowed, plants will reseed to monstrous proportions, quickly filling a large area. Reseeding may be desirable in naturalized situations, and the seeds also attract goldfinches.

OTHER MAINTENANCE Tolerates hot, dry, and lean situations. Well-draining soil is critical to survival. Will require staking, particularly in rich soil, if not pruned to control height. Often short-lived. Divide every 2–3 years. Poor performance in regions warmer than zone 7.

RELATED PLANTS *Cota tinctoria* 'Moonlight' has soft yellow flowers. Grows 2 ft. tall, often not requiring staking. 'Golden Rays' is shorter and more dense; flowers are bright yellow. Prune back hard after blooming to maintain density.

Crambe cordifolia
colewort
BRASSICACEAE

Giant cloud of tiny white flowers; bold rhubarblike basal foliage
4–7 ft. (2–3 ft.) high; 3–4 ft. wide
Sun–light shade
Blooms May–June
Zones 5–8

PRUNING Colewort blooms for only 3 weeks, but the flowering structure remains showy for a while longer and may be left standing through early summer if desired. The tiny blossoms are borne on just a few many-branched panicles, so when the time comes to cut the flowering stems down, this task is accomplished with a few quick snips. Deadleaf plants as needed to keep them looking attractive throughout the growing season. Insufficient moisture will cause leaves to crisp and curl prematurely. Cut plants to the ground in late fall or as soon as the foliage becomes an eyesore.

OTHER MAINTENANCE This broccoli and cabbage relative isn't too different from its vegetable cousins in its cultural preferences. Colewort performs best in full sun (though morning sun will do) and appreciates a fertile, neutral to alkaline soil that is regularly irrigated but well drained. Mulch plants to conserve moisture. Cabbage white butterfly larvae may chew holes in the foliage; the bacterial insecticide *Bacillus thuringiensis* (better known as Bt) is an organic control. Slugs are also fond of the tender spring foliage. *Crambe* languishes in heat and humidity; this

Crambe cordifolia

dramatic architectural plant reaches its true potential only in cool-summer climates. Plants will sometimes need staking even under ideal growing conditions. Division is possible in early spring, but isn't necessary.

RELATED PLANTS *Crambe maritima*, sea kale (zones 4–9), is a compressed rendition of colewort that tops out at 2–3 ft. It's grown primarily for its jagged, glaucous blue foliage, but its short sprays of bright white flowers are a nice bonus. Deadleaf plants as needed and cut down in late fall. This species is native to European coasts and tolerates drought, salt spray, and alkaline soils.

Crocosmia 'Lucifer'
'Lucifer' crocosmia
IRIDACEAE

Red funnel-shaped flowers; swordlike foliage

2–4 ft. high; 1–2 ft. wide

Full sun

Blooms July–August

Zones 5–9

PRUNING Deadleafing may be necessary in July or August in certain years due to spider mite damage. This may mean removing the dead leaves and leaving only the flowering stalk while still in bloom. The plant is self-cleaning and flowers simply drop off. I find the horizontal shape of the old bloom cluster and seed capsules to be attractive when first developing, so I leave these to extend interest. Then they often need to be cut down, along with any deteriorating foliage, by late summer.

OTHER MAINTENANCE Hose off spider mites when they are first visible. Divide plants every 2–3 years in the autumn to keep vigorous, or separate offsets from the mother plant in the spring as growth starts. Crocosmia prefers moist, well-draining, rich organic soil. It can be short-lived in zone 5; planting in a protected spot and mulching can improve overwintering success.

RELATED PLANTS Other cultivars

Crocosmia 'Lucifer'

may be had in a range of hot colors. 'Emberglow' is a fiery red-orange, while 'Emily McKenzie' is bright orange with a maroon ring surrounding a golden throat. 'Emily McKenzie' is a bit less hardy—to zone 6. 'George Davison' is a warm, clear yellow.

Delphinium elatum

delphinium
RANUNCULACEAE

Blue, purple, or white flower spikes;
palmately cut leaves
4–6 ft. high; 1–2 ft. wide
Full sun–part shade
Blooms June–July
Zones 3–7

PRUNING Deadhead to lateral flower
buds, if present; if not, cut off old
flowering spikes at a lateral leaf. After
all secondary flowering is completed
and the old stems start to decline, cut
back to newly developed basal foliage.
Plants will benefit from a topdressing
of compost and fertilizing with a
quick-release soluble fertilizer at this
time. Keep moist for sporadic smaller
and shorter rebloom later in the
season. When the young shoots are 6
in. tall, thin by approximately a third,
leaving at least 3–5 healthy stems per
mature clump, to avoid overcrowding
that increases susceptibility to disease.
Removing lateral flowering spikes may
increase the size of the terminal flower.
Pinching to remove the large terminal
spike spoils the main effect of the
plant, although smaller side spikes
will still bloom. Remove any flowering
stalks for the winter, but leave the
basal foliage and cut back in the
spring.

OTHER MAINTENANCE *Delphinium
elatum* is the true "maintenance
magnet." It isn't a beginner's plant,
although it seems to be one of the first
perennials new gardeners are drawn
to, perhaps because of the glorious
pictures that appear in so many British
references. It does prosper in England,
due in part to the cool summers. This
delphinium is prone to a host of
diseases, which I won't even go into,
and is a favorite food of slugs. It is also
subject to crown rot in poorly drained
soil and is short-lived. Carefully
dividing plants annually in the spring
may prolong life. Do not plant *D.
elatum* too deep. It will require staking,
and being a heavy feeder, it may need
additional fertilizer in spring or
summer. Many gardeners are better
off treating this one as an annual.

RELATED PLANTS *Delphinium
grandiflorum* 'Blue Butterflies' grows
12–18 in. tall, with no staking needed.
Dwarf forms may not respond well to
pruning back after flowering. Do not
cut back unless basal growth is evident
and strong.

Delphinium ×*belladonna* 'Bellamosum' (12–18 in.) generally isn't as prone
to disease problems as *D. elatum*, and
thinning usually isn't necessary in
more northern areas. Disbudding or
removing side flower spikes to
encourage a larger terminal flower is
not as applicable to this species as it is
to *D. elatum*, since a major appeal of
belladonna delphinium is its daintier
flowers.

Blackmore and Langdon strains of
delphinium tend to be more perennial
if divided regularly.

Connecticut Yankee Series, including 'Blue Fountains', performs well in
heat. It grows to 2 ft. tall and is one of
the best performers in the Midwest.

Delphinium elatum

Mid-Century Hybrids, such as 'Ivory Towers', 'Moody Blues', 'Rosy Future', and 'Ultra Violets', have stronger stems and are more resistant to powdery mildew.

The New Millennium Series from Dowdeswell's Delphiniums of Wanganui, New Zealand, sold as cultivars including 'Blue Lace', 'New Millenium Stars', and 'Royal Aspirations', is your best bet if you want to grow the magnificent tall hybrid delphiniums—especially if you want to grow them outside of the cool, mild, low-humidity areas where they typically thrive. Singles and doubles are available in the full color range from blue to pink to white. These delphiniums have vigor and disease resistance surpassing previous strains, but they are by no means carefree and will still need rich soil, regular irrigation, fertilizing, and staking.

Dianthus ×allwoodii

Dianthus ×allwoodii
allwood pink
CARYOPHYLLACEAE

Pink or white fragrant flowers; gray-green leaves

8–18 in. high; 12 in. wide

Full sun

Blooms June–July

Zones 5–8

PRUNING Deadheading plants to lateral buds will keep them flowering for approximately 6–8 weeks, sometimes longer—this is the main pruning that is needed. The habit of the species and most of its cultivars is tufted, and I find that the allwood pinks do not respond to shearing after flowering like the mat- or cushion-forming dianthus do. Such pruning results in weaker, thinner plants for this species. Plants have a tendency to get woody with age. They may be killed if cut back heavily into old wood, particularly if no new buds are breaking. Do not cut evergreen foliage back for the winter. Plants often need some foliage cleaned up in the spring from winter damage.

OTHER MAINTENANCE Must have well-draining soil, and prefers alkaline conditions. Usually short-lived, particularly in areas with high humidity and clay soils. I like to plant with large amounts of grit and mulch with grit around the base of the plants. Keep heavy mulch away from the crowns. Give the plants space so as to increase air circulation.

RELATED PLANTS *Dianthus plumarius*, a parent of *D. ×allwoodii*, is longer lived and offers many cultivars from which to choose. These plants are more cushion forming and will benefit from a shearing after flowering to keep them from opening in the center. Shear back by half or remove the old flower stems and at least a third of the foliage. *Dianthus plumarius* may also benefit from a trim around the edges to reduce the size of the clump and to eliminate scraggly outer growth. Lift the foliage and trim off at the base of the bare outer stems underneath. Do not prune for the winter, but cut back if needed in the early spring.

Dianthus barbatus
sweet William
CARYOPHYLLACEAE

Dense clusters of flowers atop green leaves
10–18 in. high; 12 in. wide
Full sun; tolerates part shade
Blooms May–June
Zones 3–9

PRUNING Cut back by a third to
half immediately after flowering and
before seed sets to get this biennial to
act perennial. Another route is to let it
go to seed and then enjoy the progeny.
Sweet William self-sows so easily that
it seems to be a perpetual in the
garden. May contract leaf spot under
conditions of high humidity, in which
case deadleaf and destroy affected
leaves. Do not prune for the winter,
although plants usually need cleanup
in the spring as some foliage gets
damaged with severe weather.
OTHER MAINTENANCE Plants
require frequent division (every 2–3

years) to ensure long life. Prefers
alkaline soil and cool summers.
RELATED PLANTS *Dianthus barbatus*
'Sooty' is a favorite of mine, used
frequently due to its fragrant, dark
ruby (almost blood-colored) blooms
and red stems. It is a great cut flower
and grown as a biennial.

Dianthus deltoides
maiden pink
CARYOPHYLLACEAE

Red, pink, or white flowers; mat-forming
foliage
6–10 in. high; 24 in. wide
Full sun
Blooms May–June
Zones 4–9

PRUNING Cut back by half after
flowering to keep plants from opening
up in the center. If done before seed
set, cutting back also will prevent
reseeding. You can grab a handful of
stems and cut with pruners or even old

Dianthus deltoides

grass shears, or simply use hedge shears for pruning. Pruned branches are easily cleaned up with a shrub rake. You may get a sporadic flower or two after shearing, although nothing of significance. Maiden pinks can seed to a nuisance level and take over nonaggressive perennials. This can be used to an advantage if planted between lightly traveled stepping stones, in sun or part shade, where the seeding can create a mosslike effect. The plants love the sandy and well-draining conditions that nonmortared stone walks provide. Also, plants may be short-lived, so some seeding can be desirable to ensure constancy in the garden. This species has nice evergreen foliage that adds to the winter garden, so do not cut back in the autumn.

OTHER MAINTENANCE Prefers well-draining, alkaline soil. Tolerates drought. Will spread rapidly under ideal conditions, but is often short-lived, rotting in high-moisture situations. Divide every 2–3 years in the spring.

Dianthus gratianopolitanus

cheddar pink
CARYOPHYLLACEAE

Pink flowers; blue-green leaves
12–15 in. (6 in.) high; 12–15 in. wide
Full sun
Blooms June–July
Zones 3–9

PRUNING Cut or shear off old flowering stems and about a third of the foliage after flowering to enjoy the beautiful and reliable blue-green foliage for the rest of the year. Although deadheading each old flowering stalk before seed sets will prolong bloom, it is a tedious job, particularly on large plantings. I prefer to take what flowers I can get, without the extra deadheading, and just enjoy the foliage after a quick shearing. Shearing plants with hedge shears and shaping by cleaning up any shaggy edges creates especially nice results; plantings are easily cleaned up of pruned branches with a shrub rake. Plants fill in within a week, forming a dense groundcover, and they look great the rest of the season, including into the winter. May require minimal cleanup in the spring.

Dianthus gratianopolitanus 'Feuerhexe' Firewitch

OTHER MAINTENANCE Prefers a well-draining soil, but much more tolerant of heavy soil as well as of heat and humidity than other pinks and is much longer lived. Doesn't require the frequent division to keep plants vigorous.

RELATED PLANTS *Dianthus gratiano-politanus* 'Bath's Pink' is probably the best low-maintenance pink; a good beginner plant. 'Feuerhexe' Firewitch has brilliant magenta blooms. 'Shooting Star', part of the Star Series, is a more compact, tidy plant (6–8 in.) and not as vigorous. 'Tiny Rubies', a sweet low-growing pink with tiny flowers, is one of my husband's favorite perennials—goes to show that real men like pinks. To deadhead these numerous tiny stems of flowers I grab a handful at a time and cut. The foliage usually is so low and ground hugging that it is not cut during this procedure, just the old flower stems. Again, flowering may be prolonged with jumping on deadheading before seed has a chance to set. *Dianthus carthusianorum,* cluster-head dianthus, is 2 ft. tall with deep pink flowers. Allow to seed, but not to nuisance level, to ensure longevity in garden. Cut back, after some seeding is allowed, to grassy basal growth. May need some cleanup in the spring.

Dicentra formosa 'Luxuriant'

Dicentra formosa 'Luxuriant'

fringed bleeding heart
PAPAVERACEAE

Heart-shaped, cherry-red flowers; gray-green feathery leaves
15–18 in. high; 18 in. wide
Part shade–full shade
Blooms April–September
Zones 3–9

PRUNING After all flowers fade on flower scape, deadhead down to basal foliage—this can prolong bloom into the autumn. Deadleaf any browning or fading foliage to make room for new growth from the crown of the plant. Does not die back in the summer like *Lamprocapnos spectabilis*. Plants often flower late into the autumn; wait for

several killing frosts before cutting down for the winter.

OTHER MAINTENANCE Mixed performance of this plant puts it into the high-maintenance class as far as I'm concerned. Can be short-lived, at times never even establishing in the first year. At other times it does beautifully, with no apparent reason for the difference, although it is probably related to soil drainage. Not predictable. Requires rich, high-organic but well-draining soil, particularly over the winter. Will take some sun if provided sufficient moisture. Constant summer moisture will ensure a long bloom period. The overwintering buds of *Dicentra* are high on the crown, and if planted too deeply they can rot, further contributing to losses. Divide brittle roots carefully, only if needed, in the spring.

RELATED PLANTS Cultivars may be of *Dicentra eximia* or *D. formosa,* or hybrids of the two. Pruning requirements are the same for both species and for cultivars of either.

Dicentra formosa 'Alba', a white

form, is often less vigorous than the pink forms. 'Zestful' seems a bit more reliable than 'Luxuriant', but it doesn't flower as long.

Lamprocapnos spectabilis (syn. *Dicentra spectabilis*), known as common bleeding heart, is an old-fashioned beauty that dies down after flowering. Foliage is more persistent if provided with consistent moisture and cool conditions, possibly holding into late summer in northern gardens. But normally dieback occurs in late spring or early summer, particularly if plants are allowed to dry out and if summer heat persists. Cut to the ground when foliage looks shabby. May self-sow readily, depending on the climate. Divide in late summer or early autumn when the foliage has died down. 'Gold Heart' has beautiful golden foliage, but protect it from early spring frosts.

Dictamnus albus
gas plant
RUTACEAE

Pink or white flower spikes; compound leaves
2–4 ft. high; 3 ft. wide
Full sun
Blooms May–June
Zones 3–9

PRUNING Flowers are self-cleaning. It is best to leave the seedheads, which form interesting star shapes, to add interest in the garden through the summer and often into winter. Cut plants down in the spring. If any pruning is done when the plants are not dormant, care should be taken because the flowers and foliage can cause a dermatital reaction (skin irritation) in some individuals.
OTHER MAINTENANCE Long-lived, tough plant that requires little care. Plant in fertile, humus-rich, preferably alkaline soil that does not get soggy, in sun or light shade. Plants take some time (2–3 years) to become established and are very slow growing. Usually no staking is required. Division generally is not needed or recommended, as success rate is low.

Dictamnus albus

Digitalis grandiflora
yellow foxglove
PLANTAGINACEAE

Light yellow flower spikes; green leaves
2–3 ft. high; 1¼–1½ ft. wide
Full sun, part shade, or heavy shade
Blooms June–July
Zones 3–8

PRUNING Benefits from 2 types of pruning to look its best. First dead-head to lateral buds. Then, as new basal foliage starts to develop and when all secondary flowering is finished, plants should be cut back to the basal foliage. Plants sometimes will rebloom, though usually the blooms are smaller and fewer than those of the initial flowering. Plants may seed under favorable conditions. Basal foliage looks good into the winter; cut back any dead leaves in early spring if needed. Pinching plants ruins the natural habit by removing the large terminal flower. Smaller lateral flowering stems will still develop on pruned plants.
OTHER MAINTENANCE Easy-to-grow perennial foxglove. Long-lived. Does not require division for 5 or more

Digitalis grandiflora

Digitalis purpurea
common foxglove
PLANTAGINACEAE

Pink, white, yellow, or rust-colored flowers in spikes; green leaves

2–5 ft. high; 2 ft. wide

Part shade

Blooms June–July

Zones 4–9

PRUNING Deadhead to a lateral leaf or bud when about 70 percent of the flowering on the spike is finished; this avoids having a long, spindly, unattractive spike with numerous seed capsules at the bottom and a few stray flowers at the top. Cut back to basal rosettes immediately after all flowering is finished and before seed set to promote the perennial nature of this biennial. Lifting the plants and replanting the new rosettes at this time will ensure vigor, otherwise the following year's flowers may be smaller in size. Plants can also be allowed to reseed before deadheading to ensure constancy in the garden. Common foxglove often looks tatty when going to seed, so cutting down most but not all flowering spikes will ensure some seeding, though not an overabundant amount, while keeping the plant a bit cleaner. The foliage may also get tatty by late summer if the plant is allowed to go to seed, in which case the foliage should be removed at this time.

OTHER MAINTENANCE Performs best in well-draining yet moist soils high in organic matter, preferably with an acidic pH. Prone to a variety of diseases and to Japanese beetles, all of which contribute to foxglove's ratty late-summer appearance. Leaves and seeds are toxic if ingested.

RELATED PLANTS *Digitalis purpurea* 'Foxy' blooms throughout the summer in its first year with constant deadheading. Only blooms early in the season in its 2nd year. Best treated as an annual and replanted yearly.

Digitalis purpurea Excelsior Group is a biennial with tall flower spikes in early summer.

years. Division can be done in the spring or autumn and can be accomplished simply by separating new plantlets from the mother crown.

RELATED PLANTS *Digitalis grandiflora* 'Carillon' is shorter and has a decent rebloom with deadheading.

Digitalis lutea, straw foxglove, doesn't seem to rebloom as reliably after deadheading as *D. grandiflora*, although it looks better if old foliage is cut down to new basal growth in late summer when it starts to decline. Holds up through winter. Prune in spring if needed.

Digitalis 'Mertonensis' (*D.* ×*mertonensis*), strawberry foxglove, seeds itself freely; watch for seedlings in late summer. Not as long-lived as *D. grandiflora*. Divide every couple of years to maintain vigor. This is a hybrid of *D. purpurea* and *D. grandiflora*.

dormant but often fails to return and is best treated as a cool-season annual. Afternoon shade and ample water will help keep foliage looking fresh and delay dormancy. If dormancy is unavoidable, interplant leopard's bane with perennials or annuals to cover the gaps that will appear. Clay soil is acceptable as long as it drains well and doesn't dry out. Divide plants every 3 years in fall or early spring, discarding any old, woody centers. All parts are poisonous if ingested, so keep *Doronicum* species away from young children, pets, and livestock.

RELATED PLANTS *Doronicum orientale* 'Finesse' has distinctive skinny petals that come to a point. It reaches 18 in. tall, making it especially useful as a cut flower. 'Leonardo Compact' is an extra-early bloomer and a tidy grower reaching 6 to 8 inches. 'Little Leo' is the most widely available selection of leopard's bane. It has semi-double flowers and tops out at 12 inches.

Digitalis purpurea Excelsior Group

Doronicum orientale

leopard's bane
COMPOSITAE

Yellow daisylike flowers; heart-shaped toothed leaves

12–24 in. high; 15 in. wide

Sun–part shade

Blooms April–May

Zones 4–7

PRUNING Shear doronicum after blooms fade to prevent unwanted seedlings. Plants will usually go dormant shortly thereafter; allow foliage to die down and then cut stems to the ground if they're unsightly. Leaves may reappear in fall. The flowers can be harvested for long-lasting additions to spring arrangements.

OTHER MAINTENANCE Leopard's bane is at its finest in cool climates. Where summers are hot and humid, it goes dormant after flowering, and where summers are very hot and humid, this plant not only goes

Doronicum orientale 'Little Leo'

Echinacea purpurea 'Bright Star'. The shorter plants in front were pruned in early July and the taller plants in back were left unpruned. This effectively layers the planting and delays flowering on the pruned plants, providing flowers later in the season.

Echinacea purpurea

purple coneflower
COMPOSITAE

Mauve-pink daisylike flowers with an orange cone center; coarse green leaves

2–4 ft. high; 2 ft. wide

Full sun

Blooms July–September

Zones 3–8

PRUNING Plants seem to have a long bloom period even without deadheading, although deadheading makes the new flowers more prominent and keeps the plants looking fresh. I deadhead early in the bloom season and then curtail it in September, removing only the blackest heads and allowing the other seedheads to remain for the goldfinches that will feed heavily on the seedheads during September and October. Leaving the seedheads up for the winter provides food for many birds, including the juncos. But beware, leaving the seedheads also means excessive (an understatement) seedlings to contend with in the spring. They appear to have a 100 percent germination rate. I have started to compromise (since I'm running out of friends and family to whom I haven't already given flats of echinacea), leaving only small numbers of seedheads for the winter. I enjoy the birds too much to remove them all, and the heads are so interesting when covered with snow. I know some gardeners who find the deadheads unattractive and opt to remove them for that reason.

Echinacea responds well to pruning before flowering as a means to delay bloom, providing fresh coneflowers into late September, even early October, for extended interest in the garden as well as for cut flowers at a time when unpruned plants are mostly faded and full of seedheads. Part of a drift of coneflowers can be treated this way, or coneflowers in different parts of the garden can be pruned for different peak flowering times. Two interesting approaches to pruning are described. Plants can be cut by half in early June or when they are about 2½ ft. tall. They will start to flower 2–3 weeks later than usual (mid- to late July), depending on the weather, and will bloom for 2–3 weeks longer than unpruned plants, going strong until late September. They may mature at about 1 ft. shorter than unpruned plants.

Another effective method to delay flowering is to cut off about 1 ft. of the plant while in bud in early July, or when it's about 3 ft. tall. The plants can look a bit rough at this point, but they'll recover and flower nicely from mid-August until early October. They grow about 1 ft. shorter than unpruned plants.

It is interesting to note that, with either method, some basal shoots usually will be left below the level at which the plants are pruned. If this is the case, these unpruned shoots come up through the pruned plant and will flower about 1 week or so sooner than the pruned stems. Plant height is still reduced, as these stems naturally seem to grow to about the height of the pruned stems. Flowering is still extended with the pruned stems. Cutting plants to the ground in early June will delay flowering until mid-September, and on 2½-ft. plants, so all summer flowering is missed if plants are pruned to the ground.

The pruning advice applies to all *Echinacea purpurea* cultivars.

OTHER MAINTENANCE This is an easy-to-grow perennial. Avoid high-fertility soil, which can lead to tall, leggy plants that require staking. Purple coneflower is drought and heat resistant. It seldom needs division, but seedlings are best removed in the spring to control spread. Can attract beneficial soldier beetles in late August; be certain not to harm them.

RELATED PLANTS *Echinacea angustifolia*, narrow-leaved coneflower, sports a tidy mound of slim basal leaves and mauve-pink coneflowers on 2 ft. stems. It possesses exceptional drought tolerance but requires very sharp drainage.

Echinacea pallida, pale purple coneflower, has distinctive flowers with pastel pink flowers with skinny ray petals that hang down limply around a red-orange cone. It tolerates hot, humid conditions, but needs good drainage.

Echinacea paradoxa, yellow coneflower (zones 5–8), looks more like *Rudbeckia* than *Echinacea* with its yellow petals and brown cone, although the shuttlecock shape is pure coneflower. It can reach 3 ft. and may require staking.

In recent years, all these native coneflowers have been incorporated into various breeding programs to create a staggering array of new *Echinacea* hybrids with different flower forms and colors. Some of the more popular and reliable selections include 'Bright Star' (maroon-pink), 'Pink Double Delight', 'Milkshake' (double white and one of the best overall cultivars), 'Fragrant Angel' (white), 'Sunrise' (yellow), 'Red Knee High' (bright magenta-red, dwarf habit), 'Marmalade' (orange), and 'Hot Papaya' (red-orange). Many of the new coneflowers have proved to be difficult to overwinter and short-lived. Excellent drainage, especially in the winter, is an absolute must for success. It is also a good idea to plant coneflowers in the spring rather than the fall, so they have time to establish a sturdy root system before cold weather hits.

Echinops ritro
globe thistle
COMPOSITAE

Round blue flower heads; rough, spiny leaves

3–4 ft. high; 2–3 ft. wide

Full sun

Blooms June–July

Zones 3–8

Echinops ritro

PRUNING Globe thistle benefits from a couple types of pruning to look its best and to flower longest. First deadhead or cut back by a third to half, to lateral flower buds. Then, when new basal foliage starts to develop and all flowering is finished, plants should be cut back to basal foliage. Plants normally will rebloom from this basal growth, but usually the blooms are smaller, shorter, and less numerous than that of the initial flowering. Plants may seed occasionally if not deadheaded. Seedheads are attractive to the birds, so leaving a few dead-heads from the last bloom phase may be a good compromise. Foliage may decline if not given afternoon shade in warm sunny gardens, in which case deadleafing will be necessary to keep plants attractive. Do not cut back for the winter; prune in the early spring.

OTHER MAINTENANCE Very hardy, pest resistant, and drought tolerant once established. Well-draining soil is essential for survival. Does not need staking unless sited in overly rich soil. Can also spread strongly under such conditions. Division is not needed or recommended for many years and can prove difficult due to the thick, branching taproot. I have successfully divided young plants of globe thistle cultivars in early spring.

RELATED PLANTS *Echinops ritro* 'Veitch's Blue' is particularly desirable because it's a good rebloomer.

gardeners use rotary mowers in the autumn to clean up large groundcover areas, which means missing out on the winter foliage but getting a jump on spring maintenance. This technique would also be useful for related species that have minimal winter interest. Deadheading may involve a little clipping here or there, but for the most part the maturing foliage hides old flower stalks.

OTHER MAINTENANCE Barrenwort is a tough, long-lived, low-maintenance groundcover. It prefers moist, well-draining, high-organic soil, but is great for dry shade once established; it will compete with tree roots. It is a moderate spreader. Division is seldom needed, but if desired, divide in early spring before flowering or in summer after the foliage has had a chance to mature.

RELATED PLANTS *Epimedium grandiflorum*, longspur barrenwort, increases slowly. Foliage starts to decline soon after the first frost and usually is completely gone by spring, thus not requiring cutting back. It can be somewhat difficult to grow, though it is fully hardy (to zone 5). Notable cultivars include 'Lilafee' (lilac), 'Red Queen' (rosy red), and 'Tama-no-gem-pei' (white and purple bicolor).

Epimedium ×*perralchicum* 'Frohn-leiten' is hardy to zone 5 and is evergreen to zone 6. It has red-mottled foliage and upright columns of

Epimedium ×*rubrum*

Epimedium ×*rubrum*
red barrenwort
BERBERIDACEAE

Intricate red flowers; semi-evergreen, heart-shaped foliage
Blooms April–May
8–12 in. high; 12 in. wide
Part shade–full shade
Zones 4–8

PRUNING Plants usually are semi-evergreen (actually bronze) over the winter and become unsightly by very early spring. They should be cut down at this time, so as to not detract from the early spring flowers. Some

substantial bright yellow flowers to 15 in.

Epimedium pinnatum blooms in red, pink, yellow, or white and is especially tolerant of dry soils. 'Black Sea' displays pale peach flowers and foliage that turns maroon in cool weather.

Epimedium ×versicolor 'Sulphureum' has yellow flowers and is vigorously stoloniferous. It is hardy to zone 4 and is one of the best epimediums for dry shade.

Epimedium ×warleyense has vibrant orange blooms and spreads rapidly but not densely. 'Orangekonigin' (orange queen) spreads more slowly. This hybrid is evergreen to zone 7.

Epimedium ×youngianum 'Niveum' is a white bloomer that forms compact clumps which increase relatively quickly.

Eryngium planum
flat sea holly
APIACEAE

Blue cone surrounded by spiny blue bracts on almost leafless branching stems; heart-shaped basal foliage

2–3 ft. high; 1–2 ft. wide

Full sun

Blooms July–August

Zones 5–8

PRUNING Individual flowers are ornamental for a long period of time. Deadheading doesn't seem to prolong bloom, but it makes the plant more attractive and reduces seeding.

Eryngium planum

Deadheading can be tricky business because of the spiny nature of the plant. Trying to remove each flower head as it declines would drive even the worst neatnik off his or her rocker. Waiting until most of the heads have declined on several of the flowering branches and then going in to tidy up by removing whole branches seems the most practical solution. Generally this needs to be done only once during the blooming season in early August. Then, in late August when most of the remaining flowering is finished and the unattractive brown heads develop, all flowering stems should be cut to the ground. Sometimes basal foliage will be present, other times it won't. With this regimen some seeding will occur, but it's worth it compared to the tedious and painful process of deadheading each individual flower. Leave the basal growth, which remains evergreen, for the winter.

OTHER MAINTENANCE Flat sea holly is normally self-supporting and trouble free, except for seeding. It does require well-draining soil; in fact, it thrives in dry, sandy soil and is tolerant of neglect during dry summers when you can't seem to make it out to the gardens with the sprinkler. Division is seldom necessary, and the taprooted plants resent disturbance.

RELATED PLANTS Extra-blue selections of flat sea holly include

Eryngium planum 'Blaukappe' (blue cap) and 'Blue Glitter'. 'Blue Hobbit' is a dwarf selection reaching only 8–12 in., while 'Jade Frost' offers cream-variegated foliage to go along with the blue blooms.

Eryngium amethystinum, amethyst sea holly, has large steely blue flowers. 'Sapphire Blue' is sterile and will not produce unwanted seedlings.

Eryngium yuccifolium, rattlesnake master, is a native North American prairie plant with rounded, spiky white flowers on stalks stretching to 4–5 ft. It may need staking in rich or well-irrigated soils.

Euphorbia epithymoides
cushion spurge
EUPHORBIACEAE

Yellow flowers in clustered inflorescences; green leaves
12–18 in. high; 18 in. wide
Full sun
Blooms April–May
Zones 4–8

PRUNING Plants can be sheared back by a third and shaped after flowering but before seeds mature. Plants are heavy seeders, and shearing not only quickly takes care of deadheading but also helps produce a nicely shaped plant that is less likely to open up in the center. Hedge shears work well for this task. *Euphorbia* species produce a sticky milky sap that can cause severe skin irritation in sensitive individuals. It is best to wear latex gloves when pruning these plants.

Plants can be left for the winter and cut back in the early spring. In southern areas plants may act almost like a subshrub, with buds breaking from old stems to create 3-ft.-wide plants. Plants allowed to develop this way in other parts of the country generally will not be as compact or as well formed, and pruning down to the base in the spring is likely to be more desirable.

OTHER MAINTENANCE Requires well-draining soil, tolerates drought. May be susceptible to wilt in heat and humidity. Can be invasive in overly rich soil. Resents transplanting, and often doesn't require it for 10 years or more. If desired, divide thick fleshy roots, carefully, in the spring. Benefits from afternoon shade in southern gardens.

RELATED PLANTS *Euphorbia griffithii*, Griffith's spurge, can be pruned after flowering as described above for *E. epithymoides*, or it may need to be cut back even harder (by two-thirds) to control flopping stems.

Euphorbia myrsinites, myrtle euphorbia, self-sows prolifically. Cut back flowering stems before the seeds disperse. Foliage remains an attractive blue-green through the winter if protected from afternoon sun and winds. Clean up as needed in early spring.

Eutrochium maculatum 'Gateway'
'Gateway' Joe Pye weed
COMPOSITAE

Rose-pink flower heads on tall stems; whorled leaves (in circular clusters around the stem)
Blooms July–September
5–6 ft. high; 3–5 ft. wide
Full sun
Zones 4–8

Euphorbia epithymoides

PRUNING Plants respond to several different pruning techniques before flowering either to reduce height, to create smaller flowers and fuller plants, or to stagger bloom. Reducing the height may not be an objective as the plants are lovely, 5- to 6-ft.-tall, self-supporting specimens with impressive, large (7- to 8-in.-diameter) flower heads. Shorter, fuller plants may be useful in certain situations, however—such as to achieve proper proportions for combination with other shorter perennials. Pruning also produces slightly smaller flower heads (5 in. diameter), which can be more useful in flower arranging. Pruning may be desirable for plants grown in too much shade or overly rich soil, which produces larger plants with weaker stems.

My preferred technique is to pinch plants in early June, when they are about 3 ft. tall. This causes 5 breaks to emerge from the 1 pinched stem, creating full plants with slightly smaller 5-in.-diameter flowers. The plant's height normally is not noticeably reduced with this pruning, which I like, nor is the flowering time delayed significantly. A "have your cake and eat it too" situation can be attained by leaving several center stems unpinched to get the usual larger flower heads on unbranched stems, and pinching the outer stems around it for some fuller growth and smaller heads.

Cutting back by 6 in. in early June produces shorter plants, by about 1–1.5 ft., and flowers are delayed by about 1 week. Under certain situations the flower heads may be reduced to about 4 in. × 2 in., which are not as ornamental as the flowers on pinched or unpruned plants. This technique also could be performed on only a few stems of the plant.

Some gardeners in warmer areas, where plants reach 6–10 ft., have had success with cutting plants back by half when 2 ft. tall to obtain 4-ft.-tall flowering plants. I personally have not had success with this method, getting

Eutrochium maculatum 'Gateway'

shorter plants (3 ft. tall compared to 6 ft.) that were weak and didn't flower. Variables such as climate, shade, competition, and age of plant may be responsible for the inconsistent results. Definitely a plant with which to play and experiment.

Deadheading is not necessary with 'Gateway' Joe Pye weed since it has such a long bloom season without it. The flowers fade from early October to the first frost, and the fluffy seedheads that develop further extend their interest. Seeding is usually not a problem. The old stems and seedheads are attractive in the early winter garden, but they tend to break under heavy snow and wind. Even when broken down, they make good cover for the birds, and so should be left if space is available. In a small garden where this habit isn't tolerable, cutting down in the autumn may be the pruning choice.

OTHER MAINTENANCE Plants prefer moist locations; provide supplemental watering while establishing in the first year. Once established, plants are tough and tolerate short periods of drought. It takes 2–3 years for the plants to reach maturity. Division can be done in the spring but is only needed if plants get too big for their garden spot. Full sun is best to keep plants strongly upright.

RELATED PLANTS *Ageratina altissima* (syn. *Eupatorium rugosum*), white snakeroot, has white blooms in fall and is a very heavy seeder that should be deadheaded. If the foliage declines, cut the whole plant down after flowering before seeds mature.

Ageratina altissima is best known by the selection 'Chocolate', which displays chocolate-brown foliage until hot weather turns it green. It grows 3–4 ft. tall and prefers part shade. White snakeroot is poisonous if ingested.

Eutrochium dubium 'Little Joe' resembles *E. maculatum* 'Gateway', but is a more compact Joe Pye weed that matures around 3–5 ft. × 2–3 ft. It likes a rich, moist soil that doesn't dry out.

At the other end of the spectrum, *Eutrochium fistulosum* towers over the garden at 7 ft. or more. It also prefers moist soil and can be pruned like *E. maculatum* 'Gateway'. *Eutrochium fistulosum* 'Carin' is a strong-performing dusky pink selection, while 'Bartered Bride' shines in white.

Ferns

PRUNING Deciduous ferns die back to the ground in late fall, but the fronds often remain attached to the crown. Compulsively neat gardeners may be tempted to cut the brown leaves off at this time and cart them away, and while that is certainly an option, it's better for the plant to leave them alone until the new fronds have unfurled. Food stored in the old leaf bases will help fuel new growth in spring, and the ring of spent leaves acts as mulch to help protect the plant from winter cold.

Evergreen ferns may have color all winter, but as spring approaches, their fronds, too, begin to look tattered and worn. It is easiest to cut them back then, while the new leaves are still tightly curled, but again, it is better for the plant to leave the old fronds attached to the plant for as long as possible. Doing so will turn a quick chop into a time-consuming project of hand pruning later, as the new fronds will have intermingled with the old, so

the method chosen depends on the energy of the gardener and the practicality of the approach for the situation. Ferns trimmed back early won't grow quite as large as those hand-pruned later, but they won't be damaged by the procedure.

Occasional deadleafing may be needed throughout the season to keep plants looking shipshape. For appearances you'll probably want to remove damaged fronds all the way to the base, as fern fronds don't branch or send out new growth below the cut like most other plants' leafy stems will.

Some ferns' new growth, or fiddleheads, are edible and may be harvested in early spring when they are 2–3 in. tall. Ostrich fern (*Matteuccia struthiopteris*) is the fern most often used in this way. New shoots will emerge to replace the ones taken, though removing more than a few fiddleheads from each plant may weaken it.

OTHER MAINTENANCE Ferns are nearly universal in their fondness for part shade and soil that is cool, rich, moist, organic, and well-drained. It is a misconception that ferns thrive in deep shade; dappled shade is nearly always better for plant growth, including ferns. Some ferns will even tolerate full sun in cool climates if supplied with plenty of moisture, though part shade is usually preferred. Slightly acid soil is ideal for most ferns, but a few are found naturally in alkaline soil, and many aren't too fussy one way or the other. Mulch is important; keeping the soil cool and moist and providing a steady source of organic matter makes the gardener's task easier.

Ferns aren't heavy feeders, but weak plants may be fortified with a topdressing of compost or organic fertilizer. If synthetic fertilizers are used, they should be applied at half the usual dosage and never allowed to touch the crown.

Many ferns are sensitive to the oils and soaps used in pesticides and these should be avoided in their vicinity.

Anisocampium niponicum 'Pictum'

Dryopteris erythrosora

Osmundastrum cinnamomeum

Matteuccia struthiopteris

Luckily, ferns are largely trouble-free and rarely have outbreaks that need to be addressed with action. Deer leave them alone unless they are extremely hungry. Slugs and snails can be a problem in spring in some areas of the country.

Most ferns rarely require division, but they may be split if desired. Division is least stressful to the plant in early spring but can be accomplished at any time during the growing season except late fall as long as plants are shaded and not allowed to dry out. Some ferns reproduce quite quickly via stolons or rhizomes and may need regular thinning to keep them in check. Over-abundant self-sowing is rarely an issue.

DETAILS *Adiantum pedatum*, Northern maidenhair (zones 2–8), is a deciduous fern that grows to 30 in. and spreads by rhizomes. It enjoys part shade and moist, woodsy soil and can be divided easily with a sharp knife. *Adiantum venustum*, Himalayan maidenhair (zones 5–8), is semi-evergreen and reaches 6 in. × 3 ft. It is slow to get established. ***Athyrium filix-femina***, lady fern (zones 4–8), is a deciduous fern that grows to 3 ft. It tolerates considerable sun if given steady moisture. The fronds of this plant break off easily; shield it from errant foot traffic or soccer balls. Over the years lady fern crowns tend to rise up from the ground, and they benefit from being dug up and reset at soil level. ***Anisocampium niponicum*** 'Pictum', formerly ***Athyrium niponicum*** 'Pictum', Japanese painted fern (zones 4–9), is deciduous and reaches 18 in. When happy, it will continue to put out new foliage all season and will spread steadily.

Dryopteris erythrosora, autumn fern (zones 5–8), is an evergreen fern that grows to 30 in. It is easily grown and is relatively drought tolerant once established. It often continues to send up colorful new foliage throughout the summer. ***Dryopteris erythrosora*** 'Brilliance' has stunning copper-colored spring foliage that lasts especially long and returns in the autumn. ***Dryopteris filix-mas***, male fern (zones 4–8), is deciduous and reaches 4 ft. It is more accepting of sun than other ferns. It increases steadily via short rhizomes. ***Matteuccia struthiopteris***, ostrich fern (zones 2–6), is a deciduous fern that can grow to 6 ft. It is often found in wet, mucky, alkaline soils in the wild but grows well in regular garden conditions, too. It multiplies quickly by stolons. Ostrich fern is not a fan of hot climates. ***Onoclea sensibilis***, sensitive fern (zones 2–10), is a deciduous fern that grows to 3 ft. It tolerates sun, but whether planted in sun or shade, it needs moist soil. The foliage usually looks rough late in the season. Sensitive fern is a quick spreader. ***Osmundastrum cinnamomeum***, formerly ***Osmunda cinnamomea***, cinnamon fern (zones 2–10), is a deciduous fern that grows to 4 ft. It is easily grown in part shade and moist soil. It prefers acid soil. ***Osmunda***

Filipendula rubra 'Venusta'

claytoniana, interrupted fern (zones 2–8), is deciduous and reaches 4 ft. It is native to woodlands and woodland edges and appreciates consistent moisture. ***Osmunda regalis***, royal fern (zones 2–10), is also deciduous and can reach 6 ft. or more. It will grow in full sun in boggy sites and prefers acid soil but grows reliably in alkaline soil. It commands attention during the growing season but leaves a considerable gap in the winter. ***Polystichum acrostichoides***, Christmas fern (zones 3–9), is an evergreen fern that grows to 2 ft. It requires part shade and favors moist, woodsy sites but can cope with somewhat dry soil. It forms new crowns from short rhizomes, and these may be separated carefully in early spring. Christmas fern's spores form on the terminal third of selected fronds; this section of the leaf naturally withers and falls off after the spores are released, so don't worry that there is something wrong with the plant when this happens. ***Polystichum polyblepharum***, tassel fern (zones 5–8), is evergreen and reaches 2 ft. It needs regular moisture but good drainage, especially in winter.

Filipendula rubra 'Venusta'

queen-of-the-prairie
ROSACEAE

Fluffy deep rose flowers; compound leaves
4–6 ft. high; 4 ft. wide
Full sun
Blooms July–August
Zones 3–9

PRUNING Rebloom is minimal with deadheading, and the seedheads develop a rather interesting pinkish cast into the fall, so allowing spent flowers to remain on the plant is desirable. If foliage declines in late summer, cut the plants to the ground for a low, fresh mound of leaves. Be certain to keep moist to encourage regrowth, or it may not occur that season. Plants that were cut back by half in early June—when 2½ ft. tall and in tight bud—in an attempt to reduce height and delay flowering never bloomed. Queen-of-the-prairie usually does not respond to pinching, either. Plants may fall over during the winter. If this is not welcome, cut back in the autumn; otherwise, leave for winter bird cover and then cut back in the early spring.

OTHER MAINTENANCE Best summer-long performance is in moist, high-organic soil. Prefers cool climates. Tolerant of light shade. Usually requires light support, preferably by an obliging neighbor plant. The tough, thonglike root system is best left undisturbed for many years, unless you need to control spread, in which case divide in the autumn.

RELATED PLANTS *Filipendula purpurea*, Japanese meadowsweet, has spent flower heads that develop reddish tints, so plants don't need deadheading.

Filipendula vulgaris, dropwort meadowsweet, seeds abundantly, but seedlings are easily weeded out. In contrast to other *Filipendula* plants, this species transplants easily and is tolerant of drier soil.

Filipendula ulmaria
queen-of-the-meadow
ROSACEAE

Fluffy white flowers; compound leaves
4–6 ft. high; 3 ft. wide
Full sun–part shade
Blooms June–July
Zones 3–9

PRUNING Removing deadheads may encourage some rebloom and will

Filipendula ulmaria

prevent abundant reseeding. If old foliage declines, cut the plant down for new basal growth development.

OTHER MAINTENANCE Best in moist, high-organic soils. Provide some shade in hot regions. Tough root systems do not require frequent division. Strong stems do not require staking. Prone to mildew in hot, dry, or stressed conditions.

RELATED PLANTS *Filipendula ulmaria* 'Aurea' is valued for its golden foliage, which is more outstanding into the autumn if the plant is sheared back after flowering for new basal growth. Because flowering reduces the vigor of the foliage, a still-better option might be to prevent the plant from flowering altogether by shearing the flower buds off when they are just starting to form. This also prevents any chance of mongrel seedlings developing, which are green and vigorous growers that may overtake the golden parent.

Foeniculum vulgare 'Purpureum'

Foeniculum vulgare '**Purpureum**'

copper fennel
APIACEAE

Feathery purple foliage; yellow-green umbel flowers

3–4 ft. high; 1½–2 ft. wide

Full sun

Blooms July–August

Zones 4–9

PRUNING Copper fennel is most often grown in the perennial garden for its ornamental foliage color and texture. Some gardeners remove the flowers while in bud to prevent flowering altogether so as to not detract from the foliar effect. Plants can also reseed heavily, and preventing the plants from flowering is a sure way to eliminate this problem. But fennel should really be permitted to flower, because the small flowers serve an important function in being the host for beneficial parasitic wasps. These wasps help control caterpillars, aphids, and other soft-bodied pests. Deadhead fennel after all flowering is finished and before seeds mature. Allowing a small amount of seeding can mean greater constancy of the plant in the garden, as fennel are often short-lived.

Fennel foliage can also serve an important function in the perennial garden in that it provides larval food for black and anise swallowtail butterflies. In some years, this may mean total defoliation of fennel by late summer, in which case the bare stems should be cut to the ground at this time. The leaves hang limply from the stems if hit by a heavy freeze, so cutting down for the winter may be preferred to spring pruning.

Care should be taken when working with fennel because the plant's juices can cause phytophotodermatitis in some individuals—this means that if the juice gets on the skin and is exposed to the sun a reaction will occur, creating dark purplish discoloration on the skin, which can develop into a blister or two, although usually not. (This does not resemble the irritation caused by poison ivy, as so many other plant dermatital reactions do.) The darkened areas can remain for several months and, if severe enough, can cause light scars. To avoid problems, work with the plants only on cloudy days or in the late evening when the sun is down, and wear long sleeves, long pants, and gloves.

OTHER MAINTENANCE Requires well-draining soil. Fennel is tolerant of drought and heat. Fairly short-lived.

Fragaria 'Pink Panda'
'Pink Panda' strawberry
ROSACEAE

Pink flowers; sporadic tiny edible strawberries

6–12 in. high; spreading

Full sun–part shade

Blooms May–July

Zones 4–8

PRUNING Plants require constant pruning to keep in bounds, especially when placed in the wrong location such as a perennial border. Best used as a groundcover on its own. Requires deadleafing—a tedious task—if plants get dry in the summer, which causes scorching. Plants are semi-evergreen and require spring cleanup to remove foliage damaged from harsh winters. Do not prune for the winter.

OTHER MAINTENANCE Can be extremely invasive when planted with other low-growing perennials, which strawberry will overtake. I had a single plant spread over a 9 ft. × 9 ft. area in 4 years, weaving between and over everything in its path. The spread of this particular plant was stopped by a wet and cold winter, to the point where nothing remained. Well-draining soil is essential, particularly in the winter. Hardiness is unclear.

Fragaria 'Pink Panda'

Gaillardia ×grandiflora

blanket flower
COMPOSITAE

Daisylike flower heads in combinations of reds, yellows, and oranges; gray-green hairy leaves

2–3 ft. (1 ft.) high; 2 ft. wide

Full sun

Blooms June–October

Zones 3–10

PRUNING *Gaillardia* seems to flower continuously even without deadheading. This is a nice advantage, because if you don't deadhead you can enjoy the new flowers and the attractive spherical seedheads together, either in the garden or in arrangements. Self-seeding may occur, so deadhead if seeding is not desired. Some authorities feel that the tendency toward continuous bloom, although pleasing to the gardener, can work against the plant's chances of overwintering by directing its energy to flower production, rendering the plant unable to form buds for the following year's shoots. Cutting all flowering stems down to the basal foliage in late August or early September can stimulate vegetative growth before the coming of frost. The plant may then form new basal buds and more vigorous shoots, which can improve the plant's chances of survival.

OTHER MAINTENANCE Often short-lived, usually due to wet overwintering conditions rather than cold temperatures. Well-draining soil, particularly over the winter, is vital to survival. Drought, heat, and salt tolerant. Avoid overly rich soil. Tall-growing forms require staking. Divide in the early spring every 2–3 years to maintain vigor.

RELATED PLANTS *Gaillardia ×grandiflora* 'Baby Cole' and 'Goblin' are dwarf forms not requiring staking.

Gaillardia ×grandiflora 'Goblin'

Gaura lindheimeri

gaura
ONAGRACEAE

White or pink butterflylike flowers; narrow green leaves, sometimes spotted red

3–5 ft. high; 3 ft. wide

Full sun

Blooms June–October

Zones 5–9

PRUNING Old flower petals simply drop off the plant, leaving tiny pinkish-red-tinted seed capsules on the spike. New flowers continue to open from the bottom of the flowering spike up to the top over a long period of time. Depending on the conditions and the age of the plants, flowering may continue for the entire summer and autumn even without deadheading. And because the stems are so fine and the seedheads so tiny, any finished spikes usually go unnoticed among the masses of blooming spikes. The whole appearance of the plant is wispy.

The stems take on a nice scarlet tint in the autumn, but turn brown in midwinter and may fall under the weight of heavy snow. If plants are left up for the winter, reseeding may occur, usually near the base of the parent plants. Reseeding can ensure constancy of this often short-lived perennial in the garden. In some situations plants may appear to take a rest from flowering in midsummer; deadhead at this time, or shear in half, and rebloom normally will occur from late summer into autumn.

Gaura can be cut back or sheared before flowering for a nice effect to reduce the height of the plants and to produce fuller clumps with more flowering branches. The stems are so thin and weak on this perennial, however, that it seems no matter at what height the plants end up flowering, they are still going to flop slightly or at least lean over a bit. Plants cut back in early June by half when 12–15 in. tall flower 1–2 weeks later than unpruned plants, and they start flowering at 3 ft. and mature at 4 ft. (Flower stems on gaura elongate through the bloom period.) Pruned plants will still lean on their neighbors,

Gaura lindheimeri 'Siskiyou Pink'

but not as much as the 5-ft.-tall unpruned plants. Cutting plants back by two-thirds may be more desirable to further reduce height.

Gaura responds in an interesting way to continued shearing and shaping. A couple of shearings can create full, deep green, 10- to 12-in. mounds. Flowering seems to be initiated as soon as pruning stops. Plants sheared by half in early June, again when in bud in mid-July, and when in bud in mid-August, finally flowered in early October on 18-in. plants, elongating to 2-ft.-tall plants with a slight lean. The problem with this approach is that all the summer bloom is lost. Also, the amount of flowers seems to be reduced. The shearing can be stopped in mid-July, after the second pruning, for flowering in mid- to late August on fuller, more compact plants than those that undertake only a single shearing. This could be useful in preparation for a special September event in the garden, where smaller, fuller, fresh-flowering specimens are in order.

Two shearings, or a single heavier shearing, before bloom may be useful in southern gardens, where plants can become leggy with extended heat and humidity. Shearing can be repeated throughout the season whenever buds are visible to keep plants in a vegetative state, if desired.

OTHER MAINTENANCE Adequate drainage is the primary requirement of this long-flowering, heat- and drought-tolerant perennial. Plants have a tendency to bend over, and this habit is even more pronounced in overly rich or wet soil. Use neighboring perennials for support. The stout taproot seldom needs division. Gaura can be short-lived.

RELATED PLANTS Quite a number of new gaura selections have come on the market in recent years, offering novel colors and forms. *Gaura lindheimeri* 'Corrie's Gold' is a yellow-variegated form that opens its white flowers in early summer; if cut back by half in late July, it will rebloom in September.

'Crimson Butterflies' stays compact at 18 in. × 24 in. and boasts crimson-pink flowers and maroon-colored new growth. Though it needs no trimming, occasional light pruning will keep the richly colored new leaves coming. 'Siskiyou Pink' does well with close planting or support from adjacent perennials, and may be cut back by half in late spring to control legginess. Rosy Jane ('Harrosy') features white blossoms with a pink picotee edge and also stays a neat 18 in. × 24 in. Snow Fountain ('Walsnofou') is a flurry of crisp white flowers all summer and is a compact grower. White-blooming gauras tend to be more cold hardy than pink-flowering ones. Sunny Butterflies ('Colso') has white variegation with pink flowers and tops out at 24 in.

Gentiana andrewsii
bottle gentian
GENTIANACEAE

Blue to violet flowers like swollen buds that never open; smooth, shiny leaves in pairs
1–2 ft. high; 1–1½ ft. wide
Full sun–part shade
Blooms September–October

Gentiana andrewsii

Zones 3–7

PRUNING Poorly branched plants may be cut back by half when they reach 6 in. tall to encourage side branching. Most flower buds will occur at the tips of the stems. In winter, the straw-colored plants with their interesting seedpods remain moderately attractive, and cleanup may be put off until early spring or until plants lose their modest charms.

OTHER MAINTENANCE Native to moist meadows of the Northeast and Midwest, bottle gentian prefers a fertile, organic soil that doesn't dry out for long periods. Mulch plants to conserve moisture. Full sun promotes the most prolific flowering, but afternoon shade is appreciated in hot climates, where this species may struggle. Bottle gentian develops a taproot and division is not recommended.

Gentiana septemfida var. lagodechiana

summer gentian
GENTIANACEAE

Upward-facing, cobalt-blue flowers; low mound of smooth green leaves
4–8 in. high; 12–18 in. wide
Full sun–part shade
Blooms July–September
Zones 4–7

PRUNING Summer gentian doesn't reseed much (though you may wish it did), and deadheading isn't necessary. Plants are trailing but compact and seldom need shaping. Cut them back after a killing frost.

OTHER MAINTENANCE This gentian is less exacting in its needs than others and performs well in average garden conditions provided drainage is good and the soil doesn't dry out. Afternoon shade is a good idea, especially in the warmer end of its range. Watch for slugs and snails. Plants are slow to bulk up, but older clumps may be divided in early spring.

Gentiana septemfida var. *lagodechiana*

Geranium endressii 'Wargrave Pink'

'Wargrave Pink' geranium
GERANIACEAE

1½-in. light pink flowers; palmately cut leaves
15–18 in. high; 18 in. wide
Full sun–part shade
Blooms May–June
Zones 4–8

PRUNING Sprawling, straggly stems tend to develop after the initial flowering. Cut down to new growth at the base of the plant after flowering using hand pruners, or go for speed and use hedge shears. You may hit some of the new growth, but no harm done—the plants usually fill in with fresh mounds of foliage within 2 weeks. You may even get some sporadic rebloom for your efforts. For best regrowth, avoid prolonged drought after cutting back. Flowering may last longer in cool climates, and cutting back may not be necessary. Plants hold up well until late winter, at which point they often turn to mush.

Geranium endressii
'Wargrave Pink'

relatives do. Deadheading is all that's needed to keep it looking good, and this work is a treat, as brushing against the foliage causes it to emit its pungent scent. The foliage of this evergreen to semi-evergreen plant remains an attractive gray-green with tints of scarlet-red at the junction of stem and leaf throughout most of the winter. Don't prune it back in the autumn, but in early spring simply cut off any dead foliage that developed from a harsh winter. Will readily self-seed if permitted, which along with the natural spreading habit of this plant can create a pleasant groundcover effect. If this effect is desired, do not deadhead until seeds have dropped. Plants are drought tolerant, but some leaves may yellow by late summer with prolonged periods of dry conditions. A quick deadleafing will return the plant to its fresh appearance. It displays beautiful autumn foliage color.

OTHER MAINTENANCE This is a good low-maintenance geranium and is very easy to grow. It is tolerant of drought and heat. The stoloniferous roots seldom need dividing. *Geranium macrorrhizum* can tolerate full sun in cooler climates.

RELATED PLANTS *Geranium* ×*cantabrigiense* 'Biokovo' is a wonderful groundcover for dry shade that only requires deadheading to keep it

Cutting back in the autumn after several killing frosts may be desirable. **OTHER MAINTENANCE** 'Wargrave Pink' requires well-draining soil. It prefers moist soil in areas with hot summers, although it's fairly adaptable to short periods of dry conditions. It can tolerate more sun and drier soil in cooler climates. This geranium seldom needs dividing, but if desired, divisions can be easily taken by reaching into the plant and separating pieces from the main crown in spring or autumn.

RELATED PLANTS *Geranium* ×*oxonianum* 'Claridge Druce' is similar, while 'A.T. Johnson' is more vigorous and free flowering and is also better adapted to dry situations. 'Katherine Adele' has leaves attractively mottled with bronze. Pruning is as described, although in warmer climates plants may be semi-evergreen and hold up well for the winter.

Geranium macrorrhizum
bigroot geranium
GERANIACEAE

Pink or white flowers; palmately lobed gray-green leaves with scarlet autumn color
12–15 in. high; 18 in. wide
Full sun–full shade
Blooms May–June
Zones 3–8

PRUNING Bigroot geranium doesn't require cutting back like so many of its

Geranium macrorrhizum

looking good. The blossoms are white with pink stamens, and the leaves turn scarlet and orange in the autumn. Cut back any dead foliage in the spring if desired, but tatty old foliage is usually lost among new growth. There are reports that G. ×cantabrigiense 'St. Ola', in white, might be an even better performer. *Geranium ×cantabrigiense* 'Crystal Rose' and 'Karmina' are pink versions.

Geranium phaeum
mourning widow
GERANIACEAE

Nodding black-purple flowers; palmately lobed leaves, often with dark markings
18–24 in. high; 18–24 in. wide
Part shade–full shade
Blooms late April–June
Zones 4–8

PRUNING Shearing plants after they flower will result in a flush of new foliage and will likely prompt some rebloom. Provide plenty of water after cutting them back. Where the growing season is long enough, plants may be sheared again for a third wave of flowers and fresh foliage. Shearing will also prevent reseeding, which can be excessive in some gardens. Cut *Geranium phaeum* back to basal foliage when frost kills the tops; in mild climates a small rosette of lime green leaves may persist over the winter.

OTHER MAINTENANCE Mourning widow geranium favors cool, moist, shady sites, and it is here that seedlings may appear in their greatest numbers. Like other geraniums, its seeds are flung some distance from the plant when ripe, and volunteers may show up all about the garden. They are easily dug up and transplant well. Selected varieties may or may not come true from seed; dividing clumps in spring or fall will ensure that new plants are identical to the parent. *Geranium phaeum* has decent drought tolerance, particularly when grown in shade or in cool-summer climates.

RELATED SPECIES *Geranium phaeum* 'Album' displays clear white flowers, while 'Lily Lovell' has purple blooms over light green leaves. 'Margaret Wilson' has leaves splashed liberally with creamy yellow variegation, while the popular 'Samobor' has leaves stamped with deep purple markings. *Geranium phaeum* var. *purpureum* displays rich maroon blooms spring through midsummer.

Geranium phaeum var. *purpureum*

Geranium psilostemon

Geranium psilostemon

Armenian cranesbill
GERANIACEAE

Magenta flowers with a black eye; finely
dissected palmate foliage
2½–4 ft. high; 3–4 ft. wide
Full sun–part shade
Blooms May–July
Zones 4–8

PRUNING Armenian cranesbill is a
large sprawling perennial that looks
stunning in bloom with its screaming
magenta flowers, but once the flowers
are spent, the foliage declines and the
plant may become an eyesore. Cut it
back hard after blooming. It is unlikely
to flower again in the same season, but
it will form an attractive mound of
fresh foliage to carry it quietly through
the rest of the year. The leaves may
turn crimson in the fall. Do the final
cleanup of dead foliage any time
before growth resumes in spring.
OTHER MAINTENANCE *Geranium*
psilostemon struggles in hot, humid
climates and is at its best where
summers are mild. The ideal soil
would be deep and fertile and the best
exposure, morning sun. Some support
in the form of pea sticks or strong
neighboring plants will probably be
necessary to hold up the tall stems as
they grow heavy with flowers. Armenian cranesbill tolerates competition
from other plants, so it won't suffer
from having supportive neighbors
close by. Some reseeding may occur if
deadheading isn't completed in time,
but rarely enough to be a nuisance.
RELATED PLANTS *Geranium psiloste-*
mon is a parent to *G.* 'Ann Folkard',
which has acid-yellow new foliage to
go with its hot pink blooms. It will
rebloom sporadically even if it isn't
trimmed after the first flush. *Geranium*
'Anne Thomson' is similar, but
reblooms with more gusto with or
without pruning.

Geranium ROZANNE 'Gerwat'

ROZANNE geranium
GERANIACEAE

Violet-blue flowers with a white eye; palmately lobed foliage
15–20 in. high; 2–3 ft. wide
Full sun–part shade
Blooms June–October
Zones 5–8

PRUNING ROZANNE looks great all season and has set the new standard for geraniums. It starts blooming a little later than other geraniums, but then goes nonstop until frost, even without pruning. Plants can be shaped at any time if they outgrow their allotted space; they will quickly recover and pick up where they left off. Occasional deadleafing may be needed in hot and dry locations. Cut back dead foliage in late fall or in early spring before growth resumes. This is a sterile hybrid that sets no seed.

OTHER MAINTENANCE Amazingly adaptable, ROZANNE can take sun or part shade—plants in full shade flower well but get floppy. A good, humus-rich, moist but well-drained soil will produce the lushest plants, but ROZANNE isn't too fussy and has a fair degree of drought tolerance. Staking is rarely necessary. Plants spread more than you might expect and can be used as groundcover.

RELATED PLANTS *Geranium* 'Orion' is a hybrid that looks similar to ROZANNE and performs similarly, but its flowers are bigger and bluer. It also frequently displays long-lasting red fall foliage, a feat which ROZANNE does only rarely. It may reach up to 6 ft. wide. If plants get scraggly after the summer bloom, cut back heavily for autumn rebloom. This plant was given a 4-star rating by Richard Hawke at the Chicago Botanic Garden Plant Trials.

Geranium ROZANNE 'Gerwat'

Geranium sanguineum

bloody cranesbill
GERANIACEAE

Pink, magenta, or white flowers; small, lobed leaves
6–15 in. high; 24 in. wide
Full sun–part shade
Blooms May–August
Zones 3–8

PRUNING I usually don't bother to go through the tedious process of deadheading the hundreds of little "cranes" that develop on this plant. I wait until most of the flowering, including sporadic rebloom, is

Geranium sanguineum
'Max Frei'

finished and plants are looking rough, usually in late summer, and I cut the plant back (using hedge shears) to the fresh basal foliage, which turns crimson in the autumn. Plants do not need to be pruned down for the winter. The waxy leaves hold well until spring, at which point any dead leaves can be removed, although this usually is not even necessary, as new growth quickly covers any dead foliage. Some reseeding occurs when deadheading is omitted. If deadheading is desired, rather than removing deadheads one by one with pruners, a less arduous

approach is to shear them off along with about 4 in. of foliage after the main flowering is finished. Plants can be shaped at the same time if desired, which may be helpful to keep plants from encroaching into neighboring perennials' space. Sporadic rebloom appears to be the same on deadheaded and nondeadheaded plants.

OTHER MAINTENANCE This is a very tough, long-lived, sun-loving geranium. While it is tolerant of many soil types, it requires good drainage and may spread excessively in overly rich soil. Bloody cranesbill is drought tolerant. It usually doesn't require division. Side shoots can be removed, without lifting the plant, to help confine expanding clumps.

RELATED PLANTS *Geranium sanguineum* 'Cedric Morris', a compact form (8 in.), has large flowers that bloom about 2 weeks earlier and last longer than those of the species. 'Max Frei' has diminutive leaves and a compact habit, growing 6 in. tall. It's a good choice where space is limited. 'New Hampshire' is a choice long-blooming cultivar with a wide-spreading habit.

Geum hybrids

(*Geum coccineum* × *Geum quellyon*)

geum
ROSACEAE

Yellow, orange, or scarlet flowers; fuzzy, lobed basal leaves
18–24 in. high; 18 in. wide
Full sun
Blooms May–June
Zones 5–7

PRUNING Plants flower strongly in May and June and intermittently after that, sometimes until autumn, with deadheading. Flowering spikes are branched. Deadhead to lateral flowers, then when all flowering on the spike is finished, cut it down to the foliage. If foliage declines after flowering, deadleaf or cut back once new basal growth is evident. Keep moist. Plants remain semi-evergreen into the winter; cut back as needed in the

spring. Young or newly divided plants bloom stronger and longer than old plants.

OTHER MAINTENANCE Short-lived plants. Research for my master's thesis showed geum to be not very cold hardy, nor tolerant of poorly drained conditions, particularly in the winter. Plants need a cool root run, and moisture in the summer. Performance is better in cooler climates; provide afternoon shade in hot regions. Annual division in the spring or late summer is required to maintain vigor.

Gillenia trifoliata
(syn. *Porteranthus trifoliata*)

Bowman's root
ROSACEAE

Starry white or pale pink flowers on dark stems; trifoliate serrated green leaves turn bronzy orange in fall

2–4 ft. high; 3 ft. wide

Part shade

Blooms late May–June

Zones 4–8

PRUNING Bowman's root flowers for only a few weeks and doesn't rebloom even when deadheaded. Seedheads are rather ornamental and may be left up for winter interest. Plants occasionally self-sow but never obnoxiously.

Cut stems down at any time after leaf-fall.

OTHER MAINTENANCE Native to much of the eastern United States, Bowman's root has proved itself to be adaptable to a wide range of growing conditions. It performs best in lightly shaded sites with rich, moist, well-drained, woodsy soils, but can cope with less than ideal conditions and is drought tolerant once established. Mulch to conserve moisture. This bushy plant is normally self-supporting but may flop in too-rich soil or during a particularly wet season. Stake with peony hoops early in the year if splaying is a problem. This long-lived perennial rarely if ever needs dividing, and the woody crowns make doing so difficult.

RELATED PLANTS *Gillenia trifoliata* 'Pink Profusion' has pale pink flowers. *Gillenia stipulata*, another North American native, has lacier foliage and is less floriferous than *G. trifoliata*.

Geum 'Mrs. J. Bradshaw'

Gillenia trifoliata

Grasses

PRUNING Although ornamental grasses generally don't require cutting back for the health of the plant, most will benefit from cutting back once a year, if for nothing but aesthetics. Grasses that aren't cut back in the spring may be slower to start new growth, since the old foliage will impede the sun from hitting and warming the crown of the plant.

Most grasses should be cut back just before new growth begins in the spring; this is normally mid-March to early April in the Midwest or late February to early March in milder areas. Cool-season grasses like calamagrostis break before warm-season grasses like miscanthus and will need to be cut back earlier. Certain grasses such as festuca may not need cutting back at all, only removal of dead leaves by hand. Some gardeners choose to cut their grasses down in autumn if the plants tend to fall over or lose their color in winter, or if time is limited in the spring; however, besides offering outstanding winter interest, dormant foliage left standing on the plants often provides additional winter protection to the crown against cold and excess moisture to help prevent winter losses. In some dry climates where dormant grasses may be a fire hazard, cutting them back is the law.

Cut most grasses down to within 3–4 in. of the ground. Certain grasses, particularly those that are inclined to be short-lived, resent close shearing and may not recover if cut down closer than 3–4 in. Tying the grass together with heavy twine before cutting can help tremendously with cleanup. Once it is cut at the base, the bundle can be easily transported to the compost pile. It also helps if two people are working together. Wear gloves and long sleeves as well as safety goggles when cutting back, as grass blades can be razor-sharp. Hand pruners can be used on a small-scale planting, or handheld hedge shears, electric hedge shears, a weedeater with a blade, or even a chain saw may be the tool of choice. As the size of the planting increases, so can the intensity of the tool used. I find electric hedge shears to be the most useful.

Deadheading may be necessary on spring-blooming grasses if the heads shatter or become unattractive later in the summer. Deadheading also reduces seeding on grasses so inclined. Some people feel that the flowers of certain grasses, such as blue fescue (*Festuca glauca*), only detract from the foliage, in which case the panicles can be removed before flowering occurs.

Some grasses, such as variegated forms of miscanthus, have a tendency to flop and need staking. Cutting grasses down to 3–4 in. above the ground in June or July can reduce their height, eliminate the need for staking, and possibly put a large-growing grass more in scale with the rest of the planting. It may also cause a delay in flowering, depending on the species. Bob Saul of Saul Nursery in Georgia cuts variegated miscanthus down to 4 in. in early July when plants are 5 ft. tall. The results of such pruning are plants that mature at an upright 2½–3 ft. rather than a flopping 6 ft. In the Midwest I cut plants down to 18 in. in early July, and they grow to 5 ft. within 2 weeks—obviously cutting down lower is in order. This is an area where more experimentation is needed.

OTHER MAINTENANCE Most grasses prefer full sun, although some tolerate shade. Grasses benefit from a high-organic, well-prepared soil. It generally is best to plant in early spring or early autumn to allow them time to establish before the heat of summer or the cold of winter. Keep new plantings moist. Grasses are not heavy feeders, and overly rich or high-nitrogen soils can cause floppy growth and increase the need for staking.

Grasses normally don't require division for about 5–7 years after planting. Division is best performed as the new growth emerges in the spring, although grasses will tolerate division at other times. Division can be difficult, often requiring the assistance

of a good axe and saw. If growth progresses before division is accomplished, plants should be cut back by about a third.

Pests are usually not a major problem for grasses. One pest that has become a concern on miscanthus plants is mealybug. Mealybug is very difficult to control, and digging out and destroying infested plants is the most common recommendation. Do not compost infested plant material. Rust can occur under certain conditions in the spring; if rust develops, prune off infected leaves as soon as they appear. This may even involve shearing the plants to within a few inches of the ground.

DETAILS *Achnatherum calamagrostis* (zones 5–8) is a cool-season grower to 3 ft. It struggles in areas with high humidity and warm night temperatures and flops in rich, moist soils; a mild Mediterranean climate suits it best. The plumes remain showy all winter and the foliage is evergreen where winter temperatures aren't too severe. *Calamagrostis* ×*acutiflora* 'Karl Foerster' (zones 5–9) is a cool-season grower to 6 ft. It blooms in late spring, but the spikes remain ornamental well into winter. This feather reed grass doesn't set viable seed. 'Karl Foerster' tolerates part shade; variegated varieties like 'Overdam' require afternoon shade. *Calamagrostis arundinacea*, formerly *C. brachytricha*, (zones 4–9) reaches 4 ft. and blooms in September. It also tolerates part shade. Fluffy plumes remain showy until late December and are a lovely red-violet when they emerge, maturing to a wheat color in autumn. Plants may reseed. Sedges (*Carex* spp.) are cool-season, mostly low-growing, grasslike plants. Many are evergreen or semi-evergreen in mild areas, such as *C. buchananii,*

(clockwise from top left) *Pennisetum alopecuroides* 'Hameln'; *Muhlenbergia capillaris; Calamagrostis* ×*acutiflora* 'Karl Foerster'

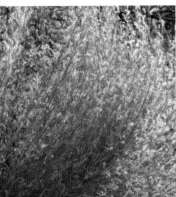

C. conica 'Snowline', **C. dolichostachya** 'Kaga Nishiki', **C. elata** 'Aurea' ('Bowles Golden'), **C. morrowii** 'Ice Dance', and **C. oshimensis** 'Evergold'. If winter hasn't been kind to them, they may be cut back in spring; otherwise, only minor grooming will be necessary. All of the above except **C. buchananii** will do well in part shade. **Chasmanthium latifolium** (zones 3–8) is a fine-textured, mid-sized grass with olive-green bamboolike foliage. Cut it back in the early spring before new growth begins. Can reseed heavily. **Chondrosum gracile**, more commonly known as **Bouteloua gracilis** (zones 3–10), is a warm-season grower to 15 in. It is easy to grow in full sun in any soil, wet or dry. It reseeds freely. Blue grama grass can also be maintained as a 2–3-in. turfgrass by regular mowing. **C. gracile** 'Blonde Ambition' has pale yellow plumes instead of the usual purple. **Deschampsia cespitosa** (zones 4–9) is a cool-season grower to 3 ft. Tufted hair grass likes moist soil and tolerates part shade. The basal foliage is semi-evergreen in protected locations. **D. cespitosa** 'Northern Lights' is a more compact form with variegated leaves. **Elymus hystrix** (zones 5–9) is also known as bottlebrush grass. A low-care, robust, but interesting addition to the garden, it requires minimal or no pruning. **Festuca glauca** (zones 4–8) is a cool-season grower to 12 in. It tolerates light shade but prefers full sun and likes heat but hates high humidity. Plants are short-lived in the Southeast. Remove spent flower spikes if you find them distracting. Blue fescue requires

minimal spring pruning; if you do shear, don't cut plants any closer than 3–4 in. from the crown. 'Elijah Blue' is a relatively durable selection.

Hakonechloa macra 'Aureola' (zones 5–9) is a warm-season grower to 18 in. It needs shade in most parts of the United States This variegated Japanese forest grass grows slowly and seldom needs division; if you choose to divide established plants, do it in early spring, not fall. The leaves of *H. macra* 'All Gold' (zones 5–9) are entirely yellow; it's fast-growing, robust, and slightly taller than 'Aureola'. **Miscanthus sinensis** (zones 5–9) is a warm-season grower and is represented by an extensive array of selections ranging in size from 4–9 ft. Avoid early-blooming maiden grasses like 'Adagio' and 'Malepartus' in the southeastern and mid-Atlantic states, where they can become rampant reseeders; late-blooming 'Gracillimus' and 'Morning Light' are safer. Plants often remain attractive all winter. Mealybug can be a problem. **Miscanthus** 'Purpurascens', of uncertain parentage, has silvery white plumes and leaves that turn orange and red in the fall. It rarely reseeds. **Molinia caerulea** 'Skyracer' (zones 5–8) is a cool-season grower that forms a tuft of basal foliage 2–3 ft. tall topped by airy plumes in July to 7 ft. It doesn't have much of a winter presence, as the stalks break off at the crown in rainy or snowy weather late in the season. The old foliage is essentially self-cleaning; just gather up the leaves in early winter. 'Skyracer' purple moor grass prefers moist soil. It is a slow-growing but long-lived plant and performs beautifully in the Midwest. ***Muhlenbergia capillaris*** (zones 6–10) is a warm-season grower to 3 ft. It needs full sun and excellent drainage and is very drought tolerant. Although pink muhly grass is native as far north as Massachusetts, plants of southern provenance may be hardy to only zone 7 or 8, which explains the overwintering difficulties many Midwest and Northeast gardeners have had with some of the selections in commerce. The similar ***M. reverchonii*** is recommended in colder zones if northern forms of ***M. capillaris*** can't be located. ***Nassella tenuissima*** (zones 7–10) is a cool-season grower to 2 ft. It requires full sun and sharp drainage, especially in winter. Mexican feather grass may go dormant in summer. It reseeds, sometimes overenthusiastically, in mild climates. In cold climates it serves as a useful annual for adding movement and fine texture to the garden. ***Panicum virgatum*** (zones 4–10) is a warm-season grower that ranges from 4–8 ft. tall. It is sun loving but tolerates part shade, and it copes with wet or dry soil once established, making it an excellent candidate for rain gardens. There's no hurry to cut switch grass back in early spring, as the plant remains standing until the bitter end, and new growth emerges later than that of just about any other perennial plant. Seedlings may become a nuisance. 'Dallas Blues' and 'Northwind' are strong performers with blue foliage; 'Northwind' was the Perennial Plant Association's Perennial of the Year for 2014. 'Shenandoah' is known for its red-tipped leaves; it is a slow grower. 'Rehbraun' has reddish brown flower panicles and foliage that is a glowing yellow in fall with hints of red in winter. 'Cheyenne Sky' is a compact switchgrass known for foliage that turns deep wine-red in early summer. ***Pennisetum alopecuroides*** (zones 6–9) is a warm-season grower to 4 ft. It favors a sunny position, regular water, and good drainage. 'Hameln' (2–3 ft.) is the most common incarnation of

fountain grass; it starts to flower in July and the plumes usually shatter by early October, though the tidy tufts of bleached foliage look good all winter. It doesn't reseed. 'Moudry' has charcoal-gray plumes and can be a rampant reseeder in moist conditions; don't set it loose near irrigated lawns unless you want a maintenance nightmare. ***P. orientale*** (zones 6–8) blooms May–September. It isn't normally an aggressive seeder. Oriental fountain grass loses winter interest in November, although I like to leave foliage up until spring to help overwinter marginally hardy ***Pennisetum*** species in our area. 'Karley Rose' has pink-tinted plumes. 'Tall Tails' has extra-long plumes and can reach 6 ft. in height. ***Schizachyrium scoparium*** (zones 3–9) is a warm-season grower to 4 ft. It likes a lean soil in full sun and will flop in moist, rich soil. It may seed to nuisance levels in a border setting. 'The Blues' is my favorite cultivar. ***Sesleria autumnalis*** (zones 5–8) is a cool-season grower to 12 in. Autumn moor grass tolerates part shade, drought, and alkaline soil but hates hot, humid summers. ***Spodiopogon sibiricus*** (zones 4–8) is a warm-season grower to 5 ft. Frost grass struggles in hot, humid climates, but provides a handsome and interesting bamboolike presence in mild regions in summer. It is best with light shade and regular water. This plant begins to break down with the first hard freeze and doesn't have a lot to offer in winter. ***Sporobolus heterolepis*** (zones 3–9) is a warm-season grower to 30 in. It is easy to grow in any soil type and is drought tolerant and long-lived. Don't attempt to divide it. Prairie dropseed begins to shatter in early December; cut plants back then rather than waiting until early spring. ***Stipa gigantea*** (zones 6–10) sports basal foliage to 2 ft. and plumes to 8 ft. Giant feather grass needs excellent drainage and prefers climates with low humidity. The clump of basal leaves is evergreen in mild areas, but should be cut back in late winter anyway.

Gypsophila paniculata

Gypsophila paniculata

baby's breath
CARYOPHYLLACEAE

Tiny white or pink flowers in large, airy clusters; linear blue-gray leaves

2–3 ft. high; 3 ft. wide

Full sun

Blooms June–August

Zones 3–9

PRUNING Deadhead gypsophila throughout the summer for more flower production and to keep it looking fresh. Deadhead to lateral flowers, and when all flowering is finished cut stems down to the rosette of foliage for rebloom in the autumn.

OTHER MAINTENANCE Well-draining soil is essential to survival. Plants prefer alkaline conditions. More compact cultivars should be selected to eliminate or reduce the need for staking. Division is not recommended due to the thick roots of baby's breath. Short-lived.

RELATED PLANTS *Gypsophila paniculata* 'Bristol Fairy', a 2-ft.-tall form, usually doesn't need staking. 'Pink Fairy' grows to 18 in. and requires no staking. 'Rosenschleier' ('Rosy Veil') is more tolerant of wet conditions, more vigorous, and longer lived than other taller cultivars. It grows to 18 in.

Gypsophila repens, creeping baby's breath, is hardier than *G. paniculata* and longer lived in heavy soil conditions.

Helenium autumnale

common sneezeweed
COMPOSITAE

Red, yellow, or orange daisylike flower heads; narrow green leaves

3–5 ft. high; 3 ft. wide

Full sun

Blooms July–October

Zones 3–8

PRUNING The species and cultivars of common sneezeweed can be pruned in a variety of ways to reduce height and possibly delay flowering. Pinching plants every couple of weeks, starting around mid-May and going until mid-June, will produce more compact plants with more flowers. Another method that offers similar results and possibly slightly delayed flowers is to simply cut plants back once by half or two-thirds in early to mid-June, layering the outer branches.

Some gardeners prefer to cut the plants back to about 12 in. in mid-July for bloom 6 weeks or so later on plants half the normal size, although a good deal of bloom time is lost with this technique. If such a drastic delay is not desired, a more practical alternative is to remove 4–6 in. off the tips of the plants when in tight bud, which will delay flowering by only a week or two. This technique is useful to delay flowering on a plant that was pruned earlier for height control. Other options for gardeners include removing the tips from a few stems on an individual plant to prolong the bloom of that plant, or removing the tips of a few plants in a large group to prolong the bloom of the planting. Deadheading also prolongs bloom.

Plants are usually spindly at planting and should be cut back by half at that time for shorter first-year plants.

Plants have dense foliage that can be prone to mildew late in the season. Plants should be cut back by half to two-thirds or even to basal growth, if present, after flowering to reduce occurrence of mildew or to remove infected foliage.

OTHER MAINTENANCE Plants require sufficient moisture during the summer for best performance. They flounder in dry conditions and tolerate wet sites. Frequent division, every 2–3 years, often is needed to maintain vigor. Staking is required, even with many of the cultivars and hybrids, unless pruned. Tall, weaker growth is promoted by hot conditions.

RELATED PLANTS *Helenium autumnale* 'Waltraut' offers an extended blooming period, and 'Moerheim Beauty' is erect and clump-forming so doesn't require support or pinching.

Helenium autumnale 'Moerheim Beauty'

Helianthemum nummularium

sunrose
CISTACEAE

Crepe paper–like flowers; gray-green narrow leaves

6–12 in. high; 12–18 in. wide

Full sun–part shade

Blooms May–June

Zones 5–7

PRUNING In the early spring, before flower formation, plants may benefit from a light trim to create denser growth. Plants should be sheared by about a third and shaped after flowering to maintain form. They may benefit from a heavy shearing every 2–3 years down to about 6 in., or lower for shorter forms, if they have gotten leggy. Heavy shearing will return the plant to a vigorous condition. All heavy pruning should be completed by mid- to late August so that these subshrubs can harden for winter. Plants are evergreen—do not prune for the winter.

OTHER MAINTENANCE Good drainage is absolutely essential. Prefers rocky, dry, alkaline conditions with cool summers and mild winters. Avoid overly rich soil. Grit can be added to heavy soil at planting to improve water movement. Plants are shallow rooted and should be mulched with evergreen boughs to reduce frost heaving and winter desiccation. Avoid planting or dividing in autumn. Divide every 4–5 years in the spring if needed.

RELATED PLANTS The *Helianthemum* cultivars 'Ben Heckla' and 'Rose Queen' perform well in heat. 'Fire Dragon' grows to 6 in tall and spreads, producing red-orange blooms in May and June.

Helianthemum nummularium 'Fire Dragon'

232

Helianthus salicifolius

willowleaf sunflower
COMPOSITAE

Golden-yellow, daisylike flower heads; long narrow leaves

5–6 ft. high; 3 ft. wide

Full sun

Blooms late September–October

Zones 4–9

PRUNING If plants are grown in full sun, the stems are usually self-supporting. If given shade or overly rich soil, plants will be more open, taller, and weaker, requiring staking. Pinching or cutting back creates more compact growth. Plants in full sun that normally reach 4–5 ft. may grow to about 3 ft. when pinched in early July, with no delay in flowering. Cutting plants back by half in mid-June also creates shorter plants with no delay in bloom. *Helianthus salicifolius* flowers so late in the season that deadheading to prolong bloom isn't really practical, and the

seedheads are attractive to humans and birds. I've never had reseeding of this species. Plants can be left up for the winter, although stems will break under the weight of snow and heavy winds. Cutting back after several frosts may be more desirable if a tidy winter appearance is the goal.

OTHER MAINTENANCE This is an easy-to-grow plant. It is seemingly tolerant of a wide range of situations, although it prefers moist, well-draining soil. It is fairly drought tolerant once established. Willowleaf sunflower is wide-spreading, so a single plant creates an impressive sight. Divide clumps, if needed, in the spring every 4–5 years.

RELATED PLANTS Maturing at 15 in., *Helianthus salicifolius* 'Low Down' is so small that it seems like another species entirely, but it is just a willow-leaf sunflower in miniature.

Helianthus angustifolius, swamp sunflower (zones 6–9), is a tall-growing sunflower with a rather

Helianthus salicifolius. Unpruned, this species reaches approximately 5 ft. in height; pruned, as here, it reaches only 3 ft.

open habit, particularly in shady sites. It benefits from pruning as described above, although Allen Bush, a well-known horticulturist, reports that plants in his North Carolina garden grew to 8–9 ft. even with cutting back by half in mid- to late June. This species might need a heavier hand with the pruners, or less southern hospitality! It requires abundant moisture, as the common name would indicate, and is a heavy feeder and seeder. Deadhead spent flowers or cut down plants before seeds have a chance to mature. Swamp sunflower may be invasive in certain sites. 'First Light' tops out at 4 ft. and is a more reasonable candidate for the average border.

Helianthus 'Lemon Queen' (zones 4–10), a hybrid sunflower, opens its cheery lemon-yellow daisies from August through September. It reaches 5–7 ft. in height but shouldn't need staking unless overfertilized or overwatered. It can be pinched as for *H. salicifolius* to reduce its height; stop pruning by mid-July to give it time to flower. 'Lemon Queen' may seed around a bit, but not obnoxiously, and the offspring will resemble the parent. Divide in spring as for willowleaf sunflower, every few years or whenever flower production slows down.

The magnificent *Helianthus maximiliani*, Maximilian sunflower (zones 4–10), is suitable for only the largest planting areas, not only because of its great height (to 10 ft. when left unpruned), but also because of its ability to spread laterally and crowd out weaker, smaller plants. It can be trimmed as for *H. salicifolius* in June to bring it down to a more reasonable height at flowering time. Untrimmed, it will need heavy-duty staking (like metal fence posts) to keep it upright, although allowing a few stalks to tumble to the ground and mingle with the plants at its feet can create a lovely effect. The blooms are 3–4 in. across and smell like cocoa.

Heliopsis helianthoides '**Summer Sun**'

'Summer Sun' heliopsis
COMPOSITAE

Golden-yellow, daisylike flower heads; green leaves
3–6 ft. high; 4 ft. wide
Full sun or part shade
Blooms June–September
Zones 3–9

PRUNING Young plants bloom all summer long, almost nonstop, with

minimal or no deadheading. With older plants, deadheading greatly increases the length of the bloom period. Deadheading also prevents seeding. Don't be too much of a neatnik, however; leave some heads for the gold finches, who feed on them heavily in August but will frequent the plants as soon as seed is available. Some seeding can create a nice effect in the garden, as plants come fairly true to seed. Since heliopsis can be short-lived, seeding may also be the only guarantee of longevity in the garden.

In certain years the entire plant may need to be cut down after flowering, around mid-September, if it has gotten tatty from sooty mold (remains of heavy aphid populations) or mildew or just wear from a long summer. Otherwise you can leave the plants up for further bird feeding. Selective cutting back of the worst stems or deadleafing of the worst leaves can also help keep the appearance presentable.

Plants respond well to cutting back before flowering to reduce the mature height and delay the bloom period. Three-foot-tall plants cut back by half in early June matured to 3½ ft., compared to the 5-ft. unpruned plants, and they started blooming 1½–2 weeks later and consequently flowered that much longer. Pruning in this way can be used to reduce the height of some individuals and create a nice layering effect for a planting, or to have different plants in different parts of the garden flowering at slightly different times. It provides flowers for arrangements over a longer period as well. Heliopsis probably could be pruned back even more for shorter plants, or pruned slightly later, perhaps in mid- to late June, for an even greater delay.

OTHER MAINTENANCE Fairly low-maintenance perennial once established. First-year plants sometimes struggle to take hold. Prefers moist, organic soil but tolerates short periods of drought. Plants grown in rich conditions may need division every 2–3 years in the spring or fall to increase longevity; otherwise plants can usually go 5 years before division is needed. Red aphids usually attack the plants starting in May. They don't do much harm, unless a plant is badly infected, in which case the unsightly sooty mold that follows can literally cover the plant. Wash heavy aphid populations off with a strong spray of water. Beneficial soldier beetles may help control pest infestations.

Heliopsis helianthoides 'Summer Sun'. Plants in the front were pruned by half in early June. They matured to 3½ ft., rather than the typical 5 ft., and started flowering about 2 weeks later than unpruned plants.

Helleborus ×hybridus

Lenten rose
RANUNCULACEAE

Rose- or cream-speckled flowers; deep green palmate leaves
15–18 in. high; 15 in. wide
Part shade–full shade
Blooms March–April
Zones 4–9

PRUNING Plants are evergreen, but the foliage can get battered by late winter. Prune off dead leaves at this time to make room for new growth and flowering. Some gardeners mow the old foliage off large plantings of Lenten rose for complete renewal. The flower sepals are attractive for a long time, even after their color has faded. Helleborus can reseed heavily, literally by the hundreds under certain conditions. Usually the seedlings are located at the base of the parent plant, and they will flower in about the third spring. This can create a nice effect in a natural setting, but it may not be desirable for every garden. Deadheading before seeds set can reduce the problem. Helleborus can be prone to disease in warm, wet, humid conditions; prune off and destroy affected parts.

OTHER MAINTENANCE Prefers high-organic, moist, well-draining alkaline soil; will tolerate some dry conditions in the summer. Plants are slow to take hold but are long-lived and don't need to be disturbed once established; division is seldom, if ever, needed. If desired, divide in the spring. Plant in the spring to allow plants to establish before winter.

RELATED PLANTS *Helleborus foetidus*, stinking hellebore, is the longest-blooming hellebore, setting yellow-green buds in the autumn and opening in the spring. Foliage stays greener than most over the winter and sometimes takes on attractive purple tinting. When flowering stems decline, cut back to basal foliage for more vigorous new growth. Tolerates short periods of drought. Can be short-lived. Allowing some seeding can ensure permanence in the garden. On the hardiness borderline in zone 5, plants performed beautifully for 4 years and then were lost in a single hard winter.

Helleborus niger, Christmas rose, prefers moister conditions than *H. orientalis* and is more difficult to establish after division. Best to leave undisturbed and avoid cultivation around its roots. Also slower spreading than Lenten rose.

Helleborus ×hybridus

Hemerocallis

daylily
XANTHORRHOEACEAE

Trumpet-shaped flowers in many colors; straplike leaves

1–4 ft. (1–3 ft.) high; 1.5 ft. wide

Full sun–light shade

Blooms June–October

Zones 3–9

PRUNING The Greek term *hemerocallis* means "beautiful for a day," but it could also be understood to mean "not beautiful for more than a day." This being the case, daylilies are a dead-heading nightmare. No matter how you refer to them—wet globs of tissue paper, slimy creatures, mush-mummies, or the like—daylily deadheads are ugly. Many flowers are borne per flower stem. Each flower can be snapped off the stem as it fades using the thumb and forefinger; be sure to get the entire flower and not just the petals, or the ovary will be left behind to develop into an unattractive seed capsule, which also detracts from the fresh flowers. Some purple-flowered forms can stain your hands like grape juice when you're deadhead-ing them. When all flowering is finished on the flowering stem, the entire stem should be cut back to the basal foliage. Deadheading not only keeps the plants looking good but is important for the subsequent bloom in reblooming daylilies. Some daylilies with smaller flowers are self-cleaning and don't require the stringent deadheading that the large flowering forms do.

After all flowering and deadhead-ing is finished, around mid-August, deadleafing begins. This involves grabbing clumps of dead leaves and pulling them out of the plant by hand. Trimming off yellow tips may also be helpful. If foliage decline is severe, and if a hole in the garden is tolerable (which in many cases is better than continually declining foliage), a more practical and time-saving approach may be to simply shear the whole plant down. The new foliage that emerges

Hemerocallis 'Pardon Me'

will be fresh and will hold through frost. The plants can either be sheared to within a few inches of the ground, or they can be cut down to new fresh leaves (6–8 in. above the ground) if the new foliage has already started to develop at the base of the plant. Hedge shears make quick work of shearing. Depending on conditions, a plant sheared to the ground can take anywhere from a couple of weeks to a month for decent regrowth. The new mound of foliage will be shorter than the normal mature size of the plant. Be certain to keep the plants moist after shearing, or regrowth may not occur. Topdressing with compost or an organic fertilizer may help ensure vigorous regrowth. Cutting plants back can also serve as a method of controlling thrips, if the pests pose a problem.

Plants do not respond to pinching or cutting back when in bud in an attempt to delay flowering; if buds are removed, plants simply won't flower

A comparison made late in the season of a daylily sheared to the ground (right) to a daylily left unsheared (left).

that season.

Daylilies can remain attractive into late autumn, and in mild areas some varieties may remain semi-evergreen. In these instances, cutting plants back in the spring is preferable to cutting them down for winter. In most cases, though, the foliage gets pretty tatty over the winter and should be cut back after several killing frosts. Sometimes the foliage can be pulled off by hand.

OTHER MAINTENANCE Despite all the pruning requirements, daylilies are tough, long-lived, cold hardy, and tolerant of neglect. As with most perennials, daylilies prefer a high-organic, well-draining soil, but they are flexible, although they will rot if the soil is too poorly drained. They are fairly drought tolerant. Daylilies are easily divided using the double-fork method, and this can be done at any time, although spring or autumn is best. Normally division is not needed for many years on older species, but the hybrids can get crowded and may require division every 4–5 years—even sooner for repeat bloomers. Part shade is preferable for daylilies with pastel-colored flowers.

Reblooming daylilies require frequent division—about every 2 years to keep them vigorous and blooming strongly—because it is the new rhizomes that produce the new flowers. They are also heavy feeders and should be given both a spring granular and a summer liquid feeding. Deadheading is critical for good rebloom. Deadleafing is more desirable than cutting back after the first bloom, as future flowers might be cut off with the foliage. If the foliage looks poor after the first bloom phase, it is probably a sign that division is needed to rejuvenate the plants.

RELATED PLANTS 'Stella de Oro' (gold) is the most reliable reblooming daylily, followed by 'Happy Returns' (lemon yellow). Other popular daylilies classified as rebloomers by the American Daylily Society include 'Apricot Sparkles' (apricot with a yellow throat), 'Big Time Happy' (lemon yellow), 'Custard Candy' (cream with maroon and green eye), 'Little Business' (cranberry red), 'Mini Pearl' (peach), 'Pardon Me' (cranberry red), 'Purple de Oro' (purple), 'Rosy Returns' (rose pink), 'South Seas' (coral), 'Stella's Ruffled Fingers' (pale pink), 'Strawberry Candy' (strawberry pink), and 'Tuscawilla Tigress' (orange). Most so-called rebloomers rebloom better in the South than they do in the North.

Hesperis matronalis

dame's rocket
BRASSICACEAE

Fragrant white or purple flowers; narrow serrated leaves

2–3 ft. high; 3 ft. wide

Full sun or part shade

Blooms May–June

Zones 3–8

PRUNING Gardeners have a few pruning options with dame's rocket. The plants can be deadheaded before seed set, which may prolong bloom, particularly if there is sufficient moisture; then plants can be cut down to the basal foliage after all flowering is finished, again before seed set, to cause this normally biennial plant to act more perennial in nature. The other option would be to allow seeding, which the plant may do somewhat heavily under certain conditions, to ensure constancy in the garden.

Allowing the plant to go to seed is often more desirable because individual plants are usually short-lived. Cutting down the majority of old flowering stems before seed set but allowing a few to set seed will decrease the number of seedlings and keep the population more under control. If seeding is allowed, the parent plant usually will die.

OTHER MAINTENANCE Prefers moist, high-organic, alkaline soil for best reseeding. Well-draining soil is essential, especially over the winter to ensure survival. Plants usually go dormant over the summer. I like to plant dame's rocket alongside or coming up through rugosa roses (*Rosa rugosa*) for a great combination, and then they will not be missed when pruned down or if they die down. Care should be taken to not plant close to natural areas where it may become invasive.

Hesperis matronalis

Heterotheca villosa

(syn. *Chrysopsis villosa*)

hairy goldaster
COMPOSITAE

Yellow daisylike flower heads; gray-green hairy leaves
3–5 ft. high; 4 ft. wide
Full sun
Blooms August–September
Zones 5–9

PRUNING Plants are full and nicely formed if cut back by half in late spring to early summer (early to mid-June in Ohio) and can be nicely layered by cutting the outer stems slightly lower than the inside stems. If pruned again with the removal of about 6 in. off the tips in early August (when in tight bud), plants respond well by sending out 3 or 4 lateral flowering stems that start blooming about 1 week later than those of unpruned plants and thus bloom 1 week longer into the season. This effect can be achieved on individual plants by shearing a section or only the outside of the plant down by 6 in. If several plants are grown in a group, or in different areas of the garden, flowering can be delayed on some to extend the bloom season of hairy goldaster. Some gardeners experience a blackening of the plants with the coming of a frost, in which case the plants should be cut down at that point. I have had a different experience, however. I don't even deadhead the plants because I find the old flowers, which form pretty daisylike brown dried seedheads, to be a nice feature of the plant, and they hold until spring with no unattractive blackening of the plants. I cut plants down in the spring.

OTHER MAINTENANCE Very drought tolerant. Provide good drainage, particularly in the winter. Give plants plenty of space to accommodate the wide habit. Divide every 4–5 years in the spring if needed.

RELATED PLANTS *Heterotheca villosa* 'Golden Sunshine' is a choice long-lived cultivar. It is clump forming.

Heterotheca villosa

Heuchera micrantha 'Palace Purple'

'Palace Purple' coralbells
SAXIFRAGACEAE

Tiny white flowers on spikes; reddish-purple, ivy-shaped leaves
15–18 in. (12 in.) high; 12–18 in. wide
Full sun–part shade
Blooms June–July
Zones 4–9

PRUNING The flowers of 'Palace Purple' coralbells get mixed reviews from gardeners. Some (and I'm one of them) feel that the flowers detract from the ornamental foliage and so remove the flowers in bud. Others find the flowers ornamental in their own right and let them do their thing. The foliage color will bleach or fade if grown with afternoon sun and the leaves will scorch if allowed to dry out. Shearing off the old top growth in late summer or early autumn reveals colorful foliage below. Plants hold their color into winter to different degrees depending on the conditions

for the year. Do not prune 'Palace Purple' for the winter. Deadleaf or shear off any damaged leaves in early spring to make room for colorful new foliage.

OTHER MAINTENANCE Heuchera usually will frost heave with fluctuating winter temperatures. Plant in the spring, in moist high-organic soil, to allow establishment before winter. Well-draining soil is critical for overwintering success. Coralbells benefit from a winter mulch after the ground freezes. Gently press plants back into the soil in early spring if they heave over the winter. Division generally is needed every 3 years in the spring. Shade plants from afternoon sun in hot climates.

RELATED PLANTS Like the genera *Baptisia* and *Echinacea*, *Heuchera* has been the subject of much breeding work in recent years, and the market has been flooded with exciting new choices. 'Chocolate Ruffles' and 'Plum Pudding' were early purple-leaved selections that whetted gardeners' appetites for more, and countless others soon followed in a wide variety of foliage colors and patterns, as well as some with an outstanding floral display. A 2014 report from a 3-year evaluation of 83 selections of coralbells at the Mt. Cuba Center in Delaware serves as a helpful guide in navigating this staggering array and choosing the ones that will perform well in the garden, at least in the mid-Atlantic region. The top performers as rated by the evaluators, who also rated the highest with visitors, included 'Apple Crisp' (green with silver, showy white flowers), 'Caramel' (amber), 'Citronelle' (chartreuse), 'Color Dream' (silver with dark veining), 'Frosted Violet' (purple with silver, showy pink flowers), 'Southern Comfort' (amber), and 'Spellbound' (silver with purple).

Heuchera sanguinea
coralbells
SAXIFRAGACEAE

Tiny red, pink, or white flowers; heart-shaped or rounded leaves
12–20 in. (8 in.) high; 12 in. wide
Full sun–part shade
Blooms May–July
Zones 3–8

PRUNING Deadhead plants to prolong bloom. Old flowering stems can be trimmed off to the basal foliage using pruners, or they can be snapped off with a sharp thumbnail. Stems can even be simply pulled out of the plant

Heuchera micrantha 'Palace Purple'

Heuchera sanguinea
'Splendens'

when they have declined enough. Plants need deadleafing if they get too dry over the summer. Evergreen foliage usually holds well over the winter; deadleaf or shear off tattered leaves, if needed, in the spring.

OTHER MAINTENANCE Prefers rich, organic, alkaline, moist soil for best performance. Moist soil conditions help to keep plants blooming, though well-draining soil is essential for overwintering. Fluctuating winter temperatures causes frost heaving. Plant coralbells in spring to allow them to establish themselves before winter, and mulch them after the ground freezes to moderate winter soil temperatures. Division often is needed every 3 years in the spring. Plants may get woody at the base, lifting the crowns up; top-dress with organic matter to keep crowns in contact with the soil. Provide afternoon shade in hot regions and avoid drought.

RELATED PLANTS *Heuchera sanguinea* 'Firefly' and 'Splendens' have bright red flowers, while 'Snow Angel' has deep pink flowers over white-splattered green foliage.

Heuchera villosa
hairy alumroot
SAXIFRAGACEAE

Small, creamy white flowers; large, triangularly lobed, hairy green leaves
2 ft. high; 2 ft. wide
Full sun to part shade
Blooms August–September
Zones 4–9

PRUNING This species blooms relatively late in the season, so deadheading isn't needed. Deadleaf or shear off any damaged leaves or old flower stalks in early spring.

OTHER MAINTENANCE Like *Heuchera sanguinea*, *H. villosa* prefers rich, organic, alkaline, moist soil and benefits from winter mulching to prevent frost heaving. It may also require division every 3 years in the spring. This species is considerably

more tolerant of summer heat and humidity than other species and hybrids of *Heuchera*—a boon to southern gardeners.

RELATED PLANTS 'Caramel' is a stunning, sturdy hybrid of *Heuchera villosa* with apricot new growth that matures to amber-orange. The flowers are negligible. Slightly more compact than *H. villosa*, with a height and spread of 12–18 in. Pruning and maintenance—as well as heat tolerance—similar to *H. villosa*.

×*Huecherella* 'Sweet Tea' was bred using *Heuchera villosa* as one of its parents; it likes more moisture than straight *H. villosa*, however. 'Sweet Tea' is a favorite for its large, bronzy orange leaves with maroon veins.

enjoy resting in them at this time and may give the deadheader a stinging surprise. Seedheads are attractive and it may be desirable to leave them on the plant later in the season to extend the interest of the plant through the winter. Stems need to be cut down in the spring for new growth. Seeding may be a problem under wet conditions; deadhead regularly during the season and cut stems down for the winter if this is the case. Deadleafing is needed during the summer if plants dry out.

Plants respond favorably to pruning before flowering in an effort to reduce height and create fuller plants. Some gardeners also do this in an attempt to avoid some early Japanese beetle

Hibiscus moscheutos
'Lord Baltimore'

Hibiscus moscheutos
rose mallow
MALVACEAE

Large red, white, pink, or bicolored flowers; triangular leaves

3–8 ft. high; 5 ft. wide

Full sun or part shade

Blooms July to frost

Zones 4–9

PRUNING Flowering is similar to that of daylilies in that individual flowers last only 1 day and then eventually turn to mush and stick together. Deadheading before this stage keeps the plant's appearance up and may prolong bloom. Take care if deadheading in the evening when the flowers have just folded down as bees seem to

damage, which can be so prominent on hibiscus. Plants that normally flower at 4 ft. bloomed at 2½ ft. when cut back by half in early June when 16 in. tall. Flowering is usually delayed by about 1–2 weeks, depending on the conditions.

OTHER MAINTENANCE Prefers rich moist soil. Good for wet sites. Although plants can grow tall, stems are strong and so staking is normally not needed. Plants are late to emerge in the spring; do not disturb area. Plants do not need division for many (10 or more) years. Division of woody crown is challenging and is best avoided. Heavy feeders; fertilize annually in the spring. Japanese beetles love hibiscus.

RELATED PLANTS *Hibiscus moscheutos* 'Lord Baltimore' and 'Lady Baltimore' grow 4–5 ft.; the Splash Series is compact, growing 30–36 in., and the Sundae Series has purple foliage. The Cordial Series of hardy hibiscus will reach 42 in.

Hosta
hosta
ASPARAGACEAE

Spikes of lavender or white flowers; green, blue, yellow, or variegated leaves
2 in.–4 ft. high; 6 in.–6 ft. wide
Part shade–full shade
Blooms June–August
Zones 3–8

PRUNING Deadheading hostas can often improve their appearance. Most hostas are not reblooming. Some set seed, which can supply food for birds, namely juncos and chickadees, over the winter. Most forms of *Hosta sieboldiana*, *H. sieboldii*, and *H. ventricosa* usually form seed and are good choices for the bird-watching gardener. Of course, seeds can also mean reseeding. Reseeding may occur some years and not others, depending on the conditions. Plantlets are usually green and may or may not resemble the parent. They are easily pulled out, so they are not normally a nuisance. *Hosta ventricosa* will produce true progeny.

Disbudding, or removing all the flower buds when they appear on a plant in an attempt to delay flowering, will not consistently result in the plant forming new flower buds later. In most cases disbudding will prevent flowering altogether, or only sporadic later bloom will form. Pruning flower buds can serve the purpose, though, of creating fuller plants, by directing the plant's energy toward vegetative rather than floral growth. This may be desirable for hostas whose flowers are not very ornamental and which take away from the appearance of the foliage.

Certain forms of hosta are susceptible to damage from late spring frosts. If damaged leaves are pruned off and the plants kept moist, they usually will send up new fresh growth without missing a beat. It would be advisable, though, to cover small plants, particularly expensive or unusual ones, if a late frost is predicted, because they may have a hard time recovering from the damage. Deadleafing may be

necessary in late summer, particularly if plants have gotten dry.

Leaving foliage on hostas over the winter can provide additional protection against cold temperatures. It can also provide cozy hangouts for slugs; the choice is up to the gardener. Hosta grower Van Wade, of Wade and Gatton Nurseries in Ohio, who has a "kajillion" hosta plants (what hosta grower doesn't!), cuts some of his plants down in the autumn and the rest in the spring to spread out the workload. Remember to leave seed-bearing hostas for bird feeding, if desired.

OTHER MAINTENANCE Best performance for hostas is in moist, high-organic, well-draining soil, but these are adaptable plants. Hostas with a thick, waxy substance to their leaves are often more tolerant of dry soils, but prolonged drought can mean the demise of most forms. Young plants should be mulched for the winter to prevent frost heaving. Van Wade recommends fresh white pine needles, which allow for good air circulation. Avoid mulching with heavy materials, as they can lead to crown rot if not removed promptly in the spring.

Hostas generally prefer high-filtered shade with perhaps a quarter to half of the day in morning sun. Hot afternoon sun, particularly in areas with hot summers, will scorch most hostas and should be avoided. Blues prefer bright filtered shade, such as that provided by high overhead trees, for best coloring, but they tolerate heavier shade as well. Green forms such as the fragrant *Hosta plantaginea*, as well as other types grown for their flowers like 'Allan P. McConnell', 'Fragrant Blue', 'Guacamole', 'So Sweet', and *H. ventricosa* benefit from morning sun for best flower production. Avoid very deep, dark shaded areas.

Division can be easily accomplished at almost any time of the year by the double-fork method or even by just cutting a pie-shaped section out of the plant. Keep plants moist and shaded, and prune off at least a third of the foliage if dividing during the warmer months or plants may flop. Springtime, when the new leaves are still curled, is the preferable and most successful time for division. Division is often not needed for many years—never in some cases.

Slugs and hostas go hand-in-hand. It's risky to claim that certain forms are more resistant than others, because some slug will be waiting to prove you wrong. But here goes: hostas with heavier or thicker foliage are usually not as badly damaged, if at all. This may include 'Abiqua Drinking Gourd', 'Big Daddy', 'Blue Angel', 'Blue Mouse Ears', 'Halcyon', 'June', 'Loyalist', *Hosta sieboldiana*, and 'Sum and Substance'. Also, forms in which the leaves don't come in contact with the soil, such as the vase-shaped 'Krossa Regal', 'Liberty', 'Praying Hands', and 'Sagae', are usually less prone to slugs. Diatomaceous earth is a form of slug control.

Hosta 'Sum and Substance'

Hypericum calycinum
St. John's wort
HYPERICACEAE

Large yellow flowers; evergreen leaves
15–18 in. high; 24 in. wide
Full sun or part shade
Blooms June–August
Zones 5–9

PRUNING Plants are evergreen to semi-evergreen, depending on the climate, although leaves are often battered by winter weather. Plants

Hypericum calycinum

have a tendency to become straggly and twiggy if neglected. They benefit from a shearing down to 6–10 in. every year or two in the early spring to remove winter damage, improve density, and keep vigorous. Removing any crowded, weak, or dead branches at this time is also beneficial.

OTHER MAINTENANCE A stoloniferous groundcover for dry, sunny, or partly shaded locations. Flowering is reduced if the shade is too great. Plants can be invasive and may require sections to be dug out to maintain control every 2–3 years in the spring or autumn. Good for bank stabilization. Benefits from part shade and moister conditions in southern gardens.

Iberis sempervirens
evergreen candytuft
BRASSICACEAE

White tufts of flowers cover entire plant; narrow evergreen leaves
6–12 in. high; 24 in. wide
Full sun
Blooms April–May
Zones 3–9

PRUNING Yearly, plants should be cut back by half after flowering to keep them full and compact. This can be easily accomplished with hedge shears or by grabbing a handful of stems at a time and cutting with hand pruners. Such pruning takes care of deadheading at the same time. Plants quickly fill in to form an evergreen mound that holds through the growing season and the winter. Some damage may occur in severe winters. Prune off damaged sections in the spring, if necessary.

OTHER MAINTENANCE
Well-draining soil is essential to survival, particularly over the winter. A good rock garden perennial. Avoid areas with high winds and strong afternoon sun in the winter if consistent snow cover is not reliable, as plants will quickly desiccate. Mulching with evergreen boughs can help alleviate the damage in such locations. Division is seldom necessary, as plants form a subshrub growth habit. Stems

Iberis sempervirens

may root as they come in contact with the soil; these can be separated from the parent plant and transplanted.

Inula ensifolia
swordleaf inula
COMPOSITAE

Yellow daisylike flowers with skinny ray petals; stiff, narrow green leaves
1–2 ft. high; 1–2 ft. wide
Full sun
Blooms June–July
Zones 3–7

PRUNING Swordleaf inula flowers for about 6 weeks in June and July, often reblooming sporadically into August and September. Shear by half after the first wave of flowers has faded to encourage stronger rebloom. Shearing is also an effective way to thicken plants that have begun to open up in the middle. Cut plants to the ground in late fall.

OTHER MAINTENANCE Given full sun and average, well-drained garden soil, this species is easy to grow. It shows considerable drought tolerance once established, but tends to contract powdery mildew in overly dry soils, so give it a drink during droughty periods. *Inula ensifolia* is happiest in cool-summer climates and melts out in the Deep South after a few years. Wherever it's grown, division in spring every 2 or 3 years is advisable to help keep plants robust.

RELATED PLANTS *Inula ensifolia* 'Compacta' makes a tight bun of foliage and flowers. It tops out at 8–12 in.

Inula ensifolia

Inula helenium

elecampane
COMPOSITAE

Shaggy yellow flowers on tall stalks; huge
oblong basal leaves
3–7 ft. high; 3 ft. wide
Full sun–part shade
Blooms June–July
Zones 3–7

PRUNING This big, bold perennial is
the star of the border during its main
bloom time in June and July, but after
flowering its foliage often yellows and
turns brown and crispy on the
margins. Deadleafing may give the
plant some semblance of dignity to
carry it through the rest of the season.
Deadheading may also be employed to
help preserve foliage quality by not
allowing precious energy to go to seed
production, and it may extend the
bloom period as well. Cut plants down
in fall—or earlier, if their raggedness
is too much of a distraction. Those
who appreciate a natural, free-spirited
look in the garden, however, may well
enjoy the presence of the tall, dark
stems and seedheads over the winter.

OTHER MAINTENANCE Elecampane
is a rugged plant that survives with
little care, but it needs plenty of
moisture and a deep, rich soil to really
thrive. Irrigate well and top-dress with
a shovelful or two of compost after
deadheading to help the plant
maintain healthy looking foliage. In
some years it may be easier to front the
plants with bushy annuals to hide the
declining foliage. Areas graced with
cool summers produce the best
specimens. *Inula helenium* flowers
most prolifically in full sun but will
accept part shade. In exposed sites
sturdy stakes may be called for, as the
tall stems can lodge in strong winds.
Divide plants in spring or fall if
performance declines or if more plants
are desired.

RELATED PLANTS *Inula magnifica*
'Sonnenstrahl' is a scene-stealer that
has striking jumbo-sized flowers with
long, drooping ray petals. Plants can
reach 8 ft. tall.

Inula helenium

Iris domestica

(syn. *Belamcanda chinensis*)

blackberry lily
IRIDACEAE

Orange star-shaped flowers; irislike leaves
3–4 ft. high; 2 ft. wide
Full sun
Blooms July–August
Zones 5–10

PRUNING Old flowers literally roll up, and the seeds turn into attractive black berries. Plants will reseed, sometimes heavily under the right conditions, but allowing some seeding is recommended to ensure the presence of this often short-lived perennial in the garden. Removing some of the fruit before the seeds drop can reduce overseeding, although seedlings are easily removed. If fruit is to be used for dried arrangements, cut before frost, as frost causes them to shrivel. The black berries add winter interest to the garden if allowed to remain. Remove any dead leaves and clean up debris at the base of the plant through the summer and for the winter, especially where borers are a problem, to reduce infestation. Do not compost.

OTHER MAINTENANCE Successful overwintering depends largely on well-draining soil. Plants are short-lived, particularly where summers are cool and moist. Tolerates colder winter temperatures in areas with long, hot summers. Mulch in regions colder than zone 5, and avoid autumn planting to prevent frost heaving. Divide carefully in the spring or late summer, although it is easier to allow seedlings to replace the parent plant after a year or two. Plant may require staking in rich soils.

RELATED PLANTS *Iris domestica* 'Freckle Face' is self-supporting and pest and disease free. 'Hello Yellow' is a shorter yellow form. It grows to 12–15 in. and requires no staking. Has proved to be reliably hardy in the central Ohio area.

Iris domestica
'Hello Yellow'

Iris ×germanica

bearded iris
IRIDACEAE

Bearded flowers in a variety of colors; swordlike flat leaves
2–4 ft. high; 1–2 ft. wide
Full sun
Blooms May–June
Zones 3–10

PRUNING Deadhead individual dead flowers, not the entire stalk, because new flower buds will open lower on the flower stalk. Old flowers turn to mush and require regular removal to keep plants attractive. When all flowering is finished, cut the flower stalk off down to the foliage. Leaves are often marred with different foliar diseases after flowering in late June, especially in the humid eastern states. If plants aren't too badly affected, try selectively pulling off and trimming the worst leaves. If badly affected,

Iris ×*germanica*

the beauty of neighboring perennials. Pruning tools should be disinfected before moving on to other perennials. Dump disease-infected foliage in a pile by itself where it can break down—do not compost. Regrowth, if any, can be slow, taking several weeks. The new foliage may be partly infested with disease again by late summer in humid climates. Cut down all foliage in autumn after killing frosts and clean up and remove all debris at the base of the plants. Borers can overwinter in old leaves and debris. Again, do not compost clippings.

OTHER MAINTENANCE Watch for foliar diseases, borers, and soft rot. Plant rhizomes high so that they're exposed to the sun in order to reduce the incidence of soft rot. Well-draining soil is also necessary to reduce rot. Rhizomes affected with soft rot should be dug out and discarded. Dark streaking in leaves is evidence of borers; prune off leaves and dig out affected rhizome. Frequent division is needed to keep plants vigorous. Divide after flowering until August, leaving 1 fan per rhizome. Although most gardeners cut the foliage back when transplanting, some leave it on. The feeling is that the foliage aids in the establishment process, and in flowering for the following season, by providing more food to the rhizome. Forms taller than 30–36 in. usually require staking. Bearded irises have excellent drought tolerance.

RELATED PLANTS There are reblooming bearded irises that can repeat bloom anytime from late July until October or November. It's fun to see bearded irises with asters, mums, and pumpkins. Be certain to cut all old flowering stalks to the ground after the initial bloom period for a chance at rebloom. In my experience, the foliage does not decline as quickly or as drastically on the reblooming beardeds as compared to other forms. Plants usually don't start to decline until early to mid-August. I simply pull off the poor foliage and trim the tips a bit, not cutting back heavily. Fresh new

shear all foliage back to about 4–6 in. above the ground. Pull off any brown leaves that have shriveled and died down at the base of the plant. Sheared plants look as though they've had a crew cut. Individual leaves can be cut with hand pruners at different angles to create a slightly more natural look. This method is preferred by some gardeners, but it is more time consuming, and personally I feel that the plants are unattractive under either pruning regimen. Nevertheless, the pruned foliage is preferable to the ugly unpruned foliage taking away from

fans are usually evident under the old ones, and these are the sites of late summer to autumn flower production. Divide plants frequently to keep them strong. Some reblooming forms include 'Baby Blessed' (dwarf yellow), 'Best Bet' (2-tone blue), 'Champagne Elegance' (white/apricot), 'Feedback' (blue-violet), 'Harvest of Memories' (yellow), 'Immortality' (white), 'Ozark Rebounder' (black-purple), 'Sugar Blues' (medium-blue), and my favorite, 'Perfume Counter'(purple), a fragrant, tall cultivar whose foliage holds up much longer than that of other forms. These are all heavy feeders and will benefit from an application of a balanced organic fertilizer once in the fall.

Iris sibirica

Siberian iris
IRIDACEAE

White, blue, or purple beardless flowers; straplike leaves
2–4 ft. high; 2 ft. wide
Full sun–part shade
Blooms May–June
Zones 3–9

PRUNING Deadheading doesn't prolong bloom of this beautiful plant, and the smaller deadheads don't distract from the plant like those of the large-flowering bearded iris. The season is extended with the magnificent seed capsules that develop. These hold through the winter and can be cut in the spring and used for dried arrangements. I remove about two-thirds of the old flowering stalks and leave the rest of the deadheads to enjoy. I have found that the plants experience reduced flowering and vigor the following season if all the seedheads are allowed to mature. Reseeding can occur if some pods are allowed to remain. Seedlings are easily removed, and friends love them. Siberian iris develops a nice golden autumn color as well, and the color holds into early winter. Wait until spring to cut the entire plant down.
OTHER MAINTENANCE Siberian

irises are good, low-maintenance, multiseason plants. These sturdy irises usually are resistant to the borers and diseases that may trouble bearded iris. They are adaptable to a variety of soils and will tolerate part shade but will flop if grown in too much shade. The fleshy-rooted plants seldom need dividing and in fact resent it, taking a year or longer to fully recover. Division can be performed in the spring if sufficient moisture is provided, although autumn is often the best time to divide them.

Iris sibirica
'Caesar's Brother'

RELATED PLANTS *Iris sibirica* 'Baby Sister' is a violet-blue dwarf form reaching 16 in. Good standard-sized Siberian irises include 'Butter and Sugar' (yellow and white), 'Caesar's Brother' (deep violet-blue), 'Super Ego' (light blue), and 'White Swirl' (white).

Iris Louisiana hybrids (zones 4–9) are composed of 5 iris species native to the Gulf Coast. These hybrids come in a rainbow of colors and are easy to grow, provided ample water can be supplied and the soil is on the acid side. They prefer full sun, though afternoon shade is a good idea in hot climates. Louisiana irises can be grown in up to 6 in. of standing water as well as in ordinary garden beds that are regularly irrigated and deeply mulched. The plants may go dormant in summer after blooming in late spring or early summer, in which case any yellowed foliage may be pruned away. They are heavy feeders and benefit from an application of a balanced organic fertilizer once in the fall and again in early spring; they make their fastest growth in fall and winter, weather permitting. Division may be necessary every 3 or 4 years and is best done in August or September. Deadheading will not cause additional flowers to form, but preventing plants from setting seed will redirect energy into stronger growth. They top out at 3–4 ft. in height. Some of the more popular selections include 'Ann Chowning' (red), 'Black Gamecock' (black-purple), 'Brushfire Moon' (yellow), and 'Geisha Eyes' (blue-lavender). Iris borers and slugs may be troublesome.

Iris spuria, butterfly iris (zones 4–8), is a good one for dry-summer climates. It goes dormant in summer and wants no water then, though it likes regular moisture during the rest of the year, sweet soil, regular feeding, full sun, and a topping of mulch. It can grow anywhere from 3 to 5 ft. tall and blooms in late spring or early summer. The sturdy stems do not need staking. Deadhead to direct energy into root growth rather than seeds. Space new

Kirengeshoma palmata

plants at least 3 ft. apart and do not disturb clumps; division isn't necessary for 10 years or more but can be accomplished in August or September if desired. Watch for borers and slugs.

Kirengeshoma palmata
yellow wax bells
HYDRANGEACEAE

Pale yellow, bell-shaped flowers; sycamore-like, light to medium green leaves that turn gold in fall

3–4 ft. high; 2–3 ft. wide

Part shade–full shade

Blooms August–September

Zones 5–8

PRUNING No pruning is needed during the growing season. In fact, you might want to leave your pruners in the shed until spring for this plant, because the curious 3-horned seed capsules contribute winter interest to the garden.

OTHER MAINTENANCE *Kirengeshoma palmata* is a bushy, shade-loving Japanese and Korean native grown for its magnificent bold foliage and its drooping sprays of delicate yellow late-season flowers. Pamper this exquisite perennial with a choice woodsy site. It relishes a well-drained, moderately acidic soil that's enriched with a generous helping of leaf mold or compost. Provide at least afternoon shade. Bait for slugs and snails in spring if they are a problem in your area and protect plants from deer. Staking shouldn't be necessary. Yellow wax bells is a slow but steady grower that seldom needs division, but if you'd like to split established clumps, early spring is the time to do it; use the double-fork method if you're unable to pry pieces apart with your hands. Sometimes this species fails to open its flowers all the way. This is no cause for alarm, and even in perpetual bud the blossoms are lovely.

RELATED PLANTS *Kirengeshoma koreana*, Korean wax bells, is very similar to *K. palmata*, but its blossoms are carried on erect flowering stems and are less droopy than those of *K. palmata*.

Knautia macedonica
crimson scabious
CAPRIFOLIACEAE

Deep crimson to pale pink pincushion flowers on wiry stems; lobed foliage, mostly basal
Blooms June–October
1½–3 ft. high; 2 ft. wide
Full sun
Zones 5–9

PRUNING This old-fashioned cottage garden flower is valued for its unusual deep wine-red coloration and its exceptionally long bloom time. Crimson scabious typically flowers for 5 months of the year; in mild climates it may offer 6 or 7 months of color. Deadheading stimulates maximum flower power, but pruning spent blossoms is tricky, because the wiry stems—which often become entangled with each other—carry a mix of buds, blooms, and seedheads. A quick fix is to cut all stems down to basal

Knautia macedonica

growth when the first flush of blooms winds down (usually in July), although doing so eliminates all flowers until the plant can recover and deprives songbirds of a favored seed source. A better method is to prune more frequently but less drastically, cutting only those stems whose flowers have mostly expired and leaving behind some blossoms and birdseed. When flower production finally shuts down for the year, plants may be left standing for migrating and winter resident birds to continue to pick at, or they may be cut back for a neater winter appearance. If you choose the tidier option, don't cut plants clear to the ground, as cutting into the basal foliage may compromise winter hardiness. Instead, leave a low mound of basal leaves and do any final tidying in spring. Basal leaves are semi-evergreen where winters are mild.

OTHER MAINTENANCE Crimson scabious is ideally suited to sunny sites in well-drained soils of average fertility. It doesn't fare well in hot, humid climates. Normally short-lived wherever it's grown, it keeps a foothold in the garden by self-sowing.

It's not a rampant seeder, however, and surplus plants are easily relocated to another part of the garden or to the compost pile. Knautia is a drought-tolerant plant but does appreciate a good drink during extended dry periods. When irrigating, use soaker hoses if possible, as overhead watering invites powdery mildew. Tall forms have a tendency to flop, which can be alleviated by selective pruning to lighten the load. Better yet, address the flopping problem ahead of time by surrounding plants with pea sticks early in the year or by giving them sturdy plant neighbors to lean on when they get a little top heavy.

RELATED PLANTS *Knautia macedon-ica* 'Mars Midget' maxes out at 12–16 in. and doesn't need staking. *Knautia macedonica* Melton pastels is a seed strain that produces crimson, mauve, lavender, and light pink flowers. Melton pastels is taller than most, reaching 3–4 ft. 'Thunder and Lightning' is a compact variety at 12–15 in. with white-edged leaves. It produces no viable seed.

Kniphofia 'Primrose Beauty'

Kniphofia hybrids
red-hot poker
XANTHORRHOEACEAE

Orange, red, or cream spikes; grasslike foliage
2–4 ft. (1¼–1½ ft.) high; 3 ft. wide
Full sun
Blooms summer (specific time depends on the cultivar)
Zones 5–9

PRUNING Diligent deadheading may prolong bloom. If earlier blooming forms are deadheaded, sporadic rebloom may occur later in the season (some reblooming cultivars are listed below). The old flower spike is unattractive anyway and should be removed by cutting it to the ground. The foliage may decline after flowering; if necessary, cut back by half to improve the appearance. Do not cut foliage back for the winter. Bundling up the leaves and tying them together over the center of the clump for the winter may help insulate the plant and prevent excess moisture accumulation in the crown, thus possibly improving survivability. Cut back in the spring when all threat of cold weather has passed, to about 3 in. from the ground, avoiding pruning too close to the crown.

OTHER MAINTENANCE Plants are tender and short-lived due to lack of cold hardiness and death from wet overwintering conditions. Provide good drainage. Mulch around plants for the winter with a fine material such as pine needles to help moderate soil temperatures. Plant and divide in the spring for establishment before winter.

RELATED PLANTS Some noted rebloomers include *Kniphofia* 'Alcazar', 'Earliest of All', 'Kingstone Flame', 'Primrose Beauty', and the Popsicle Series (compact, 14 in.); 'Pineapple Popsicle' is one of my favorites. 'Alcazar', 'Earliest of All', and 'Royal Standard' are reputed to be the hardiest cultivars.

Lamium maculatum

dead nettle
LAMIACEAE

Hooded pink flowers; green foliage with
gray-green spot on midrib

8–12 in. high; 18–24 in. wide

Full shade–part shade

Blooms April–June

Zones 3–8

PRUNING In midsummer (early July in
the Midwest) plants usually get tatty,
especially if grown in dry conditions.
Cut or shear all foliage and flowering
stems back to fresh basal leaves, which
accomplishes deadheading in addition
to refreshing the overall appearance.
The new growth that develops remains
attractive through the winter. Plants
may not even require additional
pruning in the spring, as winter
damage usually is minimal. In cooler
northern climates plants may remain
compact without summer cutting
back. Lamium will reseed if the
deadheads are not removed, and
cultivars may not grow true to type.

OTHER MAINTENANCE Vigorous
grower, but not invasive, by spreading
roots. Good groundcover for dry shade
once established. Prefers moist,
well-draining conditions. Divide if
needed in spring or autumn.

RELATED PLANTS Cultivars are
preferred over the species; prune as
above.

Lamium maculatum 'Beacon Silver'
has silver leaves with green margins
and lavender flowers. 'Shell Pink' is
light pink and is one of the longest
blooming cultivars. 'White Nancy' has
outstanding near-white foliage and
white flowers. 'Pink Pewter' has small
silver leaves with a green edge, and
salmon-colored blooms. 'Anne
Greenaway' has marbled leaves of
green, silver, and chartreuse.

Lamium galeobdolon 'Variegatum',
variegated yellow archangel, should be
sheared back to about 4–6 in. if plants
get leggy, or cut all the way down to
new leaves at the base of the plant if
present. More aggressive than *Lamium
maculatum* forms. Should not be used
in the perennial border but as a
groundcover in dry shade.

Lamium galeobdolon 'Hermann's
Pride' is more clump forming and less
aggressive than 'Variegatum'.

Lamium maculatum
'Pink Pewter'

Lavandula angustifolia

English lavender
LAMIACEAE

Purple flower spikes; narrow, fragrant silvery leaves
12–24 in. high; 24 in. wide
Full sun
Blooms June–July
Zones 5–9

PRUNING Lavender can be dead-headed after the first bloom period for a smaller second bloom later in the summer. Individual old flowering stems can be removed one-by-one or a handful at a time with pruners. Hedge shears work best though, and the plant can be shaped a bit at the same time. The old stems from the second bloom phase can be left on and then removed with spring pruning, or if neatness is the priority they can be cut off after flowering. The species may reseed under certain conditions. Avoid heavy pruning after late August so that plants are able to harden before winter. Do not prune plants for the winter. Winter-damaged tips need to be sheared off annually. Wait to prune until new growth has broken from the old stems in the spring, sometimes as late as early June. Plants can be shaped at this time as well. Because lavender breaks from the old stems it is really more a subshrub than herbaceous perennial. Many beginning gardeners lose their lavender plants by cutting them completely down in the autumn or early spring as they do to their herbaceous perennials.

Lavender has a tendency to grow straggly with age. Shear plants back heavily every 2–3 years in the spring to about 6–8 in. Do not cut low into old, nonviable wood. Neglected plants may develop thick woody stems with small bunches of foliage at the tips. Plants left unpruned for many years usually cannot be restored to their former appearance. Lavender responds so well to shearing that it is often used as a low hedge. In such situations, shear and shape plants annually in the spring. *Lavandula angustifolia* 'Lodden Blue' is a smaller, more compact shrub.

OTHER MAINTENANCE Plants require well-draining soil, especially to ensure survival over the winter. Losses can occur in severe winters without consistent snow cover. Heavy soils can exaggerate the problem by encouraging soft growth, which is more sensitive to winter injury. Alkaline conditions are preferable. Able to withstand dry conditions for extended periods once established. Susceptible to fourlined plant bug damage.

RELATED PLANTS According to lavender researcher Debra Knapke, *Lavandula angustifolia* cultivars 'Hidcote' and 'Munstead' are the hardiest choices for the Midwest and similar climates. Lavandins (*Lavandula ×intermedia*) are popular, though they seem to be more sensitive to "wet feet" than *L. angustifolia*. Highly fragrant 'Phenomenal' lavandin does well in warmer, drier winters.

Lavandula angustifolia
'Loddon Blue'

Leucanthemum ×superbum

Shasta daisy
COMPOSITAE

White daisy flowers; narrow, toothed leaves
2–4 ft. high; 2–3 ft. wide
Full sun
Blooms June–July
Zones 5–9

PRUNING Deadheading can prolong bloom to amazing lengths, particularly on first-year plants, which often will flower from June until frost. Deadhead to lateral flower buds, and after all flowering from lateral buds is finished and new basal growth is developing, cut plants down to basal growth. Sporadic rebloom may occur, though the flowers are usually smaller in size and number. The deep green basal growth looks great in the autumn garden and holds up well through the winter. Shasta daisies are often short-lived. According to some authorities, one reason for the short life span may be that they flower themselves to exhaustion. By cutting the plants down (as described above) in early September or before, vegetative growth is stimulated, and plants can form buds for next year's shoots, possibly extending their lives. Taller forms can be pinched or cut back to produce shorter, more compact plants that don't require staking and flower slightly later. This pruning can also be used to layer a planting (or an individual plant), effectively hiding the bare stems of taller unpruned daisies.

OTHER MAINTENANCE Shasta daisies need rich, moist but well-draining soil and frequent division (every 2–3 years) to maintain vigor. Division may be done with the double-fork method. Good winter drainage is essential for survival. Avoid prolonged drought. These heavy feeders benefit from a light spring fertilizer and possibly a liquid feed again in early summer. Good air circulation is helpful. Taller forms require staking—don't let them fool

Leucanthemum ×superbum 'Becky'

you. Sometimes they look like they're doing well, nice and upright, and then a good summer storm comes along and knocks them over on their sides; staking at this point is too late. I know, I've been fooled. Plants are often short-lived and aren't reliably hardy in zone 5. Don't plant Shasta daisies in the autumn.

RELATED PLANTS *Leucanthemum ×superbum* 'Banana Cream' has pale yellow blooms on 18-in. stems. The flowers fade to white as they age. 'Becky' has an outstanding thick substance to its leaves and stems. It is a 3-ft.-tall, self-supporting form. It flowers later, normally from July to October with deadheading. Good heat tolerance makes this a good candidate for the South. 'Crazy Daisy' is a seed strain that has double flowers on 30-in. stems and blooms for a long time. 'Snowcap', a charming dwarf form (12 in.), is a flowering machine. Cutting it down in September and annual division may help to keep it strong. An even better 'Snowcap' may be the new 'Woops-a-Daisy', which gives a dense mound covered in 3- to 4-in. flowers into midsummer or longer. 'T. E. Killen' has thick, sturdy stems at 24–30 in. and stands up well.

Liatris spicata

spike gayfeather
COMPOSITAE

Spikes of violet, purple, or white flowers;
linear leaves

2–4 ft. (6–10 in.) high; 1–2 ft. wide

Full sun

Blooms July–August

Zones 3–9

PRUNING Deadheading often induces
rebloom into August and September.
The flowers open from the top of the
spike to the bottom. Deadhead plants
by cutting the entire spike down to the
basal foliage when about 70 percent of
the flowering is finished. Deadheading
by cutting the spike midway may
produce several smaller (6-in.) spikes,
which can be useful for small flower
arrangements. I find the seedheads,
which turn fluffy and brown on
red-tinted stems, to be interesting in
the autumn and winter, and so I
usually elect to leave them up on
shorter growing cultivars. They are
also attractive to birds. Occasional
seeding may occur.

Further testing should be done to
determine the effects of cutting plants
back before flowering for height
reduction; results have been inconsistent to date. Branching of the flowering spike can occur, resulting in
anywhere from 2 to 10 shorter
branches from 1 cut stem; in other
cases there was no branching and
failure to flower. It appears that the
taller the plant is when cut back, the
more branches that break, possibly
due to the greater number of breaking
points on a taller stem. Plants cut back
by half when 12 in. tall formed 2
branches; those cut back when 2½ ft.
tall formed up to 10 branches. It is
believed that the vigor of the plant
may have a significant impact on the
results of such pruning, with young
strong plants responding more
favorably.

OTHER MAINTENANCE
Well-draining soil, particularly over
the winter, is critical to survival. Spike
gayfeather is tolerant of drought,
though it is native to moist meadows.
Plants may need division after 4–5
years. Flower spikes usually require
staking.

RELATED PLANTS *Liatris spicata*
'Kobold' is an outstanding, more
compact form (2–2½ ft.) that doesn't
require staking. Plants cut back by half
in early June when 15 in. tall failed to
flower.

Liatris punctata, dotted blazing star
(zones 3–9), is a smart choice for xeric
landscapes, as it's native to the arid
Midwest and Rocky Mountain states.
Sharp drainage is crucial to survival,
especially over the winter. Plants grow
from 1 to 2 ft. tall and need no staking
when they send up their violet bloom
spikes in July through September.
When well sited, dotted blazing star is
a long-lived perennial that never
needs division.

Liatris spicata 'Kobold'

Ligularia dentata

bigleaf ligularia
COMPOSITAE

Yellow-orange daisylike flower heads; large,
rounded leathery leaves
3–4 ft. (3 ft.) high; 4 ft. wide
Full shade–part shade
Blooms July–September
Zones 4–8

PRUNING Deadheading doesn't seem
to do much to prolong the bloom of
this perennial, but some gardeners may
elect to remove the spent flowers so
they don't detract from the attractive
foliage. Ligularia often is grown solely
for the lovely tropical feel provided by
the foliage. Prune off flower buds if
desired. I like the brown heads that
develop, and they usually come late in
the season when brown is a more
accepted part of the perennial garden.
They also hold well for the better part
of the winter and are attractive to the
goldfinches. The foliage often turns to
mush, so I normally cut it off before
winter. Deadleafing is necessary if
plants dry out.

OTHER MAINTENANCE Moist to wet
conditions are necessary to keep the
leaves from wilting in midday heat.
Even in wet conditions, high summer
temperatures can cause wilting. One
of the few perennials that should be
bagged to keep moisture around the
roots. After digging the hole for the
plant, line it with a plastic garbage bag,
poke a couple of holes in the bottom of
the bag, backfill with high-organic soil,
and plant. This procedure improves
the success rate with ligularia even
with short periods of dry conditions.
Plants seldom require division; if
desired, perform in the spring. Favored
by slugs.

RELATED PLANTS *Ligularia dentata*
'Britt Marie Crawford' is an amazing
dark chocolate–maroon selection with
rounded leaves and violet undersides.
It is the only cultivar I'll use in my
designs.

Ligularia stenocephala 'The Rocket'
offers deadheads that are attractive to
birds, but in some cases deadheads left
on the plant may cause decline of the
old foliage. If deadheads are removed,
new purple-tinted leaves emerge and
the old foliage holds nicely for the
remainder of the season.

Ligularia dentata
'Britt Marie Crawford'

Limonium platyphyllum

sea lavender
PLUMBAGINACEAE

Clouds of tiny violet flowers above narrow, leathery basal leaves

24–30 in. (8 in.) high; 30 in. wide

Full sun

Blooms July–August

Zones 3–9

PRUNING Deadheading can prolong bloom, but plants have a long season of interest whether deadheaded or not. The highly branched flowering stems are just as attractive after the tiny flowers fall, and they are good for dried arrangements or, better still, left as a dried arrangement on the plant in the garden. They hold well into early winter but often snap off in heavy storms in late winter. The foliage is evergreen to semi-evergreen. Do not prune for the winter. Plants can be cleaned up in the spring, or new growth normally will fill in quickly to hide any old, damaged foliage.

OTHER MAINTENANCE
Well-draining soil is essential to survival. Tolerant of drought and salt. Staking is usually not necessary except in heavy or overly rich soils. Resents division; allow clumps to remain undisturbed. Space plants at least 24 in. apart to allow for good air circulation and reduce the chance of crown and root rot.

Limonium platyphyllum

Linaria purpurea
purple toadflax
PLANTAGINACEAE

Purple or pink snapdragonlike flowers; narrow blue-green leaves

3 ft. high; 1¼–1½ ft. wide

Full sun–part shade

Blooms June–October

Zones 5–9

PRUNING Deadheading can prolong bloom for most of the season. *Linaria* has a tendency to flop onto its neighbors. Although flopping is usually done gracefully, cutting plants back after flowering by about half to lateral flowering branches can help curb this habit. Pinching or cutting back plants in early May before flowering can also produce shorter, more compact plants with heavier branching but smaller and, in my opinion, less attractive flowers. If flowering stems decline, cut them down to new foliage that develops at the base of the plant. Toadflax can seed freely—allowing some seeding to occur is a good idea to ensure constancy of this short-lived perennial in the garden. Excess seedlings are easily removed.

OTHER MAINTENANCE Plants prefer an infertile, fairly dry soil. Avoid wet conditions, particularly over the winter. Allow other plants to support flopping toadflax, or use light staking to help maintain the natural grace of the plant. Doesn't transplant well.

RELATED PLANTS *Linaria purpurea* 'Canon Went' is a pink-flowered form. Seedlings usually come true if parent plant was not planted along with the straight species.

Linaria purpurea

Linum perenne

perennial flax
LINACEAE

Sky-blue flowers; small narrow leaves
18–24 in. high; 12 in. wide
Full sun
Blooms May–July
Zones 5–8

PRUNING Each individual flower lasts only 1 day, and the old flower petals drop neatly off the plant. Young plants may bloom for a long period without pruning. With age, plants usually get straggly by midsummer, in which case they can be sheared back at this time by half to two-thirds for production of new feathery growth and often a smaller rebloom. If plants open up again they may need another lighter (by a third) shearing. Keep plants moist after pruning, particularly in hot regions, for better regeneration of foliage. Perennial flax may seed strongly; allowing some seeding can ensure permanence of this short-lived perennial in the garden. If seed is mature when plants are cut back, sprinkle some seeds onto the soil in the desired location to obtain seedlings for the following year. Shearing plants before flowering by half in early May can help produce fuller plants. This is useful for newly planted flax as well, which is often thin and spindly.

OTHER MAINTENANCE Avoid poorly drained soil, which will shorten the life of flax. Alkaline, dry soils are best. Division of the coarse and sparse roots is usually unsuccessful.

RELATED PLANTS *Linum lewisii*, prairie flax (zones 3–9), could be described as the western United States version of the European *L. perenne*, and enjoys the same conditions. Plant it in dry soil in a sunny spot (the flowers don't open in shade or on cloudy days). It is susceptible to rot if winter drainage isn't perfect and is short-lived even under the best of circumstances. It will reseed to maintain its presence in the garden. Prairie flax grows 1–2 ft. tall and is topped with sky-blue blossoms in late spring and may rebloom later in the year if deadheaded after the first wave of flowers. It shouldn't need staking. Watch for slugs and aphids.

Linum narbonense, Spanish blue flax (zones 5–8), is considered by some to be longer lived than *L. lewisii* or *L. perenne*, but still falls under the rubric of the short-lived perennial. It tops out at 2 ft. and displays the sky-blue blossoms that are typical of the genus. Spanish blue flax likes a sharply drained but not bone-dry position in full sun and holds its wispy stems up without staking unless sited in too-rich soil. Deadheading may bring another round of flowers. Cut plants down in early spring before the new growth emerges.

Linum perenne

Liriope spicata

creeping lilyturf
ASPARAGACEAE

Small pale violet to white flowers; grasslike
leaves; blue-black fruit

8–12 in. high groundcover

Full sun or shade

Blooms August

Zones 4–10

PRUNING Do not deadhead; the
blue-black berrylike fruit that follow
the flowers are attractive and can
persist into early winter. Foliage is
evergreen into midwinter and usually
browned by early spring. Shear down
or mow to the ground in spring for
fresh new growth.

OTHER MAINTENANCE This is a
tough, low-maintenance, adaptable
plant that can be used as a groundcover, as well as for erosion control in
dry shady areas. Tolerates root
competition from trees. Can be
planted in the sun, but scorching of
the foliage may occur, particularly in
southern regions. Stoloniferous habit
is too invasive for the perennial
border—if planted in such a site,
creeping lilyturf will quickly turn into
a high-maintenance perennial! Divide
in the spring if needed.

Liriope spicata

Lobelia cardinalis

cardinal flower
CAMPANULACEAE

Bright red flower spikes; narrow foliage
3–4 ft. high; 2 ft. wide
Part shade
Blooms July–September
Zones 3–9

PRUNING Deadheading can improve the overall appearance of the plant and may result in some sporadic rebloom. Do allow at least some of the flowering spikes to produce, and then drop, seed before deadheading to ensure seedlings of this short-lived perennial. Plants can also be pinched or cut back before flowering to produce more compact plants. Flowers of pruned plants usually will be more numerous but smaller and slightly delayed, depending on when the plants are pruned.

OTHER MAINTENANCE Getting the plants through the winter is the trick. Leaving the stems on the plant for the winter, as in nature, may be beneficial for overwintering. Although native to wet sites, cardinal flower in a garden setting seems to do best in moist, high-organic soil that doesn't stay overly wet in the winter. It also benefits from a light mulch for the winter, but be careful because too much mulch can kill the plants; remove mulch as soon as the soil warms in the spring to prevent losses. Self-sown seedlings are the surest bet for longevity in the garden. Division can be accomplished by separating a side rosette from the parent plant in the early autumn. Dividing and moving the clump every 2–3 years can increase vigor.

RELATED PLANTS *Lobelia cardinalis* 'Golden Torch' offers brilliant red flowers against glowing yellow to lime green foliage. 'Queen Victoria' has red flowers and bronze to red-purple foliage. 'Queen Victoria' cut back by half in mid-June when 2 ft. tall flowered at approximately 2½ ft. in mid-August. Plants normally reach 4–5 ft. tall. The smaller flowers produced with pruning are nice for smaller cut flower arrangements. 'Black Truffle' is one of the newest of several vegetatively propagated, purple-foliaged cardinal flowers that is hoped to be an improvement on 'Queen Victoria', whose foliage color has been diluted over the years, due to seed-propagated plants with weaker color making their way into the marketplace.

Lobelia siphilitica, great blue lobelia (zones 4–9), can be pruned as for *L. cardinalis*, although some prefer to just pinch plants in early July. I've also heard of good results cutting plants back by half when 4 in. tall and again when 16 in. tall.

Lobelia ×*speciosa* (zones 6–9) is a group of hybrid lobelias that includes blue, red, and purple bloomers. 'Compliment Deep Red' features wine-red flowers on 3-ft. plants, and 'Dark Crusader' has red flowers and reddish purple foliage. 'Monet Moment' has blooms of pink, while 'Fan Blue', 'Fan Burgundy', 'Fan Salmon', and 'Fan Scarlet' cover the whole lobelia spectrum. Unfortunately, many of the hybrid lobelias have proved to be short-lived like the species.

Lobelia cardinalis

Lupinus hybrids

lupine
LEGUMINOSAE

Spiked flowers in various colors; palmately compound leaves
3–4 ft. high; 1½–2 ft. wide
Full sun or part shade
Blooms June–July
Zones 4–6

PRUNING Deadheading will prolong bloom and help prevent seeding. Seedlings are usually not true to type, but some interesting forms may be produced. After the initial flowering, usually sometime in mid- to late July, cut plants down to about 6 in. or down to the new basal leaves that have developed. Plants may produce sporadic rebloom. Cutting back is also an effective control against aphids, which often trouble lupines. Plants usually do not need to be cut back again until spring, when removing winter damage is necessary.

OTHER MAINTENANCE A high-maintenance, short-lived perennial. Requires rich, high-organic, acidic, well-draining soil and cool summer temperatures for best performance. Provide afternoon shade in hot regions. Requires winter mulch in northern gardens. May require staking. Inoculating the roots with a legume inoculant before planting seems to improve performance. Divide by removing side shoots in the spring without lifting the whole plant. Yellow-flowered forms may be more tender. Cultivar 'Candy Floss' produces robust flower spikes, usually in shades of pink.

Lupinus 'Candy Floss'

Lysimachia ciliata 'Firecracker'

Lysimachia ciliata 'Firecracker'
'Firecracker' fringed loosestrife
PRIMULACEAE

Smattering of 1-inch nodding yellow
flowers; deep red-purple foliage
2½–3 ft. high; 2½–3 ft. wide
Full sun–part shade
Blooms June–July
Zones 3–8

PRUNING The burgundy leaves may
turn bronzy green in the heat of
summer. Shear plants by half after
blooming to force a fresh crop of
reddish-purple leaves and enliven the
planting during the hotter months.
Cut plants down to the basal leaves in
late fall or early winter. Rosettes of
bronzy purple foliage may persist all
winter in mild areas.

OTHER MAINTENANCE Use this
plant with caution, as it can spread
rapidly. Fringed loosestrife isn't as
rampant a grower as some other
loosestrifes, such as gooseneck
loosestrife, but that's like saying a
greyhound isn't as fast as a cheetah.
Planting it in a dryish spot rather than
the moist soil it relishes will slow it
down a bit. If you do decide to invite it
into the perennial border, frequent
division will be needed to keep it
reined in. You'll also want to patrol
regularly for runners that pop up,
which fortunately are shallow-rooted
and easy to pull. Full sun brings out
the richest color in the foliage, but
light shade gives acceptable results,
too.

RELATED PLANTS Other similar
purple-leaved versions of fringed
loosestrife include 'Purpurea' and
'Atropurpurea'. The straight species
has plain green leaves and is rarely
sold at nurseries, even though it is a
North American native wildflower. All
forms are vigorous growers.

Lysimachia clethroides

gooseneck loosestrife
PRIMULACEAE

Nodding gooseneck-shaped racemes of small white flowers; elliptical green leaves that turn red in fall

2–3 ft. high; 3–4 ft. wide

Full sun–part shade

Blooms June–July

Zones 3–8

PRUNING Gooseneck loosestrife is a charming but some would say wickedly aggressive perennial plant that will choke out its neighbors via a network of underground runners if allowed to infiltrate beds or borders. Landscape beds surrounded by paving or large containers are the only places for it that won't result in a maintenance nightmare, and in those situations the only pruning needed will be to cut down the stems in late fall. In some situations gooseneck loosestrife might deserve consideration for planting in open ground as a weed-suppressing monoculture. In that case its spread into surrounding turf could be controlled by mowing. In large-scale loosestrife plantings, the late fall cleanup in preparation for winter may also call for the use of power tools, as the stems on this plant can become rather woody by the end of the season.

OTHER MAINTENANCE This plant grows most lushly (and spreads most quickly) on moist ground. Water may be withheld to check its vigor, but in overly dry conditions the foliage will fade and wilt, eventually browning on the edges. Full sun gives the most prolific flowering, although plants perform admirably in part shade, too.

RELATED PLANTS *Lysimachia clethroides* 'Geisha' features foliage with wide irregular margins of creamy yellow on 2-ft. plants. Its growth is greatly slowed by the reduction of chlorophyll, and it may safely join other plants in the border without fear of a hostile takeover. 'Heronswood Gold' has solid yellow leaves and also grows at a moderate rate. It benefits from afternoon shade in hot climates.

Lysimachia clethroides

Lysimachia nummularia 'Aurea'

golden creeping Jenny
PRIMULACEAE

Small, bright yellow flowers; round, penny-sized golden leaves on prostrate plants

2–4 in. high; 15–20 in. wide

Full sun–part shade

Blooms June

Zones 3–10

PRUNING This creeper is often treated as an annual and is used in container plantings as a "spiller." It can also be planted in the landscape—with caution. In the lightly shaded, moist sites where it feels most at home, it can become an overzealous spreader, rooting at the nodes as it travels along the ground. Where plants don't run rampant, pruning isn't much of a chore. Spring cleanup is a matter of trimming or simply pulling away by hand whatever dead plant material remains in order to make way for new growth (which emerges early in the year). Plants may also be sheared at any time during the growing season if the foliage looks rough, and a fresh mantle of bright glossy leaves will soon follow. Creeping Jenny is semi-evergreen in protected places.

OTHER MAINTENANCE Golden creeping Jenny not only favors moist sites but can actually be grown submerged in water. It likes some shade during the hottest part of the day, particularly in warm climates. Deep shade will turn the bright yellow leaves green. Where its wandering ways are not a nuisance, this plant is a useful groundcover that provides an exciting contrast to dark-foliaged plants and acts as a living mulch throughout the growing season. Pale gray caterpillarlike sawfly larvae occasionally attack this species and can decimate a planting. The plants will usually releaf once the sawflies have moved on.

RELATED PLANTS *Lysimachia nummularia* 'Goldilocks' is likely just a more marketable name for *L. nummularia* 'Aurea'. The straight species, *L. nummularia*, has plain green leaves and is rarely found at nurseries. It is an even more rampant grower than the golden form and is considered a truly noxious weed in some areas of the United States.

Lysimachia congestiflora (zones 6–9) is a short-lived, low-growing perennial similar to *L. nummularia* for container plantings, groundcover, or edging. It's represented by purple-leaved selections such as 'Midnight Sun' and 'Persian Chocolate', as well as by yellow-and-green variegated forms like 'Walkabout Sunset'.

Lysimachia nummularia 'Aurea'

Lysimachia punctata

yellow loosestrife
PRIMULACEAE

Whorls of yellow blossoms on upright spikes; whorled elliptical green leaves

2–3 ft. high; 1–2 ft. wide

Full sun–part shade

Blooms May–July

Zones 4–8

PRUNING Shearing plants after flowering will improve appearances by encouraging a fresh crop of leaves to form and may also spur rebloom later in the year. Deadheading is especially important in the moist areas where yellow loosestrife may become

invasive. Cut plants back to the ground in late fall or any time before growth resumes in spring.

OTHER MAINTENANCE This moisture-loving perennial has invaded ditches, pond edges, and streambanks in some areas of the United States, spreading by both seed and rhizome. Use with caution. In some gardens it is perfectly well behaved. Plants accept full sun in mild summer areas, but afternoon shade is appreciated where summers get hot. Like creeping Jenny, this species is also susceptible to sawfly damage, caused by a light gray caterpillarlike insect that can devour plantings. Monitor for larvae and pick them off and destroy them should they

appear. The organic insecticide *Bacillus thuringiensis* (Bt) doesn't work on sawflies, and yellow loosestrife isn't a special enough plant to merit the risks involved in using more toxic chemical controls.

RELATED PLANTS *Lysimachia punctata* 'Alexander' is a less robust grower with creamy white variegated foliage that's flushed with pink in spring, while Golden Alexander ('Walgoldalex') features soft yellow variegation.

Macleaya cordata

plume poppy
PAPAVERACEAE

Lysimachia punctata

Creamy plumes; large, lobed leaves with gray undersides

6–10 ft. high; 6 ft. wide

Full sun

Blooms July–August

Zones 3–8

PRUNING Deadhead to lateral buds to prolong bloom and prevent abundant reseeding. Plants can be cut back by half in May for shorter, more compact growth. Cutting back later may delay flowering. Flowers tend to be smaller on pruned plants. New growth may be damaged by late frost, in which case it should be pruned off in the spring to make room for fresh foliage.

OTHER MAINTENANCE Plants are high maintenance due to their extremely invasive root system. Avoid rich soil and shade, which can prompt even more aggressive behavior. Too invasive to be planted among other perennials. Best given a bed of its own to take over. Requires division in spring every 2–3 years to control spread. Staking not usually required.

Macleaya cordata

Malva alcea 'Fastigiata'

upright hollyhock mallow
MALVACEAE

Pink hollyhocklike flowers; palmate deep
green leaves
2–3 ft. high; 1½ ft. wide
Full sun–part shade
Blooms June–October
Zones 4–8

Malva alcea 'Fastigiata'

PRUNING Deadheading plants can
prolong bloom into mid-October. The
brown capsules that develop after
flowering detract from the plant
anyway and are best removed. Deadhead to a lateral leaf after the entire
cluster of flowers is finished blooming.
The lateral leaves are the site of new
bud formation. Deadheading prevents
plants from reseeding to weedy
proportions, but allowing a few
capsules to mature and drop seed will
ensure permanence of hollyhock
mallow in the garden, as individual
plants are often short-lived. Another
approach that may be taken to try to
prolong the life of the individual plant
is to prevent seed set completely with
deadheading, then cut down to fresh
basal growth if the old flowering stems
start to decline. Plants should also be
cut down to basal foliage if they topple
in late summer, or if the foliage is
badly damaged by Japanese beetles or
foliar diseases.

Plants respond well to pinching or
cutting back to produce fuller plants.
Pinching plants in early May can
produce shorter but wider mounded
plants. They will spread out a bit,
reaching about 3 ft. in width and 1½ ft.
in height. Pinching new plants at
planting in the spring is advisable if
shorter, wider plants is the desired
result. If stems look weak, or if they
open up, plants may benefit from an
additional pinching or cutting back of
the tips in early summer to get into
form. Plants pinched in early May and
then cut back by about 6 in. in
mid-June were 2 ft. rather than 3 ft.
wide and were sturdier than plants
pinched only once in May. The species
form of hollyhock mallow (*Malva*
alcea) also benefits from such
treatment.

If plants flower into the autumn,
cut back to low basal foliage after
several frosts to reduce seeding over
the winter.

OTHER MAINTENANCE Short-lived,
high-maintenance plants.
Well-draining soil is necessary to
ensure survival. Drought tolerant.
Prefers alkaline pH, although adaptable. May require staking, particularly
if given part shade or if not pinched to
control height. Requires frequent

division, in the spring or autumn, to maintain vigor. Subject to Japanese beetles and a variety of other pests and diseases in southern regions, although it seems a bit more resistant in northern gardens.

RELATED PLANTS *Althaea zebrina*—the nomenclature is unclear about this plant, but this is the name under which it is sold. Plants should be pinched in early spring as for upright hollyhock mallow to reduce flopping. Deadheading is critical to reduce prolific seeding, but it is a tedious job as new flowers are produced all along the stem close to where dead flowers are located. Sharp pruning scissors are needed. Better still, cut all old flowering stems down to about 8–10 in. after most of the initial flowering is finished but before seeds drop. Young or vigorously growing plants cut back in this way will regrow to approximately full size and will rebloom as in the first bloom period, flowering into mid-October. If you get lazy in this next bloom period and forget to deadhead, numerous seedlings in the spring will serve as a painful reminder.

Monarda didyma
beebalm
LAMIACEAE

Red, pink, purple, or white flowers on square stems; aromatic leaves
1–4 ft. high; 2–4 ft. wide
Full sun
Blooms June–July
Zones 4–9

PRUNING Deadheading can prolong bloom, particularly on young or vigorously growing plants; older plants may not produce much rebloom, if any, with deadheading. Seeding may occur if plants aren't deadheaded, although in most cases this is minimal. Deadhead back to lateral flower buds. The plants may be infected with mildew after flowering is finished, and the foliage may become unsightly. If this is the case, cut down to the new clean foliage developing at the base of the plants. The new foliage usually will stay low, about 6–8 in., for the rest of the season. Discard diseased foliage, and do not compost.

Cutting back once or twice before flowering encourages more compact growth and delayed flowering. Plants cut back by half in early May when approximately 12 in. tall flower about 1½–2 weeks later than unpruned plants and at 3 ft. rather than 3½ ft. If plants pruned in early May start to look spindly by mid-May, cutting them back again by about a third can delay flowering by about 3 weeks and reduce

Monarda didyma

the height to 2½ ft. The number of flowers may be slightly less on plants pruned twice. This pruning can foster fresh flowers of beebalm into mid-August, rather than being finished at the end of July. Perhaps even more important is that the delay in flowering also means a delay in foliage decline. Since the foliage normally declines after flowering, plants that flower earlier also have tatty foliage earlier than plants that flower later. Thinning stems of beebalm can help reduce the incidence of powdery mildew.

OTHER MAINTENANCE Beebalms are wide-spreading plants due to rhizomes that can fill a 4 ft. × 4 ft. area. They are easily pulled out, but it is better to plant them singularly rather than in groups in most gardens. Many are highly prone to mildew. Select resistant cultivars for best performance (see below), although even these can develop some infection in years when the conditions are favorable for mildew. Provide good air circulation and avoid overly dry soil. Divide plants every 2–3 years to control spread and to keep them strong. Division also prevents a hole from developing in the center of the clump.

RELATED PLANTS The following *Monarda didyma* cultivars are resistant to powdery mildew: 'Gardenview Scarlet'(red), 'Jacob Cline'(red), 'Marshall's Delight' (pink), 'Petite Delight' (dwarf pink), 'Purple Rooster' (purple), and 'Raspberry Wine' (purplish red).

Nepeta ×faasenii 'Six Hills Giant'

'Six Hills Giant' catmint
LAMIACEAE

Lavender-blue flowers; gray-green leaves
3 ft. high; 3 ft. wide
Full sun
Blooms June–August
Zones 3–8

PRUNING Deadheading doesn't seem to do much to prolong bloom on this catmint. Snipping off the old flowering stems can improve the appearance of the plant, though. Plants are sterile, so reseeding does not occur. Shearing down the foliage is not as critical with this catmint as with others, because this one doesn't decline to the degree that the others can. In my experience, the plant may turn a bit yellowish in certain years and may open in the center with heavy rains, but normally not severely. It can be sheared and shaped after flowering, if desired, to keep it from falling over other perennials, or to induce lush new foliage. If sheared back by about two-thirds after flowering, it will stay more compact and the new growth will hold the strong gray-green color. Often rebloom will occur, but not always, depending on the vigor of the plant and the conditions for the season. 'Six Hills Giant' looks rough in the winter; pruning after several killing frosts is advisable.

OTHER MAINTENANCE This catmint is easy to grow. It requires average well-draining soil and full sun. Division is seldom required, but it can be performed in the spring.

Nepeta ×faasenii 'Six Hills Giant'

Nepeta racemosa 'Walker's Low'

'Walker's Low' catmint
LAMIACEAE

Small lavender-blue flowers; gray-green leaves
30 in. high; 36 in. wide
Full sun
Blooms June–July
Zones 3–8

PRUNING As with the previous plant, deadheading doesn't do much to prolong bloom on this perennial; it is better to simply shear plants back by about two-thirds after flowering for lush new growth and sporadic rebloom. Shearing controls sprawling stems and declining foliage. 'Walker's Low' is a sterile form, so no seedlings will pop up if plants aren't sheared after bloom. This catmint isn't very attractive over winter, and cutting it back after several killing frosts may be desirable.

Nepeta racemosa 'Walker's Low'

OTHER MAINTENANCE 'Walker's Low' catmint is easily grown in average well-draining soil. Some gardeners like to prop up the sprawling stems a bit; despite the name, the plant can reach 30 in. in height. Division is seldom needed, but it can be done in the spring if desired.

RELATED PLANTS *Nepeta sibirica* 'Souvenir d'André Chaudron' can be cut back by half in early June, or when about 2 ft. tall (plants may be in tight bud), for fuller, more compact growth and a 3- to 4-week delay in flowering. Pruned plants flower in August, while unpruned plants are usually finished blooming in mid-July. Cutting plants back before early June will not produce such a delay in bloom. Deadhead plants to lateral flowering buds and then cut down to fresh new basal foliage after all flowering is completed.

Nepeta subsessilis

Japanese catmint
LAMIACEAE

Whorls of violet-blue or pink flowers; fragrant green leaves
18–30 in. high; 18–30 in. wide
Full sun–part shade
Blooms May–September
Zones 4–8

PRUNING Plants may be pinched in early spring or midspring to encourage a fuller, more compact habit. Shearing after the blossoms fade will also promote a neater form and may spur rebloom later in the season. Leaving the stems standing, on the other hand, may allow for a modest amount of reseeding and will provide food for finches. Cut plants to the ground after several killing frosts render them unsightly.

OTHER MAINTENANCE Japanese catmint needs more moisture than other catmints and can tolerate part shade; it makes a good rain garden plant. This fast grower may need staking in windy sites. No major pests or diseases trouble it.

RELATED PLANTS *Nepeta subsessilis* 'Candy Cat' has pale mauve-pink flowers, while 'Cool Cat' has delicate lavender-blue blooms. 'Sweet Dreams' is a washed-out pink, but its purple bracts add definition to the inflorescence.

Oenothera fruticosa 'Fyrverkeri' (Fireworks)
'Fireworks' sundrops
ONAGRACEAE

Red buds and lemon-yellow flowers; narrow green leaves that may turn red in fall

15–18 in. high; 18–24 in. wide

Full sun

Blooms May–June

Zones 4–8

PRUNING Deadheads fall neatly from the plant. Plants can be sheared back by about a third and shaped after flowering to create a tidy form in the garden. If the foliage should decline, cut plants down to the low evergreen rosette. Do not prune again for the winter.

OTHER MAINTENANCE Well-draining soil is essential to survival. *Oenothera fruticosa* is tolerant of poor dry soil, though it is often short-lived. Divide plants in the spring or early autumn every 4–5 years.

RELATED PLANTS *Oenothera speciosa* var. *berlandieri* 'Siskiyou' (zones 5–9) is a low groundcover evening primrose with light pink flowers. It will bloom for most of the summer if deadheaded. It has a vigorous stoloniferous rootstock and can become very invasive.

Oenothera macrocarpa, Missouri evening primrose (zones 3–7), is a low, sprawling, nonaggressive perennial with bright yellow flowers for average to dry soil in full sun. Deadhead to extend the bloom time from May through mid- to late summer. Allowing some of the interesting large, winged seed pods to remain will allow some reseeding, but usually not to an excessive degree. Cut plants back in late fall in preparation for winter. New plants are best grown from seed, as the fleshy roots aren't amenable to division.

Nepeta subsessilis

Oenothera fruticosa 'Fyrverkeri' (Fireworks)

Origanum 'Kent Beauty'

'Kent Beauty' ornamental oregano
LAMIACEAE

Long-lasting papery pink, cream, and pale green bracts; rounded gray-green leaves with white stripes

6–8 in. high; 12–18 in. wide

Full sun

Blooms July–September

Zones 5–8

PRUNING This hybrid oregano (*Origanum rotundifolium* × *O. scabrum*) boasts a long season of color, as the large bracts remain colorful even after the tiny light purple blooms inside the flowering structure are spent. No pruning is needed until plants show life in the spring; at that point cut the stems down to the new growth. Don't trim plants after August or winter hardiness may be compromised.

OTHER MAINTENANCE While 'Kent Beauty' is the showiest of the ornamental oreganos, it is also one of the most exacting in its requirements. It must have well-drained soil, particularly during winter dormancy; amend heavy soils before planting. Provide a sunny site for this heat lover—even a site in full-on baking sun where other plants fry is quite all right. However, high heat coupled with high humidity spells trouble, and performance in the Deep South is usually poor. Water regularly during the 1st year, then hold off on supplemental irrigation except during prolonged dry spells. Mulch with gravel rather than with a moisture-conserving organic mulch of wood chips or bark. In zone 5, 'Kent Beauty' should be planted in spring to give it plenty of time to put down a good root system before winter.

Origanum 'Kent Beauty'

276

Origanum laevigatum 'Herrenhausen'

'Herrenhausen' ornamental oregano
LAMIACEAE

Tiny lavender-pink flowers on purple stems; small green leaves tinged purple in cool weather

2 ft. high; 2 ft. wide

Full sun

Blooms July–September

Zones 5–9

PRUNING 'Herrenhausen' blooms for about 2 months in summer, but plants remain colorful into fall thanks to persistent purple bracts along with dark stems and purple-flushed leaves. Don't cut back plants until growth resumes in spring, as fall pruning reduces cold hardiness.

OTHER MAINTENANCE Plant ornamental oregano in lean, preferably alkaline soil that drains freely. Well-drained soil is especially crucial in winter. This Mediterranean plant needs full sun and tolerates heat but struggles in high humidity. Divide plants every few years to keep them growing vigorously.

RELATED PLANTS Culinary oregano, *Origanum vulgare*, need not be relegated to the herb garden if you have a landscape bed that's kept on the dry side. This oregano has penny-sized green leaves and grows 1–3 ft. tall. Tall strains may splay open when the pale lavender-pink flowers begin to open; shear plants a couple of times in spring and early summer (and eat the trimmings) to keep them compact. Continue trimming to prevent plants from flowering altogether if you wish, stopping in August to give them time to harden off for the winter. Do let at least a few plants bloom, however, because the blossoms are a pollinator's paradise. Golden oregano, *O. vulgare* 'Aureum', is also a nice addition to the perennial border. It stays shorter than the green version, reaching only 6–12 in. Its glowing yellow spring foliage may change to lime green in the heat of summer.

Origanum laevigatum 'Herrenhausen'

Paeonia 'Nymphe'

Paeonia hybrids

peony
PAEONIACEAE

Pink, coral, white, or red flowers; coarse, lobed, dark green leaves

3 ft. high; 3 ft. wide

Full sun

Blooms May–June

Zones 3–8

PRUNING Deadheading peonies will not prolong bloom, but it will greatly enhance the appearance of the plant, since in most cases, particularly on double forms, the old flowers are so unattractive. Red-flowered peonies are particularly susceptible to disease and should be deadheaded immediately as flowers fade, to reduce the chance of disease affecting the decaying flower and entering the stem. The foliage on many forms becomes unsightly with the heat of August as plants are starting to form eyes at that time and don't have much strength for the bush. It is best for the health of the plant to leave the foliage on the plant as long as possible, even if it's unattractive, so that the foliage can continue to perform photosynthesis and provide food reserves. Peony experts recommend leaving foliage unpruned until after the first of September in zones 3, 4, and upper zone 5; leave until the end of September in the rest of zone 5. Gardeners in zones 6, 7, and warmer areas should try to leave the foliage until early October.

Peonies are subject to a host of diseases, particularly botrytis. Remove any infected leaves or buds. Plants that were not cut back in the late summer or autumn should be cut down for the winter to remove possible sources of infection for the following spring. Clean up any debris from around the base of the plant. Any time plants are cut down or dead leaves are removed, the clippings must be discarded—do not compost.

Peonies respond to disbudding. Removing the large terminal flower bud results in smaller flowers being produced by the plants. Often plants that are treated in this way will not require staking due to the decreased weight from the removal of the large terminal flower. Some gardeners remove the smaller lateral flower buds to increase the size of the terminal flower.

OTHER MAINTENANCE Deep, rich, well-draining, alkaline soil is preferred. Plant from September to October in the North and October to November in the South. Peonies planted in November should be mulched. Be sure to not plant the eyes more than about 2 in. below the soil surface in the North, or else flowering may not occur; planting at soil level is recommended for southern gardens. It usually takes 2–3 years for the plants to become completely established. Some other reasons peonies may fail to flower include too much shade, competition from tree roots, too much nitrogen, or late-spring frosts (or winter cold). Double forms need to be staked, and peony rings are best for this. Cool and wet spring weather can cause leggy growth, thus staking may be necessary even on lower growing forms. Plants go for eons without division. If desired, divide peonies in late summer, leaving 3–5 eyes per division. Mulch newly planted peonies to prevent frost heaving.

RELATED PLANTS Peony cultivars such as 'Nice Gal', 'Snow Swan', and 'Mister Ed' have foliage that usually holds up well through the season and may take on interesting autumn tones. 'Nymphe' is an upright bush of deep green leaves that stays attractive all season. 'Nice Gal', 'Vivid Rose', and the Bridal Series are examples of some lower growing forms that generally don't need staking.

Paeonia tenuifolia, fernleaf peony, should be deadheaded immediately after flowering to reduce chance of disease. This applies both to the species and its many cultivars.

Papaver orientale
oriental poppy
PAPAVERACEAE

Large red, orange, pink, white, or salmon flowers; large coarse leaves
2–4 ft. high; 2 ft. wide
Full sun
Blooms May–June
Zones 3–7

PRUNING Poppies have outstanding seed capsules that extend the season of interest of this perennial, and deadheading doesn't do much to prolong bloom. Some gardeners have success with cutting the old foliage and flowering stems to the ground immediately after flowering to encourage new but smaller growth that remains to fill the space through the summer. Keep plants moist after cutting back. This pruning does not always work, however, and a hole may remain until the foliage returns in late summer. If not cut down immediately after flowering, the foliage declines over time, usually by the end of July,

Papaver orientale 'Patty's Plum'

and should be cut down (or pulled off by hand) at this point. The new leaves that return in the late summer or autumn should be left for the winter. The new foliage may serve as a living mulch and help insulate the crown from extreme temperature. The leaves often stay green through the winter and into spring, depending on the conditions. If the foliage does suffer winter injury, the new spring growth that follows quickly covers it.

OTHER MAINTENANCE Well-draining soil is essential for survival. Mulch first-year plants. Plant or divide in August or September. Division generally is not needed for about 6 years or more. The plant's fleshy taproot can make it a challenge to transplant. Oriental poppy is long-lived once established.

RELATED PLANTS I adore poppies. Some of my favorite cultivars include 'Patty's Plum' (gorgeous dusky purple), 'Princess Victoria Louise' (salmon pink), 'Beauty of Livermore' (dark red), and 'Royal Wedding' (pure white).

Papaver nudicaule, Iceland poppy, is a short-lived perennial that acts almost biennial in nature. Deadheading to prevent seed set and cutting down immediately after flowering may help to extend the life of individual plants.

Patrinia scabiosifolia
patrinia
CAPRIFOLIACEAE

Clusters of tiny yellow flowers; pinnately divided leaves
3–6 ft. (1 ft.) high; 2 ft. wide
Full sun or part shade
Blooms August–September
Zones 4–9

PRUNING Deadhead for prolonged bloom and to reduce abundant seeding. When flowering is finished, but before seed sets, cut stems down to basal foliage. Leave basal foliage for the winter.

OTHER MAINTENANCE Provide rich, well-draining soil for best performance. I have had trouble establishing patrinia after several attempts in my

gardens and in clients' gardens—perhaps it has to do with the taproots. Plants are supposedly long-lived once established and seldom need division.

Penstemon barbatus
beardtongue
PLANTAGINACEAE

Tubular pink or scarlet flowers; low, narrow leaves
2–3 ft. (8 in.) high; 1–1½ ft. wide
Full sun
Blooms June–July
Zones 3–8

PRUNING Deadhead to lateral flowers or buds to prolong bloom. The overall appearance of the plant is enhanced by cutting back old flowering stems to the basal foliage. The low foliage remains evergreen over the winter and usually stays nice into spring. Pinching plants when they are 12–15 in. tall will produce more compact, fuller growth.

OTHER MAINTENANCE Beardtongue depends heavily on well-draining soil for success and is drought tolerant. It may require mulching in winter for extra protection. This species is short-lived, usually because of moisture problems or a variety of foliar diseases. It requires frequent division, about every 3 years in the spring.

RELATED PLANTS *Penstemon digitalis* (zones 3–8), foxglove penstemon, should be deadheaded to a lateral leaf after flowering and then cut down to new basal growth as old stems decline. This species is longer lived, hardier, and more tolerant of damp soil than *P. barbatus*. It is the species of choice for the lower-maintenance garden. *Penstemon digitalis* 'Husker's Red' (2–3 ft.) has spikes of white blossoms over outstanding purple-red foliage. Cut it down to new basal growth if the old foliage fades in late summer or autumn. 'Dark Towers' is similar to 'Husker's Red' and comes from the same breeder, Dr. Dale Lindgren of the University of Nebraska, but it is a hybrid plant. 'Dark Towers' has deeper burgundy foliage, pale pink flowers, and a taller habit than 'Husker's Red'. Dr. Lindgren also developed the 'Prairie' series of penstemons, which do well in the Midwest, where most penstemons don't thrive. I've had great success with 'Prairie Twilight'.

A group of hybrid penstemons that goes by the name *Penstemon ×mexicali* includes some popular and relatively adaptable selections like 'Pike's Peak Purple' (grape purple) and 'Red Rocks' (pink). They are more cold hardy and more forgiving than many other penstemons, but still need excellent drainage, especially in winter. They bloom best in spring and fall, when the weather is cool.

Penstemon 'Red Riding Hood' has bright coral-red blooms on 2-ft. plants and is hardy in zones 5–8. Seven selections make up the 'Riding Hood' series, in colors from red to pink to lavender to blue.

Penstemon barbatus

Perovskia atriplicifolia

Perovskia atriplicifolia

Russian sage
LAMIACEAE

Spikes of lavender-blue flowers; fine gray leaves
3–4 ft. high; 3–4 ft. wide
Full sun
Blooms July–September
Zones 5–9

PRUNING In the Midwest, plants flower for a long time even without deadheading. In southern gardens, where the plants may flower earlier, deadheading may be beneficial to produce rebloom. Susan Urshal, a gardener in Texas, likes to cut about two-thirds of the stems by about two-thirds after flowering; the pruned stems send out new shoots that will be reblooming by autumn.

The straight species of Russian sage has a tendency to flop or fall over a bit in most garden situations. Plants can be pinched or cut back by half when they are about 12 in. tall to obtain fuller plants.

The silvery stems and seedheads of Russian sage provide nice winter interest. Generally plants are cut back to about 6 in. above the ground annually in the spring, and new buds break from these low woody stems. Some gardeners prefer to cut plants all the way to the ground, believing that the plants are fuller if pruned in this fashion. Some people don't have a choice, as plants may be killed completely to the ground each winter.

Perovskia may be harmed by late frosts, although plants usually recover nicely. Trim off damaged foliage if necessary to improve the appearance of the plant.

OTHER MAINTENANCE
Drought-tolerant, low-maintenance plants with a long bloom period. Good for the beginning gardener. Well-draining soil is critical for survival, particularly over the winter. Seldom needs division.

RELATED PLANTS *Perovskia atriplicifolia* 'Longin' is more upright and narrower than the species. Doesn't require pinching.

Persicaria amplexicaulis 'Firetail'

'Firetail' mountain fleeceflower
POLYGONACEAE

Slim spikes of tiny crimson-red flowers; lance-shaped, leathery green leaves

3–4 ft. high; 3–4 ft. wide

Full sun–part shade

Blooms July–October

Zones 4–7

PRUNING 'Firetail' mountain fleece-flower is grown for its long-blooming flowers and not for its nondescript, rather coarse foliage. Deadheading and occasional deadleafing will help to keep this hardworking perennial looking thrifty. If plants are beyond help (dry soil and Japanese beetles can take their toll), cut them to the ground and they'll rebound with fresh foliage and flowers, blooming until frost. Plants collapse after a few freezes, so cut them down for the winter in late fall.

OTHER MAINTENANCE Like most other *Persicaria* species, mountain fleeceflower is adaptable, but does best in consistently moist soil in full sun or dappled shade. It's a strong grower but isn't considered invasive or weedy. Japanese beetles may be troublesome in some areas. Divide clumps every few years in spring or fall to maintain vigor.

RELATED PLANTS *Persicaria amplexi-caulis* 'Golden Arrow' (2–3 ft. tall and wide) has deep crimson flowers spikes over chartreuse foliage. *Persicaria affinis*, Himalayan fleeceflower (zones 3–7), forms a low, weed-smothering mat that stands less than 1 ft. tall. Its flower spikes are deep pink in bud, opening to pale pink, and last from late June through September. The foliage turns red in fall, eventually becoming a not unattractive red-brown and persisting through the winter. It prefers cool-summer climates. Cut plants back in early spring. *Persicaria affinis* is most often represented by the selection 'Superba', a.k.a. 'Dimity'.

Persicaria amplexicaulis 'Firetail'

Persicaria virginiana 'Painter's Palette'

'Painter's Palette' knotweed
POLYGONACEAE

Airy wands of miniscule red flowers; cream-splashed green leaves with maroon chevrons

18–24 in. high; 18–24 in. wide

Full sun–part shade

Blooms August–October

Zones 4–8

PRUNING This variety of our native knotweed is grown primarily for its colorful foliage. Remove the late-blooming flower spikes to prevent unwanted seedlings. 'Painter's Palette' comes true from seed, and volunteers are welcomed in most gardens, but seedlings can become excessive in others. Cut plants to the ground in

Phlomis russeliana
sticky Jerusalem sage
LAMIACEAE

Tiered whorls of pale yellow flowers; large, felty gray-green leaves

3 ft. high; 2½ ft. wide

Full sun–light shade

Blooms late May–July

Zones 4–9

PRUNING Sticky Jerusalem sage's main blooming period is in June, but deadheading may encourage more flower spikes to form, extending the bloom time possibly through September. The tiered seedheads are a wonderful addition to the winter garden, and the leaves are evergreen in mild climates; wait until early spring to cut plants back to the ground.

OTHER MAINTENANCE This Mediterranean plant needs sharp drainage and a site in full sun or very light shade to thrive. It languishes in high humidity and rots if overwatered. Mulch with gravel rather than moisture-retentive bark or wood chips. Performance may wane after several years—if this happens, divide plants in early spring or start new ones from cuttings.

RELATED PLANTS *Phlomis fruticosa*, Jerusalem sage, is similar in most respects to *P. russeliana*, but has smaller leaves and is less hardy (zones 7–10).

Phlomis tuberosa, tuberous Jerusalem sage (zones 6–9), has green leaves, deep red stems, and pink flowers. It is most often represented by the robust selection 'Amazone'.

Persicaria virginiana 'Painter's Palette'

preparation for winter.

OTHER MAINTENANCE 'Painter's Palette' tolerates sun, but is happiest in part shade. Once established it can handle considerable drought, making it a great candidate for those troublesome dry shade areas where little else will grow.

Phlomis russeliana

RELATED PLANTS *Persicaria microcephala* 'Red Dragon' (zones 6–9) is also grown for its foliage (as well as its red stems), though its sprays of tiny white flowers in late summer are also attractive. In early spring, leaves emerge a deep, dusky purple with silver chevrons, fading to green and bronze come summer. 'Red Dragon' is a clumper reaching 3–4 ft. in height with a 4-ft. spread and doesn't reseed. If plants become leggy or floppy, trim them by half or more and they'll recover quickly, pushing out bushy new growth.

Phlox divaricata

woodland phlox
POLEMONIACEAE

Light blue, white, or lavender flowers; small green leaves
10–15 in. high; 12 in. wide
Part shade–full shade
Blooms May–June
Zones 4–9

PRUNING Plants can reseed heavily to create a beautiful display in a naturalized or woodland area. If reseeding is not desired, deadhead before seed matures. One efficient way to accomplish deadheading is to shear off the old flowering stems, with hedge shears, down to the low green foliage. If the flowering stems are left on the plants for reseeding, they usually become brown and ugly by mid-July. Deadheading before this time is best for keeping plants attractive. Plants may be subject to powdery mildew in hot and humid conditions. If affected, shear down for lush new growth; do not compost diseased material. Woodland phlox is evergreen and so should not be pruned for the winter.

OTHER MAINTENANCE Plants prefer moist, humus-rich conditions. The foliage will die down if allowed to dry out in the summer or if given too much sun. Plants are shallow rooted and should be planted or divided in the spring to avoid the winter frost heaving that can occur with autumn planting.

RELATED PLANTS *Phlox divaricata* subsp. *laphamii* 'Chattahoochee' is a nice selection with more compact growth. The flowering stems of this cultivar are borne closer to the foliage than those of the species. Deadhead and shape by shearing off (with hedge shears) the old flower stems and about a third to half of the foliage. This pruning keeps the plants bushy for the rest of the season. Foliage holds up better in drought than that of the species. 'Fuller's White' is heavier blooming than the species and more tolerant of sun.

Phlox divaricata subsp. *laphamii* 'Chattahoochee'

Phlox maculata

early phlox
POLEMONIACEAE

White, pink, or rose clusters of flowers;
narrow, shiny green leaves
2–3 ft. high; 3 ft. wide
Full sun
Blooms June–July
Zones 4–8

PRUNING Deadheading can greatly
prolong the bloom of early phlox, in
some cases for up to 2 months longer.
Deadhead the main flowering truss to
above lateral buds. Plants are
self-sterile and will not self-sow, so
deadheading to prevent mongrel
seedlings is not a concern. If the stems
of the plants brown or are affected
with leaf spot, they should be cut to
the ground for regrowth and, if
vigorous, rebloom may occur,
although this is not common. Keep
moist and fertilize after cutting back
for best performance.

Pruning extends early phlox's
season to later in the summer and
provides smaller flowers, which are
better for small cut-flower arrangements. Plants can be pinched, and they
respond well to cutting back by half
and shaping at the end of May or in
early June before flowering to reduce
the height and delay the bloom. Plants
in tight bud also can be pruned by
removing 6 in. or more to obtain
shorter plants and later bloom.
Flowers are usually delayed by about 2
weeks but can be delayed by up to 4
weeks with either form of cutting back.
If plants are stressed or not growing
strongly, pruning may further reduce
the flowering and quality of bloom.
See cultivars listed below for specifics.

OTHER MAINTENANCE This species
is a good selection of phlox because of
its resistance to powdery mildew.
Plants are heavy feeders and need
moist, fertile, organic-rich soil for best
performance. Division every couple of
years will maintain vigor.

RELATED PLANTS *Phlox maculata*
'Alpha' cut back by half and shaped in
early June produces outstanding
plants that flower nicely at 1½ ft.,
rather than 2½ ft., and begin flowering
2 weeks later than unpruned plants, in
mid-July rather than late June. 'Miss
Lingard' plants cut back by half at the
end of May flowered 3–4 weeks later
than unpruned plants and at 2 ft.
rather than 3 ft. The floral display of
the pruned plants was not as effective
as that of unpruned plants, but that
was most likely because the plants
were stressed and in need of division
to improve their vigor. 'Omega' is a
white form with a pink eye; if deadheaded, it usually reblooms all white
later in the summer. 'Rosalind' did not
respond to pruning 4 in., rather than 6
in., off the tips of the plants when in
tight bud in mid-June. Pruning off less
of the stem must not have removed
already formed lateral flower buds,
which broke at the normal flowering
time to create a rather bizarre effect.

Phlox maculata 'Alpha'

Phlox paniculata
garden phlox
POLEMONIACEAE

Large flower clusters in white, pink, red, purple, or orange; dull green leaves

2–5 ft. high; 2–3 ft. wide

Full sun

Blooms July–September

Zones 4–8

PRUNING Deadheading prolongs bloom on plants and prevents reseeding. Seedlings are not desirable, because they are not true to type and often take over the more desirable parent plant. Thinning phlox by a third or to 4–6 stems is often recommended to reduce the incidence of powdery mildew, but this is not always effective and in some years plants get mildew whether thinned or not. The gardener needs to decide whether it's worth the effort. Plants badly infected with powdery mildew should be cut to the ground, making sure to keep them moist and fertilized for regrowth. Do not compost clippings. All this being said, selecting mildew-resistant cultivars in the first place is really the best way to avoid the extra maintenance; see the listing of cultivars.

Plants can be pinched or cut back and shaped to produce shorter plants and to delay flowering. 'Flamingo' can be cut back by half in early to mid-June, or 6 in. or more can be cut off when the plants are in tight bud. Flowering normally will be delayed by 2 weeks with pruning, but it can be delayed by as much as 4 weeks. If plants are cut back earlier, say in mid-May, flowering may not be as greatly delayed. Pruning can be used to produce flowers later in the season on a few plants or on a few stems of an individual plant. Flower size is also reduced with pruning before flowering, which is nice for smaller cut arrangements. Stressed plants or plants in need of division may have weaker than normal flower production if pruned.

Be sure to prune down phlox for the winter if they are affected with mildew. Clean up and destroy all debris around the plants to reduce the chances of infection the following spring.

OTHER MAINTENANCE Garden phlox plants are heavy feeders. They prefer moist, rich, high-organic soil. Avoid wet conditions. Give plants space, good air circulation, and regular irrigation to help reduce incidence of mildew. Frequent division, every 3 years, in the spring helps keep plants vigorous; the double-fork method can be used. Discard the deteriorated center of divided plants and leave at least 3–4 shoots per division. Some cultivars may require staking.

RELATED PLANTS The cultivars listed below are less prone to mildew. The occurrence of disease may vary depending on the cultural and growing conditions for the season or on the weather, but at least the chances are better if these more resistant forms are selected over other more susceptible cultivars. Some resistant forms of *Phlox paniculata* include: 'David', 'David's Lavender', 'Delta Snow', 'Jeana', 'Laura', 'Lichtspel' (light show), 'Natascha', 'Peppermint Twist', Pink Flame ('Bartwelve'), 'Robert Poore', 'Shortwood', and 'Speed Limit 45'.

Phlox paniculata 'Flamingo'. Shorter, fuller, later flowering results from cutting plants back by half in mid-June.

Phlox stolonifera

creeping phlox
POLEMONIACEAE

Purple, red, blue, or white flowers; small oval leaves

6–12 in. (2 in.) high; 12–15 in. wide

Part shade–full shade

Blooms April–May

Zones 4–9

PRUNING Cut or shear deadheads down to creeping basal foliage to improve the overall appearance of the plant. Plants remain evergreen over the winter, so do not prune in the autumn. Although winter damage is not common, any branches that decline over the winter should be pruned off in early spring. Creeping phlox spreads by stolons, which can be pruned off to control spread if desired.

OTHER MAINTENANCE Great low-maintenance perennial. Useful as a groundcover even in shady spots. Nice between stepping stones in a low-traffic path. Prefers moist, acidic, humus-rich soil, although plants are fairly adaptable. Avoid prolonged drought. Can take some sun in all but southern gardens. Not susceptible to mildew, as with other phlox. Divide, if needed, in the spring or summer after flowering. 'Blue Ridge' features soft blue flowers over a compact plant.

Phlox stolonifera 'Blue Ridge'

Phlox subulata
moss phlox
POLEMONIACEAE

Pink, magenta, red, white, lavender, or blue flowers; matlike foliage

3–6 in. high; 24 in. wide

Full sun

Blooms April–May

Zones 3–9

PRUNING After flowering is completed, cut plants back with hedge shears by half to prevent the plants from opening up in the center later in the season. Shearing before the seeds set also prevents reseeding of untrue types. Cut plants back if needed to control spread. Plants are evergreen; do not prune in the autumn, and clean up any winter-damaged growth in the spring.

OTHER MAINTENANCE Well-draining soil is key to survival. Moss phlox prefers slightly alkaline conditions. Division may be needed every 3 years to maintain vigor, and it should be done after flowering in the spring. Be certain to cut back foliage by half on new divisions. 'G.F. Wilson' is an evergreen groundcover with lavender flowers.

Phlox subulata 'G.F. Wilson'

Physostegia virginiana

obedient plant
LAMIACEAE

Tubular pink or white flowers; narrow green leaves
2–4 ft. high; 3 ft. wide
Full sun–part shade
Blooms August–October
Zones 3–9

PRUNING Deadhead to a lateral flower bud or leaf to improve the overall appearance of the plant and possibly to prolong bloom. Pinch or cut back plants by half in the spring to prevent flopping, particularly in rich moist soils or shaded sites. Cut plants down to new basal growth if they develop a ratty appearance after flowering.

OTHER MAINTENANCE Best growth occurs in full sun, although plants may still require staking. Obedient plant prefers moist soil. This is a rather high-maintenance plant, because it spreads aggressively, requiring frequent digging out of sections of the plant to keep it in bounds. Division every couple of years helps to maintain a decent plant. It is best relegated to a naturalized garden where a spreading and flopping growth habit is more acceptable.

RELATED PLANTS *Physostegia virginiana* 'Crystal Peak White' is a dwarf form (to 18 in.) that is somewhat less aggressive than the species; at the other end of the spectrum, 'Eyeful Tower' is a fun, but fairly aggressive, novelty plant reaching 6–7 ft. 'Rose Queen' is an upright, spreading cultivar with pink flowers. 'Miss Manners' (white) is a well-behaved clumping form that doesn't roam, reseed, or need staking; 'Pink Manners' is similar, but in pale lilac-pink. 'Variegata' is a less rambunctious form, and it also has cream-edged foliage to offer. 'Vivid' is more compact and upright than the species, normally not requiring pruning, yet it's still a spreader.

Platycodon grandiflorus

balloon flower
CAMPANULACEAE

Blue, pink, or white inflated flowers that
pop open with maturity; oval green leaves

2–3 ft. high; 2 ft. wide

Full sun

Blooms July–September

Zones 3–8

PRUNING Deadheading of balloon
flower can greatly prolong bloom and
keep the plants attractive. Each
individual dead flower needs to be
removed without damaging new buds,
which are produced all along the
flowering stem—sharp pruning
scissors work best for this task.
Removing the entire flowering stem
will remove future flowers. Snipping
off the old flowers and simply letting
them drop to the ground helps speed
up this tedious deadheading. Minimal
reseeding can occur, so you should
deadhead before seeds mature if
reseeding is not desired.

Balloon flower responds well to
pinching or cutting back before
flowering to control its flopping
nature. Cutting plants back by half in
late May to early June, or about 1
month before they flower, produces
nicely branched, well-shaped, shorter
plants with delayed flowering that will
not require staking. Plants that
normally mature at 2½–3½ ft. tall will
mature at 1½–2 ft. tall with this
pruning regimen, and flowering can
be delayed by 2–3 weeks. Plants cut
back in mid- to late June may be
delayed by as much as 4 weeks. After
the foliage turns attractive colors in
the autumn it blackens with several
killing frosts. If you cut plants down at
this time, leave about 6 in. of the old
stems to mark the location of the
plants, since they are late to emerge in
the spring. The old stems can be
further pruned down once new growth
is visible in the spring.

OTHER MAINTENANCE Plants are
slow to establish, but once they take
hold they are long-lived and low
maintenance. Provide high-organic,
well-draining soil and a location
where the plant won't be disturbed by
cultivation around its roots. Can be
difficult to transplant, and balloon
flower doesn't need to be divided for
20 years or more. If division is desired,
take plenty of soil, for deep roots, with
the clump in the spring. Spring
planting is required for best establishment. Plants are late to emerge in the
spring, so be careful to not disturb the
area. Usually requires staking, unless
plants are pruned or shorter growing
cultivars are selected. It's worth noting
that popping the balloons does not
damage the flowers—so enjoy!

RELATED PLANTS *Platycodon
grandiflorus* 'Mariesii' is a shorter form
(1–2 ft.) that normally doesn't require
staking.

Platycodon grandiflorus

291

Podophyllum pleianthum
Chinese May apple
BERBERIDACEAE

Foul-smelling deep red flowers; huge glossy umbrellalike leaves

24–30 in. high; 24 in. wide

Part shade–full shade

Blooms April–May

Zones 6–9

PRUNING Do not prune. Plants will die back to the ground with the first fall freeze. Foliage may be left in place to decompose or cleaned up in fall.

OTHER MAINTENANCE Chinese May apple is a stunning foliage plant for moist, shady gardens. Loamy, humus-rich, slightly acidic soils will produce the huskiest specimens. Avoid chemical fertilizers, which may burn the leaves. Protect plants from late frosts in spring. Many of the Asian May apples resent disturbance, and some will disappear for no apparent reason, though this species is more durable than most.

RELATED PLANTS Other Asian May apples include *Podophyllum delavayi* (also known as the Chinese May apple), which has fantastic mottled red-brown markings, and *P. hexandrum* (Himalayan May apple), which has pale pink or white flowers followed by vivid red fruit underneath its deeply lobed leaves. Hybrids like 'Galaxy', 'Kaleidoscope', and 'Spotty Dotty' have amazing checkered foliage, but are difficult to propagate and may take some hunting to locate at nurseries. Our native American May apple, *Podophyllum peltatum*, is easier to grow than its Asian cousins, but makes less of an impact in the garden. Unlike the Asian types, which hold their foliage all season (unless drought-stressed), *P. peltatum* naturally goes dormant in summer. It forms a groundcover of jagged green umbrellas reaching 8–18 in. tall and spreads quickly once it has settled in. Mark their location to divide plants in early spring or after dormancy in late summer or fall.

Podophyllum pleianthum

Polemonium caeruleum
Jacob's ladder
POLEMONIACEAE

Small blue flowers on spikes; pinnately compound leaves
18–24 in. (10 in.) high; 18 in. wide
Part shade
Blooms June
Zones 3–7

PRUNING Cutting plants down to lush basal foliage after all flowering is finished may produce some sporadic rebloom later in the summer. Stems decline by late summer anyway, so cutting them down early also keeps the plants looking fresh. Plants can be prolific seeders. If reseeding is not desired, cut plants down before seed has a chance to mature. Although long-lived in the North, plants can be short-lived in southern regions and so allowing some seeding may be the only way to ensure constancy of the plant in such warmer conditions. Leave the basal growth for the winter and cut off any damaged material if needed in the spring.

OTHER MAINTENANCE Plants prefer rich, moist, humus soil. They will take some sun in cooler climates. Foliage scorches in very hot, sunny locations, requiring cutting back. Plants seldom need to be divided, but if desired, perform in late summer.

Polemonium caeruleum

Polygonatum odoratum 'Variegatum'

Polygonatum odoratum 'Variegatum'
variegated Solomon's seal
ASPARAGACEAE

White bell-shaped flowers; broad green and creamy white variegated leaves

2–3 ft. high; 2 ft. wide

Shade

Blooms May–June

Zones 3–9

PRUNING Deadheading is not required for this perennial, as the old flowers simply drop off the plant. Minimal, if any, fruit is produced on this cultivar of Solomon's seal. The foliage holds up beautifully all season with no pruning. It turns an outstanding yellow in the autumn, and the leaves fall off the stems after several killing frosts. The stems usually loosen from the rhizome and fall over after killing frosts; they are easily pulled off at this time. Do not tug on the stems as this will pull the rhizome out of the soil. Cut off the stem if it has not loosened itself for the winter.

OTHER MAINTENANCE Wonderful low-maintenance perennial. Slow to establish—be patient with young plants—but long-lived once it takes hold. Prefers rich organic soil. Tolerant of drought and competition from tree roots once established. The slow-spreading rhizome roots seldom need division, but it can be done in the early spring. Leave several buds per division for best success with transplanting.

Potentilla nepalensis
Nepal cinquefoil
ROSACEAE

Pink, 1-in. flowers on thin stems; strawberrylike foliage with 5-toothed leaflets

12–18 in. high; 24 in. wide

Full sun

Blooms May–August

Zones 4–7

PRUNING After the first flush of blooms winds down in mid- to late July, foliage declines and plants look unruly, so trim them hard at this time and water well. Fresh foliage and an encore of blooms will follow. Cut them again when flowering ceases for the season, and a tidy mound of frost-resistant leaves will form, keeping plants looking thrifty until the worst of winter cold descends.

OTHER MAINTENANCE Nepal cinquefoil is a long-blooming perennial for cool-summer climates. It struggles where nighttime summer temperatures are regularly above 65°F. Full sun and good drainage are essential, and although it possesses decent drought tolerance, regular irrigation will prevent the foliage browning that occurs when plants are stressed. *Potentilla nepalensis* is short-lived if left in place year after year, but if dug up and divided every 2 or 3 years, it will continue to contribute its cheery blossoms to the summer garden. Tall plants may flop in rich soil, though generally not unattractively. Staking isn't much help; choose compact cultivars like 'Ron McBeth' if the relaxed look isn't for you.

RELATED PLANTS 'Melton Fire', 'Miss Willmott', and 'Ron McBeth' are the most common selections of *Potentilla nepalensis* found at nurseries. *Potentilla atrosanguinea*, ruby cinquefoil, is similar in habit and culture and offers single and double flowers in more intense flower colors, like flame-red, orange, and yellow. 'Gibson's Scarlet', 'Vulcan' (deep red), 'William Rollinson' (orange with a yellow eye), and 'Flamenco' (orange-red) are some of the more popular *P. atrosanguinea* cultivars.

Potentilla nepalensis
'Miss Willmott'

Primula denticulata

drumstick primrose
PRIMULACEAE

Spherical umbels of lavender, pink, or white flowers on 12-in. scapes; long, oval basal leaves

8–12 in. high; 12 in. wide

Part shade

Blooms March–April

Zones 4–7

PRUNING Flowers arise very early from winter-dormant aboveground buds. Deadheading will not result in additional blooms and will prevent self-sowing, which most gardeners would appreciate from this lovely species. The frost-resistant foliage is evergreen in mild climates; wait until late winter to tidy up clumps if the leaves are still decent at fall cleanup time.

OTHER MAINTENANCE Like most primroses, drumstick primrose prefers areas with moderate summer temperatures, but this species is more adaptable in this respect than many. Plant it out of direct sun in soil enriched with lots of organic matter—ideally near a pond or other water source where the ground remains constantly damp. Cover plants with evergreen boughs or some kind of noncompactable cover in the winter in the colder parts of its range where snow cover is iffy. This primrose does need a cold period in order to bloom, but the buds—exposed as they are—may be damaged by extreme cold snaps without protection. Divide plants after flowering every few years to keep them vigorous, or allow seedlings to take the place of declining plants.

Primula denticulata

Primula japonica

Japanese primrose
PRIMULACEAE

Tiers of pink or white flowers on 1- to 2-ft. stems; bold basal foliage like romaine lettuce

12–24 in. high; 18–24 in. wide

Part shade

Blooms May–June

Zones 5–7

PRUNING Japanese primrose self-sows when content, so leave spent flower stalks standing unless seeding becomes a nuisance. Remove any yellowed foliage at the end of the season. A small rosette of semi-evergreen foliage may remain throughout the winter in mild-climate areas.

OTHER MAINTENANCE Grow Japanese primrose in constantly moist soil, such as near a stream or in a well-mulched border with regular

irrigation. Areas with moderate summers produce the prettiest specimens. This species prefers a somewhat acid site and will need light or medium shade in all but the coolest regions. Dig and split plants in early spring or fall to maintain vigor, or simply allow self-sown seedlings to replace tired plants. Top-dress with compost in late fall or early spring before new growth emerges.

RELATED PLANTS 'Miller's Crimson' and 'Postford White' are the most popular named varieties of *Primula japonica* and should come true from seed.

Pseudofumaria lutea

(syn. *Corydalis lutea*)

yellow corydalis
PAPAVERACEAE

Tubular yellow flowers; fernlike green leaves
12–15 in. high; 15–18 in. wide
Part shade
Blooms May–September
Zones 5–7

PRUNING Deadheading seems to prolong bloom and reduces prolific seeding. Do be certain, though, to allow some seeding, or the species may be lost from the garden. Plants scorch

Primula japonica

297

yellow corydalis receives mixed reviews. Sometimes it almost reaches weed status in the garden, reseeding with great ambition. I unfortunately have not had this experience. On the contrary, *Pseudofumaria lutea* (formerly *Corydalis lutea*) has been very short-lived in my own gardens and in clients' gardens, seeding only sparingly if at all. Plants are difficult to establish, but even if you make it past this phase, losses occur later or over the winter. Wet soils could be the main culprit. It prefers well-draining, even gravelly soils and slightly alkaline conditions. It likes to grow among rocks. Plants may be divided in the spring or autumn.

Pulmonaria saccharata
lungwort
BORAGINACEAE

Pink buds that open to blue flowers; scratchy silver-spotted leaves
9–15 in. high; 18 in. wide
Part shade–full shade
Blooms March–April
Zones 3–8

PRUNING Old flowering stems of *Pulmonaria saccharata* have a tendency to fall to the outside of the plant after flowering, leaving a clump of basal leaves in the center. The old stems can be grabbed by the handful and pruned off at ground level, which also serves to thin the plants. Such pruning greatly enhances the plant's appearance and reduces the chance of seeding. If the foliage declines or if plants are infected with powdery mildew in midsummer, plants should be deadleafed or, if damage is severe, cut completely down to the ground. Do not compost diseased leaves. Keep plants moist after cutting down. Lush new growth will appear in about 2 weeks. *Pulmonaria* plants may remain semi-evergreen through winter, depending on the weather conditions, planting site, and the particular cultivar or species. If the foliage looks good going into the winter, you may want to leave the plants unpruned

Pseudofumaria lutea

or yellow if given too much sun or if allowed to dry out or, on the other hand, if it stays too wet. In any of these conditions, cut plants back to fresh basal foliage. Basal foliage does not need to be pruned for the winter and may remain semi-evergreen. If plants are not cut down to basal growth in the summer, prune down after several killing frosts for the winter if seeding is not desired.

OTHER MAINTENANCE Even though no pests or diseases afflict this plant,

until spring. If this is the route taken, early spring pruning will be necessary to clean up any damaged foliage before the early flowering begins.

OTHER MAINTENANCE Plants do best with rich, high-organic, moist soil. Avoiding dry conditions can reduce the incidence of powdery mildew and leaf scorch. Plants do not need division for many years, and it's only necessary if the clump becomes crowded. Divide in late summer or early autumn, and keep roots moist, so plants have a chance to establish before winter.

RELATED PLANTS *Pulmonaria saccharata* cultivars and hybrids with *P. saccharata* parentage include striking plants with all-silver or nearly all-silver leaves like 'Majeste' and 'Samouri'. 'Mrs. Moon' is an older selection with the typical spotted leaves; it may seed itself prolifically under wet and cool conditions. 'Pierre's Pure Pink' has spotted foliage and no blue coloration in the blossoms.

'Leopard' has attractive mottled foliage with white splashes.

Pulmonaria longifolia, narrow-leaved lungwort, has also spawned many cultivars and hybrids, such as the classic 'Bertram Anderson' with pink-to-blue flowers over spotted leaves. 'Raspberry Splash' has an upright growth habit. 'Roy Davidson' has flowers that mature to sky blue and foliage that seems to hold up well over the winter in most cases. 'Trevi Fountain' has rich blue flowers and mounds of lush spotted foliage.

Pulmonaria officinalis selections are few, because it is susceptible to mildew. 'Sissinghurst White' is a snow-white cultivar.

Pulmonaria rubra, red lungwort, is represented by selections like 'David Ward' and 'Redstart'. It is among the first of the lungworts to bloom (in coral-red with no blue) and has plain green foliage that is evergreen in protected locations. Red lungwort performs poorly in hot climates.

Pulmonaria saccharata 'Leopard'

Rheum palmatum var. *tanguticum*

Rodgersia 'Bloody Mary'

Rheum palmatum var. tanguticum
ornamental rhubarb
POLYGONACEAE

Stately panicles of pink flowers; enormous jagged leaves that are bronzy red in spring
6–8 ft. (3–5 ft.) high; 4–6 ft. wide
Full sun–part shade
Blooms May–July
Zones 4–7

PRUNING This statuesque perennial is grown for its colossal jagged leaves, which are colored a rich bronze-red until late spring or early summer, when they turn green on the top sides. The towering flower plumes in early summer are a fitting accent. The entire plant dies back to the ground with the first freeze; clean up the big leaves then so they don't smother the crown.
OTHER MAINTENANCE Give ornamental rhubarb plenty of elbow room in a sunny or partly shaded site

in deep, loamy, moist soil. It needs above-average moisture to support its magnificent foliage, but will rot in constantly wet conditions. Top-dress with a generous helping of compost each year. Like edible rhubarb, this plant is a poor performer in hot, humid climates. Look for vegetatively propagated plants, as seed-grown specimens vary in the amount of red pigment expressed in their leaves. Division, though seldom necessary, may be accomplished in early spring. All parts are toxic if ingested.

Rodgersia pinnata
featherleaf rodgersia
SAXIFRAGACEAE

White, pink, or red goatsbeardlike flowers; large, pleated, compound green or bronze leaves
3–4 ft. (2–3 ft.) high; 3–4 ft. wide
Light shade–part shade
Blooms late May–June
Zones 5–7

PRUNING Deadhead flowers after they fade so as to better enjoy the outstanding foliage. The foliage is often damaged by late spring frosts; prune off damaged leaves to make room for new growth. Leaves become scorched and tatty in late summer if not provided with sufficient moisture. In

such cases, deadleaf to clean up the plant and be sure to increase the moisture provided to the plants in the future. Plants are not attractive over the winter and are best pruned down after a killing frost.

OTHER MAINTENANCE Rodgersia requires moist, fertile, humus-rich soil for best growth. Although it prefers constant moisture, it doesn't tolerate standing water. Protect plants from hot sun and strong winds and avoid planting in frost pockets. Rodgersia is slow growing and seldom needs division, but it can be done in the autumn. Watch for slugs.

RELATED PLANTS Some rodgersias, such as *Rodgersia pinnata* 'Chocolate Wings' and *R. pinnata* 'Fireworks', have interesting chocolate-brown foliage in spring that normally changes to green later on. *Rodgersia* 'Bloody Mary' has prominent, heavily texture leaves and dark pink flowers. Several species besides *R. pinnata* are available at nurseries, including *R. aesculifolia*, *R. podophylla*, and *R. sambucifolia*. All are similar in appearance, and even experts have a hard time telling them apart. They require the same care, although *R. pinnata* is considered somewhat less demanding of water than the others.

Rudbeckia fulgida 'Goldsturm'

'Goldsturm' black-eyed Susan
COMPOSITAE

Golden daisylike flowers with black centers; broad coarse leaves
18–30 in. (12 in.) high; 24–30 in. wide
Full sun
Blooms July–September
Zones 3–9

PRUNING Plants have a long bloom period even without deadheading. Seedheads are attractive after the petals fall and are usually left on the plant for winter interest. They also provide good food for the birds in the autumn and winter. Plants may seed to almost weedy proportions in some situations, however, and if this is not desired some or all of the seedheads should be cut down. Stems may topple a bit over the winter as well. Pinching can produce more but smaller flowers on sturdier plants.

OTHER MAINTENANCE Tough, long-blooming perennial. It is so widely used that it could be considered the juniper of the perennial world! Plants have a rhizomatous habit that can form fairly large colonies. Holes may develop in planting. Divide every 4 years to keep strong and to control spread. More frequent division may be needed in light soils where the spread can be fast. Not affected by powdery mildew and doesn't require staking.

RELATED PLANTS *Rudbeckia fulgida* var. *speciosa* (*R. newmanii*), orange coneflower, can seed prolifically. Deadhead most of the seedheads to reduce the population if desired, but leave a few for the birds. Stems hold up well and basal foliage remains evergreen over the winter.

Rudbeckia maxima, giant coneflower, is gorgeous, with towering 5-ft. stems and large, waxy, blue-green leaves. It has attractive seedheads that are favorites of the birds. Tall stems often break over the winter. Minimal seeding. This plant is native to the south-central United States and is great for scale in the border.

Rudbeckia fulgida 'Goldsturm'

Rudbeckia triloba, 3-lobed coneflower, is biennial in nature but usually lives more than 2 years. Very prolific seeder. Cutting most of the flowering stems down to basal foliage after flowering will prevent literally hundreds of offspring from developing, although you should allow some seeding to ensure permanence of the species in the garden. The stems that are allowed to remain will fall over in the winter but are still enjoyed by the birds. The basal foliage remains evergreen.

Plants have a tendency to flop during flowering and may require staking. In a garden setting, pinching or cutting back may be desirable for sturdier growth. Plants pinched or cut back by about a third when 2 ft. tall in early June flowered at about 4 ft., rather than 5 ft., with only a slight delay in bloom time. Cutting back further may be desirable to produce even shorter plants with a greater delay in bloom. Flower size is not noticeably reduced after pruning. A native plant, it is good in a naturalized area where free seeding and flopping are permissible.

Rudbeckia nitida 'Herbstsonne'

'Herbstsonne' coneflower
COMPOSITAE

Golden-yellow, daisylike flower heads with drooping petals; bright green leaves
7 ft. (2½ ft.) high; 3 ft. wide
Full sun
Blooms July–August
Zones 4–10

PRUNING This coneflower has a long season of interest even without deadheading. Not a plant that could easily be deadheaded anyway by all but the tallest of gardeners without the aid of a step ladder. Attractive seedheads extend the season of interest and bring birds into the garden for feeding. Seeding is not usually a problem with this species. Although often touted as having self-supporting stems (perhaps in more northerly gardens), plants in my garden topple over unless given light support. The wonderful height is one of the main reasons to grow this plant, but cutting back or pinching could be used for height control where shorter plants are desirable. Cutting back by half in early June when plants are 2 ft. tall can produce 4½- to 5-ft.-tall plants, rather than the typical 7-ft. height. Flowering may be delayed by a week or so. A few stems still may fall over at this height, but staking is not required. Cut any fallen stems down to the basal foliage before winter and leave the rest.

stake to stake as light support for any wayward stems. Divide every 4–5 years in the spring or early autumn.

RELATED PLANTS *Rudbeckia nitida* 'Goldquelle' has large double flowers that need deadheading or else they look horrendous. Deadheading can also prolong bloom. May need staking in rich soil.

Rudbeckia nitida 'Herbstsonne'

Usually all stems will fall over some-time in the winter, but they are still enjoyed by the birds. If this untidy winter habit is not tolerable, cut all stems down late in the autumn, leaving the basal growth.

OTHER MAINTENANCE Trouble-free plants except for light staking or pruning to handle massive height. Three or 4 sturdy stakes can be placed around the perimeter of the foliage in the early summer with twine tied from

Ruta graveolens
common rue
RUTACEAE

Blue-green aromatic foliage; small yellow flowers
1–3 ft. high; 2 ft. wide
Full sun
Blooms July–August
Zones 4–9

PRUNING Common rue is actually a woody subshrub that may need to be

Ruta graveolens

sheared back to 6–8 in. in the early spring to maintain a full form. Do not do any hard pruning in late summer or plants may not harden in time for the winter. Plants can be grown exclusively for foliar effect, in which case the flowers are best sheared off when in bud. If flowering is permitted, shear off deadheads and shape plants before seed formation, or the foliage may yellow and decline due to energy expended toward seed production. Wear gloves and long sleeves when pruning rue, as some individuals may develop a skin irritation upon contact, which can be accelerated by hot, sunny weather.

OTHER MAINTENANCE Well-draining soil is essential for survival. Tolerates heat and drought. Can be short-lived. Mulch in northern gardens for the winter. Seldom needs division.

RELATED PLANTS *Ruta graveolens* 'Jackman's Blue' is a compact, 18- to 24-in.-tall form that doesn't seem to require as much pruning to maintain its form as compared to the species. The new growth of 'Variegata' is forced by early spring pruning, which consequently enhances the variegation.

Salvia ×sylvestris

(syn. *Salvia nemorosa*)

meadow sage
LAMIACEAE

Spikes of violet-blue, pink, or white flowers; oblong green leaves

18–36 in. high; 24 in. wide

Full sun

Blooms May–August

Zones 4–7

PRUNING Deadheading of perennial salvia encourages a long bloom period. Deadhead to lateral buds. The reddish purple bracts that remain after flowering further extend the interest of the plant, and many gardeners opt to leave the bracts on the plants for a while before deadheading. Plants, particularly older ones, have a tendency to get leggy and open up as the season progresses. If the appearance declines, cut the plant down to newly developed fresh basal foliage. Later rebloom may sometimes occur, although the blooms are usually smaller and fewer in number than in the initial bloom phase. If plants are open and ratty after the initial flowering, it may be best to simply cut the plants down to basal growth, skipping the deadheading. Although this may leave a hole in the garden earlier in the season, fresh low foliage will return and is usually more appealing than the previous shaggy growth. Keep plants moist after cutting back to encourage stronger regrowth. If plants have not been previously cut back, remove top straggly growth for the winter, leaving the low basal growth.

OTHER MAINTENANCE Provide well-draining soil for best performance. These are drought-tolerant, tough plants. They have a tendency to flop if given too much shade or overly rich soil, or if division is needed. Any dividing should be done in the spring.

RELATED PLANTS Select cultivars of *Salvia ×sylvestris* over the species form for more compact growth and longer bloom periods. 'Blue Hill' ('Blauhügel') and 'Rose Queen' both reach 20 in. and have distinctive sky-blue and rose-pink flowers, respectively. 'Caradonna' has tall, strong, slim spikes of violet-blue flowers on dark stems and is a favorite among many garden designers. 'East Friesland' ('Ostfriesland') is a deep violet-blue sterile form that tolerates heat and humidity better than others. Marcus ('Haeumanarc') is a purple-blue dwarf reaching only 12–14 in., and 'Sensation Rose' is a comparable-sized plant in pink. 'May Night' ('Mainacht') grows to 18 in. in height and has been the Perennial Plant Association's Perennial Plant of the Year. 'Plumosa' is 18 in. tall with dense, plumelike, rosy lilac flowers. The New Dimension Series has 8- to 10-in. plants with blue and rose flowers.

Salvia argentea 'Artemis' is a silver sage, a drought-tolerant biennial grown for its striking silver foliage. Allow some flowering for seeding.

Salvia azurea, blue sage, is a 5-ft.-tall leggy plant for which pinching or cutting back is often recommended to control laxness. Plants cut back by half in early June when 15 in. tall reached 2–3 ft. in height, but the stems were still weak and very floppy.

Salvia coerulea (formerly *S. guaranitica*), blue anise sage, has a preference for full sun and moist but well-drained soil and can reach 6 ft. tall or more where growing seasons are long and warm. It normally needs no staking. Its cobalt-blue flowers are a favorite waystation for hummingbirds. Anise sage is hardy to zones 8–10; in colder zones it is often used as an annual. In 'Black and Blue', a handsome black calyx holds each dark blue flower.

Salvia greggii, autumn sage, is a woody but fine-textured sage native to Texas and central Mexico. It requires full sun and well-drained soil and copes well with heat and humidity. Most selections are hardy only to zone 7 or 8, but gardeners in zone 6 have had luck overwintering 'Cold Hardy Pink', 'Furman's Red', 'Pink Preference', 'Texas Wedding' (which may even

Salvia ×sylvestris 'May Night'

survive in the warmer parts of zone 5), and 'Wild Thing'. For the best chance of success, don't cut back *S. greggii* in the fall, but wait until it shows signs of life in spring.

Salvia uliginosa, bog sage (zones 6–10), is spangled with true-blue blooms and reaches 4–6 ft. tall. It grows well in moist or dry soil and may require some staking or pinching early in the season to maintain a good habit throughout its long season of summer and fall bloom. It has a tendency to spread in damp soil, but it isn't hard to control. It may reseed modestly, though not enough to make itself a pest—only enough to make it more likely to return after a hard winter. Don't cut into the woody part of the stem until signs of new growth appear in spring.

Salvia verticillata 'Purple Rain' will have its bloom time greatly prolonged with deadheading. Plants may require cutting back to basal growth after flowering to promote fresh growth and rebloom. Cut plants back if infected with powdery mildew.

Sanguisorba obtusa
Japanese burnet
ROSACEAE

Reddish-pink fluffy flowers; gray-green divided leaves
3–4 ft. (2 ft.) high; 2–3 ft. wide
Full sun
Blooms July–August
Zones 4–8

PRUNING Deadhead after flowering to

Sanguisorba obtusa

enjoy the attractive blue-green leaves. The outer leaves often decline by late summer, particularly with dry conditions; deadleaf or shear foliage down to fresh lower growth. Foliage crisps with autumn frost. Cut plants down for the winter, or leave up and prune back in the early spring.

OTHER MAINTENANCE Burnet isn't an overly exciting garden perennial, but the foliage effect is different. It is a tough, low-maintenance plant. Avoid dry conditions, or leaf scorching will occur. Plants can be subject to Japanese beetle attacks. Divide clumps every 4–5 years in the spring.

RELATED PLANTS *Sanguisorba officinalis*, greater burnet (zones 3–8), has maroon flower heads on 3–4 ft. stems. Plant it in full sun in the North, but give it afternoon shade in hotter climates. In exposed sites it may need the support of ornamental grasses or other plants to help keep it upright during its bloom period in midsummer. The seedheads have ornamental interest in fall, but be careful not to let too many seeds drop, because greater burnet can become an overenthusiastic reseeder.

Sanguisorba tenuifolia 'Purpurea' (zones 4–7) should be also deadheaded to prevent heavy seeding.

Santolina chamaecyparissus
lavender cotton
COMPOSITAE

Bright yellow buttonlike flower heads; tiny gray leaves
18 in. high; 18–24 in. wide
Full sun
Blooms July–August
Zones 6–8

PRUNING Plants should be sheared and shaped as needed in the spring. In most years shearing off the dead tips after the plant breaks bud is all that is necessary. A hard spring shearing to 6–8 in. every 2–3 years is usually beneficial to prevent the plants from becoming leggy. The flowers are enjoyed by some and considered a

Santolina chamaecyparissus

distraction from the foliage by others; those in the latter camp may choose to shear off the flower buds to prevent flowering. Plants also tend to lose their form if flowering is allowed. If buds are not removed before flowering, deadheads should be sheared off before seed formation, and plants can be shaped at the same time. Light shearing throughout the summer can help keep the plants in shape at the expense of flowering, and this is particularly useful if plants are being utilized as a low hedge. Plants may not tolerate hard shearing in the summer, particularly in hot regions. Also avoid any hard shearing after August so that plants have a chance to harden for the winter.

OTHER MAINTENANCE Well-draining soil is essential to survival. Drought tolerant. May melt out in humid conditions. Winter mulching is beneficial in areas colder than zone 6.

RELATED PLANTS *Santolina chamaecyparissus* var. *nana* is a 10-in. dwarf form that holds its shape better than the straight species.

Saponaria ocymoides
rock soapwort
CARYOPHYLLACEAE

Small deep pink flowers; small oval leaves
5–10 in. high; 12 in. wide
Full sun
Blooms May–June
Zones 3–7

PRUNING Plants should be sheared back by half after flowering to keep them full and compact. Sporadic rebloom may occur. Shearing back before seed set prevents self-seeding, which can be troublesome in some gardens. Do not prune for the winter. Clean up any winter damage in the spring as needed.

OTHER MAINTENANCE Good drainage, particularly over the winter, is essential. Avoid overly rich soil, which promotes rank growth. Divide in the spring or autumn.

RELATED PLANTS *Saponaria* ×*lempergii* 'Max Frei' flowers in midsummer. Cut back by half to two-thirds for sporadic autumn rebloom.

Saponaria ocymoides

Saxifraga stolonifera

Saxifraga stolonifera

strawberry begonia
SAXIFRAGACEAE

Airy sprays of delicate white flowers; rounded leaves with scalloped margins and silver veining

12–18 in. (4–8 in.) high; 12–18 in. wide

Part shade–full shade

Blooms May–June

Zones 6–9

PRUNING The blooms last for only a few weeks in late spring. The flower stems then collapse and disappear; gardeners impatient for this to happen naturally may wish to prune out spent blooms promptly. Plants spread by means of strawberrylike runners with plantlets attached, and growth may be easily curtailed by pulling or digging out any unwanted sections. The foliage is evergreen in a protected spot. After harsh winters, the leaves may look rough and need some tidying with a quick shearing. Fresh new foliage will follow in spring.

OTHER MAINTENANCE This lovely old-fashioned foliage plant is often grown as a houseplant. It appreciates moist but well-drained shady sites and a woodsy soil or one amended with compost or leaf mold.

RELATED PLANTS *Saxifraga stolonifera* 'Maroon Beauty' has burgundy-infused leaves. 'Harvest Moon' sports bright yellow leaves and must be carefully sited so it receives enough light to bring out the yellow tones but not so much that the foliage burns. *Saxifraga* is a diverse genus represented by hundreds of species, but only a couple are mentioned here because the vast majority of them are poor performers in the average American perennial border; they prefer the sharp drainage of the rock garden and a cooler, gentler climate than most areas of the United States can provide.

Saxifraga ×*urbium* (London pride) is another relatively adaptable selection that could be given a try. Its leathery evergreen rosettes are topped with white flowers in late spring; *S.* ×*urbium* 'Aureopunctata' is an especially charming form with yellow-splotched foliage for year-round interest.

Scabiosa columbaria 'Butterfly Blue'

'Butterfly Blue' pincushion flower
CAPRIFOLIACEAE

Light blue flowers; green leaves
12 in. (6 in.) high; 12 in. wide
Full sun or light shade
Blooms May–October
Zones 3–7

PRUNING Deadheading prolongs bloom and keeps plants looking fresh. It can be a tedious job, as an established plant can produce hundreds of flowers in a season! And be careful, because it is easy to confuse the round bristly deadheads and the flat bristly new buds. The flowering stems usually branch with 2 or more flowers per stem. Deadhead by cutting the old flower and its stem down to a new lateral flowering stem or bud, and when that lateral stem is finished flowering it should be cut down to another lateral flowering stem or bud, if present, or to the basal foliage. Sometimes the stems will not branch; in that case, simply deadhead down to the basal foliage. First-year plants give the gardener a little honeymoon period by requiring only a couple of deadheading sessions to keep the plants going strong. In future years more frequent deadheading will be required. Also, with age, plants may tend to get slightly woody, developing a central leader, rather than staying in a nice herbaceous mound. Simply pinch back the woody central leader as it develops. Any severe pruning can kill the plant if no basal growth is breaking. Old flowering stems can be cut back before winter, but the basal foliage should not be cut back because it remains evergreen to semi-evergreen for most of the winter. Simply cut off any dead outer leaves in early spring before new growth begins.

OTHER MAINTENANCE Without well-draining soil, plants are usually short-lived, especially in heavy soils. High-organic, fertile soil is best, and plants prefer a neutral to alkaline pH. They like a cooler, more humid climate than is found in Ohio, but our summer heat hasn't seemed to ruffle them. Divide every 3–4 years, but only if the plants are crowded.

RELATED PLANTS *Scabiosa caucasica*, pincushion flower, bears fewer flowers than *S. columbaria*, but deadheading will help prolong bloom through the summer.

Scabiosa columbaria 'Butterfly Blue'

Sedum rupestre 'Angelina'

Sedum rupestre 'Angelina'
'Angelina' stonecrop
CRASSULACEAE

Starry yellow flowers; succulent, yellow, needlelike foliage

4–6 in. high; 15–24 in. wide

Full sun–part shade

Blooms June–July

Zones 4–8

PRUNING The yellow flowers are practically invisible against the yellow foliage, but the bees love them, so leave them up while they have pollen to provide. After the blooms are spent, cut the flower stalks down, as they aren't ornamental at that stage, and seed production may sap energy from the foliage, making it deteriorate a bit. Plants can be trimmed at any time if the foliage looks tired, and sections can be cut, dug, or yanked out by hand if plants spread too far (and they probably will). 'Angelina' takes on deep golden, orange, and bronze tones in cold weather and is evergreen or semi-evergreen most winters, so wait until early spring to clean them up.

OTHER MAINTENANCE Plant 'Angelina' in full sun and well-drained soil. It likes average to low moisture, but not bone-dry conditions. This is an easy-to-grow plant, but it may get pushy and overtake smaller, weaker plants if left unchecked, so it does require some maintenance. That said, it makes an excellent groundcover. Too much shade will turn the bright yellow foliage lime green.

RELATED PLANTS Countless other low-growing stonecrops make valuable contributions to the garden.

Sedum album, white stonecrop (zones 3–8), has white or pink flowers in summer and tiny nubbly evergreen leaves. Varieties like 'Orange Ice' have colorful foliage that intensifies in cold weather.

Sedum makinoi 'Ogon' (zones 6–9) has tiny, round, lemon-yellow leaves. It needs afternoon shade in hot climates or it will scorch.

Sedum rupestre 'Blue Spruce' is the blue-leaved brother to 'Angelina' and holds its blue "needles" through the winter.

Sedum sieboldii, October daphne (zones 3–9), has pink flowers late in the year and blue-green leaves that take on pink and orange tones in fall. It's a slow-growing deciduous clumper whose stems radiate out from a single point. The stems break off easily.

Sedum spathulifolium 'Capo Blanco' (zones 5–9) is a silvery white ground-cover stonecrop that struggles in the eastern United States. Where it can be grown well (on the West Coast), it is fantastic.

Sedum spurium, two-row stonecrop (zones 3–8), is variable in quality depending on variety. 'John Creech' is an excellent glossy green groundcover. 'Dragon's Blood' is the most common purpleleaf form, but it doesn't hold its color well; 'Fuldaglut' is a better red-leaved performer. *Sedum spurium* is evergreen or semi-evergreen in protected sites.

Sedum telephium 'Matrona'

'Matrona' stonecrop
CRASSULACEAE

Light pink flower heads; fleshy gray-green leaves on purple stems
24–30 in. high; 18–24 in. wide
Full sun–part shade
Blooms August–September
Zones 3–9

PRUNING Sedum 'Matrona' should not be deadheaded, as it is among the most outstanding of perennials for winter interest. The spent flowers look amazing when coated with frost and snow. In the early spring, they stand tall above light blue-green nubs of new growth at the base of the plant, and it is best to cut them off at this time.

Plants may flop if grown in too much shade or in overly rich soil. They respond well to pinching or cutting back for height control. Smaller, more numerous flowers are produced and flowering may be delayed slightly. Plants can be cut back to 4 in. when they are about 8 in. tall, normally in early June. They could also be pinched at this time. Many gardeners prefer the results obtained from pinching as compared to cutting back, claiming that cutting back causes the plants to callus and break off in winter weather, whereas pinching does not.

OTHER MAINTENANCE This is a low-maintenance, undemanding perennial that's great for the beginning gardener. 'Matrona' is normally pest free but occasionally may be troubled by aphids. Provide well-draining soil and full sun to part shade for best performance. It is a drought tolerant plant. Division is not needed for many (6–10) years and should be performed in the early spring when necessary.

RELATED PLANTS Other upright stonecrops make easy and colorful garden additions.

Sedum 'Autumn Joy' (zones 3-10), with pink flowers that turn bronze-red, is a classic that's simple to grow. Prune as for 'Matrona'. Sedum 'Neon' is similar to 'Autumn Joy', but with amped-up, vivid pink flower heads. Autumn Charm ('Lajos') is a sport of 'Autumn Joy' with cream-variegated leaves. You'll want to prune out any all-green branches if they appear on Autumn Charm, though this form, unlike the earlier 'Frosty Morn', is quite stable.

Sedum maximum subsp. ruprechtii 'Hab Gray' (zones 3–8) has cool blue-gray leaves and pale yellow to white flower heads. It is easy to please.

Sedum 'Purple Emperor' (zones 3–7) benefits from a pinch to add fullness. Like most of the purple-leaved upright stonecrops, it wants to sprawl, and also like most of the really dark stonecrops, the foliage tends to go downhill in mid- to late summer. 'Postman's Pride' has glossy, chocolate-brown leaves and suffers from the same problems, but early in the year it is glorious.

Sedum telephium 'Matrona'

Sidalcea malviflora

checker-mallow
MALVACEAE

Pink flower spikes; round or lobed glossy green leaves

3–4 ft. high; 2 ft. wide

Full sun or part shade

Blooms June–August

Zones 5–7

PRUNING Deadhead plants to lateral flowering spikes to keep them blooming into September and to prevent prolific seeding. Cut plants down to the ground if the stems should decline (usually due to hot and dry conditions), or when all flowering is finished. Some authorities feel that deadheading the plants regularly and cutting them down when all flowering is done will prolong the life of this often short-lived perennial. Keep plants moist after cutting down. If cut back in midsummer, low new growth and possible rebloom may occur. In especially hot summers, however, new growth may not develop until the return of cooler autumn weather, usually sometime in late September. If plants have not already been cut down, do so for the winter.

OTHER MAINTENANCE Performs best in moist, cool climates. Foliage often declines with hot and humid weather and dry soil in summer. Keep plants moist during such conditions, but provide well-draining soil. Divide in the autumn after about the 3rd year if needed; be careful when dividing, because of the taproot. May need support unless more compact cultivars are selected. Often short-lived.

RELATED PLANTS Sidalcea 'Loveliness', 'Oberon', and 'Puck' are dwarf cultivars that reach 2–2½ ft. tall and normally do not require support.

Silene coronaria

(syn. *Lychnis coronaria*)

rose campion
CARYOPHYLLACEAE

Vivid magenta flowers; fuzzy gray stems and leaves

2–3 ft. high; 1½ ft. wide

Full sun

Blooms June–July

Zones 4–8

PRUNING Regular deadheading, every week or so through July and August, can prolong bloom by several weeks or

Sidalcea malviflora

more. Deadheading each small individual seedhead to a new lateral flower or bud is a tedious job. Snipping with sharp pruning scissors and just letting the deadheads drop to the ground appears to be the most efficient method. Deadheading before seed sets can prevent prolific reseeding. Plants are so narrow, though, that seedlings pop up along walks and between plants without much harm in large gardens, and they add a spontaneous charm. My son Zachary fell in love with this plant when he was 2 years old, and rose campion continues to be his favorite. He saved it from the compost pile, inspiring in me a whole new attitude toward the plant, and hence allowing innumerable seedlings to make a home in all our perennial gardens. Seeding ensures this short-lived plant's presence in the garden, and an approach to prevent overabundance is to allow only a few of the stems to seed, or leave up only some of the late flowers to set seed. But gardeners with limited space may still find them imposing.

Cutting the old flowering stems down to the fuzzy basal leaves before seed set, and thus preventing seeding, may prolong the life of the existing plant in the garden. These normally biennial plants may act more perennial in nature if treated in this way. Plants can be deadheaded and then cut down, or they can be cut down after the majority of the initial flowering is completed, skipping the arduous task of deadheading but also missing the prolonged bloom. If plants are cut down without deadheading, it is usually performed in late July. Plants may send up sporadic rebloom after being cut back, but not always.

Rose campion responds well to pinching or cutting back before flowering to reduce height and create more compact and attractive plants. Plants cut back by half when 15 in. tall in early June, while in bud, flowered at 2 ft. rather than 3 ft. and were strong even in partial shade. Flowering was delayed by 2–3 weeks. Plants pinched

Silene coronaria 'Alba'

at 6 in. tall were also shorter and sturdier but with no flower delay.

Periodic deadleafing may be needed to clean up plants if summer humidity and moisture are high. The gray basal foliage on the plants holds well into winter. Cutting off winter-damaged leaves in early spring is often necessary to improve the overall appearance of the plant.

OTHER MAINTENANCE Well-draining soil, particularly over the winter, is key to preventing death from rotting. Clumps often open up in the center if the soil is too heavy. Frequent division is necessary to maintain vigor. A short-lived perennial.

RELATED PLANTS *Silene coronaria* 'Alba' is a white form of rose campion that will bloom from late spring into early autumn.

Silene dioica 'Firefly' is a great cut flower. Its fully double bright magenta flowers appear in early summer to midsummer. Cut it back to its semi-evergreen basal foliage after flowering. Well-drained soil is required and it is drought tolerant. 'Firefly' can be short-lived, but it is worth replacing if needed.

Silphium laciniatum

Silphium laciniatum
compass plant
COMPOSITAE

5-in.-wide golden daisies on tall stems; sandpapery, deeply lobed basal foliage
6–9 ft. (2–4 ft.) high; 2–3 ft. wide
Full sun
Blooms July–August
Zones 3–8

PRUNING This rugged native prairie plant has a respectable presence in the winter garden, and its seedheads serve as bird food; don't cut plants down until late winter. Occasional deadleafing may be in order during the growing season.

OTHER MAINTENANCE Compass plant is a striking addition to the informal wildlife-friendly border. Plant it in full sun in any type of soil provided it has decent drainage. Allow a couple of years for it to become established and don't try to move or divide it once it's settled in. *Silphium laciniatum* develops a deep taproot, which enables it to survive periods of drought and live for upward of 100 years on the moderate amount of rainfall typical of tallgrass prairielands in the Midwest. Flower stalks may flop in bad storms. Stakes may be used to support flower stems if lodging is a problem, but be sure to use heavy-duty stakes—the stalks are hefty. Left on their own, the leaning stems do bring the flowers down to eye level, which isn't all that bad.

RELATED PLANTS *Silphium terebinthinaceum*, prairie dock, is a similar taprooted species with bold, unlobed basal leaves and yellow daisy flowers on stems that rise as high as 10 ft. Plant it in all-day sun, or it will lean toward the light.

Silphium perfoliatum

cup plant
COMPOSITAE

3-in.-wide yellow daisies on tall stalks; pairs of coarsely toothed leaves that form cups around the stems

5–9 ft. high; 2–3 ft. wide

Full sun–light shade

Blooms July–September

Zones 3–8

PRUNING Cup plant can self-sow abundantly. You may want to curb reseeding by deadheading, but because the seed is a finch favorite, a better plan might be to only plant this overenthusiastic prairie native in spacious naturalistic gardens where it has permission to spread. Plants may lean or bend in strong storms but can be made sturdier by cutting them back by half when they reach about 4 ft. tall. Bloom time won't be delayed if trimming is accomplished by mid-June. Cleanup of dead stems is most easily accomplished by waiting until late winter or early spring if winter weather persists. By then the stalks will have dried completely and may be cleanly snapped off at the base and carted away to the compost pile. Any remaining debris may be left in place to decompose.

OTHER MAINTENANCE Cup plant prefers more moisture than other *Silphium* species, and its lower leaves will turn brown and begin to drop if it becomes drought stressed. It tolerates a bit of shade but is best in full sun. This plant spreads by rhizomes as well as by seed and may need to be contained by regular mowing around the planting perimeter or by roguing out unwanted plants. The hordes of butterflies it brings to the garden (especially tiger swallowtails) make it worth the effort to maintain.

Silphium perfoliatum

Sisyrinchium angustifolium

blue-eyed grass
IRIDACEAE

Tiny blue flowers with yellow throats; grasslike leaves
10–12 in. high; 8–12 in. wide
Full sun
Blooms May–June
Zones 3–8

Sisyrinchium angustifolium

PRUNING Deadheading old flowering stems doesn't seem to prolong bloom, and the flowers melt away nicely when finished. Shear plants back by half after all flowering is done and before seed set to keep foliage fresh and to prevent self-seeding. Do not prune again for the winter. Prune as needed in the spring.

OTHER MAINTENANCE Plants require moist yet well-draining soil for best performance. May require frequent division (every 1–3 years) to maintain vigor; divide after flowering.

Solidago hybrids

goldenrod
COMPOSITAE

Yellow plumes; green leaves
1–5 ft. high; 1–3 ft. wide
Full sun
Blooms July–October
Zones 3–8

PRUNING When goldenrods are grown in a border situation, rather than in a wild setting, they may benefit from the following pruning. Taller growing forms develop a better habit when cut back by half in early June, which reduces their height and creates more compact growth that doesn't require staking. Similar cutting back can also delay flowering on early bloomers. Another method that can be used with goldenrod is to pinch plants in May. Pinching will not reduce the plant's height as dramatically as will cutting back, but it creates more heavily branched growth, which may be desirable for shorter forms. Pinching in May usually delays the bloom of July-flowering forms into August, when flowering may be preferable. Early bloomers may get tatty by late summer and so can be cut down to the base if needed. Goldenrods often reseed; although plants can provide interest over the winter, cutting down the stems after flowering can prevent unwanted offspring.

OTHER MAINTENANCE Goldenrods are tolerant of a variety of soil conditions, except extremes. Avoid overly rich soil, which contributes to lanky

Solidago. Pruning at the proper time (late May–early June) for height control creates an appealing plant.

growth. Goldenrods can be either clump formers or spreaders. Rapid-spreading rhizomes often require division or removal of the outside of the expanding clump to control spread. Clump-forming types may not need division until about their 4th year. *Solidago* plants should be divided in the spring or after flowering in the autumn.

RELATED PLANTS Most *Solidago* hybrid cultivars are shorter growing than the native species. Some of the more notable such cultivars include 'Cloth of Gold', 18–24 in. tall; 'Crown of Rays', 24 in., which often starts flowering in July but can be delayed until August with pinching or cutting back; and 'Golden Fleece', a 15- to 18-in.-tall, heavily branched and spreading form that flowers in late summer to autumn.

Solidago caesia, wreath goldenrod, is a woodland type that grows in part shade and dry conditions. Avoid deep shade. It grows 1–3 ft. tall.

Solidago sempervirens, seaside goldenrod, tolerates poor, high-sodium, sandy soils. It grows 4–6 ft. tall and benefits from cutting back before flowering for height control.

Solidago speciosa, showy goldenrod, is at home in average to dry conditions and will get floppy in soils that are too rich or too moist. It reaches 2–4 ft. tall, with most of the flowers concentrated at the top of the stems. It may be pinched to control height and add fullness.

Many hybrid cultivars, which most likely derive from *Solidago canadensis*, *S. sphacelata*, and *S. virgaurea*, can be rapid spreaders that require frequent control.

Spigelia marilandica
Indian pink
LOGANIACEAE

Upward-facing, tubular red flowers with yellow throats; smooth elliptical leaves in pairs

12–24 in. high; 12–18 in. wide

Part shade–full shade

Blooms June

Zones 5–9

PRUNING Indian pink blooms for about a month in late spring or early summer and will often rebloom in August. No pruning is needed for shaping or for seedling control; a few self-sown plants may appear, but never enough of them to be a nuisance.

OTHER MAINTENANCE This native wildflower of the Southeast is easy to please. The ideal site would be in part shade with regular water, but *Spigelia marilandica* isn't rigid in its requirements and will tolerate full sun with a bit more water. It will also grow in dry shade without much complaint, once established. Division is rarely necessary but may be accomplished in early spring if more plants are desired.

Spigelia marilandica

Stachys byzantina
lamb's ears
LAMIACEAE

Scraggly pink flowers on a silvery spike; woolly, soft gray leaves

12–15 in. (8 in.) high; 18 in. wide

Full sun

Blooms June–July

Zones 4–8

PRUNING Deadheading keeps the plants attractive and reduces the decline of the foliage, which can occur for several reasons, including if the plant is allowed to go to seed. Removing the flowering spikes before they bloom may be desirable since the flowers are not especially significant and their appearance can detract from the outstanding silver foliage for which the plant is primarily grown.

Plants may benefit from thinning in midsummer to open them up to more sunlight and better air circulation, thus reducing the chance for rot.

Deadleafing often is needed periodically throughout the summer to remove rotted or generally declined foliage. Leaves snap off easily with a sharp thumbnail. Cut back any large sections of the plant that may have rotted. Regrowth usually will occur in the autumn. Do not prune plants for the winter; cut off winter-damaged foliage in the early spring.

OTHER MAINTENANCE Good drainage is the primary requirement for good growth. Foliar diseases and rot can occur in conditions of high moisture and humidity. Avoid overhead irrigation, and make sure foliage is dry going into the evening. Divide in the spring every 4–5 years to maintain vigor.

RELATED PLANTS *Stachys byzantina* 'Helene von Stein' has dynamic large leaves that normally hold up well with minimal summer deadleafing in my garden. Thinning of some of the large leaves may be beneficial in southern gardens, although this cultivar appears to be more heat tolerant, as well as more winter hardy, than most forms. It rarely flowers. 'Silver Carpet'

has normal-sized fuzzy silver leaves and also flowers very little. 'Primrose Heron' has interesting chartreuse spring foliage. Mighty Velvet ('Bello Grigio') is a new lamb's ears with amazing narrow, foot-long leaves that are nearly white with fuzz. Mighty Velvet is rated hardy only to zones 7–9.

Stachys macrantha, big betony, is grown mainly for its attractive violet flower spikes. Deadheading usually doesn't prolong bloom, but it does improve the overall appearance of the plant and prevents reseeding. Plants benefit from cutting tatty foliage down to fresh basal foliage later in the summer. Foliage decline is likely to occur if plants are subjected to dry conditions. Plants can spread to form large colonies in rich, moist soil, but spread is minimal in drier conditions. Flower quality and overall plant

performance is improved if the plant is grown in part shade in hot climates and provided with supplemental water.

Stachys officinalis, wood betony (zones 4–8), is also grown for its flowers, which are purplish pink and bloom in June and July. The scalloped foliage is nice, too, and is evergreen in mild-winter areas. Deadhead when blooms are spent to put the focus back on the foliage. The plant usually grows to around 18 in. and creeps outward, forming a groundcover if left unchecked; it is easily controlled if it strays too far. Plant wood betony in full sun or part shade in average, well-drained soil. 'Hummelo', a lavender-pink bloomer and strong performer, is by far the most common incarnation of the species, but with a little hunting, the attractive 'Pink Cotton Candy' may be found as well.

Stachys byzantina

Stokesia laevis 'Klaus Jelitto'

Stokesia laevis

Stokes' aster
COMPOSITAE

Lavender-blue fringed daisylike flowers;
straplike green leaves
12–15 in. (8 in.) high; 15 in. wide
Full sun
Blooms July–August
Zones 5–9

PRUNING Deadheading can prolong
bloom through the summer. Several
flowers are borne per flower stalk and
they usually open from the top down.
Deadhead old flowers down to new
lateral flower buds, then cut the entire
stalk off at the base when all the
flowering is finished. Sporadic
rebloom may occur. Deadheading
often requires close inspection
because the old buds and the new buds
resemble each other after the petals
fall off. The basal foliage remains
evergreen into the winter. Cut off any
dead foliage in the spring.

OTHER MAINTENANCE
Well-draining soil, particularly in the
winter, is essential to survival of
Stokes' aster. It is drought tolerant.
May frost heave with fluctuating soil
temperatures, so spring planting is
recommended; avoid fall planting.
Division in the spring is required about
every 4 years to maintain vigor.

RELATED PLANTS *Stokesia laevis*
'Alba' is a white form that is rather
unattractive as the flowers fade.
Deadhead regularly to keep up the
appearance of the plant. 'Blue Stone'
has a longer bloom period than most.
It may bloom for up to 12 weeks with
deadheading. 'Klaus Jelitto' was rated
by many people as their favorite out of
hundreds of perennials during an
open tour of my gardens, probably due
to the plant's large 4-in.-diameter
sky-blue flowers and glossy, leathery
leaves.

Stylophorum diphyllum
wood poppy
PAPAVERACEAE

Bright yellow poppylike flowers; lobed green leaves with silver undersides
18–24 in. high; 18 in. wide
Shade
Blooms May–June
Zones 4–9

PRUNING Plants self-seed nicely if not deadheaded, creating a naturalized effect in woodland plantings, and the drooping, silvery, poppylike seed capsules are attractive. Deadhead if seeding is not desired. Foliage may yellow and completely deteriorate in hot, dry summers. Deadleafing helps to maintain a decent appearance for a bit longer; if foliage damage is severe, cut back to new basal growth if present. Keeping plants moist will also help the foliage hold longer. Sporadic rebloom may even occur. Plants usually completely die down in the autumn.

OTHER MAINTENANCE Best performance of this native plant is obtained in high-organic, moist soils. Water during periods of drought to maintain foliage. Plants prefer to be left undisturbed. Divide in early spring or fall, taking care to not damage the thick, long roots.

RELATED PLANTS *Stylophorum lasiocarpum* is an Asiatic relative of *S. diphyllum* that has larger, more deeply lobed leaves. It reportedly has a longer bloom period in the spring and summer.

Stylophorum diphyllum

Symphyotrichum novae-angliae

(syn. *Aster novae-angliae*)

New England aster
COMPOSITAE

1½-in. purple, pink, or white daisy flowers; hairy dark green foliage

3–6 ft. high; 2–3 ft. wide

Full sun

Blooms August–October

Zones 4–8

PRUNING Deadhead or cut plants completely to the ground after flowering to prevent growth of seedlings, which do not develop true to cultivar type. Cutting plants to the ground can often come as a relief, because foliage may blacken or deteriorate due to foliar diseases such as powdery mildew. Do not compost infected clippings. Tall-growing forms of New England aster respond well to pinching or cutting back to reduce height, eliminating the need for staking. Such pruning usually produces more flowers per plant as well. Asters can be treated like mums (*Chrysanthemum ×morifolium*) and pinched several times before mid- to late July. Pinching into late July will usually delay flowering. A lower-maintenance approach is to simply cut asters back once by half to two-thirds, depending on the ultimate size of the plant and the gardener's objectives, in early to mid-June. Plants can be anywhere from 12–24 in. tall at the time of pruning. Pruning again later can delay flowering, and the floral display may be slightly reduced. Asters cut back by half in mid-June and then cut back by half again in mid- to late July will flower 2 weeks later than plants pruned only once, and they will flower at 18 in. rather than 3 ft. Plants cut back twice in this way were full and nicely formed, with what appeared to be just a minor reduction in the number of flowers.

Plants can be shaped by cutting the outer stems lower than inner ones and thinned at the same time as they are initially cut back. Thinning is often recommended to improve the overall form of the plant and to increase the air circulation around the plant in the hope of reducing foliar diseases that often affect asters. Thin asters by about a third or more, removing the weakest stems and leaving about 1 in. between stems. Personally, I have not seen much improvement in the plants' resistance to disease with thinning, but thinning does make room for branching of pruned or pinched stems.

Shaping for lower outer branches can help hide the ugly legs that are often associated with asters.

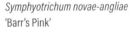

Symphyotrichum novae-angliae 'Barr's Pink'

Deadleafing can also help keep plants attractive. Some asters are attractive over the winter and may provide food for birds, but leaving the plants up can also result in undesirable seeding. Be certain to cut down any diseased plants before winter and clean up debris from the base of the plant.

OTHER MAINTENANCE Asters prefer rich, high-organic, well-draining soil. Watering during periods of drought can reduce leaf decline. Good air circulation can help prevent foliar diseases. If aster wilt should occur, destroy the plants and the roots, as this is where the pathogen resides. Well-draining soil reduces the incidence of aster wilt. Asters benefit from being divided every year or two in the spring to keep them vigorous and to control their spread. Staking is required if plants are not pruned. Chicken wire held up by stakes is an effective method for staking asters.

RELATED PLANTS *Symphyotrichum novae-angliae* 'Andenken an Alma Pötschke' is an older pink variety that's one of the most readily available New England asters, although in an evaluation of asters by the Chicago Botanic Garden, 'Harrington's Pink' and 'Honeysong Pink' New England asters both performed better than 'Alma Pötschke'. 'Purple Dome' is a good, compact, 18- to 24-in.-tall plant that doesn't require pruning for height control. It is often listed as disease free, but this has not been my experience. 'Barr's Pink', 36–48 in., flowers summer through fall and is moderately heat tolerant.

Symphyotrichum dumosum, rice button aster, is a garden-worthy eastern United States native that has gained popularity in recent years via the dwarf (about 12–16 in.) selections 'Wood's Light Blue', 'Wood's Pink', and 'Wood's Purple'. 'Wood's Light Blue' is especially disease-resistant.

Symphyotrichum laeve, smooth aster, is another pest-resistant native. It is best known by the cultivar 'Bluebird', which reaches 3–4 ft. tall and benefits from a trim in June to control its height and reduce its chances of flopping.

Symphyotrichum lateriflorum, calico aster, is yet another excellent native and was a 5-star performer in the Chicago study. It is covered in small white flowers in autumn. Calico aster tops out at about 3 ft., and while a June pinch isn't usually required, doing so will result in an even bushier, more floriferous plant.

Symphyotrichum lateriflorum 'Lady in Black', with deep, smoky purple to bronze foliage is especially attractive.

Symphyotrichum laeve 'Bluebird'

Symphyotrichum novi-belgii, New York aster, is more popular in Europe than here in its native country. It often falls prey to rust. Select dwarf cultivars of New York aster if pruning and/or staking is not desired; even medium forms often need staking. Some notable dwarf forms include 'Professor Anton Kippenburg', 'Raspberry Swirl', and 'Tiny Tot'.

Symphyotrichum oblongifolius var. angustatus, aromatic aster, in the form 'Raydon's Favorite' was another 5-star winner in the Chicago evaluations and is also my favorite aster. I cut it back by half in mid-June, as with other asters, and it flowers at about 2 ft., rather than

3 ft., around early to mid-October. It is dense and full and has lavender flowers, flowering at a time when most of the rest of the garden is finished. It has excellent disease resistance. Divide aromatic aster every couple of years to maintain vigor.

Eurybia divaricate 'Eastern Star' is one of the few asters that grows well in shade but benefits from some morning sun. It has white flowers that are borne heavily on lax plants. This cultivar has received a 5-star rating and benefits from preemptive pruning.

Symphytum ×uplandicum 'Axminster Gold'

'Axminster Gold' comfrey
BORAGINACEAE

Small, nodding, pale lavender-pink flowers; bold scratchy leaves with wide yellow margins
Blooms late May–June
30–36 in. (18 in.) high; 24–30 in. wide
Full sun–part shade
Zones 5–7

PRUNING The mauve flowers are nothing special, but the foliage is fantastic. Some gardeners like to prune out the flowering stems when they appear, holding the plant to about 18 in. tall. Alternatively, you can let it bloom, cutting it back as soon as it's done flowering. Trimmed plants may rebloom later in the season. Remove any all-green leaves should they appear, as well as any leaves that become scorched from drought stress. Cut 'Axminster Gold' back hard at any time if more than a few leaves become unsightly, and new foliage will quickly follow; provide plenty of water when rejuvenating plants this way. The frost-resistant foliage often remains in good shape until late in the year, especially if plants were cut back earlier and are on their second flush of foliage. Prune symphytum any time before growth resumes in spring. Wear gloves when working with scratchy comfrey plants if you have sensitive skin.

OTHER MAINTENANCE Grow 'Axminster Gold' in full sun or bright shade in any soil. It appreciates a yearly topdressing of compost and regular irrigation. This fleshy rooted perennial rarely needs division, but clumps may be split in early spring if more plants are desired.

RELATED PLANTS 'Axminster Gold' is hands down the most garden-worthy symphytum available. Other comfreys are valued more for their durability than for their good looks.

Symphytum ibericum, large-flowered comfrey, reaches 18 in. tall and is a trouper in dry shade where little else will grow. It has red flower buds but the blossoms are creamy white. 'Hidcote Blue', a hybrid, is a vigorous groundcover that also works well in difficult dry, shady spaces. It reaches 18 in. as well.

Symphytum officinale has pink to violet-blue flowers and tops out at 4–5 ft. It may need some support when it blooms. Established comfreys do become deeply entrenched, so think twice about including them in places where you might not want them forever. However, in challenging spots they can be a godsend. If plants look stressed, most will rebound with fresh foliage and flowers after being cut back.

Symphytum ×uplandicum 'Axminster Gold'

Telekia speciosa

RELATED PLANTS *Buphthalmum salicifolium*, willowleaf oxeye, has shorter, 1- to 2-ft.-tall stems, but they are weak and require support. Cutting back by half at planting or in late spring will often help to reduce the flopping problem, although it does not offer a complete cure. Deadheading will prolong bloom. Cut plants back after flowering to clean up toppled stems.

Teucrium chamaedrys

germander
LAMIACEAE

Purple flowers; shiny evergreen leaves
12 in. high; 12–24 in. wide
Full sun
Blooms June–July
Zones 4–9

PRUNING Shear and shape plants in the early spring to about 6 in. from the ground if they grow leggy or woody, or if they are being used for hedging.

Teucrium chamaedrys

Thalictrum aquilegiifolium

Shear off flower buds if bloom is not desired on hedge plants. An annual shearing of winter-damaged branch tips generally is needed in the spring, at least in the Midwest and colder areas, as germander invariably is injured over the winter. Plants can also be sheared by about a third and shaped after flowering to promote fuller growth. Any heavy pruning should be done by late August to allow the plants to harden for the winter.

OTHER MAINTENANCE Requires well-draining soil. Usually suffers winter burn in areas of high winds. Protect plants with evergreen boughs. Not really a reliable hedge plant in the Midwest, as winter damage is more the norm. Divide in the spring, if needed.

Thalictrum aquilegiifolium

meadow rue
RANUNCULACEAE

Fuffy pink flower heads; columbinelike leaves

2–3 ft. high; 2–3 ft. wide

Part shade

Blooms May–June

Zones 5–8

PRUNING Plants often benefit from cutting down to the ground after flowering, when fresh new growth is emerging and old growth is declining, particularly in dry locations. In rich, moist soil the foliage remains attractive all season long, and interesting seedheads develop that further add to the display. Meadow rue may seed itself if not deadheaded. If plants are not cut down after flowering, do so for the winter.

OTHER MAINTENANCE Fairly low maintenance. Prefers rich, moist soils. No staking required. Division generally not needed for many years, but when it is, it should be performed in the early spring or early autumn for establishment before winter. Pest free if given sufficient moisture.

RELATED PLANTS There are a number of outstanding related species. Most of these are taller (3–5 ft.) and flower in the summer rather than the spring. They may benefit from pinching or cutting back when half

Thalictrum 'Elin'

their mature size, sometime in late May or early June, to reduce height and eliminate the need for staking. Foliage may decline after flowering, in which case the plants can be cut back partially or all the way down to basal growth if necessary.

Some of the more notable relatives include *Thalictrum delavayi* 'Hewitt's Double', *T. flavum* subsp. *glaucum*, and *T. rochebrunianum*.

Thalictrum 'Elin' is a lofty 8-ft. meadow rue that has great vigor, stately self-supporting stems, and lavender and pale yellow blooms June through August.

Thermopsis villosa

(syn. *Thermopsis caroliniana*)

southern lupine
LEGUMINOSAE

Yellow lupinelike flowers; palmately compound leaves

3–4 ft. high; 3 ft. wide

Full sun

Blooms May–June

Zones 3–8

PRUNING Interesting seedpods develop if the plants are not dead-headed. The foliage may decline by midsummer; cut the plants to the ground if this occurs.

OTHER MAINTENANCE Southern lupine is often hard to establish because of its taproot, but once plants take hold they can survive with a good deal of neglect for many years. Tolerates low-fertility soil and drought. Avoid disturbing.

Thermopsis villosa

Thymus. Thyme's tendency to self-sow can be a benefit in the garden or landscape, particularly among stepping-stones.

Thymus

thyme
LAMIACEAE

Small pink or purple flower spikes; tiny, scented, oblong leaves

3–12 in. high; 12–18 in. wide

Full sun

Blooms June–July

Zones 5–8

PRUNING Shearing off old flower stems on thyme before seed set will prevent reseeding, but allowing some seeding can be effective in the perennial garden. The tips of the plants are often damaged over the winter. Shear off dead branches to new growth in the early spring. Several distinct forms of thyme exist. Some are subshrubs and some are mat-forming ground covers. The larger, more upright-growing shrub forms may get leggy and woody with age. Shear down to about 6 in. above the ground and shape in the spring every 3 years or so to rejuvenate. Heavy pruning should be completed by late August so that plants have time to harden for the winter. Plants remain evergreen; do not prune for the winter.

OTHER MAINTENANCE Well-draining soil is necessary to prevent rot. Tolerates low fertility and sandy, dry soil. Divide if plants die out in the center.

Tiarella cordifolia

Tiarella cordifolia

foamflower
SAXIFRAGACEAE

White flower spikes; green heart-shaped leaves
12 in. (6 in.) high; 12–24 in. wide
Part–full shade
Blooms May–June
Zones 3–8

PRUNING Deadheading improves the overall appearance of the plant and often produces sporadic rebloom later in the season. The foliage remains evergreen to semi-evergreen, so do not prune for the winter. Plants spread by stolons, and these are easily pulled up and cut off to prevent invasion.

OTHER MAINTENANCE Requires humus-rich, acidic soil. Avoid sunny locations. Tolerates brief periods of drought. Stoloniferous habit is good for use as a groundcover and spread is easy to control. Divide in the spring as needed, or remove and replant runners at any time.

RELATED PLANTS *Tiarella wherryi*, Wherry's foamflower, is a clump

former. Shallow rooted. Plant in the spring for establishment before winter. Press back into the soil if frost heaving occurs.

Tradescantia ×andersoniana

spiderwort
COMMELINACEAE

Purple, blue, white, or pink triangular flowers; straplike leaves
18–24 in. high; 24 in. wide
Full sun–part shade
Blooms June–July
Zones 3–9

PRUNING Plants usually are in flower for 2 months or more, but individual flowers last for only half a day and then the petals neatly dissolve away. Normally all buds are closed by late afternoon (an important feature to keep in mind when designing an evening garden!). Once all flowering is finished in the cluster of buds, deadhead down to new lateral flowers. Deadheading requires close inspection to be sure that all the flowers in the bud cluster have finished. Deadheading is particularly useful to prolong the bloom of young or vigorously growing plants, which may flower for the entire summer. Most often, though, the plant's foliage browns after the initial bloom, or it is infected with rust, normally by midsummer, and the plant will benefit from being cut back by two-thirds or to the ground. New, lush foliage emerges within about 3 weeks. The foliage remains low (6 in.) and plants often repeat bloom, although usually only sparsely. Keep plants moist for more vigorous regrowth. Plants that are stressed by drought, heat, or competition from other plants, or are in need of division, may not put on much, if any, new growth that season after pruning to the ground. Some plants in such conditions will put on a small amount of regrowth when the cool weather of autumn arrives. Cutting plants back or deadheading before seed sets will reduce reseeding, which can be prolific in certain cases.

Spiderwort has a tendency to flop and often requires staking. Cutting the plants back by half in early May or when they are about 12 in. tall can produce more-compact plants. I have even cut plants back by about a third later in May when they were in tight bud—I had forgotten to do it earlier in the month—and although the flowering was slightly reduced with the removal of many of the terminal buds, the plant's habit was more pleasing.

If plants are cut to the ground in the summer, pruning again for the winter is usually not necessary except to remove any flowering stalks that may be present. The new low foliage often remains fairly green into the winter. Plants that are not cut back in the summer should be pruned after a killing frost, as the old flowering stems turn to mush.

OTHER MAINTENANCE This is a good plant for moist areas. Better flowering occurs in sunny locations. Staking may be necessary unless plants are pruned or short-growing cultivars are selected. Divide plants in the early spring or autumn to keep them vigorous or to control their spread.

RELATED PLANTS *Tradescantia ×andersoniana* 'Bilberry Ice' (white with a touch of lavender), 'Concord Grape' (purple), 'Red Grape' (violet-pink), and 'Zwanenburg Blue' (deep blue) are all readily available varieties and are strong performers. Amethyst Kiss ('Redtrad') is an extra-long-blooming blue form. 'Little Doll' stays under 1 ft. tall and doesn't need pruning to stay compact. 'Blue and Gold' (also known as 'Sweet Kate') sports blue flowers and neon-yellow foliage; it appreciates afternoon shade.

Tradescantia ×andersoniana 'Zwanenburg Blue'

Tricyrtis hirta

Tricyrtis hirta

toad lily
LILIACEAE

Starry white or lilac flowers, heavily speckled purple; soft, hairy, oval leaves
2–3 ft. high; 2 ft. wide
Part shade
Blooms September–October
zones 4–8

PRUNING If the seeds have a chance to ripen before being hit by a frost (this is seldom the case in my Ohio gardens), young seedlings will appear at the base of the plant in the spring, though *Tricyrtis hirta* doesn't seed aggressively. If shorter, fuller plants are desired, toad lily responds well to cutting back by half in early June. Flowering may be slightly delayed with pruning. Plants turn to mush when hit by a heavy freeze, so cut them down for the winter.

OTHER MAINTENANCE Best performance is in rich, high-organic soil. Toad lilies are long-lived and easy to grow, and seldom need division. Division should be done in the spring, if desired.

RELATED PLANTS *Tricyrtis hirta* 'Miyazaki' is a seed strain with the typical purple-speckled flowers on 2-ft.-tall stems. 'White Towers' is a pure white form that comes true from seed.

Tricyrtis formosana spreads by stolons but not aggressively so. Cutting it back by half in early June produces a fuller plant that flowers at 2 ft. rather than 3 ft. and with 2 breaks per stem. 'Gilt Edge' and 'Samurai' are similar *T. formosana* selections that feature yellow-margined leaves.

Tricyrtis hybrids include 'Empress', known for its large flowers that open wide (many toad lilies don't seem to want to open fully); 'Sinonome', which has handsome foliage and more drought tolerance than most; and 'Tojen', which has extra-large leaves and opens its unspotted blossoms for a long period, beginning in August.

Tricyrtis pruned before flowering creates fuller, more heavily branched plants, as shown here, comparing the stem of a pruned plant (left) with that of an unpruned plant (right).

Trollius ×*cultorum*

hybrid globeflower
RANUNCULACEAE

Yellow or orange globelike flowers; dark green leaves

18–24 in. high; 24 in. wide

Part shade

Blooms June

Zones 3–7

PRUNING The foliage on hybrid globeflower usually declines after all flowering is finished; cut the plants back at this time and keep them moist. Slight rebloom may occur in the autumn. Feeding the plants after cutting them back may help to encourage rebloom.

OTHER MAINTENANCE Constantly moist, high-organic soils and cool climates foster best performance of this perennial. Not a good perennial for dry, hot regions. Provide supplemental irrigation during dry periods. Plants do not like to be disturbed, and division is not needed for many years. Divide in the spring only if essential, as plants are slow to establish afterward.

Trollius ×*cultorum*

Verbascum

mullein
SCROPHULARIACEAE

Yellow, rose, or white flower spikes; soft, often hairy, coarse leaves
3–6 ft. high; 1½–2 ft. wide
Full sun
Blooms summer (varies with the species)
Zones 5–8

PRUNING Most species of *Verbascum* are either short-lived perennials or biennials. Cutting the old flowering spikes down immediately after flowering may encourage plants to be more perennial in nature. It can also prevent the abundant seeding that often occurs with mullein, and pruning after flowering encourages some species to have a slight rebloom in the autumn. Allowing some seeding in the garden, though, may be the only way for the plants to persist.

OTHER MAINTENANCE Plants need a lean, very well-draining soil for survival. Sandy or rocky soil is preferred. Drought tolerant. Death from "wet feet" is a common occurrence in heavy soils. Avoid high fertility, which can lead to lanky plants. Staking is usually required with the taller forms. Division is seldom necessary. Often attacked by spider mites.

RELATED PLANTS *Verbascum* 'Southern Charm' has lavender or pinkish flowers with purple centers; deadhead spent flower spikes for additional bloom.

Verbascum chaixii, nettle-leaved mullein, is a short-lived perennial.

Verbascum olympicum, Olympic mullein, and *V. phoeniceum*, purple mullein, survive in zones 6–8 and are long-lived under the right conditions. *Verbascum olympicum* may rebloom in the autumn if deadheaded.

Vernonia noveboracensis

New York ironweed
COMPOSITAE

Deep purple, flat-topped flower clusters; coarse green leaves
3–9 ft. high; 2 ft. wide
Full sun
Blooms September–October
Zones 5–9

PRUNING Deadheading plants before seed set can reduce prolific seeding, which may occur particularly in moist areas. First-year seedlings may be desirable, though, as they are interesting, usually short 12- to 14-in.-high plants with intense purple flowers that may be more attractive than the parent plant.

When grown in rich, moist soil,

Verbascum 'Southern Charm'

plants can tower to 9 ft. tall, too large for many perennial gardens. Plants respond to a variety of pruning methods to reduce their height, to create fuller plants, to stagger bloom time, or to layer plantings. One such method is to cut the plants down to the ground when they reach 2 ft. tall. Another is to cut plants back by 1 or 2 ft. when they are 3–4 ft. tall. Plants cut back by 1 ft. won't be that much reduced in height, but they will flower about 1 week later than unpruned plants. Plants cut back by 2 ft. may have about a 3-week delay in bloom and will flower nicely at 2–2½ ft. rather than 4–4½ ft.

OTHER MAINTENANCE Interesting native plant that prefers moist, slightly acidic conditions. The moister the soil, the taller the plants may be. Pruning to reduce seeding and size may be desirable in most perennial gardens.

RELATED PLANTS *Vernonia fasciculata* has a 4-ft. mature height and may be more manageable than V. *noveboracensis* for most garden settings.

Vernonia noveboracensis

Veronica austriaca subsp. *teucrium*

(syn. *Veronica teucrium*)

Hungarian speedwell
PLANTAGINACEAE

Blue flower spikes; narrow, toothed leaves
18 in. high; 24 in. wide
Full sun
Blooms May–June
Zones 3–8

PRUNING Plants have a tendency to sprawl and become weedy. Shear them back by half after flowering; hedge shears work well for this. A low mound develops 2–3 weeks after shearing and the plants stay compact for the remainder of the season. No additional

Veronica austriaca subsp. *teucrium* 'Royal Blue'

pruning is needed until the following spring. If plants are not sheared before seeds mature, reseeding can occur. Plants that are not cut back during the summer may develop long, straggly growth that is unattractive over the winter, so if plants are not cut back in summer it is best to prune stems down to tiny basal growth in late autumn. 'Royal Blue' appreciates well-drained soil in full sun to part shade.

OTHER MAINTENANCE Easy to grow. Provide good drainage. Pea staking can help support the plant during flowering. Divide in the spring or autumn if the plants get too big for their space. Excessive flopping may be a sign that division is in order.

Veronica spicata

spike speedwell
PLANTAGINACEAE

Pink, blue, or white spike flowers; narrow, toothed leaves
10–24 in. high; 12–24 in. wide
Full sun
Blooms June–August
Zones 3–8

PRUNING Deadheading will prolong bloom, and first-year plants often flower all summer if deadheaded. Deadhead plants by cutting them back to lateral buds or, if buds are not visible, to the first lateral leaves. Many forms, particularly the lower-growing cultivars such as 'Red Fox' and 'Goodness Grows', should then be sheared down to the new basal foliage when all secondary flowering is finished. Hedge shears make quick work of this step. The low basal growth remains attractive for the rest of the season, and sporadic rebloom may occur. Some taller forms look best cut down to basal growth as well if their stems start to fall over or if they decline in late summer. Keep plants moist after cutting down.

Taller forms of *Veronica spicata*, such as 'Blue Charm' and 'Blue Peter', can be a bit floppy at times, particularly in overly moist or partly shaded sites; cutting these plants back before flowering produces nice results. 'Blue Charm', when cut back by about 6 in. in early June, flowered at 2–2½ ft., rather than 3–3½ ft., with about a 1-week delay. 'Blue Peter' cut back by half in early June flowered at 1½ ft., about 1 ft. shorter than normal. If tall-growing forms are not cut down earlier in the season, tidy gardeners may opt for pruning plants down for the winter, as the plants are not especially attractive at that point. Magic Show™ 'Enchanted Indigo' is a newer addition—very floriferous and a good rebloomer late in the season.

OTHER MAINTENANCE Provide well-draining soil, particularly over the winter. *Veronica* prefers fairly fertile soil. Staking may be required. My experience has shown that most cultivars and related species—including V. 'Sunny Border Blue', V. *spicata* 'Goodness Grows', and V. *spicata* 'Icicle'—require frequent division to maintain a strong plant, usually by about the 2nd or 3rd year.

RELATED PLANTS *Veronica spicata* subsp. *incana*, woolly speedwell, is a gray-foliaged plant that must have good drainage for survival. Deadheading can prolong bloom. The foliage often gets tatty in midsummer; shear it down for quick regrowth. It is drought tolerant.

Veronica alpina 'Alba', white alpine speedwell, is long blooming with deadheading. Shear when all flowering is finished. The basal foliage remains evergreen through the winter in the Midwest and the South.

Veronica spicata 'Blue Charm'. This species can be pruned before flowering for height control and a slight delay in flowering (foreground); an unpruned plant is in the background.

Veronicastrum virginicum

prior to flowering. Performance may be improved with a summer feeding. Divide plants in the spring as needed. May be subject to fourlined plant bug damage.

RELATED PLANTS *Veronicastrum virginicum* 'Adoration', 'Apollo', 'Fascination', and 'Lavendelturm' ('Lavender Towers') are similar cultivars whose pale lilac-pink spires reach 5 ft. 'Diane' is a pure white selection. 'Pointed Finger' is a fun variant with spikes that point every which way but up, but it was a poor performer in a Chicago Botanic Garden *Veronica* and *Veronicastrum* trial.

Viola cornuta and hybrids
horned violet
VIOLACEAE

Purple, yellow, or white flowers; heart-shaped leaves
4–8 in. high; 6–8 in. wide
Part shade–full shade
Blooms May–July
Zones 4–9

PRUNING Deadheading horned violets can prolong bloom or cause repeat bloom later in the season, but it can be a tedious job. Use a sharp thumbnail to quickly snap off old flowers, or use sharp pruning scissors. Just let the old blooms drop to the ground, as trying to gather such small flowers could drive the gardener over the edge. Deadheading before seed sets can help reduce abundant seeding. I have used hedge shears to shear large areas after most of the bloom is finished to encourage fresh growth and a light repeat bloom later in the season. Plants spread by runners; prune them back to keep plants in control. Shear back any rank growth in the autumn for better spring performance. Pinch plants before flowering if growth looks leggy.

OTHER MAINTENANCE Plant horned violet in moist, well-drained soil enriched with organic matter; good drainage is especially important in winter. Part shade is best. Plants will

Veronicastrum virginicum
Culver's root
PLANTAGINACEAE

Spikes of white or mauve flowers; whorled green leaves
3–6 ft. high; 2–4 ft. wide
Full sun–part shade
Blooms July–September
Zones 3–8

PRUNING Deadhead plants to lateral flower buds for a longer bloom period by 1 month or more. If the old foliage should brown, which often occurs after all flowering is finished, cut it down to new basal growth. Plants may flop in part shade, but cutting them back by half in May or early June can result in more compact, self-supporting plants. Plants cut back by half in early May flowered at 18 in. rather than 3 ft.

OTHER MAINTENANCE This native plant prefers moist, well-draining soil. Best growth is in full sun. Staking will be necessary if plants are grown in too much shade or if they are not pruned

sulk in hot weather and won't live long in warm climates. Like pansies, they are often treated as cool-season annuals where summers get hot and are even used for winter color where winters aren't too severe. Divide violets regularly to keep clumps vigorous, or encourage self-sown seedlings to replace declining plants. **RELATED PLANTS** *Viola* 'Starry Night' is a dense, compact plant with flowers that transition from yellow-orange throats to lavender outer petals. 'Columbine' has a purple and white tie-dye pattern to the petals and comes true from seed. 'Etain' has creamy yellow blooms edged in lavender and is one of the most reliable forms for perennializing. 'Rebecca' is creamy white with purple markings and has a vanilla scent.

Viola 'Starry Night'

Chelone lyonii

For best results, select the right plant for the right place based on maintenance needs. If you have wet soil or are creating a rain garden, Pink turtlehead (*Chelone lyonii*) is a great choice.

Perennials by Maintenance Needs

These lists are to be used as guidelines only. As has been stressed throughout this book, a variety of factors, including climate, annual weather conditions, soil conditions, and even other cultural practices employed by the gardener, will affect a plant's performance. Refer to the Encyclopedia of Perennials and other chapters for more information on individual plants and specifics on maintenance.

1. Perennials that tolerate wet soil

Actaea	*Iris* Louisiana hybrids	*Primula denticulata*
Aruncus dioicus	*Ligularia dentata*	*Primula japonica*
Carex elata 'Aurea'	*Lobelia cardinalis*	*Rheum*
Chelone lyonii	*Lysimachia*	*Rodgersia*
Eutrochium	*Matteuccia struthiopteris*	*Salvia uliginosa*
Filipendula rubra 'Venusta'	*Onoclea sensibilis*	*Silphium perfoliatum*
Filipendula ulmaria	*Osmunda*	*Telekia speciosa*
Helenium autumnale	*Panicum virgatum*	*Tradescantia* ×*andersoniana*
Hibiscus moscheutos	*Physostegia virginiana*	*Trollius* ×*cultorum*

2. Perennials that tolerate dry soil once established

Achillea

Agastache

Armeria maritima

Thermopsis villosa

Artemisia

Asclepias tuberosa

Baptisia australis

Bergenia crassifolia

Boltonia asteroides 'Snowbank'

Centaurea montana

Cerastium tomentosum

Ceratostigma plumbaginoides

Chondrosum gracile

Clinopodium nepeta

Coreopsis

Cota tinctoria

Crambe maritima

Dianthus

Echinacea

Echinops ritro

Epimedium

Eryngium

Euphorbia epithymoides

Festuca glauca

Foeniculum vulgare 'Purpureum'

Gaillardia ×grandiflora

Gaura lindheimeri

Geranium macrorrhizum

Geranium sanguineum

Gillenia trifoliata

Helianthemum nummularium

Helleborus

Heterotheca villosa

Hypericum calycinum

Inula ensifolia

Iris ×germanica

Iris spuria

Knautia macedonica

Lamium maculatum

Lavandula angustifolia

Liatris punctata

Limonium platyphyllum

Linaria purpurea

Linum

Liriope spicata

Malva alcea 'Fastigiata'

Muhlenbergia capillaris

Nassella tenuissima

Oenothera

Origanum

Panicum virgatum

Penstemon barbatus

Perovskia atriplicifolia

Phlomis

Ruta graveolens

Salvia

Santolina chamaecyparissus

Schizachyrium scoparium

Sedum

Silene coronaria

Silphium laciniatum

Silphium terebinthinaceum

Solidago hybrids

Spigelia marilandica

Stachys byzantina

Stipa

Stokesia laevis

Symphytum

Thermopsis villosa

Thymus

Verbascum

3. Clay busters

The following list includes wildflowers and native grasses recommended for clay soils. Reprinted with permission of Neil Diboll, Prairie Nursery, Westfield, Wisconsin.

Andropogon gerardii

Asclepias syriaca

Desmodium canadense

Echinacea pallida

Echinacea purpurea

Elymus canadensis

Eryngium yuccifolium

Helianthus ×laetiflorus

Heliopsis helianthoides

Liatris pycnostachya

Liatris spicata

Monarda fistulosa

Panicum virgatum

Parthenium integrifolium

Ratibida pinnata

Rudbeckia hirta

Silphium integrifolium

Silphium laciniatum

Silphium perfoliatum

Silphium terebinthinaceum

Solidago rigida

Sorghastrum nutans

Spartina pectinata

Symphyotrichum novae-angliae

Vernonia fasciculata

Liatris spicata

Tradescantia
×andersonia

4. **Higher-maintenance perennials**

Achillea millefolium

Achillea 'Moonshine'

Ajuga reptans

Alcea rosea

Anchusa azurea

Artemisia ludoviciana
'Silver King'

Artemisia schmidtiana
'Nana'

Campanula carpatica

Campanula persicifolia

Campanula rotundifolia
'Olympica'

Centaurea montana

Cerastium tomentosum

Chrysanthemum
×morifolium

Coreopsis grandiflora

Cota tinctoria

Delphinium elatum

Dianthus ×allwoodii

Dianthus barbatus

Dicentra formosa
'Luxuriant'

Digitalis purpurea

Fragaria 'Pink Panda'

Gaillardia ×grandiflora

Geum hybrids

Helenium autumnale

Helianthus maximiliani

Iris ×germanica

Kniphofia hybrids

Leucanthemum
×superbum

Lupinus hybrids

Lysimachia ciliata
'Firecracker'

Lysimachia clethroides

Macleaya cordata

Malva alcea 'Fastigiata'

Monarda didyma

Oenothera speciosa

Physostegia virginiana

Primula

Silphium perfoliatum

Symphyotrichum

Tanacetum parthenium

Tradescantia
×andersoniana

Verbascum

5. Lower-maintenance perennials

Boltonia asteroides
'Snowbank'

Acanthus spinosus

Achillea
'Coronation Gold'

Actaea

Amsonia

Anemone pulsatilla

Arisaema

Artemisia abrotanum

Artemisia lactiflora

Aruncus dioicus

Asarum europaeum

Asclepias tuberosa

Aster tataricus 'Jindai'

Astrantia major

Baptisia australis

Bergenia crassifolia

Boltonia asteroides
'Snowbank'

Brunnera macrophylla

Calamagrostis ×acutiflora
'Karl Foerster'

Ceratostigma
plumbaginoides

Chelone lyonii

Chondrosum gracile

Clinopodium

Coreopsis verticillata

Dianthus
gratianopolitanus

Dictamnus albus

Digitalis grandiflora

Echinops ritro

Epimedium

Eutrochium

Filipendula rubra
'Venusta'

Filipendula ulmaria

Gaura lindheimeri

Gentiana septemfida var.
lagodechiana

Geranium macrorrhizum

Geranium ROZANNE
'Gerwat'

Geranium sanguineum

Hakonechloa macra
'Aureola'

Helleborus ×hybridus

Heterotheca villosa

Hibiscus moscheutos

Iris sibirica

Kalimeris mongolica

Liatris

Ligularia dentata

Limonium platyphyllum

Liriope spicata

Origanum

Panicum virgatum

Pennisetum alopecuroides
'Hameln'

Perovskia
atriplicifolia

Phlox divaricata

Phlox maculata

Phlox stolonifera

Podophyllum,
Asian types

Polygonatum
odoratum 'Variegatum'

Pulmonaria

Rodgersia

Rudbeckia fulgida
'Goldsturm'

Rudbeckia nitida
'Herbstsonne'

Salvia ×sylvestris

Saponaria ocymoides

Spigelia marilandica

Stylophorum diphyllum

Telekia speciosa

Thalictrum
aquilegiifolium

Thermopsis villosa

Tiarella cordifolia

Tricyrtis hirta

6. Short-lived perennials

Achillea millefolium

Achillea 'Moonshine'

Agastache, Western hybrids

Alcea rosea

Anchusa azurea

Anemone ×hybrida

Aquilegia hybrids

Armeria maritima

Artemisia absinthium 'Lambrook Silver'

Artemisia 'Powis Castle'

Aster ×frikartii 'Mönch'

Cota tinctoria

Crocosmia

Delphinium elatum

Dianthus ×allwoodii

Dianthus deltoides

Dicentra formosa 'Luxuriant'

Festuca glauca

Foeniculum vulgare 'Purpureum'

Gaillardia ×grandiflora

Gaura lindheimeri

Lupinus hybrids

Malva alcea 'Fastigiata'

Nassella tenuissima

Oenothera fruticosa

Penstemon barbatus

Potentilla

Primula

Pseudofumaria lutea

Ruta graveolens

Scabiosa

Sidalcea malviflora

Silene

Begonia grandis

Begonia grandis

Campanula carpatica

Campanula persicifolia

Campanula rotundifolia 'Olympica'

Centranthus ruber

Cerastium tomentosum

Chrysanthemum ×morifolium

Clinopodium nepeta

Coreopsis grandiflora

Geum hybrids

Gypsophila paniculata

Helianthemum nummularium

Iris domestica

Knautia macedonica

Kniphofia hybrids

Leucanthemum ×superbum

Linaria purpurea

Linum

Lobelia cardinalis

Tanacetum parthenium

Teucrium chamaedrys

Verbascum

7. Perennials to prune for pest and/or disease control

Achillea 'Coronation Gold'

Achillea 'Moonshine'

Ajuga reptans

Alcea rosea

Anaphalis triplinervis

Anemone ×hybrida

Aquilegia hybrids

Chrysogonum virginianum

Clematis recta

Coreopsis grandiflora

Crocosmia

Foeniculum vulgare 'Purpureum'

Helenium autumnale

Heliopsis helianthoides

Helleborus ×hybridus

Hemerocallis

Hibiscus moscheutos

Iris domestica

Iris ×germanica

Lupinus hybrids

Lysimachia punctata

Malva alcea 'Fastigiata'

Monarda didyma

Paeonia hybrids

Persicaria amplexicaulis 'Firetail'

Phlox divaricata

Phlox maculata

Phlox paniculata

Pulmonaria

Stachys byzantina

Symphyotrichum

Malva alcea 'Fastigiata'

8. Deer-resistant perennials

Adapted with permission from the Cornell Cooperative Extension Service.

Achillea

Aconitum

Actaea racemosa

Ajuga reptans

Alchemilla mollis

Allium

Coreopsis

Amsonia

Angelica

Aquilegia

Artemisia

Aruncus dioicus

Asclepias tuberosa

Aster

Astilbe

Baptisia

Bergenia

Boltonia

Campanula

Ceratostigma plumbaginoides

Chelone

Coreopsis

Dennstaedtia punctilobula

Dianthus

Dicentra eximia

Dictamnus albus

Digitalis

Echinacea purpurea

Echinops

Epimedium

Eryngium

Euphorbia

Eutrochium

Filipendula

Geranium macrorrhizum

Geum

Goniolimon tataricum

Gypsophila paniculata

Helleborus

Heuchera

Iberis sempervirens

Iris (occasionally eaten)

Kirengeshoma palmata

Lamium

Lavandula

Leucanthemum

Liatris

Lilium lancifolium

Linaria

Linum perenne

Lupinus

Macleaya cordata

Matteuccia struthiopteris

Monarda didyma

Myosotis scorpioides

Nepeta

Oenothera

Onoclea sensibilis

Origanum

Ornamental grasses, most

Osmunda

Paeonia (occasionally eaten)

Papaver orientale

Penstemon

Perovskia atriplicifolia

Platycodon

Polemonium caeruleum

Polystichum acrostichoides

Primula

Pulmonaria

Ranunculus

Rodgersia

Rosmarinus officinalis

Rudbeckia

Salvia officinalis

Saponaria

Sedum 'Matrona'
(occasionally eaten;
tall sedums are
bothered, low
sedums are left
alone)

Silene

Solidago

Stachys byzantina

Symphyotrichum

Tanacetum

Thalictrum (occa-
sionally eaten)

Thelypteris
noveboracensis

Thymus

Tiarella

Tricyrtis

Verbascum

Veronica austriaca
subsp. *teucrium*

Viola labridorica

9. Perennials that require staking

Achillea 'Moonshine'

Aconitum*

Actaea racemosa

Alcea rosea*

Amsonia*

Anchusa azurea

Aquilegia hybrids

Artemisia lactiflora*

Baptisia australis*

Boltonia asteroides
'Snowbank'*

Campanula
glomerata

Campanula
persicifolia*

Cephalaria gigantea

Crambe cordifolia

Delphinium elatum

Filipendula rubra
'Venusta'

Gaillardia
×grandiflora

Gaura lindheimeri*

Gillenia trifoliata*

Gypsophila
paniculata

Helenium autumnale*

Helianthus
maximiliani*

Heterotheca villosa*

Iris domestica

Iris ×germanica

Leucanthemum
×superbum*

Liatris spicata

Linaria purpurea

Lupinus hybrids

Malva alcea
'Fastigiata'*

Nepeta*

Paeonia hybrids

Platycodon
grandiflorus*

Rudbeckia nitida
'Herbstsonne'*

Salvia uliginosa*

Silphium laciniatum*

Symphyotrichum*

Tradescantia
×andersoniana*

Veronica spicata*

Veronicastrum
virginicum*

Gaillardia ×grandiflora

*can be pruned to avoid the need for staking

10. Perennials that may require division every 1–3 years

Achillea millefolium

Achillea 'Moonshine'

Ajuga reptans

Alcea rosea

Anchusa azurea

Artemisia ludoviciana 'Silver King'

Aster ×frikartii 'Mönch'

Astilbe ×arendsii

Campanula carpatica

Campanula persicifolia

Centaurea montana

Centranthus ruber

Cephalaria gigantea

Cerastium tomentosum

Chrysanthemum ×morifolium

Coreopsis grandiflora

Coreopsis tripteris

Coreopsis verticillata

Cota tinctoria

Crocosmia

Delphinium elatum

Dianthus barbatus

Dianthus deltoides

Digitalis purpurea

Doronicum

Fragaria 'Pink Panda'

Gaillardia ×grandiflora

Geum hybrids

Helenium autumnale

Helianthus 'Lemon Queen'

Heuchera micrantha 'Palace Purple'

Heuchera sanguinea

Hypericum calycinum

Inula

Iris domestica

Iris ×germanica

Leucanthemum ×superbum

Lobelia cardinalis

Lysimachia

Macleaya cordata

Malva alcea 'Fastigiata'

Matteuccia struthiopteris

Monarda didyma

Oenothera speciosa

Origanum laevigatum 'Herrenhausen'

Penstemon barbatus

Persicaria amplexi-caulis 'Firetail'

Phlox maculata

Phlox paniculata

Phlox subulata

Physostegia virginiana

Potentilla

Primula

Sidalcea malviflora

Silene coronaria

Sisyrinchium angustifolium

Symphyotrichum

Tanacetum parthenium

Veronica spicata

Campanula 'Pink Octopus'

Lamium maculatum

11. Perennials that may require division every 4–5 years

Acanthus spinosus

Achillea 'Coronation Gold'

Anaphalis triplinervis

Armeria maritima

Artemisia lactiflora

Aster tataricus 'Jindai'

Astrantia major

Bergenia crassifolia

Boltonia asteroides 'Snowbank'

Campanula glomerata

Campanula rotundifolia 'Olympica'

Ceratostigma plumbaginoides

Chelone lyonii

Chrysogonum virginianum

Dianthus gratianopolitanus

Dicentra formosa 'Luxuriant'

Digitalis grandiflora

Eutrochium

Geranium phaeum

Helianthemum nummularium

Helianthus salicifolius

Heliopsis helianthoides

Hemerocallis

Heterotheca villosa

Iris Louisiana hybrids

Kalimeris mongolica

Lamium maculatum

Liatris spicata

Oenothera fruticosa

Phlox stolonifera

Podophyllum peltatum

Rudbeckia fulgida 'Goldsturm'

Rudbeckia nitida 'Herbstsonne'

Sanguisorba

Scabiosa columbaria 'Butterfly Blue'

Silphium perfoliatum

Solidago hybrids

Stachys byzantina

Stokesia laevis

Thymus

Tiarella cordifolia

Tradescantia ×*andersoniana*

Veronica austriaca subsp. *teucrium*

Veronicastrum virginicum

12. Perennials that may require division every 6–10 years

Alchemilla mollis

Amsonia*

Arum italicum 'Pictum'

Echinops ritro*†

Epimedium*

Ferns, most

Geranium

Iberis sempervirens*

Iris sibirica

Kniphofia hybrids

Ligularia dentata

Limonium platyphyllum*

Nepeta

Ornamental grasses, most

Papaver orientale*

Patrinia scabiosifolia

Phlomis

Polygonatum odoratum 'Variegatum'

Pulmonaria

Rodgersia

Ruta graveolens

Salvia ×sylvestris

Sedum 'Matrona'

Spigelia marilandica

Symphytum ×uplandicum 'Axminster Gold'

Telekia speciosa

Thalictrum aquilegiifolium

Tricyrtis hirta

Trollius ×cultorum*

Verbascum

Iris sibirica

Asarum europaeum

Begonia grandis

Brunnera macrophylla

Echinacea purpurea

Filipendula rubra 'Venusta'†

Filipendula ulmaria

Gaura lindheimeri

Gentiana septemfida var. lagodechiana

*resents disturbance
†tough woody or thonglike roots or taproot

13. Perennials that may require division every 10 years or more

*Aconitum napellus**

Actaea racemosa*†

Anemone ×*hybrida**

Anemone pulsatilla

Aquilegia hybrids

Aruncus dioicus*†

Asclepias tuberosa*†

*Baptisia australis**

Crambe cordifolia

*Dictamnus albus**

Eryngium*†

Euphorbia epithymoides

Gentiana andrewsii

Gillenia trifoliata*†

Gypsophila paniculata*†

Hakonechloa macra 'Aureola'

Helleborus ×*hybridus*

Hibiscus moscheutos

Hosta

*Iris spuria**

Kirengeshoma palmata

Liatris punctata

Molinia caerulea 'Skyracer'

Oenothera macrocarpa*†

Paeonia hybrids*

Perovskia atriplicifolia

Platycodon grandiflorus*†

Podophyllum, Asian types*

Polemonium caeruleum

Rheum

Silphium laciniatum†

Silphium terebinthinaceum†

Sporobolus heterolepis

Stylophorum diphyllum

*Thermopsis villosa**

Asclepias tuberosa

*resents disturbance
†tough woody or thonglike roots or taproot

14. Perennials to deadhead to prolong bloom or for rebloom

Achillea

Aconitum

Agastache

Alcea rosea

Anchusa azurea

Agastache

Aquilegia hybrids

Armeria maritima

Asclepias tuberosa

Aster ×frikartii 'Mönch'

Astrantia major

Begonia grandis

Campanula

Centaurea montana

Centranthus ruber

Clinopodium

Coreopsis

Cota tinctoria

Delphinium

Dianthus ×allwoodii

Dianthus gratianopolitanus

Dicentra formosa 'Luxuriant'

Digitalis

Echinacea purpurea

Echinops ritro

Filipendula ulmaria

Gaillardia ×grandiflora

Gaura lindheimeri

Geranium phaeum

Geum hybrids

Gypsophila paniculata

Helenium autumnale

Heliopsis helianthoides

Hemerocallis

Hesperis matronalis

Heuchera sanguinea

Hibiscus moscheutos

Inula

Knautia macedonica

Kniphofia hybrids

Lavandula

Leucanthemum ×superbum

Liatris spicata

Limonium platyphyllum

Linaria purpurea

Lupinus hybrids

Lysimachia punctata

Malva alcea 'Fastigiata'

Monarda didyma

Oenothera macrocarpa

Oenothera speciosa

Patrinia scabiosifolia

Penstemon barbatus

Persicaria amplexi-caulis 'Firetail'

Phlomis

Phlox maculata

Phlox paniculata

Platycodon grandiflorus

Potentilla

Pseudofumaria lutea

Salvia ×sylvestris

Scabiosa

Sidalcea malviflora

Silene coronaria

Spigelia marilandica

Stokesia laevis

Symphytum

Tiarella cordifolia

Tradescantia ×andersoniana

Veronica spicata

Veronicastrum virginicum

15. Perennials that do not rebloom with deadheading

Acanthus spinosus

Actaea

Amsonia

Arisaema

Artemisia absinthium 'Lambrook Silver'

Artemisia lactiflora

Artemisia ludoviciana 'Silver King'

Arum italicum 'Pictum'

Aruncus dioicus

Astilbe ×arendsii

Bergenia crassifolia

Brunnera macrophylla

Crambe cordifolia

Crocosmia

Epimedium

Eutrochium

Gillenia trifoliata

Helianthus maximiliani

Helianthus salicifolius

Iris Louisiana hybrids

Iris sibirica

Iris spuria

Kirengeshoma palmata

Ligularia dentata

Liriope spicata

Paeonia hybrids

Papaver orientale

Phlox divaricata

Podophyllum

Primula denticulata

Rheum

Stachys monieri 'Hummelo'

Teucrium chamaedrys

Acanthus spinosus

16. Perennials to deadhead to improve overall appearance

Achillea

Alcea rosea

Alchemilla mollis

Anaphalis triplinervis

Anemone ×hybrida

Armeria maritima

Artemisia

Aruncus dioicus

Bergenia crassifolia

Campanula glomerata

Chrysanthemum ×morifolium

Chrysogonum virginianum

Coreopsis grandiflora

Crambe

Delphinium elatum

Dianthus ×allwoodii

Echinops ritro

Festuca glauca

Geranium

Gypsophila paniculata

Helenium autumnale

Heliopsis helianthoides

Helleborus ×hybridus

Hemerocallis

Heuchera

Hibiscus moscheutos

Hosta

Inula

Iris ×germanica

Iris spuria

Knautia macedonica

Kniphofia hybrids

Leucanthemum ×superbum

Nepeta

Paeonia hybrids

Penstemon barbatus

Phlox maculata

Phlox paniculata

Phlox stolonifera

Phlox subulata

Physostegia virginiana

Polemonium caeruleum

Potentilla

Primula vulgaris

Pulmonaria

Rodgersia

Ruta graveolens

Salvia ×sylvestris

Sanguisorba

Santolina chamaecyparissus

Scabiosa

Sedum rupestre 'Angelina'

Stachys byzantina

Symphytum

Tanacetum parthenium

Teucrium chamaedrys

Tradescantia ×andersoniana

Verbascum

Veronica austriaca subsp. teucrium

Veronica spicata

Stachys byzantina

Dicentra formosa 'Luxuriant'

Echinacea purpurea

Lysimachia

Malva alcea 'Fastigiata'

17. Perennials to deadhead to a lateral flower, bud, or leaf

Many of these perennials can also be deadheaded by shearing; refer to Encyclopedia of Perennials for details.

Achillea

Aconitum napellus

Alcea rosea

Amsonia

Anaphalis triplinervis

Anchusa azurea

Angelica gigas

Aquilegia hybrids

Artemisia

Aruncus dioicus

Asclepias tuberosa

Aster

Astilbe ×arendsii

Astrantia major

Baptisia australis

Begonia grandis

Campanula

Centaurea montana

Centranthus ruber

Cephalaria gigantea

Chelone lyonii

Chrysanthemum ×morifolium

Clematis recta

Coreopsis grandiflora

Coreopsis verticillata

Cota tinctoria

Delphinium

Digitalis

Echinacea purpurea

Echinops ritro

Eryngium

Filipendula ulmaria

Foeniculum vulgare 'Purpureum'

Gaillardia ×grandiflora

Gaura lindheimeri

Geranium sanguineum

Geum hybrids

Gypsophila paniculata

Helenium autumnale

Heliopsis helianthoides

Helleborus ×hybridus

Hemerocallis

Hesperis matronalis

Hibiscus moscheutos

Iris

Knautia macedonica

Lavandula

Leucanthemum ×superbum

Ligularia dentata

Linaria purpurea

Lupinus hybrids

Macleaya cordata

Malva alcea 'Fastigiata'

Monarda didyma

Nepeta

Paeonia hybrids

Aster

Persicaria amplexicaulis 'Firetail'

Phlox maculata

Phlox paniculata

Phlox subulata

Physostegia virginiana

Platycodon grandiflorus

Pseudofumaria lutea

Rodgersia

Ruta graveolens

Salvia ×sylvestris

Scabiosa

Sidalcea malviflora

Silene coronaria

Solidago hybrids

Spigelia marilandica

Stokesia laevis

Symphyotrichum

Tanacetum parthenium

Telekia speciosa

Teucrium chamaedrys

Thalictrum aquilegiifolium

Thymus

Tradescantia ×andersoniana

Veronica austriaca subsp. teucrium

Veronica spicata

Veronicastrum virginicum

18. Perennials to deadhead to the ground or to basal foliage

Acanthus spinosus

Ajuga reptans

Alchemilla mollis

Armeria maritima

Bergenia crassifolia

Brunnera macrophylla

Crambe

Crocosmia

Dicentra formosa 'Luxuriant'

Doronicum

Epimedium

Geranium endressii 'Wargrave Pink'

Geranium macrorrhizum

Geranium phaeum

Heuchera

Hosta

Kniphofia hybrids

Limonium platyphyllum

Liriope spicata

Phlox divaricata

Phlox stolonifera

Polemonium caeruleum

Pulmonaria

Stachys byzantina

Tiarella cordifolia

Alchemilla mollis

19. Reseeding plants

Deadhead before seeds mature if seeding is not desired.

Achillea millefolium

Agastache*

Ageratina altissima 'Chocolate'

Ajuga reptans

Alcea rosea*

Alchemilla mollis

Amsonia

Anchusa azurea

Angelica gigas*†

Aquilegia hybrids*

Asclepias tuberosa

Astrantia major

Begonia grandis

Brunnera macrophylla

Campanula carpatica

Campanula persicifolia

Campanula rotundifolia 'Olympica'

Centaurea montana

Centranthus ruber

Chondrosum gracile

Chrysogonum virginianum

Clinopodium*

Coreopsis grandiflora

Coreopsis verticillata

Cota tinctoria*

Dianthus barbatus*†

Dianthus deltoides

Digitalis grandiflora

Digitalis purpurea*†

Doronicum*

Echinacea purpurea

Echinops ritro

Eryngium planum

Euphorbia epithymoides

Filipendula ulmaria

Foeniculum vulgare 'Purpureum'

Gaillardia ×grandiflora

Gaura lindheimeri*

Geranium macrorrhizum

Geranium phaeum

Geranium sanguineum

Helianthus 'Lemon Queen'

Heliopsis helianthoides

Helleborus ×hybridus

Hesperis matronalis†

Hibiscus moscheutos

Iris domestica

Iris sibirica

Knautia macedonica*

Lamium maculatum

Linaria purpurea*

Linum*

Lupinus hybrids

Lysimachia punctata

Macleaya cordata

Malva alcea 'Fastigiata'*

Miscanthus sinensis

Monarda didyma

Nassella tenuissima*

Oenothera macrocarpa

Panicum virgatum

Patrinia scabiosifolia

Pennisetum 'Moudry'

Persicaria virginiana 'Painter's Palette'

Phlox divaricata

Phlox paniculata

Phlox subulata

Platycodon grandiflorus

Polemonium caeruleum

Primula

Pseudofumaria lutea

Pulmonaria

Rudbeckia fulgida 'Goldsturm'

Echinops ritro

Salvia uliginosa

Schizachyrium scoparium

Sidalcea malviflora*

Silene coronaria*

Silphium perfoliatum

Solidago hybrids

Stylophorum diphyllum

Symphyotrichum

Tanacetum parthenium

Thalictrum aquilegiifolium

Thymus

Tradescantia ×*andersoniana*

Tricyrtis hirta

Verbascum*†

Vernonia noveboracensis

*plants are often short-lived; seeding may ensure permanence in the garden
†biennial plants; allow seeding to foster new plants, or deadhead to promote
  perennial nature of existing plant

20. Perennials with attractive seedheads

Actaea

Anemone pulsatilla

Arisaema

Arum italicum 'Pictum'

Crocosmia

Dictamnus albus

Echinacea purpurea

Eutrochium maculatum 'Gateway'

Iris domestica

Iris sibirica

Kirengeshoma palmata

Liatris

Ligularia dentata

Limonium platyphyllum

Liriope spicata

Oenothera macrocarpa

Ornamental grasses, most

Papaver orientale

Phlomis

Rudbeckia fulgida 'Goldsturm'

Ceratostigma plumbaginoides

Asclepias tuberosa

Astilbe ×*arendsii*

Baptisia australis

Begonia grandis

Ceratostigma plumbaginoides

Chelone lyonii

Clematis heracleifolia

Clematis recta

Filipendula rubra 'Venusta'

Fragaria 'Pink Panda'

Gaillardia ×*grandiflora*

Gentiana andrewsii

Gillenia trifoliata

Helianthus salicifolius

Heterotheca villosa

Rudbeckia nitida 'Herbstsonne'

Sedum 'Matrona'

Stylophorum diphyllum

Telekia speciosa

Thalictrum aquilegiifolium

Thermopsis villosa

21. Perennials with self-cleaning flowers

Amsonia

Arisaema

Aster ×frikartii 'Mönch'

Ceratostigma plumbaginoides

Clinopodium

Crocosmia

Dictamnus albus

Fragaria 'Pink Panda'

Gaura lindheimeri

Iris domestica

Kalimeris mongolica

Kirengeshoma palmata

Limonium platyphyllum

Linum perenne

Origanum 'Kent Beauty'

Phlox divaricata

Phlomis

Polygonatum odoratum 'Variegatum'

Salvia coerulea

Saxifraga

Silene coronaria

Spigelia marilandica

Stylophorum diphyllum

Tanacetum parthenium

Tradescantia ×andersoniana

Stylophorum diphyllum

22. Perennials that do not require deadheading

This list includes plants that do not rebloom, that normally do not reseed or have minimal reseeding, that have attractive seedheads, or that have deadheads that contribute to a more attractive overall winter form.

Actaea

Anemone pulsatilla

Arisaema triphyllum

Arum italicum 'Pictum'

Asarum europaeum

Aster tataricus 'Jindai'

Astilbe ×arendsii

Baptisia australis

Boltonia asteroides 'Snowbank'

Ceratostigma plumbaginoides

Chelone lyonii

Clematis heracleifolia

Clematis integrifolia

Clematis recta

Clinopodium nepeta

Crocosmia

Dictamnus albus

Epimedium

Sedum 'Matrona'

Eutrochium macula-
tum 'Gateway'

Filipendula rubra
'Venusta'

Fragaria 'Pink Panda'

Gentiana septemfida
var. lagodechiana

Gillenia trifoliata

Helianthus
salicifolius

Heterotheca villosa

Hypericum
calycinum

Kalimeris mongolica

Kirengeshoma
palmata

Liriope spicata

Origanum 'Kent
Beauty'

Ornamental grasses,
most

Papaver orientale

Perovskia
atriplicifolia

Phlomis

Podophyllum

Polygonatum
odoratum
'Variegatum'

Rudbeckia nitida
'Herbstsonne'

Salvia coerulea

Sedum 'Matrona'

Thermopsis villosa

23. Perennials with seedheads that attract song birds

Rudbeckia maxima

Agastache
foeniculum

Coreopsis tripteris

Cota tinctoria

Echinacea purpurea

Echinops ritro

Eutrochium

Helianthus

Heliopsis
helianthoides

Hosta

Knautia macedonica

Liatris

Ligularia dentata

Monarda didyma

Rudbeckia

Silphium

Telekia speciosa

24. Perennials to cut back to keep in their own space

Achillea millefolium

Aconogonum 'Johanniswolke'

Ajuga reptans

Alchemilla mollis

Artemisia

Aster tataricus 'Jindai'

Baptisia australis

Campanula glomerata

Cerastium tomentosum

Ceratostigma plumbaginoides

Clematis heracleifolia

Dianthus deltoides

Fragaria 'Pink Panda'

Geranium

Monarda didyma

Nepeta

Phlox stolonifera

Phlox subulata

Salvia coerulea

Sedum rupestre 'Angelina'

Telekia speciosa

Tiarella cordifolia

Sedum rupestre 'Angelina'

25. Perennials to cut back after flowering for aesthetics in the spring

Phlox subulata

Aquilegia hybrids

Brunnera macrophylla

Cerastium tomentosum

Clematis recta

Dianthus barbatus

Dianthus deltoides

Dianthus gratianopolitanus

Doronicum

Hesperis matronalis

Iberis sempervirens

Iris ×germanica

Lamium maculatum

Nepeta

Paeonia hybrids

Papaver orientale

Phlox divaricata

Phlox subulata

Polemonium caeruleum

Pulmonaria

Saponaria ocymoides

Stylophorum diphyllum

Thermopsis villosa

Thymus

Veronica austriaca subsp. *teucrium*

26. Perennials to cut back after flowering for aesthetics in the summer

Acanthus spinosus

Alchemilla mollis

Amsonia

Artemisia abrotanum

Artemisia absinthium 'Lambrook Silver'

Artemisia 'Powis Castle'

Artemisia schmidtiana 'Nana'

Baptisia australis

Centaurea montana

Centranthus ruber

Coreopsis grandiflora

Coreopsis verticillata

Crocosmia

Digitalis purpurea

Euphorbia epithymoides

Filipendula rubra 'Venusta'

Geranium endressii 'Wargrave Pink'

Geranium sanguineum

Geum hybrids

Helianthemum nummularium

Heliopsis helianthoides

Hemerocallis

Hemerocallis

Heuchera micrantha 'Palace Purple'

Inula

Knautia macedonica

Kniphofia hybrids

Lavandula

Linum

Lysimachia

Nepeta

Phlox maculata

Phlox paniculata

Potentilla

Ruta graveolens

Salvia ×sylvestris

Sanguisorba

Santolina chamaecyparissus

Sisyrinchium angustifolium

Solidago hybrids

Symphytum

Teucrium chamaedrys

Thalictrum aquilegiifolium

Tradescantia ×andersoniana

Trollius ×cultorum

27. Perennials to deadhead to a lateral leaf, bud, or flower and then cut back to basal foliage

Patrinia scabiosifolia

Achillea

Aconitum napellus

Alcea rosea

Anaphalis triplinervis

Anchusa azurea

Aquilegia hybrids

Artemisia lactiflora

Astrantia major

Campanula

Centaurea montana

Coreopsis grandiflora

Cota tinctoria

Delphinium

Digitalis grandiflora

Echinops ritro

Eryngium

Filipendula ulmaria

Gaillardia ×grandiflora

Gypsophila paniculata

Helenium autumnale

Hesperis matronalis

Iris ×germanica

Leucanthemum ×superbum

Linaria purpurea

Lupinus hybrids

Malva alcea 'Fastigiata'

Monarda didyma

Oenothera fruticosa

Patrinia scabiosifolia

Penstemon barbatus

Physostegia virginiana

Potentilla

Pseudofumaria lutea

Salvia ×sylvestris

Sidalcea malviflora

Silene coronaria

Solidago hybrids

Stokesia laevis

Symphytum

Tanacetum parthenium

Telekia speciosa

Tradescantia ×andersoniana

Veronica spicata

Veronicastrum virginicum

28. Summer- and autumn-flowering perennials to cut back before flowering for height control

Achillea millefolium

Aconitum napellus

Aconogonum 'Johanniswolke'

Agastache foeniculum

Alcea rosea

Artemisia

Aster

Boltonia asteroides 'Snowbank'

Chrysanthemum ×morifolium

Cota tinctoria

Echinacea purpurea

Eutrochium maculatum 'Gateway'

Gaura lindheimeri

Helenium autumnale

Helianthus

Heliopsis helianthoides

Heterotheca villosa

Hibiscus moscheutos

Hypericum calycinum

Kalimeris mongolica

Lavandula

Linum perenne

Lobelia cardinalis

Macleaya cordata

Malva alcea 'Fastigiata'

Monarda didyma

Perovskia atriplicifolia

Persicaria microcephala 'Red Dragon'

Phlox maculata

Phlox paniculata

Physostegia virginiana

Platycodon grandiflorus

Rudbeckia

Ruta graveolens

Salvia coerulea

Salvia uliginosa

Santolina chamaecyparissus

Sedum 'Matrona'

Silene coronaria

Silphium perfoliatum

Solidago hybrids

Symphyotrichum

Tanacetum parthenium

Teucrium chamaedrys

Tradescantia ×andersoniana

Vernonia noveboracensis

Veronica spicata

Veronicastrum virginicum

Tanacetum parthenium

29. Perennials that will not flower if their terminal flower buds are removed

Acanthus spinosus

Arisaema

Aruncus dioicus

Astilbe ×arendsii

Crambe

Dictamnus albus

Filipendula rubra
'Venusta'

Filipendula ulmaria

Geum hybrids

Hemerocallis

Heuchera micrantha
'Palace Purple'

Hosta

Iris ×germanica

Iris sibirica

Kniphofia hybrids

Lupinus hybrids

Papaver orientale

Rheum

Stachys byzantina

Lupinus hybrids

30. Perennials that can be pinched

Achillea millefolium

Agastache

Alcea rosea

Artemisia

Aster

Begonia grandis

Boltonia asteroides
'Snowbank'

Campanula
persicifolia

Chelone lyonii

Chrysanthemum
×morifolium

Clematis heracleifolia

Cota tinctoria

Eutrochium macula-
tum 'Gateway'

Gentiana

Helenium autumnale

Helianthus

Leucanthemum
×superbum

Linaria purpurea

Lobelia cardinalis

Malva alcea
'Fastigiata'

Monarda didyma

Penstemon barbatus

Perovskia
atriplicifolia

Phlox maculata

Phlox paniculata

Physostegia
virginiana

Platycodon
grandiflorus

Rudbeckia

Salvia uliginosa

Sedum 'Matrona'

Silene coronaria

Solidago hybrids

Spigelia marilandica

Symphyotrichum

Tanacetum parthenium

Vernonia noveboracensis

Veronica spicata

Veronicastrum virginicum

Sedum 'Matrona'

31. Perennials that do not respond well to pinching

Acanthus spinosus

Alchemilla mollis

Aquilegia hybrids

Armeria maritima

Aruncus dioicus

Astilbe ×arendsii

Crocosmia

Delphinium

Dianthus

Dictamnus albus

Digitalis

Filipendula rubra 'Venusta'

Filipendula ulmaria

Gaillardia ×grandiflora

Geranium

Geum hybrids

Hemerocallis

Heuchera

Hosta

Iris

Kniphofia hybrids

Ligularia dentata

Limonium platyphyllum

Lupinus hybrids

Papaver orientale

Polygonatum odoratum 'Variegatum'

Primula

Rodgersia

Telekia speciosa

Verbascum

Dianthus

32. Perennials that require deadleafing

Acanthus spinosus

Achillea 'Coronation Gold'

Achillea 'Moonshine'

Actaea

Ajuga reptans

Alcea rosea

Brunnera macrophylla

Chrysogonum virginianum

Clematis heracleifolia

Clematis integrifolia

Crambe

Crocosmia

Inula

Iris Louisiana hybrids

Ligularia dentata

Limonium platyphyllum

Persicaria amplexi-caulis 'Firetail'

Rodgersia

Alchemilla mollis

Anaphalis triplinervis

Angelica gigas

Aquilegia hybrids

Artemisia 'Powis Castle'

Arum italicum 'Pictum'

Aruncus dioicus

Asarum europaeum

Astilbe ×arendsii

Astrantia major

Begonia grandis

Bergenia crassifolia

Dianthus barbatus

Dicentra formosa 'Luxuriant'

Digitalis purpurea

Fragaria 'Pink Panda'

Gaillardia ×grandiflora

Geranium

Geum hybrids

Helleborus ×hybridus

Heuchera micrantha 'Palace Purple'

Heuchera sanguinea

Hibiscus moscheutos

Hosta

Phlox paniculata

Potentilla

Primula

Rodgersia

Sanguisorba

Silene coronaria

Silphium

Stachys byzantina

Stylophorum diphyllum

Symphyotrichum

Symphytum

Telekia speciosa

33. Perennials that normally do not need pruning for the winter

These perennials normally do not need pruning before winter, assuming that other recommended pruning has been performed during the season.

Acanthus spinosus

Achillea

Aconitum napellus

Aconogonum

Actaea

Agastache

Ajuga reptans

Alchemilla mollis

Amsonia

Anaphalis triplinervis

Anchusa azurea

Anemone pulsatilla

Angelica gigas

Aquilegia hybrids

Armeria maritima

Artemisia

Arum italicum 'Pictum'

Asarum europaeum

Asclepias tuberosa

Aster ×frikartii 'Mönch'

Aster tataricus 'Jindai'

Astilbe ×arendsii

Astrantia major

Baptisia australis

Bergenia crassifolia

Boltonia asteroides 'Snowbank'

Campanula

Centaurea montana

Centranthus ruber

Cerastium tomentosum

Ceratostigma plumbaginoides

Chelone lyonii

Chrysanthemum ×morifolium

Chrysogonum virginianum

Clematis heracleifolia

Clinopodium nepeta

Coreopsis grandiflora

Coreopsis verticillata

Cota tinctoria

Crocosmia

Delphinium

Dianthus

Dictamnus albus

Digitalis

Echinops ritro

Epimedium

Eryngium

Euphorbia epithymoides

Eutrochium maculatum 'Gateway'

Filipendula

Fragaria 'Pink Panda'

Gaillardia ×grandiflora

Gaura lindheimeri

Geranium macrorrhizum

Geranium sanguineum

Geum hybrids

Gypsophila paniculata

Helianthemum nummularium

Helianthus salicifolius

Helleborus ×hybridus

Hemerocallis

Heterotheca villosa

Heuchera

Hibiscus moscheutos

Leucanthemum ×superbum

Hypericum calycinum

Iberis sempervirens

Iris domestica

Iris sibirica

Kalimeris mongolica

Kniphofia hybrids

Lamium maculatum

Lavandula

Leucanthemum ×superbum

Liatris

Limonium platyphyllum

Linaria purpurea

Linum

Liriope spicata

Lobelia cardinalis

Lupinus hybrids

Oenothera fruticosa

Origanum

Ornamental grasses, most

Papaver orientale

Patrinia scabiosifolia

Penstemon barbatus

Perovskia atriplicifolia

Persicaria amplexi-caulis 'Firetail'

Phlomis

Phlox divaricata

Phlox stolonifera

Phlox subulata

Polemonium caeruleum

Pulmonaria

Rudbeckia

Ruta graveolens

Salvia coerulea

Salvia greggii

Salvia uliginosa

Santolina chamaecyparissus

Saponaria ocymoides

Saxifraga

Scabiosa

Sedum 'Matrona'

Sedum rupestre 'Angelina'

Silene coronaria

Sisyrinchium angustifolium

Stachys byzantina

Stokesia laevis

Tanacetum parthenium

Teucrium chamaedrys

Thymus

Tiarella cordifolia

Veronica austriaca subsp. teucrium

34. Perennials that require maintenance in the spring

Acanthus spinosus

Achillea

Aconitum napellus

Aconogonum 'Johanniswolke'

Agastache

Ajuga reptans

Alcea rosea

Alchemilla mollis

Amsonia

Anaphalis triplinervis

Anchusa azurea

Angelica gigas

Aquilegia hybrids

Armeria maritima

Artemisia

Arum italicum 'Pictum'

Asarum europaeum

Asclepias tuberosa

Aster

Astilbe ×arendsii

Astrantia major

Baptisia australis

Bergenia crassifolia

Boltonia asteroides 'Snowbank'

Brunnera macrophylla

Campanula carpatica

Campanula glomerata

Centaurea montana

Cerastium tomentosum

Ceratostigma plumbaginoides

Chelone lyonii

Chrysanthemum ×morifolium

Chrysogonum virginianum

Kniphofia

Clematis heracleifolia

Clinopodium

Coreopsis grandiflora

Coreopsis verticillata

Cota tinctoria

Crocosmia

Delphinium

Dianthus

Dictamnus albus

Digitalis

Echinacea purpurea

Echinops ritro

Epimedium

Euphorbia epithymoides

Eutrochium maculatum 'Gateway'

Ferns

Filipendula

Foeniculum vulgare 'Purpureum'

Fragaria 'Pink Panda'

Gaillardia ×grandiflora

Gaura lindheimeri

Gentiana andrewsii

Geranium macrorrhizum

Geum hybrids

Gypsophila paniculata

Helenium autumnale

Helianthemum nummularium

Helianthus salicifolius

Helleborus ×hybridus

Hemerocallis

Hesperis matronalis

Heterotheca villosa

Heuchera

Hibiscus moscheutos

Hypericum calycinum

Iberis sempervirens

Iris domestica

Iris sibirica

Kalimeris mongolica

Kirengeshoma palmata

Knautia macedonica

Kniphofia hybrids

Lamium maculatum

Lavandula

Leucanthemum ×superbum

Liatris

Limonium platyphyllum

Linaria purpurea

Linum

Liriope spicata

Lobelia

Lupinus hybrids

Lysimachia nummularia 'Aurea'

Macleaya cordata

Malva alcea 'Fastigiata'

Monarda didyma

Oenothera speciosa

Origanum

Ornamental grasses, most

Patrinia scabiosifolia

Penstemon barbatus

Perovskia atriplicifolia

Phlox

Physostegia virginiana

Polemonium caeruleum

Primula denticulata

Pulmonaria

Rudbeckia

Ruta graveolens

Salvia coerulea

Salvia greggii

Salvia uliginosa

Santolina chamaecyparissus

Saponaria ocymoides

Saxifraga stolonifera

Scabiosa

Sedum 'Matrona'

Sedum rupestre 'Angelina'

Silene coronaria

Silphium

Sisyrinchium angustifolium

Solidago hybrids

Stachys byzantina

Stokesia laevis

Symphyotrichum

Symphytum

Tanacetum parthenium

Teucrium chamaedrys

Thymus

Tradescantia ×andersoniana

Tricyrtis hirta

Veronica austriaca subsp. teucrium

Veronicastrum virginicum

35. Perennials that require maintenance in the summer

Acanthus spinosus

Achillea

Aconitum napellus

Actaea

Agastache

Ajuga reptans

Alcea rosea

Alchemilla mollis

Amsonia

Anaphalis triplinervis

Anchusa azurea

Anemone ×hybrida

Anemone pulsatilla

Angelica gigas

Aquilegia hybrids

Armeria maritima

Artemisia

Arum italicum 'Pictum'

Aruncus dioicus

Asclepias tuberosa

Aster ×frikartii 'Mönch'

Astilbe ×arendsii

Astrantia major

Baptisia australis

Begonia grandis

Bergenia crassifolia

Boltonia asteroides 'Snowbank'

Brunnera macrophylla

Campanula

Centaurea montana

Centranthus ruber

Cephalaria gigantea

Cerastium tomentosum

Ceratostigma plumbaginoides

Chelone lyonii

Chrysanthemum ×morifolium

Chrysogonum virginianum

Clematis heracleifolia

Clematis recta

Coreopsis

Cota tinctoria

Crambe

Crocosmia

Delphinium

Dianthus

Dicentra formosa 'Luxuriant'

Digitalis

Echinacea purpurea

Echinops ritro

Eryngium

Euphorbia epithymoides

Eutrochium

Filipendula

Foeniculum vulgare 'Purpureum'

Fragaria 'Pink Panda'

Gaillardia ×grandiflora

Gaura lindheimeri

Geranium

Geum hybrids

Gypsophila paniculata

Helenium autumnale

Helianthemum nummularium

Helianthus

Heliopsis helianthoides

Helleborus ×hybridus

Hemerocallis

Hesperis matronalis

Heterotheca villosa

Heuchera

Hibiscus moscheutos

Hosta

Iberis sempervirens

Inula

Iris ×germanica

Iris sibirica

Knautia macedonica

Kniphofia hybrids

Lamium maculatum

Lavandula

Leucanthemum ×superbum

Liatris

Ligularia dentata

Linaria purpurea

Linum

Lobelia cardinalis

Lupinus hybrids

Lysimachia

Macleaya cordata

Malva alcea 'Fastigiata'

Monarda didyma

Nepeta

Oenothera

Paeonia hybrids

Papaver orientale

Patrinia scabiosifolia

Penstemon barbatus

Phlox

Physostegia virginiana

Platycodon grandiflorus

Polemonium caeruleum

Potentilla

Pseudofumaria lutea

Pulmonaria

Rodgersia

Ruta graveolens

Salvia ×sylvestris

Sanguisorba

Santolina chamaecyparissus

Saponaria ocymoides

Scabiosa

Sidalcea malviflora

Silene coronaria

Silphium

Sisyrinchium angustifolium

Solidago hybrids

Stachys

Stokesia laevis

Stylophorum diphyllum

Symphyotrichum

Symphytum

Tanacetum parthenium

Telekia speciosa

Teucrium chamaedrys

Thalictrum aquilegiifolium

Thermopsis villosa

Thymus

Tradescantia ×andersoniana

Trollius ×cultorum

Verbascum

Vernonia noveboracensis

Veronica

36. Perennials that require maintenance in the autumn

Alcea rosea

Anemone ×hybrida

Artemisia ludoviciana 'Silver King'

Aruncus dioicus

Begonia grandis

Brunnera macrophylla

Centranthus ruber

Cephalaria gigantea

Clematis recta

Clematis integrifolia

Crambe

Delphinium

Dicentra formosa 'Luxuriant'

Echinacea purpurea

Foeniculum vulgare 'Purpureum'

Gentiana septemfida var. lagodechiana

Geranium endressii 'Wargrave Pink'

Geranium phaeum

Geranium Rozanne 'Gerwat'

Helenium autumnale

Helianthus maximiliani

Heliopsis helianthoides

Hosta

Inula

Iris ×germanica

Iris Louisiana hybrids

Kniphofia hybrids

Ligularia dentata

Lysimachia

Malva alcea 'Fastigiata'

Molinia caerulea 'Skyracer'

Monarda didyma

Nepeta

Oenothera

Paeonia hybrids

Papaver orientale

Persicaria

Phlox maculata

Phlox paniculata

Platycodon grandiflorus

Polygonatum odoratum 'Variegatum'

Potentilla

Primula vulgaris

Pseudofumaria lutea

Rheum

Rodgersia

Salvia ×sylvestris

Sanguisorba

Sidalcea malviflora

Solidago hybrids

Spigelia marilandica

Stachys monieri 'Hummelo'

Symphyotrichum

Telekia speciosa

Thalictrum aquilegiifolium

Thermopsis villosa

Tradescantia ×andersoniana

Tricyrtis hirta

Vernonia noveboracensis

Veronica spicata

Veronicastrum virginicum

Clematis recta

377

Perennial Garden Planting and Maintenance Schedule

I f you have a perennial garden, there will always be something for you to do with your time. It may be a large physical undertaking, such as renovating the whole thing, or perhaps it's the small, simple mental pleasure of thinking about the garden and how beautiful it is, or was, or is going to be next year.

The information here provides a guideline to the seasonal tasks involved in managing a perennial garden, and it is meant to be just that—a guideline. Only by working with your garden will you gain a more thorough understanding of what needs to be done and when. I am quite a taskmaster, with a penchant for list writing. I think you will find it helpful to do the same. Walk around your garden and take notes on what needs to be done. Such notes can be used to organize a priority list with target times or dates for the various tasks—put the timeline on your calendar. In the spring, when things are beyond hectic in the garden, there's a pretty good chance you'll forget which plant you wanted to move and where, which one you intended to divide, or which one you wanted to remove from the garden altogether. If you have the schedule and list that you started compiling the previous year, you will have one less thing to think about at the moment. This is particularly critical in the landscaping industry; with maintenance work to be done on many different gardens, it's almost impossible to remember what you wanted to do and when in each of them.

A word on garden journals. I'd like to be able to tell you that I keep one—one of those sweet journals with pretty drawings and inspirational phrases. I have made the best efforts in that direction but, to date, have failed. I do keep records in my weekly calendar so that I can see when I performed a certain task in my own or my clients' gardens. I keep notes, although brief, on specific maintenance tasks performed at each client's gardens on certain dates. For instance: "The tradescantia and coreopsis were cut back, the alchemilla were deadleafed, we did general deadheading and weeding, and we staked the hillside aster that the dog stepped on at the Brown residence on 20 July. There were two of us there and it took 1½ hours." All these notes are helpful for planning in future years. It's a good idea to keep some kind of records, either in a book or on notebook pages (as I do, although they are usually covered with splashes of soil), in your personal garden files or, for professionals, in each client's file. Such notes have allowed me to compile the schedule contained here.

Large garden plantings are often best done in phases. In this massive border, many trees and shrubs were planted in the autumn. Perennial placement and planting began in late April (taking several weeks), followed by annual planting in mid-May. Training and consulting the landscape crew on the maintenance schedule is an ongoing process.

Adding conifers, small trees, and shrubs to a perennial garden can help reduce the burden of maintenance.

The garden planting and maintenance schedule that follows is a guideline for Midwest gardens; you will need to adjust it according to your regional conditions. Contact your local county extension agent for clarification on details specific to your growing area. Different annual weather conditions may affect the schedule as well. I have indicated here the ideal times for certain tasks. But, as we all know, you can't always get to things during the ideal time. It is best to adhere to these guidelines whenever possible, but keep in mind that perennials are very forgiving and are willing to bend on certain issues. Greater details on the how-to of each of the jobs can be found throughout the book, and especially in the first 2 parts. Specifics on individual plants are found in the Encyclopedia of Perennials. After the plant listings, I have compiled lists of plants by season to show when different species may require some form of maintenance. There is also pruning information.

SPRING

There is usually so much to be done in the spring, it's not even funny. Fortunately, we've had the winter to regroup a bit, and in the spring our energy is high to get us through all the work. A busy spring is the time of year when some things may have to be put off until later when more time opens up—be willing to accept this and move on. Spring is the key time for cleanup, planting, transplanting, and dividing.

MARCH

The early part of March is usually still too cold and wet for any major activity. In milder years more can be done during the second half of the month, and this is when spring cleanup should get under way.

PLANTING

- Plant orders should be completed in the first week or two, if not already done; quantities may already be limited, particularly on the more unusual species.
- Ordering and purchasing tools and supplies should be done in early to mid-March. Clean and oil your tools if you didn't get to it in the autumn.
- March generally is too early for planting container-grown plants, as most are not yet available and the soil is normally too wet.
- Bare root plants may be available in March and, if the beds are workable, can be planted at this time. They also can be potted into containers in March to allow them to get acclimated, and once they've had a chance to establish a bit they can be planted into the garden later—this is what I often do, particularly if plants arrive small.
- Take soil tests of future or existing beds. Be sure to test for organic matter content.

GENERAL MAINTENANCE

- Remove any evergreen bough mulch, but keep handy in case of emergency cold weather. It's best to do this on a cloudy day to prevent burning of tender, pale growth.
- Remove any other winter mulch from around the crowns of the perennials, but leave the mulch on the ground surrounding the plants for a couple weeks, or until early April (early May in colder areas). Again, mulch removal is best saved for a cloudy day.
- Press back into the ground any perennials that frost heaved over the winter.
- Fertilize gardens, end of March to early April.
- Topdressing of beds can be done in late March and into April.
- Touch-up mulching can be done at the end of March.

PRUNING

- In mild years, spring cleanup can begin in the last couple of weeks of March and continue into early April.
- Cut back plants that were left for winter interest. Watch for feather reed grass (*Calamagrostis* ×*acutiflora*) and other early emerging perennials

such as pulmonaria and epimedium, which should be cut back before new growth has a chance to mature.

- ✿ Check evergreen plants for removal of dead leaves.
- ✿ Mow liriope.

APRIL

April and May are usually the 2 busiest months in the perennial garden. I always remind myself to remain calm. This can be an unnerving time, to say the least, especially if you are in the industry. A good deal of planting, along with any spring maintenance that didn't get done in March, happens in April, provided the weather is cooperating.

PLANTING

- ✿ Renovation of perennial gardens should get under way in early April.
- ✿ Perennials can be divided and transplanted when growth is 3–4 in. high. If growth has gotten any larger, plants may benefit from cutting back by a third to half.
- ✿ Divide woodland wildflowers after flowering. This applies only to plants in your gardens or on your own property—never collect from the wild.
- ✿ Add compost if transplanting or planting into an existing garden.
- ✿ A nonselective, nonresidual herbicide (such as Roundup) can be applied starting in about the 2nd week of April when grass and weeds are actively growing.
- ✿ Installations and plantings usually begin around the 3rd week of April.
- ✿ Be patient with late-emerging perennials such as *Begonia grandis*, *Ceratostigma plumbaginoides*, and *Platycodon grandiflorus*. Do not disturb or plant over them.

GENERAL MAINTENANCE

- ✿ Fertilizing, topdressing, and mulching that wasn't completed in March continues in April.
- ✿ April is a good time to aerate the soil with a fork or hoe; take care to not damage roots.
- ✿ All winter mulch should be removed by now in most gardens. In colder climates (perhaps zone 4 or colder) leave mulch until early May.
- ✿ Weeding begins with a bang, as the perennials haven't yet filled in enough to smother them out.
- ✿ Pea staking may need to be applied in the 3rd or 4th week of April, particularly to fast-growing perennials like *Clematis recta* and *C. integrifolia* that undergo rapid growth at this time.
- ✿ Continue to fill bird feeders, as many birds migrate during late April into May and will reward you with a visit.

PRUNING

- ✿ Early spring cleanup continues in April if not completed in March.
- ✿ Once warm weather is assured, prune down tender perennials such as mums and *Aster* ×*frikartii* 'Mönch'.
- ✿ Pinching may be needed on perennials at planting.

MAY

Any planting that didn't get done in April should happen in May. I like to have the majority of the installations and planting for my business completed before the end of May, if possible, when the weather usually is still fairly cool. A good deal of pruning for height control also begins in May. Refer to the chapters on pruning for details; consult the Encyclopedia of Perennials for information on individual species and genera.

This beautiful sculpture by Thomas Yano reminds me to take time to look up, reach up, and stretch my neck and lower back during long work sessions in the garden, particularly in the busy months of April and May.

PLANTING

- ❀ Lots and lots of planting.
- ❀ In the home garden, for your records, take notes of locations of new plantings.
- ❀ Transplanting and division of summer- and autumn-flowering perennials can continue in May. Spring-flowering species can be divided after flowering.
- ❀ This is a good time to move or remove any unwanted perennial seedlings.
- ❀ Once everything has sprouted, take note of any empty spots for new plantings.

GENERAL MAINTENANCE

- ❀ Topdressing can continue early in the month if new growth isn't too large to interfere.
- ❀ Weeding continues; especially strong are the dandelions and thistle.

All irrigation for Hiddenhaven is pumped from the pond, which acts as a giant rain barrel—a very sustainable practice.

✿ Continue placement of pea stakes; hoops are needed on peonies.

✿ Mulch.

✿ Be on the lookout for the fourlined plant bug nymphs and crush them.

✿ Slug control should be placed now.

✿ Aphids are active.

✿ Hang hummingbird feeders, as the birds are starting to dance in the columbine now.

PRUNING

✿ Many summer-flowering perennials, including leucanthemum, monarda, phlox, physostegia, and tradescantia, can be pinched or cut back for height control and possibly to stagger bloom.

✿ Thinning can be done now, especially for delphinium.

✿ Lavenders and other subshrubs may still be breaking dormancy.

✿ Spring-flowering perennials should be deadheaded or cut back or sheared after flowering.

✿ Do not deadhead biennials if seeding for the following year is desired.

✿ It is a good idea to pinch or cut back perennials by half at planting.

✿ Cutting back may be needed during divisions and transplanting.

✿ Prune off any growth damaged from late frosts. (In the Columbus, Ohio, area the last frost date is generally May 20; one year a freeze on May 12 nipped the new growth on some perennials.)

SUMMER

In summer, my gardens are kept fresh with irrigation when needed, every 4 days or so.

Pruning, staking, and general maintenance are in order during the summer months. If you go away for an extended period in the summer, make sure there is someone around to water the gardens if needed, especially for a new planting. You may want to experiment with cutting back some or many of your summer-flowering plants before you leave for a long period so that you can enjoy their regrowth and flowering upon your return. You may also want to get weeds under control before you leave so that you don't have to face them when you return. Pruning in midsummer is done to promote the autumn display. Take notes throughout the summer of plants to move or remove or divide or add, of new pruning techniques to try, of new colors to incorporate, and any other changes you may want to consider in planning for autumn and next year.

JUNE

Planting usually continues into and sometimes through June, but if the weather starts to get too hot by late June, the perennials will have a more difficult time establishing. Also, plants that have been in containers all spring should be planted at this time. June is a big month for pruning, including cutting back, thinning, deadheading, and deadleafing.

Dense plantings of reseeding perennials such as this black-eyed Susan (*Rudbeckia fulgida* var. *speciosa*) help reduce weeds and create harmony.

PLANTING

✿ Try to finish all planting by mid-June, if possible.

✿ Transplanting and dividing can continue, but plants will need to be cut back and possibly shaded.

✿ Old-fashioned bleeding heart (*Lamprocapnos spectabilis*) can be transplanted now.

GENERAL MAINTENANCE

✿ Be certain to keep new plantings well watered.

✿ Weed.

✿ Linking staking and single stakes should be placed in June.

✿ Prop up any stray branches off neighboring plants, if needed.

✿ Watch for fourlined plant bug adults.

✿ Japanese beetles are the problem for the month.

✿ Baby grasshoppers are evident; apply garlic sprays now.

PRUNING

✿ Continue to cut back spring-flowering plants, especially any that may be flopping, such as *Veronica austriaca* subsp. *teucrium* and its cultivars.

✿ Autumn-flowering plants should be pinched or cut back for height control as well as thinned and shaped.

✿ Numerous summer-flowering plants, including echinacea, heliopsis, phlox, platycodon, and veronica, among others, can be cut back to extend flowering of plant groups or to create staggered or delayed flowering.

- ✿ Deadhead, deadhead, deadhead—to extend bloom of a variety of perennials and to reduce seeding of heavy seeders such as aquilegia and *Iris sibirica*.

- ✿ Prune or thin plants to keep them in their desired space. Make certain that any new perennials planted in an existing garden are not being overtaken or shaded by established neighbors widening with the warm weather.

- ✿ Deadleafing of spring-flowering perennials may be needed; the leaves of some summer bloomers, like daylilies (*Hemerocallis*), also may be starting to yellow.

- ✿ Shear down any declining foliage, if needed. Tall bearded iris may be a particular culprit, and columbine foliage may start to deteriorate later in the month.

- ✿ Cut back and shape amsonia and baptisia if desired toward the end of the month.

- ✿ Near the end of the month, certain hardy geraniums will need to be deadheaded or sheared back.

- ✿ Don't forget to cut flowers for fresh arrangements and for drying.

JULY

Early July is often the peak bloom time for traditional perennial borders. This can be an ideal time to take some great photos. Enjoy!

PLANTING

- ✿ Keep planting in July to a minimum, if possible.
- ✿ Transplant and divide with care.

GENERAL MAINTENANCE

- ✿ Continue to keep new plantings moist, with deeper but less frequent waterings. For established plantings that have been dry for several weeks, watering may be in order now.

- ✿ Perennials that have been heavily pruned back also need to be kept moist.

- ✿ Weed.

- ✿ Heavy-feeding perennials or perennials that have been cut back for rebloom may benefit from fertilizing in July.

- ✿ Aerating may be needed in compacted areas.

- ✿ Staking may be needed for certain autumn bloomers.

- ✿ Watch for mites and black blister beetles and other pests.

PRUNING

- ✿ Perennials that bloom a second time, including delphinium and *Digitalis grandiflora* 'Temple Bells', should be cut back to basal foliage.

- ✿ Older plants of tradescantia may need to be cut to the ground now.

- ✿ Most pinching or cutting back of autumn-blooming plants is completed in mid- to late July.

- Deadleaf plants that bloom in early summer, as needed.
- Deadhead more and more—perennials such as 'Moonbeam' coreopsis (*Coreopsis verticillata* 'Moonbeam') may need shearing now for a second bloom phase.
- Prune crowded or sprawling perennials to keep them in their space.
- Cut back any insect-ridden foliage, such as on columbine.
- Subshrubs that have gotten straggly may need hard pruning. Lavandula that is in good condition can simply be deadheaded in July to promote another flowering period in September.

AUGUST

Perennial gardens often take a bit of rest during the month of August. It is a busy month for cutting back "tired" plants that have finished blooming and dead-leafing any scorched subjects.

PLANTING

- Any planting during August should be done with caution. Keep plantings moist and shaded.
- Bearded iris, Oriental poppies, and peonies can be divided now.
- Design beds and order plants for autumn planting.

GENERAL MAINTENANCE

- Weed.
- Don't forget to water the spring-planted gardens. Established gardens may also benefit from watering, as this is usually the key dry month.
- Aerating continues.
- Staking may be needed, particularly after storms.
- Do not apply fertilizer, so as to allow plants to harden better before winter.
- Grasshoppers can be a problem this month.

PRUNING

- Many plants require cutting back for aesthetics.
- Lots of deadleafing.
- Continue with deadheading.
- Prune plants to keep in desired space.
- Cut back finished, "tired" plants to make room for later bloomers.
- Asters and mums can be cut back by 4–6 in. to delay bloom, though at the expense of floral abundance.
- Cut back any insect- or disease-plagued foliage.
- Do not cut back subshrubs after late August, so that they can harden for the winter.
- Try cutting back short-lived species of genera such as *Gaillardia* and *Centranthus* at the end of the month to stimulate vegetative growth.

AUTUMN & WINTER

Planting starts again in autumn as the cooler weather approaches. Pruning is the major maintenance that continues in this season. It's enjoyable to be in the garden again—get your fill before winter sets in.

Autumn, my favorite season, is such a welcome relief after a busy spring and summer in the garden. Enjoy the lush regrowth and rebloom on the many perennials you pruned earlier.

SEPTEMBER

September is the month to start getting back into planting. Enjoy all the summer-flowering perennials that are reblooming in September because you took the time to cut them back and/or deadhead them earlier in the season.

PLANTING

- Division and transplanting of spring- and summer-flowering perennials is accomplished with ease as the days start to cool down. Try to finish this by the end of the month so that plants can establish before winter.
- Move self-sown biennials as needed.
- Continue to order plants for autumn installations and planting.
- Bed preparation and planting can begin again.
- Peonies, poppies, and bearded iris (best planted by mid-September) are available for planting now.

- ✿ Continue weeding.
- ✿ Keep new autumn plantings moist.
- ✿ Apply touch-up mulch if needed.
- ✿ Generally, no more fertilizer should be applied to the plants.

PRUNING

- ✿ Deadhead late-summer and autumn bloomers such as echinacea and heliopsis.
- ✿ Cut back short-lived perennials in early September, if it was not done in late August.
- ✿ Continue to cut back faded summer-flowering perennials as needed.

OCTOBER

In the Midwest, planting can continue until about October 15; finish before then if possible.

PLANTING

- ✿ Finish planting in early October.
- ✿ Beds can be prepared for spring planting throughout the month.
- ✿ All divisions and transplanting should be finished by October.

GENERAL MAINTENANCE

- ✿ Continue to keep new plantings watered if the weather is dry; established gardens may need water as well so that they can go into winter with sufficient moisture.
- ✿ Weeding is usually needed less by October.
- ✿ Rake leaves.
- ✿ Mulch tender plants once the ground is frozen.

PRUNING

- ✿ October 15 is the approximate first frost date, at least in the Midwest. Some perennials may turn to mush at this time and should be pruned, if desired. Otherwise, wait for several killing frosts and prune in November.

NOVEMBER

November is the time for pruning to prepare for winter after several killing frosts.

PLANTING

- ✿ No more planting of herbaceous plants in the Midwest.
- ✿ Beds can be prepared for spring if weather permits.

GENERAL MAINTENANCE

- ✿ Topdressing with organic matter, if not done in the spring, can be done after autumn cleanup.
- ✿ Be certain all water and irrigation systems are turned off and drain all hoses.

- ✿ Clean and oil tools after all cleanup is complete.
- ✿ Keep your pruners and a basket handy for work on a mild day.
- ✿ Recycle or return used pots, which have been accumulating all season, to accepting nurseries.
- ✿ Rake leaves. Mow or shred to speed composting.

PRUNING

- ✿ Cut back perennials that are not desired over the winter or that harbor insects and disease.
- ✿ Deadhead some of the heavy seeders, but leave some for the birds.
- ✿ Do not prune evergreens, mums, tender perennials, or anything with attractive winter interest.

DECEMBER

Enjoy the holidays. Ask for gardening gifts. (Buy this book for all your friends!) Feed and watch the birds.

PLANTING

- ✿ Only in our dreams!

GENERAL MAINTENANCE

- ✿ Mulch with old Christmas tree boughs once the ground has frozen.

PRUNING

- ✿ On a mild day go out and prune some fallen plants to keep your mind clear.

JANUARY/FEBRUARY

Take vacations. Attend gardening conferences for inspiration. Design and plan for the new year using all your notes. Relax and regroup. Start ordering plants and seeds. Take some time on a mild day to go out and prune something to relieve your cabin fever. Watch the perennials when the snow melts to see what is happening. Keep track of temperatures, recording lows as well as temperature fluctuations, to help understand overwintering results. Press in perennials that may have frost heaved during times of thaw. Be sure your winter garden is what you have in mind; now is the time to note changes. Keep your bird feeder full. Remember that sunflower seed hulls can inhibit plant growth, and uneaten sunflower seeds and other bird seeds can sprout in gardens in the spring, creating a mess. Keep bird feeders out of the beds.

Metric Conversions

INCHES	CENTIMETERS	FEET	METERS
¼	0.6	1	0.3
⅓	0.8	2	0.6
½	1.3	3	0.9
¾	1.9	4	1.2
1	2.5	5	1.5
2	5.1	6	1.8
3	7.6	7	2.1
4	10	8	2.4
5	13	9	2.7
6	15	10	3
7	18		
8	20		
9	23		
10	25		

TO CONVERT LENGTH:	MULTIPLY BY:
Yards to meters	0.9
Inches to centimeters	2.54
Inches to millimeters	25.4
Feet to centimeters	30.5

TEMPERATURES

degrees Celsius = $0.55 \times$ (degrees Fahrenheit - 32)
degrees Fahrenheit = $(1.8 \times$ degrees Celsius$) + 32$

Bibliography

Aniśko, Tomasz. 2008. *When Perennials Bloom: An Almanac for Planning and Planting*. Portland, OR: Timber Press.

Armitage, Allan M. 2008. *Herbaceous Perennial Plants: A Treatise on their Identification, Culture, and Garden Attributes*. 3rd ed. Champaign, IL: Stipes Publishing.

Avent, Tony. 2010. *An overview of Epimedium. The Plantsman* 9 (March): 10–17.

Avent, Tony. 2011. Arisaema, Arisaema, Arisaema: Jack-in-the-pulpits and cobra lilies for the garden. *Plant Delights Nursery Perennial Plant Articles*. plantdelights.com/Article/Arisaema-Jack-in-the-Pulpit.

Avent, Tony. 2015. Ornamental sages for the garden. *Plant Delights Nursery Perennial Plant Articles*. plantdelights.com/Article/Salvia/Perennial-Salvia/Salvia-greggii/Salvia-nemorosa/.

Avent, Tony. 2015. Pulmonaria, Pulmonaria, Pulmonaria: The world of lungworts. *Plant Delights Nursery Perennial Plant Articles*. plantdelights.com/Article/Pulmonaria-Lungwort.

Bakalar, Elsa. 1994. *A Garden of One's Own*. New York: William Morrow.

Best of Fine Gardening. 1995. *Healthy Soil*. Newtown, CT: Taunton Press.

Bir, Richard E. and Joseph L. Conner. 2002. Mildew resistant garden phlox. North Carolina State University. ces.ncsu.edu/fletcher/staff/rbir/phloxmildew.html.

Brickell, Christopher. 2003. *The American Horticultural Society Encyclopedia of Gardening*. Revised ed. Ed. Fern M. Bradley. London: Dorling Kindersley.

Capon, Brian. 2010. *Botany for Gardeners*. 3rd ed. Portland, OR: Timber Press.

Carey, Dennis and Tony Avent. 2010. Tricyrtis: Perennial toad lilies for the woodland garden. *Plant Delights Nursery Perennial Plant Articles*. plantdelights.com/Article/Tricyrtis-Toad-Lily.

Chinery, David. n.d. *Annuals, Biennials, Perennials, Groundcovers and Vines Useful when Gardening with Deer*. New York: Cornell Cooperative Extension of Westchester County.

Clausen, Ruth Rogers and Thomas Christopher. 2014. *Essential Perennials: The Complete Reference to 2700 Perennials for the Home Garden*. Portland, OR: Timber Press.

Coombs, Duncan, Peter Blackburne-Maze, Martyn Cracknell, and Roger Bentley. n.d. *The Complete Book of Pruning*. England: Ward Lock.

Coombs, George. 2014. Heuchera for the mid-Atlantic region. Research Report. Hockessin, DE: Mt. Cuba Center. mtcubacenter.org/images/PDFs-and-SWFs/Heuchera_Report.pdf.

Cresson, Charles. 1993. *Charles Cresson on the American Flower Garden*. New York: Prentice Hall.

Cullina, William. 2009. *Understanding Perennials*. Boston, MA: Houghton Mifflin Harcourt.

Daigle, Jean-Yves and Hélène Gautreau-Daigle. 2001. *Canadian Peat Harvesting and the Environment*. 2nd ed. Ottawa, ON: North American Wetlands Conservation Council.

Darke, Rick. 2007. *The Encyclopedia of Grasses for Livable Landscapes*. Portland, OR: Timber Press.

Diblik, Roy. 2014. *The Know Maintenance Perennial Garden*. Portland, OR: Timber Press.

DiSabato-Aust, Tracy. 1991. Pruning herbaceous plants. In *Pruning Techniques*. New York: Brooklyn Botanic Garden.

DiSabato-Aust, Tracy. 1992. *Pruning perennials for peak performance*. Proceedings, Perennial Plant Association. Steven M. Still, ed. Hilliard, OH.

DiSabato-Aust, Tracy. 1994. Deadheading and cutting back. *The Best of Fine Gardening: Plant Care*. Newtown, CT: The Taunton Press.

DiSabato-Aust, Tracy. 2003. Off with their heads! Removing spent blossoms keeps perennials tidy and triggers more flowers. *Fine Gardening* 92: 64–66.

DiSabato-Aust, Tracy. 2003. *The Well-Designed Mixed Garden: Building Beds and Borders with Trees, Shrubs, Perennials, Annuals, and Bulbs*. Portland, OR: Timber Press.

Eddison, Sydney. 2011. Can you see the stakes? Give your garden an invisible support system that will help it look its best. *Fine Gardening* 140: 36–39.

EPA. 2015. Advancing sustainable materials management: 2013 fact sheet. EPA Bulletin 530-R-15-003.

Frett, Jeanne and Victor Piatt. 2006. Asters for the mid-Atlantic region. Research Report. Hockessin, DE: Mt. Cuba Center. mtcubacenter.org/images/PDFs-and-SWFs/Mt_Cuba_Report-Asters_for_Mid-Atlantic.pdf.

Frett, Jeanne and Victor Piatt. 2009. Coneflowers for the mid-Atlantic region. Research Report. Hockessin, DE: Mt. Cuba Center. mtcubacenter.org/images/PDFs-and-SWFs/Mt_Cuba_Report_Coneflowers_for_Mid-Atlantic.pdf.

Gleason, Mark L., Margery L. Daughtrey, Ann R. Chase, Gary W. Moorman, and Daren S. Mueller. 2009. *Diseases of Herbaceous Perennials*. St. Paul, MN: American Phytopathological Society Press.

Hansen, Richard and Friedrich Stahl. 1993. *Perennials and Their Garden Habitats*. Portland, OR: Timber Press.

Harper, Pamela and Fred McGourty. 1985. *Perennials: How to Select, Grow and Enjoy*. Tucson, AZ: HP Books.

Hawke, Richard G. 2005. A comparative study of cultivated *Stachys*. Chicago Botanic Garden Plant Evaluation Notes 27. chicagobotanic.org/downloads/planteval_notes/n027_stachys.pdf.

Hawke, Richard G. 2007. A comparative study of cultivated catmints. Chicago Botanic Garden Plant Evaluation Notes 29. chicagobotanic.org/downloads/planteval_notes/n029_catmint.pdf.

Hawke, Richard G. 2007. A report on *Leucanthemum ×superbum* and related daisies. Chicago Botanic Garden Plant Evaluation Notes 30. chicagobotanic.org/downloads/planteval_notes/n030_leucanthemum.pdf.

Hawke, Richard G. 2010. Comparative studies of *Veronica* and *Veronicastrum*. Chicago Botanic Garden Plant Evaluation Notes 33. chicagobotanic.org/downloads/planteval_notes/n033_veronica.pdf.

Hawke, Richard G. 2010. A comparative study of *Tradescantia* cultivars. Chicago Botanic Garden Plant Evaluation Notes 34. chicagobotanic.org/downloads/planteval_notes/n034_tradescantia.pdf.

Hawke, Richard G. 2011. A comparative study of *Phlox paniculata* cultivars. Chicago Botanic Garden Plant Evaluation Notes 35. chicagobotanic.org/downloads/planteval_notes/n035_phloxpaniculata.pdf.

Hawke, Richard G. 2013. A comparative study of cultivated asters. Chicago Botanic Garden Plant Evaluation Notes 36. chicagobotanic.org/downloads/planteval_notes/n036_asters.pdf.

Hawke, Richard G. 2014. A comparative study of Joe Pye weeds (*Eutrochium* spp.) and their relatives. Chicago Botanic Garden Plant Evaluation Notes 37. chicagobotanic.org/downloads/planteval_notes/n037_joepyeweed.pdf.

Hoitink, H.A.J., M.A. Rose, and R.A. Zondag, 1995. Properties of materials available for formulation of high quality container media. *The Buckeye* (June): 1–7.

Kashmanian, Richard M., and Joseph M. Keyser. 1992. The flip side of compost: what's in it, where to use it and why. In *The Environmental Gardener*. New York: Brooklyn Botanic Garden.

Lovejoy, Ann. 1993. *The American Mixed Border*. New York: Macmillan.

Lowenfels, Jeff and Wayne Lewis. 2010. *Teaming with Microbes: The Organic Gardener's Guide to the Soil Food Web*. Revised ed. Portland, OR: Timber Press.

McGourty, Fred. 1989. *The Perennial Gardener*. Boston: Houghton Mifflin.

Mickel, John T. 2003. *Ferns for American Gardens*. Portland, OR: Timber Press.

Norris, Kelly. 2013. Clod-busters: These plants scoff at heavy clay soils. *Fine Gardening* 151:46–51.

Olsen, Sue. 2007. *Encyclopedia of Garden Ferns*. Portland, OR: Timber Press.

Ondra, Nancy J. 2009. *Perennial Care Manual*. North Adams, MA: Storey Publishing.

Patterson, J.C., J.J. Murray, and J.R. Short. 1980. The impact of urban soils on vegetation. *M.E.T.R.I.A. Proceedings* 3: 33–56

Perennial Plant Association. Standards. Steven M. Still, ed. Hilliard, OH.

Phillips, Ellen and C. Colston Burrell. 1993. *Rodale's Illustrated Encyclopedia of Perennials*. Emmaus, PA: Rodale Press.

Schmidt, Genevieve. 2013. Stop! Don't prune that grass. *Fine Gardening* 153: 48–54.

Sheldon, Elisabeth. 1989. *A Proper Garden*. Harrisburg, PA: Stackpole Books.

Smith, Elton and Sharon Treaster. 1990. Application of composted municipal sludge in the landscape. Columbus: The Ohio State University Department of Horticulture.

Smith, Elton and Sharon Treaster. 1991. Production of herbaceous perennials in mineral soil amended with composted municipal sludge. Columbus: The Ohio State University Department of Horticulture.

Still, Steven M. 1994. *Manual of Herbaceous Ornamental Plants*. Champaign, IL: Stipes Publishing.

Tyler, Rodney W. 1991. Organic matter: the life blood of soils. *The Buckeye* (October): 25–37.

Tyler, Rodney W. 1993. Calculating compost capacity. *Lawn & Landscape* (March).

Tyler, Rodney W. 1993. Cashing in on compost. *Lawn & Landscape* (March)

Tyler, Rodney W. 1996. *Winning the Organics Game*. Alexandria, VA: ASHS Press.

United States Composting Council. 2008. *Keeping Organics Out of Landfills*. USCC Position Statement. Ronkonkoma, NY: U.S. Composting Council.

Walliser, Jessica. 2014. *Attracting Beneficial Bugs to Your Garden: A Natural Approach to Pest Control*. Portland, OR: Timber Press.

Woods, Christopher. 1991. Notes on the propagation and maintenance of herbaceous perennials. In *Perennials: A Gardener's Guide*. New York: Brooklyn Botanic GardPhoto Credits

Photography, Illustration, and Garden Credits

All photographs by the author with the exception of the following:

Boerner Botanical Gardens, courtesy of Milwaukie County Parks, WI, page 123 bottom

Amy Campion, pages 62, 152, 154 top, 168, 170, 177 top and bottom, 184, 185, 190 bottom, 192, 193 top, 196, 199 bottom, 203 bottom, 205, 211 all, 212, 218, 223, 227 top and bottom left, 228 all but far right, 236, 237, 239, 241, 248, 250, 257, 258, 264, 267, 268, 269 top and bottom, 271, 289, 294, 305, 308, 310, 314, 315, 316, 318, 324, 326, 330, 333, 337, 341, 342, 344, 345, 346, 347, 348, 349, 351, 353, 355, 359, 360, 361, 362, 363, 364 top, 365, 366 top and bottom, 368, 370, 372, 374, 376

© Ruth Rogers Clausen, page 277

Alan and Linda Detrick, pages 275, 292, 336

GAP Photos
  © Adrian Bloom, page 209
  © Carole Drake, page 284 top
  © GAP Photo, page 171
  © Neil Holmes, page 266
  © Dianna Jazwinski, page 329 top
  © Howard Rice, page 188 top
  © Jan Smith, page 295
  © Nicola Stocken, page 276

GardenPhotos.com
  © Graham Rice, page 325
  © judywhite, pages 251, 354

Mark A. Garland, hosted by the USDA-NRCS PLANTS Database, page 304

© Global Book Publishing/Quarto Group, pages 144, 146, 150, 154 bottom, 155 left, 157, 161 top, 163 top, 164, 169, 171 bottom, 173, 181 bottom, 182, 193 bottom, 200, 203, 214, 216, 217, 220 bottom, 224, 232, 242, 243 bottom, 246, 254, 255, 256, 265, 273, 282, 285, 290, 299, 307 top and bottom, 312, 313, 321, 328 bottom, 334 top, 369

Chris Hansen, pages 298, 302

iStock
  © mikfoto_pl, page 296
  © zorani, page 145

© Clive Nichols, pages 159, 180

© Photoshot, pages 148, 153, 156, 161 bottom, 162, 163 bottom, 165, 167 top and bottom, 175, 176, 179 top and bottom, 183 top and bottom, 187, 191, 195, 206, 207 top, 208, 213, 215, 225 top, 230, 240, 260, 261, 262, 263, 272, 281, 288, 291, 293, 306, 309, 319, 327, 328 top, 332, 335, 340

Dr. David Shetlar, page 70

Shutterstock
  © Bildagentur Zoonar GmbH, pages 244–245
  © Kefca, page 202

Nanette Welch, page 46 bottom

Wikimedia
  Used under a GFDL, version 1.2:
    Ram-Man, page 243
  Used under a Creative Commons CC0 1.0 Universal Public Domain Dedication:
    Ayman Hikari, pages 189, 377
  Used under a Creative Commons Attribution 3.0 Unported license:
    A. Barra, page 225
    Sandstein, page 322
    Kor! An, page 178
    Epibase, pages 253, 278
  Used under a GFDL and Creative Commons Attribution-Share Alike 3.0 Unported license:
    Fritzflohrreynolds, page 160
    Frank Vincentz, page 222
    H. Zell, page 219
    Jean-Pol GRANDMONT, pages 142–143
    KENPEI, pages 252, 280, 297, 367
    Meneerke bloem, page 190
    Mnemo, pages 311, 370
    Pethan, page 199
    Qwert1234, page 275
    Rasbak, page 194
    Rolf Engstrand, page 247 bottom
  Released into the Public Domain:
    Daderot, page 283
    Georges Jansoone, page 284 bottom

George Weigel, page 274

ILLUSTRATIONS

Black and white illustrations by Beth Ann Daye.
Color illustrations by Kerry Cesen.

GARDENS

Mike and Trish DiSabato garden, author's design, pages 18–19

Sandy Harbrecht garden, author's design, pages 22–23, 58, 59, 60

Hiddenhaven, author's garden and design, pages 2, 5, 8, 10, 13, 14, 15, 16, 17, 34–35, 38, 84, 101, 102, 106, 129, 130–131, 140, 380, 383, 384, 385, 386, 389

Martha and Carl Lindner garden, author's design, pages 28, 41, 44, 46, 47, 48, 56, 350

Edwards Communities, Hayden Run Garden, author's design, pages 20–21, 24, 27, 78, 231, 249, 320, 323, 378

Susan Rector garden, author's design, pages 23, 30, 31, 53, 74

Acknowledgments

I'd like to first thank *you* for reading this book and supporting this work. Without the continued support and encouragement of those who follow and use this reference, it would not have remained so popular all these years.

I'd like to also thank the many organizations that have brought me in to lecture, thus promoting and enforcing the lessons within these pages. Thanks to my faithful clients, many of whom have remained with me for countless years—it has been an honor and a pleasure to design and help you maintain your gardens and to share them in this book. A huge thanks to the women who have helped me in all aspects of my business—from my three books, to office work, to client designs and maintenance, to my own gardens at Hiddenhaven: Virginia Terry, Amber Darst, Andrea Dunlap, the late Nanette Welch, and the late Antoinette Ellis. Thanks to Hidden Creek Landscaping, especially Jason Cromley, for installing my designs with respect and patience. Thanks to Chris Baker, owner of Baker's Acres Greenhouse, and George Pealer, owner of Millcreek Gardens, for more than 20 years of growing gorgeous plants for my designs.

As always, thanks to the great people at Timber Press for continuing to believe in me: my project editor Julie Talbot, senior acquisitions editor Tom Fischer, and publisher Andrew Beckman. Thanks also to Amy Campion for her assistance in shaping this new edition and for her beautiful photographs.

And finally, I can't thank my husband and best friend, Jim, enough for all his love, constant understanding, ridiculous amount of patience, and never-ending help in all aspects of our lives. I know I promised more than 16 years ago, "This is the last book!" Glad you didn't hold me to it!

Index

About the Author

NANETTE WELCH

Tracy DiSabato-Aust has worked in the horticulture industry for over 40 years, earning international acclaim as one of America's best-known and most knowledgeable garden writers and designers. She is the author of the best-selling books *The Well-Designed Mixed Garden* and *50 High-Impact, Low-Care Garden Plants*, also published by Timber Press.

A dynamic speaker, Tracy is a frequent guest on national television and radio gardening shows and is in great demand on the lecture circuit both nationally and internationally. Her speaking venues have included England's Royal Horticultural Society Garden, Wisley; The Royal Botanic Gardens, Kew; The English Gardening School; the University of Oxford botanical gardens; and venues in Argentina, Uruguay, Australia, New Zealand, and Switzerland.

Tracy has contributed to or been featured in numerous magazines and newspapers including *Fine Gardening*, *Horticulture*, *Garden Design*, *Real Simple*, *The New York Times*, *The Telegraph* (London), and the *National Post* (Toronto).

When not pursuing all things plant related, Tracy is racing triathlons. She and her husband Jim and son Zach proudly represent Team USA at the world level. She is an ITU World Triathlon Age-Group Champion (Budapest) and ITU World Triathlon Age-Group Champion Runner-up (Beijing), as well as a three-time National Champion and nine-time All-American triathlete. What time is left is spent with her horses, competing in dressage, driving, and trail riding. Her website may be found at www.tracylive.com.